EARLY MODERN LITERARY GEOGRAPHIES

General Editors
JULIE SANDERS   GARRETT A. SULLIVAN, JR.

EARLY MODERN LITERARY GEOGRAPHIES
Oxford University Press

Series Editors: JULIE SANDERS, Royal Holloway, University of London and GARRETT A. SULLIVAN, JR., Pennsylvania State University

Early Modern Literary Geographies features innovative and agenda-setting research monographs that engage with the topics of space, place, landscape, and environment. While focused on sixteenth- and seventeenth-century English literature, scholarship in this series encompasses a range of disciplines, including geography, history, performance studies, art history, musicology, archaeology, and cognitive science. Subjects of inquiry include cartography or chorography; historical phenomenology and sensory geographies; body and environment; mobility studies; histories of travel or perambulation; regional and provincial literatures; urban studies; performance environments; sites of memory and cognition; ecocriticism; and oceanic or new blue studies.

ADVISORY BOARD

Dan Beaver, Pennsylvania State University
Nandini Das, University of Oxford
Stuart Elden, University of Warwick
Bernhard Klein, University of Kent
David McInnis, University of Melbourne
Andrew McRae, University of Exeter
Evelyn Tribble, University of Connecticut
Alexandra Walsham, University of Cambridge

Shakespeare Beyond the Green World

Drama and Ecopolitics in Jacobean Britain

TODD ANDREW BORLIK

Great Clarendon Street, Oxford, OX2 6DP,
United Kingdom

Oxford University Press is a department of the University of Oxford.
It furthers the University's objective of excellence in research, scholarship,
and education by publishing worldwide. Oxford is a registered trade mark of
Oxford University Press in the UK and in certain other countries

© Todd Andrew Borlik 2023

The moral rights of the author have been asserted

First Edition published in 2023

Impression: 1

All rights reserved. No part of this publication may be reproduced, stored in
a retrieval system, or transmitted, in any form or by any means, without the
prior permission in writing of Oxford University Press, or as expressly permitted
by law, by licence or under terms agreed with the appropriate reprographics
rights organization. Enquiries concerning reproduction outside the scope of the
above should be sent to the Rights Department, Oxford University Press, at the
address above

You must not circulate this work in any other form
and you must impose this same condition on any acquirer

Published in the United States of America by Oxford University Press
198 Madison Avenue, New York, NY 10016, United States of America

British Library Cataloguing in Publication Data
Data available

Library of Congress Control Number: 2022941381

ISBN 978–0–19–286663–9

DOI: 10.1093/oso/9780192866639.001.0001

Printed and bound in the UK by
Clays Ltd, Elcograf S.p.A.

Links to third party websites are provided by Oxford in good faith and
for information only. Oxford disclaims any responsibility for the materials
contained in any third party website referenced in this work.

Acknowledgements

During the decade or so in which this rainbow of a book acquired its stripes, a number of wonderful people helped to burnish its lustre. Among the many to whom I owe a debt of gratitude the following stand out: Julie Sanders and Garrett Sullivan, for finding the book a desirable niche in the Early Modern Literary Geographies series and offering many helpful suggestions on tightening its arguments; two anonymous reviewers for OUP for their painstaking comments on the typescript; Karen Raber and Holly Dugan, for their sage advice on performing animals; Bill Streitberger, who long ago taught me to see Shakespeare as a court dramatist; Clare Egan, for uncovering the manuscript of the petition to King James transcribed in the Introduction; Jeffrey Cohen, whose *Prismatic Ecology* inspired this book's title and scope; Lowell Duckert, for calling my attention to Poole's polar bears; Randall Martin, for sharing his then unpublished work on *Coriolanus*; Daniel Patterson, for his input on some difficult transcriptions; my colleague Steve Ely, *il miglior naturalista*, for his insights into English wildlife and his companionship on a quest to find Tiddy Mun in the Hatfield Moors; and my former neighbour, Gerald Strauss, who kindly gave me his battered copy of *Annals of English Drama*, which fell open to a page listing the Admiral's productions of 'Nebuchadnezzar', 'Cutlack', and 'Pythagoras' after I had already written on Shakespeare's inter-textual allusions to Nebuchadnezzar, Guthlac, and Pythagoras. A six-month sabbatical from the University of Huddersfield in 2019 was instrumental in completing this book, although the portions dealing with the plague had to be revised during the dark days of the 2020 lockdown. The University of Huddersfield Research Fund covered the fees to reproduce the images. Many thanks to the libraries, estates, and museums who granted the permissions and to their staff who handled my requests.

Portions of Chapters 2, 3, 4, 5, 6, and 8 were presented at, respectively, the University of London Shakespeare Seminar, the MLA convention in Washington, DC, the Spiritual/Material Symposium at Sheffield Hallam University in 2020, the British Shakespeare Association meeting in Swansea and a Medieval and Early Modern Research Seminar at the University of Leeds in 2019, the Rewilding Symposium at the University of Huddersfield in 2016, and the 2015 ASLE-UKI conference in Cambridge. During these events the following people offered valuable input: Dan Cadman, Drew Daniel, Simon Estok, Coen Heijes, Brett Greately-Hirsch, Lisa Hopkins, Sujata Iyengar, Gwilym Jones, Ben Spatz, Peter Smith, Daniel G. Williams, and Gillian Woods. The book was also enriched by the participants in the 2019 SAA seminar on Ecomaterialism and Performance:

Craig Dionne, Christopher Foley, David Goldstein, Laurie Johnson, John Joughin, Natasha Korda, Evelyn O'Malley, Gretchen Minton, Hillary Nunn, Chloe Preedy, and Jeffrey Theis. A conversation with Ben Crystal set me thinking about the puns lurking in early modern pronunciation. The international environmental humanities network Earth-Sea-Sky provided the initial impetus for the *Pericles* chapter. My profound thanks to the co-organizers—Vin Nardizzi, Tiffany Jo Werth, and Tom White—and our funders: The Oxford Research Centre for the Humanities (TORCH), the John Fell Fund, and the University of California Research Institute for the Humanities. A sizeable extract of Chapter 5 appeared in *The Routledge Handbook of Shakespeare and Animals*. An early version of *The Tempest* chapter was published in the *Shakespeare* journal in 2013, and benefited greatly from the cogent feedback of two anonymous reviewers.

As ever, my greatest debts are to my parents, for their unconditional support over the years, and to my wife and children: you chase the greyness from the scholar's life.

Contents

List of Figures ix
List of Abbreviations xi
A Note on Texts xiii

    Introduction: From Tudor England's Green World to
    Stuart Britain's Iridescent Empire   1

1. The 'Blasted Heath' and Agrilogistics in *Macbeth*   24

2. *Timon of Athens* and Scottish Mines: The Folio's Gold as Vibrant Matter   46

3. 'Watery Empire' in *Pericles*: British Sea Sovereignty, the Fisheries, and the Eco-material History of Purple   63

4. Welsh Mountains, Alpine Pastoral, and Eco-Masculinity in *Cymbeline*   87

5. Performing *The Winter's Tale* in 'the Open': Bears, Ermines, Rural Girlhood, and the White Sea Fur Trade   112

6. Caliban and the Fen-Demons of Lincolnshire: The Englishness of *The Tempest*   138

7. 'Purple Plagues or Crimson War': Population Control in *Measure for Measure*, *Coriolanus*, London, and Ulster   167

8. Staging Darkness at Whitehall and Blackfriars: Nocturnalization in the Stuart Masque and Shakespeare's Late Tragedies   193

    Conclusion: King-Man and the Anthropocene as Species Tyranny   217

Endnotes 225
References 253
Index 283

List of Figures

0.1	Unknown Artist, *King James VI of Scotland with a Peregrine Falcon* (1574). © National Portrait Gallery, London.	13
1.1	*Macbeth* at the Park Avenue Armory (2014). © Stephanie Berger.	28
1.2	A Muirburn in Scotland. Simon Butterworth/Alamy Stock Photo.	38
1.3	Gervarse Markham, *Hungers Prevention: Or, the whole Arte of Fowling* (1621). Courtesy of the British Library, digitized by the Google Books project.	41
1.4	The Dovecote at Temple Grafton, outside Stratford-upon-Avon. SOTK2011/Alamy Stock Photo.	43
3.1	Jan Porcellis, *A Storm at Sea* (c.1606–10). RCIN 402633. Royal Collection Trust. © Queen Elizabeth II 2021.	73
3.2	Henry Shaw, The Fishmongers' pageant, from Anthony Munday, *The Golden Fishing* (1616). © British Library Board.	75
3.3	Joachim Beuckelaer, *Fish Market with Ecce Homo* (1570). Nationalmuseum Stockholm PD.	83
4.1	Robert Peake, *Prince Henry and Robert Deveraux, 3rd Earl of Essex, in the Hunting Field* (c.1605). RCIN 404440. Royal Collection Trust. © Queen Elizabeth II 2021.	92
4.2	Roelandt Savery, *Mountain Landscape with Castle* (1609). © Fundación Colección Thyssen-Bornemisza, Madrid.	93
4.3	Inigo Jones, Mountainscape for *Oberon* (1611). © Devonshire Collection, Chatsworth. Reproduced with permission of Chatsworth Settlement Trustees.	94
5.1	The Barentsz expedition killing and skinning polar bears on Novaya Zemlya in 1596, from Gerrit de Veer, *The true and perfect description of three voyages…on the north sides of Norway, Muscovia, and Tartaria* (1609). Science History Images/Alamy Stock Photo.	114
5.2	Paul van Somer, *James VI & I* (c.1620). RCIN 404446. Royal Collection Trust. © Queen Elizabeth II 2021.	119
5.3	The ermine as emblem of purity, from Henry Peacham, *Minerva Britanna* (1612). Beinecke Rare Book and Manuscript Library, Yale University.	121

5.4 Nicholas Hilliard, The 'Ermine Portrait' of Queen Elizabeth (1585).
    Reproduced with permission of the Marquess of Salisbury, Hatfield House. 122
6.1 The Lincolnshire fens in the nineteenth century.
    De Luan/Alamy Stock Photo. 141
6.2 William Hole, The Lincolnshire fens, from Michael Drayton, *Poly-Olbion* (c.1622).
    Royal Geographic Society. 149
6.3 Guthlac journeys to the island of Crowland, from Harley Roll Y.6. (c.1200).
    © British Library Board. 159
6.4 Guthlac tormented by bestial demons, from Harley Roll Y.6. (c.1200).
    © British Library Board. 159
6.5 Marcus Sadler (after Maerten de Vos), Saint Guthlacus of Crowland, from *Sylvae sacrae monumentum anachoretium* (1594).
    Rijksmuseum, Amsterdam. 160
7.1 Richard Bartlett, *A Generalle Description of Ulster* (c.1603).
    Special Collections, The Library, Queen's University Belfast. 188
7.2 Anonymous, *The Over-throw of an Irish Rebell... Carey Adoughterie* (1608).
    Reproduced with permission of the Master and Fellows of Trinity College, Cambridge. 191
8.1 Inigo Jones, Nightscape for *Luminalia* (1636).
    © Devonshire Collection, Chatsworth. Reproduced with permission of Chatsworth Settlement Trustees. 198

List of Abbreviations

BL	British Library
CSP	Calendar of State Papers
CUA	Cambridge University Archives
CWBJ	Ben Jonson. 2012. *The Cambridge Edition of the Works of Ben Jonson*, ed. David Bevington et al. 7 vols. Cambridge: Cambridge University Press.
DC	Dudley Carleton. 1972. *Dudley Carleton to John Chamberlain: 1603–1624 Jacobean Letters*, ed. Maurice Lee. Newark: Rutgers University Press.
GMS	Stephen Atkinson. 1825. *The Discoverie and Historie of the Gold Mynes of Scotland: Written in the Year 1619*. Edinburgh: Ballatyne.
HD	Philip Henslowe. 2002. *Henslowe's Diary*, ed. R. A. Foakes. Cambridge: Cambridge University Press.
JC	John Chamberlain. 1965. *The Chamberlain Letters: A Selection of the Letters of John Chamberlain*, ed. Elizabeth McClure Thomson. London: John Murray.
KJSW	James I. 2003. *King James VI and I: Selected Writings*, ed. Neil Rhodes et al. Farnham: Ashgate.
LPD	Lost Plays Database
NLW	National Library of Wales
ODNB	*Oxford Dictionary of National Biography*
OED	*Oxford English Dictionary*
OFB	Francis Bacon. 1996–. *The Oxford Francis Bacon*, ed. Brian Vickers et al. 16 vols. Oxford: Oxford University Press.
PPMF	John Nichols. 1828. *The Progresses, Processions, and Magnificent Festivities of King James the First*. London.
REQ	Court of Requests
SBT	Shakespeare Birthplace Trust
SD	Stage Direction
SPD	State Papers Domestic
SPF	State Papers Foreign
SPO	*State Papers Online*
SRP	James Larkin and Paul Hughes, eds. 1973. *Stuart Royal Proclamations*. Oxford: Clarendon.
TLN	Through Line Numbers
TMCW	Thomas Middleton. 2007. *Thomas Middleton: The Collected Works*, ed. Gary Taylor and John Lavagnino. Oxford: Clarendon.
TNA	The National Archives
TRP	Paul Hughes and James Larkin, eds. 1969. *Tudor Royal Proclamations*. 3 vols. New Haven: Yale University Press.

A Note on Texts

Citations of Shakespeare are taken from the Third Series of the Arden Shakespeare, unless otherwise noted. To relay the ecocritical implications of rhetorical capitalization, this study in several places reverts to the First Folio, supplying the through line numbers (TLN) from the Norton facsimile. When citing it and early editions of other Renaissance texts, I have preserved original spelling, altering only i/j and u/v/w to conform with modern conventions.

Introduction

From Tudor England's Green World to Stuart Britain's Iridescent Empire

This book pursues two lines of argument that may seem parallel but will be shown to intersect with surprising regularity and force. First, it helps propel ecocriticism and Shakespearean studies beyond the green sliver of the colour spectrum by charting how the early modern economy exploited the underdeveloped hinterlands as green England engulfed the more varied topographies of multihued Britain and acquired overseas colonies. Secondly, it proposes that the most compelling case for Shakespeare as an eco-conscious dramatist can be made by locating him not in the semi-mythical greenwood of Arden or the sheep-dotted Cotswolds but within the corridors of power in urbane Whitehall and uncovering how his plays pointedly intervene in environmental policy disputes at the Jacobean court. The launch points for both these claims rest on firm bedrock. That Shakespearean drama ranges beyond pastures and woodscapes is undeniable, although his sylvan comedies have received a disproportionate amount of attention. Likewise, numerous theatre historians have long insisted on the necessity of casting Shakespeare as a court dramatist. Inspecting Shakespeare's plays through the bifocal lens of environmental history and theatre history will disclose startling new contexts for and unsuspected glimmers of meaning in some of the most familiar works in English literature. Through an eco-historicism of innuendo, this book reasserts Shakespeare's relevance in the Anthropocene by tracing the current predicament of our human-dominated planet back to the anthropocentricism of early modernity and the imperial poetics of Stuart absolutism. It demonstrates that the court-oriented drama of the King's Men's leading playwright achieves a poetic grandeur that 'make[s] Nature afraid' by replicating the Orphic power of the monarch over the realm but ultimately and even more insistently 'maketh Kings feare to be Tyrants' by debunking or repudiating fantasies of environmental sovereignty.[1]

That Shakespeare colour codes landscape has been a critical commonplace since Northrop Frye unfurled his theory of the 'green world' (1957, 182). In identifying a recurrent structural pattern in Shakespearean drama of a journey from a corrupt and oppressive civilization to a wilder space of revelry, passion, and freedom, Frye made an indelible contribution to Shakespearean scholarship.

Shakespeare Beyond the Green World: Drama and Ecopolitics in Jacobean Britain. Todd Andrew Borlik,
Oxford University Press. © Todd Andrew Borlik 2023. DOI: 10.1093/oso/9780192866639.003.0001

Although this concept had lost much of its gloss by the turn of the millennium, the greening of the humanities has given it a felicitous ring, and some ecocritics have been irresistibly tempted to upcycle it.[2] As ecocriticism has blossomed and diversified, however, confining our attention to a narrow, chlorophyll-dominated strip of our planet's kaleidoscopic spectrum has come to seem myopic and reductive. England's 'sheep-wrecked' (Monbiot 2013a) and chemical-laced pastures, for instance, can hardly be considered natural bastions of biodiversity. It is no longer 'easy being viridescent' (2013, xxii), as Jeffrey Jerome Cohen quips in the scintillating collection *Prismatic Ecology*. As a result of the lazy bandying about of green as shorthand for the non-human environment, the colour has been 'oversold as a lumping term, thereby foreshortening one's sense of other spectral possibilities' (Buell 2013, ix). Anthropological studies indicate English speakers have an 'enlarged' green, but examining the literature of other eras as well as places can help elucidate how perceptions of our polychromatic world are linguistically and culturally conditioned.[3] In early modern usage, green could connote not only freshness and fertility but also naïvete, unripeness, sickliness, fickleness, and transience.[4] The popularity of Shakespeare's pastoral comedies *A Midsummer Night's Dream* and *As You Like It* has rendered green world almost synonymous with greenwood, despite the facts that early modern descriptions of shadowy woodscape skew towards black as much as green and most of England's dwindling forests were hardly havens of liberty.[5] Since the Norman Conquest, forests were heavily regulated places managed by a local bureaucracy with their own courts known as swainmotes, and the word forest itself is a juridical term designating a royal game preserve. While Frye does recognize that the green world is not a monochrome, and admits both Portia's refined Belmont and Falstaff's gritty Eastcheap into this league of quasi-utopian places, the ensuing study does question his idealization of a timeless and mythic nature in opposition to the 'red and white world' of history and commerce.[6] As we shall see, Shakespeare frequently depicts the natural world not only in tension with but also as subject to the forces of history, law, and commerce, and this fact will become sparklingly clear by reading his Jacobean plays alongside the geo-political, legal, and economic-environmental policies of the Stuart court—which were by no means confined to green spaces.

While Shakespeare scholars (myself included) have devoted considerable attention to verdant woodlands and pastures, and two separate monographs have examined the valences of green in early modern culture, the past decade has seen a greater willingness to traverse not so lush environments marked by greater chromatic diversity.[7] Steve Mentz—perhaps the most vocal champion of post-green and post-equilibrium ecologies—and Dan Brayton have charted the tidal force of the ocean's blue hues on Shakespeare's imagination. Early modern ecocritics are thrusting spades into the brown beneath our feet (Eklund 2017) and recognizing that the English writers and explorers in the Little Ice Age were also fascinated by its white-encrusted icescapes (Duckert 2017). Meanwhile, Mentz

(2010), Gwilym Jones (2015), and Sophie Chiari (2019) have craned their gaze upwards to the skies to canvass Shakespeare's representations of dark and stormy weather. In foraying outside green and idyllic landscapes, these studies have been emboldened by second-wave ecocriticism's mandate to move beyond the celebration of nature writing that characterized much early ecocritical work and instead embrace more intersectional theorizing and a properly complex view of nature-culture as a continuum or 'mesh' (Morton 2012). This sceptical bent informs Robert Watson's path-breaking *Back to Nature*, which decodes the pastoral's musings on the green as expressions of epistemological anxieties about the real. In a similar spirit, Mary Thomas Crane has shown that innovations in astronomy, medicine, and mathematics eroded 'an intuitive connection with nature' (2014, 9) but that Elizabethans were reluctant to abandon Aristotelian naturalism and its trust in the embodied experience of the world. In contrast, Simon Estok characterizes early modern attitudes as defined less by apprehensions of drifting too far from nature but more by revulsion that humans were too close to it. In his important but controversial monograph on 'ecophobia', Estok diagnoses a widespread fear and loathing of the non-human in Shakespeare's culture and demonstrates that such sentiments were often entwined with misogyny, racism, and homophobia. The pivot towards less pristine environs can also be discerned in muck-raking studies by Ken Hiltner (2011) and Bruce Boehrer (2013) of the polluted and overcrowded streets of seventeenth-century London, as well as work by Randall Martin (2015) and Benjamin Bertram (2018) on the collateral damage warfare inflicts on the environment.

Even as Shakespeareans still beachcomb for treasures washed ashore by this second wave, a third has surged up behind, lifting critics to gaze beyond regional or national (predominantly Anglo-American) literary traditions to take a more global outlook on the collective challenges facing our warming planet.[8] According to Scott Slovic and Pippa Marland, a fourth wave has been gathering momentum since 2012 from the material turn, billowed by the likes of Bruno Latour, Karen Barad, Jane Bennett, Stacy Alaimo, Serenella Iovino, and Serpil Opperman. Ecocriticism 3.0's impact on Shakespeare studies can be discerned in essays on bioregionalism and eco-cosmopolitanism in *As You Like It* and *Cymbeline* (Martin 2015), while the fourth dispensation underwrites the archival labours of material ecofeminists, who have revealed that many early modern women in their traditional roles as preparers of food and medicine possessed an intimate knowledge of plants and other animals, albeit the application of that knowledge sometimes betrays a disregard for animal suffering rather than some innate feminine nurturing (Laroche and Munroe 2017).

Given the relentless pace at which eco-theory has developed since the turn of the millennium, it would be unwise to assume that earlier approaches have been completely superseded. As Buell cautions, the wave analogy is overly tidy and misleading; he instead proposes that ecocriticism functions more like a 'palimpsest' (2005, 17), in which various methodologies might overlap. Rather than surf one discrete wave or trend, this book wades into the eddies and crosscurrents, responding to the particularities of Shakespeare's plays rather than employing a single theoretical sieve for all of them. It follows the second-wave in incorporating relevant concepts and insights from gender studies, queer theory, race studies, night studies, the legal humanities, and animal studies, while also pursuing the ecocritical implications of the bountiful scholarship on Shakespeare and the spatial turn.[9] Although the Stuart court stands at its epicentre, *Shakespeare Beyond the Green World* also strives to overcome the metropolitan bias of much theatre history by venturing into Suffolk, Lincolnshire, Wales, Scotland, the North Sea, Ulster, Bermuda, Western Russia, and Arctic outposts in the White Sea. It is precisely because so much of the green space of lowland England had already been tamed and developed by the agrarian economy at the dawn of the seventeenth century that Shakespeare's contemporaries increasingly set their sights on the remaining pockets of wilderness at home and abroad, and sought to 'reclaim' or exploit these 'wastes'. This process accelerated in the early seventeenth century thanks to King James and his dream of unifying and expanding Great Britain. Accordingly, this book also makes a modest contribution to redefining the scope of English studies as 'archipelagic', issuing a corrective to the fixation on England in the Anglo-American academy and the still persistent conflation of it with Britain.[10]

While this attention to local identity dovetails with ecocriticism 3.0, other chapters follow an eco-materialist trajectory in tracing the agential force of nonhuman actants, such as metal, fish, fur, and dye. The last of these is particularly important for *Shakespeare Beyond the Green World*, which takes a cue from Julian Yates's theorization of colour 'as a multispecies sensory process or network that generates biosemiotic-material effects' (2013, 85). Early moderns would have been more inclined to think in such terms since they were 'colour realists', regarding colour not as a trick of the light as Descartes and Newton would postulate but as materially engrained within the natural world.[11] That Shakespeare's contemporaries might conceive of colour as a multispecies process is suggested by the 1586 inventory of a Stratford draper, John Browne, which affords a precious glimpse of the vivid and evocative colour world that Shakespeare would have encountered in his hometown, adorning the bodies of his fellow Stratfordians as he strolled past Browne's shop on the High Street: 'violet', 'stammel' [a type of red], 'medlow color' [mallow], 'sade new color', 'iron graye', 'horseflesh color', 'russette', 'frost uppon greene', 'fryers grey', 'fryer penyston black', 'sky color', 'sea water color', 'hart brayn color', 'maydon heare color', 'awmbe gilder' [amber golden?], and 'mylkie water color' (SBT PR234/12). More than advertising gimmicks, these names preserve terse biosemiotic narratives, whispers of the ecological intimacy of an era when extracting organic dyes required botanical knowledge, dyeing was often done at home (mainly by women) with local ingredients, and garments were redyed in shades selected to match the changing colourscape of the seasons.[12] However, an eco-materialist approach also entangles the vibrant, exotic hues fetishized by Renaissance courtiers to distinguish themselves from the earth-tones of the peasantry in the material histories of political and environmental conquest. Scale insects, saffron, starch, woad, and logwood coloured thousands of household objects, fashion accessories, and theatrical costumes, from Malvolio's yellow stockings to Cardinal Wolsey's scarlet robes, but the chromatic splendour of London's courts and theatres was often leeched from the natural world in unsustainable ways that degraded biodiversity.[13] With this in mind, *Shakespeare Beyond the Green World* attends to colour not only in the variegated landscape but also upon the bodies of royals, courtiers, and actors, resolving the vibrant colourscape of Renaissance drama back to its eco-material origins: gold and silver from mines (Chapter 2), purples from murex harvesting (Chapter 3), blacks and whites in the traffic for furs of sable and ermine (Chapter 5), and blues and greens from woad cultivation in the drained fens (Chapter 6), as well as the myriad colours rendered visible in indoor playhouses by the burning of candles made from suet and beeswax (Chapter 8). Since many of these luxurious dyes were extracted from provincial and colonial environments to adorn the courts of European cities and palaces, colour often served to emblazon class and race-based divisions that replicate and are materially dependent upon the anthropocratic dominion of humans over other species.[14]

Anthropocratic Absolutism and Ecopolitics at the Jacobean Court

In King James's coronation procession, in which Shakespeare marched wearing the king's scarlet livery, the monarch was saluted by a flock of colourful figures personifying London and the abundant resources of his new domains. The Thames appeared 'in a skincoat made like flesh, naked and blue, his mantle of sea-green or water colour' and leaning on a pot full of live fish (Dutton 1995, 41); Sylvanus, the god of woods, 'dress'd up in green ivy'; Peace, in a 'garment of carnation'; Plenty, clad in a gown of 'changeable colours', and cradling a cornucopia filled with fruit and flowers; Chrusos, 'a person figuring gold' in a golden robe; Argurion, or Silver 'all in white tinsel'; Pomona, the goddess of fruit, 'attired in green, a wreath of fruitages circling her temples'; and Ceres, crowned with wheat and wearing a 'straw-coloured robe' (75–9). Such a spectacle presenting England as a garden of plenty or '*Arabia Felix*' explains the Scottish courtier Roger Aston's reply when asked how the king felt about his long-desired succession: 'like a poor man wandering about forty years in a wilderness and barren soil, and now arrived at the land of promise'.[15] The attention lavished upon the performers' costumes in Thomas Dekker's transcription of the pageant is typical of Stuart entertainments, where the wide variety of colour on display signifies the pomp and grandeur of the occasion. The grandeur of the 1604 procession reached its zenith when it entered the Strand and James was treated to the sight of an enormous rainbow arcing over seventy-foot pyramids and invited to imagine it as the goddess Iris spreading 'her roseate wings in compass of a bow / About our state' (109). Curiously, the word 'state' here designates not only the realm but also the throne on which James processed through the streets as well as the portable canopy toted over it. On its way to the Strand, the procession had passed under seven monumental arches intended to duplicate the architecture of the Roman triumph, mirrored here in the finale by the arc of the ersatz rainbow, whose parabolic shape effectively renders it an eighth triumphal arch. Like Prospero conjuring Iris in *The Tempest*, James's entry conflates royal authority over the realm with a dramaturgical mastery of the colour spectrum as materialized in the pageantry's costumes and properties. Such flattering pageants had been staged for Tudor monarchs as well, but *The Magnificent Entertainment* merits special scrutiny because of James's imperial ambitions and pretensions to absolute dominion. It is noteworthy that the 1604 entertainment also included personifications of the four elements (Earth, Water, Air, and Fire) followed by the four realms of England, Scotland, France, and Ireland 'in rich robes...lined with the coats of their particular kingdom' (90), all professing their fealty to the Stuart king. This awe-inspiring spectacle must have lingered in Shakespeare's memory, likely inspiring Iris's cameo in *The Tempest*, as it levied the power of theatre to set sky-high expectations for the reign of his new patron, and to endow the king with a magus-like mastery over the land, sea, sky, and their legions of creatures.[16]

Theatre historians have often found James's thumbprints in Shakespeare's plays but it remains to be seen how the coronation of a Scottish hunter-king and self-proclaimed absolute monarch colours, in both the figurative and literal senses, the depictions of the environment in Shakespearean drama.[17] As James waged a public relations campaign to unify his realms and expand them into an empire, Shakespeare's oeuvre registers a corresponding chromatic-cum-geographic shift from green England to prismatic Britain. While Shakespeare's Elizabethan plays wander happily through the familiar woodlands and tamed farmlands of Warwickshire, Gloucestershire, and Windsor, the Jacobean plays venture farther afield into the wilds of Scotland and Wales, and gaze outward to the North Sea, Ireland, Bermuda, the Levant, and even the Arctic.[18] It has been suggested that Shakespeare's post-1600 abandonment of the greenwood comedy betrays a loss of faith in 'nature's redemptive capacities' and that the wild spaces in late romances such as *Cymbeline* afford little more than 'a place to hide' (Boehrer 2013, 78). This book instead proposes that Shakespeare's willingness to venture beyond the English greenwood stems from a chorographic impulse to encompass the broader range of multi-hued topographies within a more global-minded Britain. When England acquired a Scottish king, a Prince of Wales, and a Danish queen in 1603, followed by an Arctic outpost on Bear Island and a Virginia colony, it also acquired wider horizons and expanded frontiers that changed the parameters of the nation's borders and identity. The fact that Great Britain was much wilder than England forced a reappraisal of wilderness in the national consciousness as James sought to amalgamate the outlying kingdoms and lay the foundation for a British empire. Indeed, the conspicuous mingling of nature and art in Shakespeare's late romances corresponds to the geo-political grafting of a wilder Britain onto England.

Many on both sides of the divide would resist this assimilation, however. As Richard Helgerson (1992, 105–47), Garrett Sullivan (1998), and John Adrian (2011, 51–73) have outlined, resentment of James's grand vision of a homogenous Britain awakened an oppositional pride in the shire, town, parish, or local environment as the cornerstone of identity. To claim, as Helgerson does, that some people in early modern Britain show 'loyalty to the land…[and] even uninhabited geographic features' (132) does not mean they valued unspoiled wilderness for its own sake or the sake of its non-humans. Rather an entrepreneurial class increasingly valued it in an economic sense as a repository of natural resources— what Heidegger calls *bestand* (1993, 22)—upsetting local communities who had their own cottage economies to skim a livelihood from the land and certain emotional/utilitarian ties (the two are not mutually exclusive) to the native flora and fauna on whom their well-being depended. Caught in the middle, King James wished to defend his humble subjects from dispossession by engrossing landlords while also endearing himself to wealthy courtiers and landowners. He protected some customary rights while also endorsing sweeping agrarian reforms. He sought to prevent enclosure, rural depopulation, deforestation, and species loss, but simultaneously commandeered resources through purveyance, overhunted, liquidized Crown forests, and invested in development projects in the hope of bankrolling his extravagant spending.[19] Moreover, the king's power to award letters patent granting monopolies on lucrative (often destructive) industries and goods meant that dubious lobbying to control the natural wealth of the nation was an abiding preoccupation of the court, while fears of shortages compelled the Privy Council to engage in environmental oversight. It should come as no surprise if debates over carving up the spoils of the realm receive a hearing in the plays of Shakespeare and the King's Men.

That critics have sometimes exaggerated or oversimplified the court's impact on Shakespeare has provoked some sceptics to overstate the counterargument. The proposition that he tailored his plays for upcoming court performances as 'occasional' drama (Nosworthy 1965) was challenged by Leeds Barroll, who objects that James's patronage of Shakespeare's company is not a reliable indicator of royal interest or influence (1991, 32–41). Rather than see James as Shakespeare's implied spectator (Kernan 1995), Barroll points to evidence that his consort Queen Anna and her circle were much closer to the artistic heart of court life

(2001b).[20] Nevertheless, Barroll admits James's attention could be piqued by plays dealing with law and governance, especially if they spoke to his own agendas and philosophies (2001b, 152), and Curtis Perry, who echoes some of Barroll's caveats, rightly insists that Shakespeare's Jacobean plays are 'powerfully motivated by their observation of and interest in issues of public government' (1997, 10). Over the past decade, studies such as James Shapiro's *1606* (2016), Richard Dutton's *Shakespeare, Court Dramatist* (2016), *Performances at Court in the Age of Shakespeare* (Chiari and Mucciolo 2019), and Lucy Munro's *Shakespeare in the Theatre: The King's Men* (2020) have fed an emerging consensus that 'a key unifying element of the late plays can be found in their engagement with topical concerns related to the person, politics, and court of the King' (Kurland 2013, 210). *Shakespeare Beyond the Green World* simply endeavours to prove that many of these topical issues of public governance Shakespeare touches upon in his Jacobean plays relate to the management of the environment.

Paradoxically, the case for Shakespeare as an environmentally engaged dramatist can be best advanced by situating him in the milieu of the court, where his plays comment upon debates over the exploitation and stewardship of the nation's resources and might even sway, however modestly, the opinions of the king, the privy councillors, lawmakers, and investors. Theoretically shrewd studies celebrating literature's power to deconstruct crude binaries such as nature/culture or human/animal are well and good, but as the world warms there is a growing impatience among ecocritics for cultural texts to inform or even impact policy. Few writers over the past four centuries can rival Shakespeare's privileged access to the inner sanctum of power and the collective ear of the ruling class. This is especially true during the first decade of King James's reign, when Shakespeare's company averaged fourteen court performances per year, four times as often as they played before Elizabeth (Kernan 1995, xvi–xvii). The scenario of a court production at Whitehall is rather like the modern London Globe or Folger Theatre in D.C. staging a private performance for the prime minister or president and their cabinets. It is inevitable that such a coterie audience would dissect the play for its political sub-text. Current events might even give an old play a new topicality as happens with Hamlet's 'Mousetrap' or when, say, a revival of *The Tempest* is timed to coincide with a climate summit. To state the obvious, Shakespeare is not writing eco-agit prop and it would be 'quixotic', as Jonathan Bate cautions, to expect that literature spell out a 'practical program for better environmental management' (2000, 266). Shakespeare is not tilting *for* windmills, so to speak. But his works intervene on a deeper level of consciousness to pose questions about humanity's niche in the natural world and the ethics of how we treat it that invite his audiences to consider their actions more carefully. The line between consciousness-raising and political action is fuzzier than data-driven reports on research impact can capture but that need not be a cause for regret or despair; indeed, art's efficacy may be greater for the subtlety of the provocation.

The twenty-first-century Shakespeare industry is less beholden to monarchy than corporate sponsors but environmental matters could create friction in these relationships in the past just as they do today: consider, for example, the 'To BP or not to BP' imbroglio, in which the Royal Shakespeare Company was pressured to 'conclude' its partnership with British Petroleum after 'actorvists' protested against Big Oil using Shakespeare to burnish its public image.[21] It therefore seems worthwhile for theatre historians to investigate Shakespeare's ambivalence towards his patron and the influence on Crown policy wielded by agrarian reformers, projectors, patent holders, livery companies, joint-stock companies, and Lord Chancellors. While agreeing with the basic tenet that Shakespeare often wrote with the Stuart court in mind, this book does not sketch a portrait of a 'palace Shakespeare' who happily acted as a 'propagandist for the monarchy, a radical conservative' (Kernan 1995, xxii). On the contrary, it frames many of his late plays as a proleptic reversal of Rubens's *Apotheosis of James* that adorns the ceiling of Whitehall's Banqueting House in that they bring the god-like king back down to earth where he learns his hand, too, smells of earthbound mortality. Seeking to command or colonize the environment, Shakespeare's royal protagonists find themselves colonized in return by wild spaces and elements that defy human control, like the storm that invades Lear to the skin. Through plot twists, metaphors, and wordplay, Shakespeare's monarchs are not simply humanized but also bestialized, forced to partake of the agony they inflict on non-human nature in their ritualistic imposition of dominion over it. In one extreme form of this ironic turnabout, the hunter becomes the hunted, as in the myth of the metamorphosed Actaeon. James's *vox regis vox dei* claims 'bred generally much discomfort' among England's political classes, who were unhappy to hear 'our monarchical power and regal prerogative strained so high and made so transcendent', and Shakespeare appears to have shared these reservations.[22] The late plays instead dramatize nature's power to dismantle and reforge autocratic identity in a process of psychological rewilding that affirms the immanence and vulnerability of the supposedly transcendent subject. Informed by an Ovidian phenomenology, Shakespeare's Jacobean plays often riff on Hamlet's insight (via Montaigne) that even a king can be deposed and digested by a worm, 'your only emperor' (4.3.21), in an ecological 'revolution' (5.1.85). Nature proves the true suzerain or absolute monarch. To claim that Shakespeare rebukes absolutism as eco-hubris is not to hail him as a deep ecologist *avant la lettre*. But his plays do present a commoner's-eye view of an absolute monarch's-eye view of the natural world, and the gulf between these perspectives shapes what stories he tells and how he tells them.

For several reasons Shakespearean drama does not unequivocally or consistently endorse the policies of James, which were themselves inconsistent. First, cultural historians have established the Stuart court was not monolithic; Queen Anna, Prince Henry, and Princess Elizabeth each had their own circle with their independent agendas, to which, I will argue, Shakespeare appeals in plays such as *Pericles*, *Cymbeline*, and *The Winter's Tale*.[23] Secondly, Shakespeare simultaneously needed to please a public audience at the Globe. His late plays often flirt with constitutionalist politics, and the fact that he never composed a court masque, where overt flattery would be compulsory, is suggestive.[24] If plays devised or adapted for court performance seem at times to lend qualified support to royal policies for agrarian development or conservation and equate a total collapse of monarchical authority with cosmic disorder, others that did not likely receive a royal performance, such as *Timon*, might be more outspokenly critical (or, conversely, unstageable because too critical). Yet the staging of *King Lear* at Whitehall attests that Shakespeare, like Lear's fool, was not afraid of rubbing the royal furs the wrong way. The stripping of Lear mirrors the Commons' efforts to abolish royal purveyance, which entitled the Crown to requisition an extravagant share of natural resources—timber trees, coal, hay, horses, hounds, food—and reimburse the owners at a fraction of the market price.[25] James's claim to be *dominus omnium bonorum* ['lord of all goods'] and 'the overlord over the whole lands' (*KJSW* 269–70) asserts this right, but many Jacobean plays are fiercely sceptical of absolutism and equate royal purveyance with ecological tyranny. A third complicating factor in Shakespeare's ecopolitics is that he wrote not only for the court but also for the lawyers of the Inns of Court, and may have done so more consciously after the King's Men acquired Blackfriars in 1608. Many perspicacious studies bear witness to Shakespeare's intense fascination with legal matters and procedure, but the scholarship is only beginning to recognize that cases concerning jurisdiction and ownership often fall under the purview of what we would now call environmental law.[26] In brief, much of the complexity of Shakespearean drama springs from its conflicting loyalties to the royal, public, and private audiences at Whitehall, Bankside, and Blackfriars, as it generates dramatic tension from political and legal disputes as to whom the nation's natural resources properly belonged.

To capture this complexity, *Shakespeare Beyond the Green World* reads the late plays through an archive that ties together royal proclamations, court entertainments, parliamentary legislation, and environmental history. It juxtaposes the view from the monarch's 'state' or elevated throne with the occluded, earthy perspectives of marginal communities, examining little-known texts such as 'Marchan Wood', Khanty Bear Plays, 'The Powte's Complaint', and 'Where have the Gaels gone?', in which the wild growls back against the metropolitan centre. Such sources exemplify the tendency of the subaltern to ventriloquize the non-human to champion local knowledge-systems and traditional, sustainable environmental management over the disruptive, extractive practices of money-minded outsiders. Recovering these lost ecologies and muted voices will require some forays into eco-historical contexts. But undertaking them is well worth the effort for the new vistas they open up on the play-texts and readers may be fortified in the knowledge that the journey is also the destination. If the climate crisis worsens as projected, producing yet another reading fixated narrowly on a literary classic may start to feel like golfing under the volcano. We must also acquire a deeper understanding of environmental history, study how past societies devised more organic methods (or rejected them) to manage a volatile climate and finite resources to cope with chronic precarity, and adapt critical skills such as close reading and thick description to narrativize human entanglement in an ecological epic more dynamic and convoluted than the Great Chain of Being.

Some of the arguments advanced in the ensuing chapters are perforce speculative. As is true of New Historicism, the interpretations do not hinge on whether or not Shakespeare in fact read all the texts or saw all the performances referenced here. I do not claim, for instance, that Shakespeare galloped across a misty Scottish heath, climbed Mount Snowdon, stowed away on a Muscovy Company voyage to the Arctic, or paddled through the fens to hear tales of Tiddy Mun. Rather the intent is to establish a keen interest in environmental-economic issues among Shakespeare's audience and thereby enable us to comprehend how his plays would have been perceived as unavoidably commenting on them. Moreover, the eclectic medley of sources seeks to mitigate the Anglocentric and anthropocentric bias of the historical archive to catch murmurs that seventeenth-century English culture and even its most celebrated playwright struggled to hear. Yet scholarship has underestimated Shakespeare's willingness to lend non-human nature agency and voice through paronomasia, apostrophe, and personification. If some of the transpecies quibbles uncovered in this book make high-minded mavens like Dr Johnson wince, as they grate against post-Enlightenment canons of taste, they cannot but make the ecocritic rejoice, for they expand the Shakespearean stage to accommodate the drama of a more-than-human world.[27]

Many cultural factors conspired to buttress anthropocentrism in the early modern era but Shakespeare's Jacobean plays afford insights into the role of absolute monarchy in underwriting fantasies of human dominion. Despite the considerable body of scholarship on James's reign, the ideological and eco-material impact of his divine-right-of-kings' theory on the environment and environmental policy in early Stuart Britain remains underexplored. James's self-proclaimed status as 'overlord' of lands and goods trumpets a God-given prerogative to expropriate the natural resources of the realm and its colonies. As this book will unfold, James did become an investor in ecologically destructive schemes to mine moors and mountains, expand British fisheries in the Atlantic, drain wetlands, and colonize wilderness in Ireland, Russia, and Virginia. Imperial kingship enthroned a proprietary and top-down view of the natural world that was co-opted by those acting in the Crown's name. Viewed in a more charitable light, however, the Stuart monarch's standing as overlord might also entail a duty to steward the nation's resources from reckless development. Throughout his reign James issued a number of royal proclamations and sought to influence Parliament to pass laws that would now be classified as acts of environmental conservation. Both these assessments deserve serious consideration, as they have direct bearing on the environmental politics of Shakespearean drama.

Any inquiry into James's views of the environment must foreground his consuming passion for the chase, the ramifications of which are more complex than modern readers might assume. Accustomed to hunting in Scotland where game was still plentiful, James was more aware of and alarmed by the human-driven disappearance of England's fauna than his Tudor predecessors.[28] One of his earliest proclamations as king of England calls for stricter enforcement of anti-poaching laws and bans the unsportsmanlike use of nets, crossbows, and guns that have 'excessively and outrageously spoiled & destroyed' the wildlife (*SRP* 14–16). He reissued it in 1609 and the following year urged Parliament to pass legislation to protect at-risk species 'now almost utterly destroyed through all the Kingdome' (*KJSW* 346). As Chapter 1 uncovers, the decline of England's ground-nesting birds was so severe that James wished that he could 'cast a roof over all the ground' (346) to transform Crownlands into giant aviaries, and Chapter 4 further documents his campaign to outlaw nest-robbing. His menagerie housed many endangered or near-extirpated British species such as beavers, wolves, and eagles, and in 1608 and 1611 he imported sounders of wild boars from France and released them in Windsor Great Park in an early example of what ecologists now call rewilding (Yamamoto 2017, 92). The courtier Francis Osborne, recalling a time the furious king drafted a proclamation for the nationwide manhunt of a stag-poacher, half-joked that during James's reign 'one man might with more safety have killed another than a raskall-deare' (Scott 1811, 1:194). While many of his contemporaries smirked at James's hunting (as have subsequent historians) as an unbecoming dereliction of duty, his earnest desire to conserve Britain's fauna no longer seems quite so ridiculous. Osborne's portrait of a literally green James in the guise of a forester 'as greene as the grasse he trode on' (Scott 1811, 1:195–6) offers a vivid reminder that he could be classed as a forerunner of hunter-conservationists like Theodore Roosevelt and Aldo Leopold. Of course, hunting for the king's pleasure seems more ethically questionable than poaching by the hungry poor and one might cast a cynical squint on James protecting certain species to monopolize the privilege of killing them, but even today many reputable naturalists defend the unfashionable position that the ecological benefits of regulated sports-hunting far outweigh the harm (Loveridge et al. 2006).

On an ideological level, however, James's devotion to the hunt appears a disturbing enactment of the monarch's dominion over the realm. It is apt that one of the first portraits of the then 8-year-old king depicts him posing proudly with a falcon perched on his begloved hand, advertising the obedience of the wild to his authority (see Fig. 0.1). Three years later, James's government renewed legislation ordering the barons to conduct mandatory wolf hunts three times each year 'in the time of their quhelps' (Hull 2007). His attraction to divine right, despite the best efforts of his republican tutor George Buchanan, can be seen as a reaction to

Fig. 0.1 Unknown Artist, King James VI of Scotland with a peregrine falcon (1574). © National Portrait Gallery, London.

the unstable political climate of Scotland, with its recurrent blood feuds between rival clans, but Scotland's harsher geophysical climate, with its inclement weather and wolf-haunted moors and highlands, would likewise have encouraged a view of the natural world as unruly and hence requiring the firm hand of a quasi-omnipotent monarch. After his arrival in England, James continued to find the hunt a gratifying performance of an absolute authority over his non-human subjects that eluded him in his quarrels with Parliament. One typical letter of his closes with the self-satisfied boast, 'going to bed after the death of six hares, a pair of fowls, and a heron' (Akrigg 1984, 278–9). Well into late middle age, James relished the ritual known as the assay, thrusting his hands or feet into the bowels of a slain deer and daubing the blood on his face or that of his favourites in the magical belief it conferred a rejuvenating power. Gervase Markham's bold claim, 'A Husbandman is the Maister of the earth' (1613, 4) indicates how agricultural manuals and other georgic texts could instil (particularly among male landowners) a will to dominate the natural world echoed in tropes of monarchical husbandry, but the mythos of the hunter-king may have been equally important in sanctioning human dominion in early modern Britain.[29]

In the negative column on King James's decidedly mixed scorecard on the environment one must also factor in the impact of his royal absolutism in emboldening natural philosophers to entertain the possibility of an absolute knowledge of the cosmos. What had been a divine prerogative was claimed by the intelligence networks of the god-like king and his Privy Council and gradually placed under the jurisdiction of secular science. In one of his final seminars, Derrida unspools a similar argument, citing the menagerie at Versailles and the dissection of an elephant before Louis XIV, a 'Sun King, a king of light... who is the condition of possibility of appearing and of knowledge' and to whom 'everything is subject' (2009, 1:281). This lends a grander significance to the expansion of the royal menageries by James, who was also glorified as a *roi soleil* (see Chapter 8). The king's animal subjects included herons, cormorants, a kingfisher, otters, a flying squirrel, a porcupine, an Indian antelope, ostriches, a peccary, a cassowary, an Indonesian cockatoo, sables, polar bears (see Chapter 5), a walrus, monkeys, lynxes, crocodiles, tigers, lions, camels, and an elephant.[30] Much has been made of the Globe's proximity to the Bankside bear-pits, but it is equally significant that Whitehall, where Shakespeare's plays were staged before the king, abutted the royal menagerie in the Spring Gardens of St James Park.[31] Shakespeare's allusions to exotic beasts would put some Jacobean playgoers in mind of the king's zoo and afford a vicarious glimpse inside. Although there is no record of James attending an elephant's dissection, he ordered a major refurbishment of the Lion Tower in 1605 to include more open space and a viewing platform so he and his guests could see the beasts more easily. According to Derrida, the reincarnation of the royal menagerie as a zoological garden in the Jardin des Plantes following the French Revolution signifies a transfer of sovereign mastery over nature from the monarch to the public and the scientific community. A similar transfer was already underway in Stuart England when sections of the royal menagerie were opened to visitors, an actor turned Master of the Royal Game staged animal baitings for the masses, and James's Lord Chancellor, Francis Bacon, penned a scientific romance envisioning a society governed by a cabal of technocrats known as Saloman's House.[32]

Given Bacon's role as a prophet of the Anthropocene, it is revealing that he dedicated *The Advancement of Learning* (1605) to James as the monarch-naturalist Solomon (see 1 Kings 4:33). The compliment hinges on the correspondence between James's imperial vision and Bacon's dream of extending human empery over the planet. Citing Proverbs 25:2, 'the glorie of God is to conceale a thing, But the glorie of the King is to find it out', Bacon elevates the scientist to the level of the sovereign as 'Gods play-fellowes' (*OFB* 4:36) in a cosmic game of hide-and-seek. As Julie Solomon (1999) illustrates in her analysis of Bacon's influence upon the Royal Society, scientific discourse achieves a pretended objectivity by simulating the perspective of the monarch. There is, in other words, a symbiosis between James's political absolutism and Bacon's anthropocratic absolutism that will restore Eden by rendering nature entirely transparent to the human intellect and malleable to human desires. In his political tracts and parliamentary speeches, James expounds an absolutism that flowed from the monarch to gentlemen naturalists, who commandeered and stimulated the labours of the mercantile and artisan classes, and was eventually rebooted as the technocratic absolutism of capitalist modernity.[33]

To most of Shakespeare's contemporaries, however, Salomon's House must have seemed a castle in the sky. A very different snapshot of the environment of Jacobean Britain can be found in two petitions to the king. In late 1604, the exasperated townsfolk of Royston pinned a letter to the collar of James's favourite hound, Jowler, complaining that the Crown's purveyance of provisions had created a local famine: 'Good Mr. Jowler, we pray you speak to the King... to go back to London or else the country will be undone' (*PPMF* 1:464–5). The prank illustrates a recurrent literary phenomenon examined in this book: how the non-human might be made to speak for disempowered local communities who resisted the destructive environmental practices of the Jacobean state. A similarly grim assessment of James's stewardship can be found in a petition dated March 1606. Rather than depict the realm as a new Eden or garden of plenty overseen by a second Solomon, it blames the king's mismanagement and the greed of his underlings for aggravating a number of environmental problems. As the manuscript has not, to my knowledge, been printed before, I cite it at length:

Most gracious King,
Hear the cries of your poor distressed subjects who have secretly writ letters to your majesty, the last was set upon a door going into the presence Sunday last, wherein you should understand the oppressions, wrongs, [and] miseries, with the great alterations and impositions, which [are] offered upon your poor subjects since her late majesty's death.... If you [are] an absolute prince, for God's cause, hear and help your poor subjects and God will bless you and yours....

Your majesty shall understand the great wrongs which [are] daily offered, required, and imposed upon your subjects by your lords and great persons for their own private gain. First, it is generally said that the covetous bloody Popham[34] offereth to lend ten thousand pounds towards the draining of the fens, thereby to take many poor men's countries from them for his own profit.... He is cursed of all the poor of that part of England and [they] swear they will kill him or such as shall be employed therein.

Also this Popham and your great lords, with the glasshouses and iron mills for their own profit maintain them saying they are very profitable to the commonwealth, who have and shortly will consume all timber and wood in England and have made it so scant and dear that it is ten times dearer in price than before, which they are daily cursed for of all poor in all England.

Also, of late years, woad is grown to be in most parts of England so commonly sown that all sorts of people England do curse them that let their lands for that use, for that it hath set such dear price of all land as no poor subjects are able to live, in that their lords by that means do ask so great fines and rents for their lands as ten times double, which is most lamentable; and this is maintained by the Lord Popham and other lords and justices for their great profit, not respecting the good of the commonwealth.

Also starch consumes abundance of flour and bran which would succour many poor subjects and feed horses. All these things were but lately used in England but brought from beyond seas, whereby the merchant gained much and her late majesty had great custom....

It is said they ['your great devouring lords'] give your majesty leave to go hunting and make show of good husbandry towards your majesty and will you to follow your pleasures, but the end and drift of their actions is to rob and spoil your poor sort of subjects for their own good; your majesty doth not understand their English policy....

What greater dishonor can be to your majesty's person and the whole state that in so short time your majesty [would] give over your housekeeping? Your majesty shall find great ease and much honor in commanding many of your lords, knights, and gentlemen into their countries to keep good houses, to feed their tenants and poor subjects, who lie at court with two lackeys and spend their revenues in apparel and whores. Noblemen and gentlemen were wont to keep two hundred persons in their houses daily ready to serve the king.

Also it is generally reported that your lords have persuaded your majesty to impose a great fine upon all your tenants and subjects for assarts [forest converted to arable land], which is very troublesome to your subjects, and it is feared that your majesty shall not have half the profit which is raised thereof.

Also there is one great abuse offered since your majesty came in: killing [and] eating of flesh in the Lent times, as common almost as before Lent, odious to God and man in making no difference of time. In her majesty's time there was [a] proclamation in all cities and towns at Shrovetide straitly [strictly] for the same, as your Council knoweth.

For all your laws [and] parliaments, there was never less care or reformation used amongst your Council, for it is said they now care for nothing but their own profits and let the commonwealth slide, for they know that all these most horrible abuses are true.... They study nothing but to get wealth and honour and to oppress the poor subjects. It were good your majesty would ask them all what good they have done since your coming to the commonwealth. We beseech your majesty, for the love of God, not to be persuaded by them, but to believe that all these are true: or wherefore should we complain? It is said that the lower house of Parliament would take away your prerogative. In her majesty's time all the subjects in England durst not once think of it or cross her in whatsoever. Your majesty wanteth some of her knowledge, breeding, and stomach.

Many thousands of your loving subjects do desire you, for God's sake, to remember these petitions and griefs, and to reform them with all speed, and they will daily pray for your majesty's long and prosperous reign.

(SPD James I 14/19 f. 97)

Composed shortly before the Midlands Rising, when dearth provoked riots over enclosure, the letter paints a picture of a society with widely disparate experiences of the environment: the middling sort and underclass straining to cope with a mounting list of problems amidst chronic fears of scarcity, while those in power aggressively manipulate the natural world for personal gain.[35] The petitioner taunts James to wield his much-vaunted absolute authority to curtail the abuses of his lords, questions the efficacy of his laws, and faults his neglect of 'housekeeping', which in early modern English prefigures the concept of ecology (derived from the Greek *oikos* for household management).[36] If the complaint endorses a utilitarian or shallow ecology, and even decries fines against assarts or woodland clearings, it is nonetheless a remarkable document in its advocacy of environmental justice and sustainability.

There is some evidence that James took such petitions to heart. He refused at first to invest in fen-draining schemes, issued proclamations ordering the nobility to return to their country estates (*SRP* 44, 323, 356), sought to curtail abuses of purveyance (136–7), eventually banned starch (188, 250), encouraged the unpopular Lenten fast (413, 536), knighted Hugh Plat in 1605 for, amongst other things, inventing new methods to improve agricultural efficiency and reduce coal pollution, and in 1610 urged Parliament to undertake 'the framing of some new Statute for the preservation of woods', calling it 'a thing so necessary for this Kingdome that it cannot stand nor be a Kingdom without it' (*KJSW* 345). Heartened by James's speech, Arthur Standish would dedicate *The Commons Complaint* (1611), his manifesto for a nationwide tree-planting campaign, to the king, who in turn commended Standish for his labours and ordered that his proposal be 'willingly received & put in practice' (A1^v). When Standish published an updated version in 1616, he reproduced the king's endorsement, complete with his royal seal, lauding James for his 'princely care' (A2^v) in helping regenerate the nation's woodlands.[37] Other assessments, however, were less enthusiastic. Like Standish, Michael Drayton's chorographical survey *Poly-Olbion* sounds the alarm about deforestation but its tone is closer to the 1606 petition in faulting the current regime for its lack of environmental oversight. Whereas Standish added the royal insignia to his text, Drayton strips it from *Poly-Olbion*'s maps and instead hails the land as the focal point of allegiance (Helgerson 1992). Despairing of

James, Drayton dedicates the poem to Prince Henry in the hopes he would surpass his father in living up to their surname, which the poem spells Steward as a nod to the dynasty's descent from a former High Steward of Scotland.

Unfortunately, Henry died young and the Crown's financial hardships meant that James proved a poor steward in practice. The centralized system of state-led environmental management developed by Elizabeth's Lord Treasurer, William Cecil, became more urgent and contested in the Jacobean period when his son Robert Cecil took charge of the frayed purse-strings and had to rein in James's expenditures and find new sources of revenue.[38] Dogged by chronic insolvency, James invested in gold, silver, and lead mining operations, sought to expand and tax British fisheries, and backpedalled on his initial opposition to fen-draining.[39] After refusing Sir Julius Caesar's overtures to sell off Crown woods, James eventually relented, ordering a survey to determine which regions could best afford to spare timber. Out of a desire to ingratiate himself to his subjects, James, like Shakespeare's Lear and Timon, indulged in a reckless liberality that diverted many of the Crown's revenue streams to grasping courtiers. His liberality was particularly excessive in the early years of his reign, when the 'King's generosity was fed by his easy assumption that the resources of his new realm were inexhaustible' (Croft 2003, 58)—an assumption encouraged by spectacles like the garden of plenty in his coronation procession. This ecopolitical context provides a vital framework for understanding Shakespeare's Jacobean plays in which coddled, profligate elites confront a recalcitrant, not-so-green wilderness and are disabused of the cornucopian fallacy.

Theatre might seem a lofty cultural enterprise remote from the mundane task of governing the nation's resources, but some of the king's advisors regarded his players simply as another part of his economic portfolio that could be milked for revenue. In October 1604, Lord Say put forward three proposals for raising his and the Crown's cash flow: (1) increasing fish days and charging an exemption fee for the sale of meat; (2) securing the right to collect fines on the illegal clearing and converting of woodlands to pasture; and (3) charging an additional penny tax per head to enter a London playhouse (Roberts 2006, 96). In the end, Say's proposals never bore fruit, but such schemes demonstrate why the King's Men would be eager to encourage their patron to find alternative means of income, possibly by investing in development projects, or levying steeper fines against environmental abuses. Jacobean playing companies, in other words, could not afford to ignore the environmental issues of their day.

For the literary historian, it is especially significant that James's faith in his divine absolutism may have been nurtured by his youthful dabbling in what he called the 'divine art of poesy'. In his oft-quoted sonnet that begins 'God gives not Kings the stile of Gods in vaine' (*KJSW* 200), the word stile means title but also signifies a literary style that elevates the poet-king above nature and endows his words with the force of divine fiats. In another verse he composed as leader of the

'Castalian band' of Scottish writers, James again revels in the physics-defying Orphic power of poets, who:

> Can change the course of Planets high or lowe
> *And make the earthe obeye them everie way*
> Make rockes to danse, hugge hills to skippe and playe
> Beasts, foules, and fishe to follow them allwhere.
>
> (*KJSW* 121)

Reversing Jonathan Goldberg's insight that Shakespeare 'represents his powers as playwright as coincident with the powers of the sovereign' (1983, 232), Jane Rickard has uncovered how James's authorship bolstered his conviction in his own God-given authority (2007), which included, I would add, the authority to reshape the natural world as he saw fit.[40] An overarching thesis of this study is that the poetics of Stuart absolutism had a profound impact in turn on Shakespeare's late plays in that James's vision of himself as a god-like ruler—a royal huntsman, royal poet, divine naturalist, or second Solomon—spurred the playwright to dramatize the limitations imposed on monarchy by the unruliness of the natural world. The *locus classicus* for this is Lear's ordeal in the storm, but Shakespeare composes variations on this theme in the sea-storms of *Pericles* and *The Tempest*, and in the wild hinterlands of *Macbeth*, *Timon*, and *Cymbeline*.

To his credit, James was painfully aware that the best laid plans of mice and monarchs oft go awry. In the late 1580s he undertook a translation of a section of Du Bartas's *La Seconde Sepmaine*, which bemoans the revolt of post-lapsarian nature against its divinely appointed sovereign, 'man':

> The soveraigne greate, I say,
> Does feele his subjects all enarm'd
> Against him everie way.
> The air by winds sturr'd, AMPHITRITE
> Doth stormie make a gild [clamour],
> The Heaven most sadlie black, the earth
> With briere thornes fulfild.
>
> (59)

Raymond Williams observed that medieval and Renaissance literature often personifies nature as 'an absolute monarch' (1983, 221), but James reworks this trope by anointing 'Man' as a just sovereign whilst unmasking nature as a tyrant or rebel. James's description of other species and the elements (often gendered female) as man's 'slaves', who have rebelled against their proper ruler to 'Become our tyrants strong' (*KJSW* 63) connives not only with Stuart absolutism and patriarchy but with Baconian science in foregrounding environmental disorder to justify the restoration or *instauratio magna* of human dominion. The sea 'by her debording [overflowing] steales / His Isles from him withal' while the earth 'a Step-mother cruell…doth ingratelie barren harv'sts / Produce us now a dayes', sabotaging the fields with thistles and 'the vaporous Darnell' (60–1). These passages afford some valuable insight into how King James would have responded to nature's assault on the monarch in plays like *King Lear* and *Pericles*. In court performance, these scenes would confirm James's belief that the environment's intransigence resulted from the subject's disobedience to the king. Investing more authority in the monarch and Privy Council will impose order on unruly nature, while the discourse of environmental crisis conspires to justify the imperialist control through which the state would siphon resources from the provinces, Scotland, Wales, Ireland, and beyond.

At the Globe, however, storms, floods, air-borne diseases, barren heaths, sodden fens, and stony mountains might act as checks on absolute monarchy. The very pomposity of Stuart absolutism spawned a proportionate backlash in which counterattacks on political tyranny made it possible to question whether human mistreatment of nature amounts to species tyranny. Seconding the bold accusation of Philip Sidney's 'Ister Bank', Shakespeare enlists nature in a critique of political absolutism but Jaques's rant against the hunter and Prospero's abjuration of his technomagic indicate that the vehicle and tenor of the metaphor are reversible. Unpacking this complex political ecology may prove a crucial means by which ecocriticism can help reassert the relevance of Shakespearean drama beyond its own historical era and the coterie audience of the court. The late plays issue barbed reminders that '[the ruler's] authority over the land is highly precarious' (MacFaul 2015, 67) and the same goes for human rule. The chapters that follow show that King-Man or Emperor Adam does not fully control heaths, mines, seas, skies, mountains, fens, fertility, the harvest, disease, suburbs, colonies, or the night. In transfiguring the absolutist king into an anthropocratic everyman, Shakespeare exposes the limitations of human (especially patriarchal) sovereignty over nature in ways that both register the onset of the Anthropocene and protest the self-crowning of homo sapiens as planetary emperor.

Examining Shakespeare's late plays as a sustained experiment in dramatic chorography—infused by the zeitgeist that produced Carew's *Survey of Cornwall* (1602), Owen's *Description of Pembrokeshire* (1603), the English translation of Camden's *Britannia* (1610), Speed's *Theatre of the Empire of Great Britaine* (1611), and Drayton's *Poly-Olbion* (1612)—the chapters in this study link them to particular locales, habitats, or chronotopes, each with their distinctive hues and eco-material histories. The first chapter ventures onto the 'blasted heath' to consider how *Macbeth* adjudicates disputes between agrarian capitalists, poor cottagers, and aristocratic hunters like the Scottish king over the management of this terrain. Whereas the first group, who wished to convert heaths to enclosed farmland, took a dim view of this landscape as the sinister abode of witches and fortune-telling vagrants, the latter two valued it as a habitat for grazing livestock or wildlife. Shakespeare's tragedy encompasses the opinions of all three in portraying the heath as a battleground between the forces of fertility and sterility. This anthropocentric dualism also clamps its tags on the play's avian imagery. In promoting selective conservation of some species such as doves (with whom Duncan, Malcolm, and Macduff are associated) and the persecution of others like the kite (identified with Macbeth), the tragedy espouses an inter-generational but shallow ecology, in contrast to the childless Macbeths, who renounce 'reproductive futurity' whilst bestowing a perverse glamour on inhuman wildness.

Chapter 2 roots *Timon of Athens* in the context of a Scottish gold boom to argue that the monarchy's superficial control over the subterranean world and its minerals perpetuated dubious views of the natural world as a gift economy. Entranced by the glittering promises of mining entrepreneurs like Bevis Bulmer, the king's faith in chimerical reserves of gold and silver encouraged a fiscal recklessness mirrored in Shakespeare and Middleton's tragic satire. Assaying the Folio's rhetorical capitalization of Gold, the chapter argues that Shakespeare imbues the metal with a vitalist power far more absolute than that of the insolvent king.

The third chapter reveals that the depleted North Sea fisheries were a whale-sized bone of contention in Anglo-European politics around the time Shakespeare and Wilkins co-wrote *Pericles*. As a court entertainment centred on a sea-faring ruler whose name evokes naval supremacy, *Pericles* lends qualified support to royalist fantasies of oceanic sovereignty not only over the blue fisheries but also over sea-creatures harvested to manufacture purple dye, a key signifier of monarchy synonymous with Pericles's hometown of Tyre. While the play's tragic sea storms throw cold water on the representation of the ocean in court masques and seascapes—debunking human dominion over the sea and the apotheosis of the Stuarts as the heirs of Neptune by alluding to the 1607 Bristol Channel Flood and the threat of coastal erosion—the comic resolution holds out hope that the Stuarts might achieve a sustainable pan-European fisheries policy through inter-dynastic marriage.

Chapter 4 scales the Welsh mountains of *Cymbeline* to challenge the prevailing view that early moderns despised mountains as barren warts prior to the Romantic sublime. Classifying Shakespeare's romance as an early example of alpine pastoral, I argue that the development of Renaissance landscape art, the Cambrophilia of early modern antiquarians, the installation of a new Prince of Wales, and the Jacobean elite's belief in hunting as the pastime of the manly warrior combined to bestow a more picturesque glow on mountains in the early seventeenth century. In tension with the georgic impulse to plunder uplands for timber, minerals, and stone, *Cymbeline* hints that the preservation of both Britishness and masculinity may depend on the preservation of mountain wilderness.

The fifth chapter pursues the bear in *The Winter's Tale* back to the Arctic to expose the involvement of the Jacobean state and theatre industry in the global fur trade. Whereas theatre historians police boundaries in seeking to determine whether Renaissance bear plays featured 'real' bears or fur-clad actors, Shakespeare's play revels in the indistinction promoted by animal studies. The creature that chases Antigonus is not the only inhuman performer in a play that transmogrifies the royal menagerie: Perdita resembles an orphaned polar bear cub, Leontes a lion, Autolycus a wolf, and Hermione (whose name or rather pet name we have mispronounced for 400 years) an ermine, a creature emblematic of the wintry north and queenly chastity. Although humans cannot literally metamorphose into other species, *The Winter's Tale* attempts the next best thing: recovering the child's epistemological proximity to the animal condition. Leontes' sexual jealousy is symptomatic of an adult male desire to control nature, but the play prescribes an antidote in rural girlhood, idealizing the upbringing of James's daughter as a feral princess and milkmaid, turning to pastoral romance to model a more benign relationship to the natural world than that exhibited by menageries and Skinners' pageants, which naturalized royal and mercantile dominion over the icy north and its fur-bearers.

Chapter 6 mires *The Tempest* in the brownish muck of the English fens and establishes that the play generates dramatic conflict out of the furore incited by campaigns to drain them. While Prospero's magical dominion over the island recalls hydro-engineering works in the swamps and bogs of America and Ireland, his masque of sedge-crowned naiads dancing with reapers more immediately gestures towards the domestic colonization of England's wetlands by agrarian developers in the early seventeenth century. This claim is buoyed by a number of sources overlooked due to the constraints of periodization and the lacunae of the print archive: medieval legends of a fen-dwelling and demon-quelling hermit, a lost play, a manuscript ballad from the point of view of a fish, and oral legends of a fen spirit who acts as a kind of Lorax for the wetlands. Invoking the fens to curse the invader Prospero, Caliban, too, speaks for the fens albeit more loudly for the fen-folk, tapping into their outrage over the confiscation of their aquatic commons and echoing doubts about the feasibility and ethics of controlling nature. Although the chapter zooms in on Lincolnshire and southern Yorkshire, managing wetlands was a familiar problem in early modern London as well. Lambeth Marsh could be glimpsed across the river from Whitehall and extended much farther east towards Southwark, where Shakespeare's Globe stood on tidal floodplains reclaimed by crumbling embankments that might someday be re-submerged.

Whereas the preceding sections in this book chart the expanding jurisdiction of the early modern state over heaths, mines, seas, mountains, fur country, and fens, Chapter 7 inspects its efforts to impose authority over London, its suburbs, and Irish plantations—efforts that were underwritten by the emergent discipline of demography. It turns out that Shakespeare's Jacobean plays share the king's acute anxieties about urban overpopulation in the aftermath of the 1603 plague. The chapter detects proto-Malthusian rhetoric in *Measure for Measure*, implicating the levelling of Overdone's bawdy houses in legislative crackdowns on overcrammed tenements, urban sprawl, and unwanted pregnancies. While such measures sought to avoid the 'positive' catastrophic check of mass mortality, the preventative solution of curbing the birth rate undergirds the dark view of human sexuality in Shakespeare's problem comedy. Population pressures reached a boiling point again after the 1607 dearth but *Coriolanus* poses tough questions about the state's attempt to vent them through war or through the colonization of the brutally depopulated Ulster.

The final chapter fades to black, recuperating the nocturnal ecologies of pre-Edisonian Britain that were gradually retreating before the human conquest of the night. Significantly, the theatre industry proved a cultural driver of nocturnalization, and the late-night revels of the Stuart court in particular enacted both onstage and off the vanquishing of darkness through artificial illumination that symbolized the absolute authority of the sun-like monarch. The chapter juxtaposes the nocturnal carnivalesque in plays like *Antony and Cleopatra* and *Timon of Athens* with fears of night-induced disability in *Macbeth* and *King Lear*, and links these divergent responses to the respective lighting levels in the hyper-illuminated Whitehall and the more dimly lit Blackfriars. Detecting an ugly correlation between nyctophobia and racism, the chapter gauges whether Shakespearean drama reinforces prejudice against other races, species, and abilities, or might instil a salutary acceptance of darkness and difference.

Collectively, the chapters in the book traverse a spectrum from brown, gold, blue, purple, white, red, and black in a bid to capture some of the diverse topographies of Great Britain and the great Globe itself. In doing so, this book re-stakes claims for Shakespeare's greatness in the depth and range of his engagement with the natural world, and in his willingness to wield his influence as a member of the King's Men to tell inconvenient truths to power about the environmental challenges of his time with a force and complexity that can illuminate our own.

1
The 'Blasted Heath' and Agrilogistics in *Macbeth*

While there is no hard evidence to confirm the supposition that *Macbeth* was written expressly for a royal performance at Hampton Court Palace in August 1606, and Shakespeare's tragedy is certainly far more complex than an obsequious bid to flatter his patron, the notion that it deliberately appeals to the witchcraft-obsessed Scottish king has become an unshakeable commonplace of Shakespearean criticism.[1] And for good reason. The play not only trumpets James's ancestral claim to the throne through Banquo, whitewashing Banquo's complicity in the assassination of Duncan, but also features a number of elements that seem designed to snare the king's attention. Every undergraduate who studies the play learns that James had presided over witchcraft trials; authored a treatise on the topic, *Daemonology*; strengthened England's anti-witchcraft statutes; and that Shakespeare drew from these sources as much as from Holinshed's *Chronicles* when creating his 'weird sisters'. While arguably no aspect of the play is more familiar than its traffic with the supernatural, far less attention has been paid to how *Macbeth* reflects King James's interest in the natural world. To be sure, the play has inspired a number of canny ecocritical readings: Robert Watson (1984, 88–9) and Robert Pogue Harrison (1992, 104) both construe the march of Birnam wood as ecological retribution for the Macbeths' unnatural crimes; Gabriel Egan (2006, 51–91) remarks on the correlation between political microcosm and environmental macrocosm; Richard Kerridge (2011) unpicks its problematically dichotomous views of nature; Steve Mentz (2011) plumbs its oceanic imagery; Randall Martin interprets the witches as 'a feminized threat to masculine dominance of the natural world' (2015, 105–6); and Rebecca Laroche and Jennifer Munroe contend that the witches' brew 'evokes women's domestic medicine and cookery' (2017, 101). Despite these eye-opening studies and the voluminous criticism situating *Macbeth* in the context of Jacobean politics, comparatively little has been done to locate the Scottish play in the landscape of Scotland. While there has been an understandable interest in the figure of the moor as a racial other in Shakespeare's England, eco-historicists might also seek to chart the topographical otherness of the moor in the early modern imagination, and *Macbeth* seems the ideal starting-point.[2]

In the absence of ecology, Shakespeare's tragedy envisions nature as an epic struggle between the forces of fertility and sterility, as it grapples with the

Shakespeare Beyond the Green World: Drama and Ecopolitics in Jacobean Britain. Todd Andrew Borlik,
Oxford University Press. © Todd Andrew Borlik 2023. DOI: 10.1093/oso/9780192866639.003.0002

anthropocentric dualisms of an agrarian society bent on eliminating scarcity—a mentality Timothy Morton derides as 'agrilogistics' (2016, 38). Recognizing the heath as a battlefront for agrilogistics in Stuart Britain lends new importance to its representation in *Macbeth*. If audiences at the Globe might view the play as demonizing the heath—portraying it as the abode of witches, 'gypsies', and lunatics—the royal play of *Macbeth* foments a tension between James's desire to extirpate hotbeds of witchcraft and his wish to protect heath and moors as breeding grounds for game-fowl. The dreary images of heath sketched by georgic writers and agrarian improvers would have been checked by the king's fondness for this landscape as a game preserve. In light of this contradictory picture of the heath as foul wasteland and fair habitat, this chapter argues that *Macbeth* intervenes in early modern debates between farmers and hunters over the management of heaths and 'wastes', and reinterprets its well-known avian imagery and infanticide allusions as voicing contemporary anxiety about the overkilling of fledglings, fry, and weanlings, resulting in species declines that prompted several bills and proclamations in Shakespeare's day resembling modern acts of environmental conservation. Although sceptical of prophecy, *Macbeth* demonstrates the towering importance—for better and worse—of 'reproductive futurity' in early modern politics and modern ecological philosophy.

Representing the Heath

In the tour de force opening scene, Shakespeare plays on the sonic affinity between the Scottish name of his eponymous protagonist and a prominent feature of the Scottish landscape. The three witches agree to rendezvous again after the battle, 'Upon the heath. / There to meet with Macbeth' (1.1.6–7). In modern received pronunciation, the couplet sounds like a slant rhyme; as a result, audiences and readers today do not register the connection between place and person as forcefully. In the midst of the Great Vowel Shift, however, heath could have been pronounced with a lower 'ɛ' sound (as in 'death') as 'hethe', which was a common seventeenth-century spelling. The fact that the first utterance of the protagonist's name yokes it with 'heath' in an incantatory trochaic couplet creates a subliminal association between Macbeth and barrenness—one that this chapter hopes to show is central to the play's tragic vision. The heath is more than an atmospheric backdrop; it is embroiled in ideological contestations, and Shakespeare's enormously influential description of it as 'blasted' reflects the increasingly pejorative views of this terrain that arose in his era and linger to this day.

Before further tracking Macbeth and Banquo onto the heath, a few definitions and a quick survey are in order, particularly for readers outside Britain unfamiliar with this landscape. Heath designates an area of open shrubland with poor, acidic soil that renders it unsuitable for cultivation. Since only a few hardy, low-growing plants, such as common heather (also called ling), bell-heather, furze (or gorse), and sphagnum moss can tolerate this harsh terroir, many early moderns regarded heaths as 'wastes', fit only for summer grazing.[3] Lowland heaths are mainly found in the English counties of Staffordshire, Suffolk, Norfolk, Cornwall, Dorset, and Surrey; swathes of heath also remain in south and west Wales and in the lowlands of eastern Scotland. In Britain, upland heaths (above 300 metres) with higher annual rainfall and concentrations of peat are commonly referred to as moors, and are clustered chiefly in the southwest at Bodmin Moor, Dartmoor, and Exmoor, and to the north in Yorkshire, Lancashire, and especially the Scottish Highlands.[4] Riding towards Forres from Fife, Macbeth and Banquo would likely have passed near the moorlands to the south of Duncan's castle, which raises the possibility that the heath in the Scottish play might be a moor. In *Hamlet*, Shakespeare seems to recognize the upland nature of the moor (as well as its proverbial barrenness) when the prince chides his mother for failing to discriminate between his father and his uncle in a line that derisively racializes both Claudius and this dark-hued biome: 'Could you on this fair mountain leave to feed / And batten on this moor?' (3.4.65–6). Since heath and moor are virtually interchangeable it makes sense to discuss them side by side, but there is one salient difference that makes Shakespeare's decision to label the setting a heath all the more significant: 'heaths are clearly the product of human activities' and—in comparison to colder, wetter moors—may more readily be reclaimed by either woodlands or enterprising farmers.[5] And reclaim them the Jacobeans did. If *Macbeth*'s heath demarcates the natural 'limits' imposed by a landscape 'violently severed from sustainable nature' (Scott 2014, 125), Shakespeare's tragedy also registers apprehensions about heathland reclamation and other ambitious agricultural practices that roll back those limits to extend human dominion over the earth.

Since psychological studies reveal that Westerners have a strong aesthetic preference for green landscapes (Ulrich 1986), a corresponding aversion to heaths and moors as dark, dreary places might seem to be hard-wired. Their depiction in several literary classics, such as *Wuthering Heights*, *Jane Eyre*, *Lorna Doone*, *The Return of the Native*, *The Hound of the Baskervilles*, and 'The Colour out of Space', only add to their ominous aura. Significantly, however, many of these texts take their cue from *Macbeth*, which was composed at a time when perceptions of the heaths were changing for the worse. As environmental historian Oliver Rackham notes, in the Middle Ages 'heath was a valued resource: the sentiment that regards it as useless land had yet to develop' (1986, 291), and prices for heathland were little below that of arable. In the iconic General Prologue to *The Canterbury Tales*, Chaucer celebrates the return of spring to 'holt and heeth', associating this landscape with fertility not sterility. The chief reason for this was that most heathlands were village commons, utilized by the landless or under-landed classes (the vast majority of the population) for hardscrabble subsistence gardening (Wordsworth's Simon Lee being a late example), livestock grazing, and recreation. As this chapter will unfurl, views of heath began to sour in the sixteenth century with the rise of the enclosure movement, as the prices for arable land soared along with England's population. The Diggers' famous occupation of St George's Hill and Little Heath in 1649 and insistence that heaths should remain a 'common treasury' was not an unprecedented or utterly utopian idea but the revival of an old-fashioned practice.[6] When *Macbeth* was first staged Britain's heaths were considerably larger—approximately six times their current size—but increasingly targeted by agrarian improvement schemes. In the intervening centuries, an estimated 84 per cent of the United Kingdom's lowland heath would be destroyed. Since the United Kingdom contains more of it than any other country, heathland is now 'rarer than rainforest' (Natural England 2002, 1) and many conservationists wish to protect heaths, especially those with carbon-sequestering peatlands, as a distinctive and fascinating part of Britain's organic heritage.

Not all environmentalists agree, however. When the Scottish government in 2016 raised taxes on large game estates that manage hundreds, sometimes thousands, of acres of moorlands many eco-activists rejoiced (Newman 2017). Although these shrublands are home to a handful of rare species—such as the Dartford warbler, the nightjar, the smooth snake, and the silver-studded blue butterfly—they support a scant number of plants and hence do not rate highly in terms of biodiversity. Moreover, gamekeepers not only cull predators, such as hen harriers and foxes, but also burn strips of heather to encourage grouse-nesting so that many moorlands resemble 'the self-shaved head of a madman' (Atkins 2014, 169).[7] When reassessing *Macbeth* through the lens of environmental history, it is essential to remember that the perceived barrenness of the heath implied in Macbeth's 'blasted' is in fact the result of human impact. Heaths may look wild but they are not genuine wilderness; they are by and large the result of centuries of deforestation by humans in the Bronze Age, when a cool, wet climate fostered peat formation and discouraged trees regenerating in the acidified soil of the manmade clearings, which gradually coalesced to create vast windswept heaths. Emphasizing their unnaturalness, George Monbiot, England's most outspoken advocate of rewilding, has repeatedly hectored UK environmental organizations to convert heaths back into woodlands, sniffing at them as a 'burnt, blasted and largely empty land with the delightful ambience of a nuclear winter' (2013). Monbiot here curiously echoes the same adjective deployed by Shakespeare four centuries earlier, when Macbeth and Banquo encounter the weird sisters upon a 'blasted heath'. Given that heaths and moorlands remain contentious sites for environmental policy-makers in Britain, it seems worthwhile to re-examine the cultural history of this landscape as refracted through the works of the national poet.

Although sketched with a few deft strokes, like the moors in *Wuthering Heights*, Shakespeare's 'blasted heath' nevertheless achieves, even on the page, what William Hazlitt termed 'a real subsistence in the mind' (1838, 15). But how would

Fig. 1.1 *Macbeth* at the Park Avenue Armory (2014).
© Stephanie Berger.

the heath be presented to audiences at the Globe or Blackfriars? It seems unlikely that Jacobean performances of *Macbeth* featured any elaborate set designs on the scale of Romantic landscapes by the likes of John Martin or George Robson (featured on the cover), much less the stunning recreation of a Scottish heath in the 2014 production at New York's cavernous Park Avenue Armory (see Fig. 1.1). But Shakespeare's acting company did not need to strew the playing space with ersatz heather and lichen-splattered monoliths. In evoking the landscape of a heath, the comparative barrenness of the Renaissance stage would actually be advantageous, reinforcing perceptions of the heaths as barren. Moreover, the King's Men could have supplemented Shakespeare's word-painting with the use of squibs to create the 'fog' through which the weird sisters hover. Jonathan Gil Harris (2009, 119–39) has ingeniously argued that the sulphur-tinged scent of playhouse pyrotechnics constitutes an olfactory pun on the Gunpowder Plot, but the more immediate purpose would be to serve as a visual evocation of the misty heaths and moors of Scotland, intensifying the negative impression of them as places of bewilderment and disorientation. An ecocritical reading might even sniff in *Macbeth*'s smoke or 'filthy air' an olfactory allusion to the widespread but controversial practice of burning heath (known as swealing, swithening, or swiddening), adding another semantic layer to Shakespeare's description of this landscape as 'blasted'.

The heath in *Macbeth* is so influential that it continues to warp cultural perceptions of this landscape to this day and even to colonize Shakespeare's other plays. While this chapter focuses on *Macbeth*, its findings have implications for *King Lear* as well, since the heath on which the crazed king wanders in the storm is to some extent retrospectively derived from William Davenant's Restoration adaptation of the Scottish play.[8] As James Ogden (1997) has proposed, Davenant's 1671 *Macbeth* at the Duke's Theatre likely featured a painted backdrop of heath, which seems to have so impressed Nahum Tate that he repurposed it for his adaptation of *King Lear* at the same London theatre.[9] Tate's *Lear*, in turn, influenced Nicholas Rowe's decision—licensed by Gloucester's declaration that the countryside surrounding his estate contains 'scarce a bush' (2.2.492)—to add stage directions to his 1709 Shakespeare edition specifying that the storm scene in *Lear* transpires on a heath. Informed by Ogden, critics such as Henry Turner and Gwilym Jones have challenged the presumptive setting of Lear's storm on the heath as a fallacy that blinds us to Shakespeare's refusal to pin down his scenes in a specific recognizable topography, unlike the *Leir* source play which identifies the setting of the king's attempted murder as a 'thicket'. While such caveats are valid apropos of *Lear*, they do not apply to *Macbeth*, which twice identifies the locale of scene 3 as a heath. The more pressing question, then, is not whether *Lear* features a heath but why did Shakespeare include one in *Macbeth* and what are the ecocritical ramifications of this decision?

It seems Shakespeare was not following his source, Raphael Holinshed's *Chronicles*. Holinshed describes Macbeth and Banquo on their journey toward Forres 'passing thorough the woods and fields, when suddenlie in the middest of a laund, there met them three women in strange and wild apparell' (1587, 86). The word 'laund' usually signifies a glade or clearing, which does not at first glance tally with Shakespeare's locating the fateful encounter upon a desolate heath. Yet the two terms are not entirely dissimilar.[10] A 'laund' or glade could eventually become heath, but only after the passage of many decades or centuries. This basic process of ecological succession was already understood in Shakespeare's day, and mentioned in one of his most beloved books. In his chorographical text prefixed to the 1587 edition of Holinshed's *Chronicles*, William Harrison describes the treelessness of the Orkneys and observes that heath is an anthropogenic landscape:

> And yet it seemeth that (in times past) some of these Ilands also have beene well replenished with wood, but now they are without either tree or shrub, in steed whereof they have plentie of heath, which is suffered to grow among them, rather thorough their negligence, than that the soile of it selfe will not yeeld to bring foorth trees & bushes. (1587, 42)

Employing his antiquarian and philological skills, Harrison also deduces that England's moors too had formerly been wooded.

> The hills called the Peak were in like sort named Mennith and Orcoit, that is, the Woody hills and forests. But how much wood is now to be seen in those places,

let him that hath been there testify if he list. For I hear of no such store there as hath been in time past by those that travel that way. (1587, 214)

Fittingly, the book that supplied the source material for *Macbeth* was among the first works to decry humanity's role in the heathification of Britain's primeval ecology. In substituting heath for laund, Shakespeare almost seems to be fast-forwarding history, updating the chronicles to reveal the long-term consequences or 'slow violence' (to borrow Rob Nixon's evocative phrase) of environmental mismanagement: medieval clearings have become early modern heaths, a process that would have been accelerated by population growth and the cool, damp climate of the Little Ice Age.

It is therefore curious that Simon Forman, who attended a performance of *Macbeth* at the Globe in 1611, makes no mention of a heath but reports that Macbeth and Banquo met the three women while 'riding thorowe a wod'.[11] Perhaps the woodcut in Holinshed contaminated his memory (Brooke 1990, 234) or he may have simply mistaken Forres for forest. Alternatively, an artificial property tree (later pruned by Malcolm's forces to conceal their numbers) may have adorned the rear of the stage in the opening act. Although mists obscure the play's early performance history, the replacement of the 'wod' that Forman saw in 1611 by a heath in the 1623 text is uncannily appropriate in that it encapsulates the ecological dynamics of succession. During the late medieval era, woodlands had increasingly given way to heath throughout the British countryside, a phenomenon that aroused concern in James's reign. Reversing this damage, the tragedy's memorable finale in which Birnam wood marches on Dunsinane, seat of the barren Macbeths, visually enacts the reconquest of heath by treescape.

A more immediate, aesthetic explanation, however, for the Folio's transformation of glade into heath would be that Shakespeare recognized its dramatic potential as an appropriate mis-en-scène for witchcraft. The link between wilderness and misbelief is an ancient one, and pre-dates the Old English word *háed*. In the Book of Jeremiah, the prophet exclaims, 'Cursed be the man that trusteth in man, and maketh flesh his arme, and withdraweth his heart from the Lorde. For hee shalbe like the heath in the wildernes' (17:5–6). This well-known verse, cited in a book of similes from 1600, would have reinforced the etymological kinship between heath and heathen, which was already something of a commonplace in the fourteenth century, when William Langland expounded it in *Piers Plowman*, 'Hethen is to mene after heath and untiled erthe' (15.457–8).[12] The derivation is not hard to fathom. Since heaths are extremely difficult to farm, the small communities who inhabited these sparsely populated regions were some of the most poverty-stricken in the kingdom. With schools and churches few and far between, heaths, like fens, gained notoriety as havens of paganism; unsurprisingly, these regions spawned a large number of witch hunts in early modern Britain.[13]

If there be any truth to the theory that Shakespeare spent some of his lost years in Lancashire as a schoolmaster for the Hoghton family, he would have been familiar with the kind of terrain depicted in act 1, scene 3 of *Macbeth*. The Hoghton's Lancashire land-holdings included, according to a 1590 survey, over 6,000 acres of moorlands and 1,000 acres of heath.[14] Indeed, the West Pennine Moors are clearly visible from the Hoghton's hilltop estate, and Pendle, the site of an infamous Jacobean witchcraft case, is only twenty miles to the northeast. Performances of *Macbeth* after 1612 would have gained verisimilitude from the trial of the Pendle witches, who had vowed 'they should all meet upon Romelys moor' (Potts 1613, 131), rendering the play's demonization of this landscape all the more compelling.[15] But Shakespeare need not have ventured to Lancashire to become acquainted with heath. Lowland heaths dotted the West Midlands, including northern Warwickshire, and Shakespeare undeniably knew a hamlet outside Stratford named Barton-on-the-Heath, where his wealthy uncle Edmund Lambert lived, and where Christopher Sly in *The Taming of the Shrew* proudly asserts he was born (Induction 2.17). Not simply a feature of the remote wilds of the far north, many heathlands could be found in the vicinity of early modern London, such as Dartford and Blackheath (which features as the home of a wizard-hermit in the comedy *Look About You*) to the east, Moorfields and Hampstead Heath to the north, and Hounslow Heath and the heathlands on which Heathrow airport now stands to the west—all of which were substantially larger than they are today. In other words, the 'blasted heath' of *Macbeth* was perhaps not such an exotic locale to Shakespeare or his audience as we imagine.

In addition to being a haunt of witches, heaths and moors also hosted another disreputable group of people on the margins of early modern society: the Romani, or 'Gypsies', as they were commonly called in the mistaken belief they originated from Egypt. In his 1621 masque, *The Gypsies Metamorphosed*, Ben Jonson describes the Romani encampments on the moors of the Peak District: 'where we yearly keep our musters, / Thus th'Egyptians throng in clusters' (*CWBJ* 5:489.55–6). Thomas Dekker's *Lanthorne and Candlelight* (1608) asserts that Romani habitually reside on some 'large heath or a fir [furze] bush common'— furze being synonymous with heaths and moors. Dekker even offers a jocoserious description of a group of Romani women slaughtering and cooking stolen animals around a pot as a 'conjuring circle' for the raising of spirits, and compares the spectacle to a 'bloody tragedy' played upon the 'stage' of a heath in a text written shortly after *Macbeth* (1608, H2ʳ). As nomads who squatted on commons and who did not subscribe to conventional notions of private property, the Romani frequently fell afoul of the authorities and were subject to a series of increasingly stringent laws calling for their deportation.[16] The Vagrancy Act of 1531 targets the so-called Egyptians by denouncing those who 'feigning themselves to have knowledge in physic, physiognomy, palmistry, or other crafty sciences, where they bear the people in hand, that that they can tell their destinies, deceases, and fortunes'.[17] When Duncan proclaims 'There's no art / To find the mind's construction in the face' (1.4.11–12) he alludes to the art of physiognomy that was a notorious speciality of the Romani. In his *Discoverie of Witchcraft*, a work Shakespeare almost certainly knew, Reginald Scot describes these 'counterfeit Egyptians' as 'cosening vagabonds' performing 'divinations' (1584, 112), and his contemporary John Harvey condemned their 'wizardly fortune-tellings' (1588, 63). In other words, early modern discourse on witches often lumped them with the Romani. Revealingly, a band of 'Gypsies' feature in Thomas Middleton's *More Dissemblers Besides Women* (c.1614), written around the same time as *The Witch* and his supposed revisions to Shakespeare's *Macbeth*. Furthermore, Shakespeare himself exhibits a greater fascination with the Romani after 1603 as witnessed by the magical handkerchief Othello's mother had from an Egyptian (read Gypsy) and the comparison of Cleopatra to a cheating 'Gypsy' in a play contemporaneous with *Macbeth*.[18]

Significantly, the English often associated the Romani with Scotland, where they had received a much warmer welcome (Hopkins 2004, 232–3). King James IV paid a group of 'Egyptians' seven pounds for entertaining him at Stirling in 1505, and another group performed at Holyrood Palace in 1530; some bands of Travellers even claimed they had letters of endorsement from James IV or V, which fed rumours that they had first arrived in Scotland and thence migrated southward into England. However, the favour they had enjoyed in Scotland cooled following the 1571 Act of Stringency, and in 1603 and 1609 the Scottish Privy Council followed England in banishing them from the realm.[19] As the Romani were fortune-tellers who camped on heaths and were linked with Scotland, it is worth considering how they may have influenced Shakespeare's recreation of Holinshed's 'weird sisters' as much as the masque featuring three sibyls performed before James at Oxford in 1605.[20] The drive to reclaim and enclose heath may even be connected to xenophobic campaigns to expel the Romani who squatted on these commons.

Approaching *Macbeth* from the heath also brings to light an unheralded influence on the play: the ghastly crimes committed by Sir John Fitz in the summer of 1605 and reported in a tract entitled *The Bloudy Booke*. Fitz was a wealthy landowner from Tavistock in Devon, whose ancestral home stood alongside Dartmoor. In a scene not unlike the assassination of Banquo, the hot-headed Fitz along with four servants murdered one of his former friends by ambushing him while he was out riding near his estate. Wracked with guilt, Fitz began to suffer from insomnia and exhibit symptoms of paranoid schizophrenia, hallucinating that his victim's family lurked in every corner. On his way to London to stand trial, he 'straied uppon the Heath a long while' in the dark before arriving at the Anchor Inn in Twickenham at two in the morning. 'But the Gentlemans mind being troubled, he could by no meanes sleepe, or take any rest, but (oftentimes starting verie suddenlie as if he had been scard) alwaies...uttering much disjointed talke' (D2ᵛ). Around four in the morning, the guests heard a loud crash and discovered Fitz stomping around the inn in his night shirt with his rapier drawn. When the innkeeper tried to shut him out, the deranged Fitz ran him through and then attempted to murder the innkeeper's wife before finally stabbing himself. He was found 'wallowing in his owne bloud, like a Pigge that had beene latelie sticked'. Shakespeare must have been acquainted with this grisly affair. The sensational crimes of Sir John Fitz would have been the talk of London between August 1605 and the Gunpowder Plot in November. In addition to *The Bloudy Booke*, which, like *Macbeth*, revels in images of blood, the crimes were reported in two ballads (now lost), *The Lamentable Murthers of Sir John Fitz*, printed by Thomas Pavier in August 1605, and *Sir John Fitz his ghost*, licensed on 13 September 1605.[21] The publicity surrounding the incident would have been an embarrassment to the Jacobean court, as King James had knighted Fitz shortly after his coronation, and it was reported that Fitz's knighthood had accelerated his dissipation by making him think himself immune to prosecution.

As a dramatist, Shakespeare would have been struck by *The Bloudy Booke*'s declaration, 'didst thou ever read a thing more tragical?' (E3ʳ), the coincidence that the homicidal lunatic's name (spelled Fites) meant a 'paroxysm of lunacy'—cf. 'then comes my fit again' (3.4.19)—and its vivid depiction of the murderer's addled psyche:

In his dreames he muttered fearefull wordes, grievous sighes, & deep-fetcht grones: most fearefull were his visions, and so terrible unto him, that where hee lay in rest hee suddainly start up, and called for his horses, intending to post presently away...so strange & dreadfull was his owne minde unto him.   (C4ᵛ)

Macbeth's 'restless ecstasy', his exclamation, 'O, full of scorpions is my mind, dear wife' (3.2.37), and Lady Macbeth's sleep-walking and sleep-talking, have a real-world analogue in the true-crime saga of Sir John Fitz. To be sure, the criminal's guilty conscience is a commonplace, and Holinshed remarks how those 'pricked in conscience for any secret offense committed have ever an unquiet mind' (1587, 13). While it would be misguided to hail *The Bloudy Booke* as a source for Shakespeare's bloody tragedy, it and the lost ballads would doubtless have sparked contemporary interest in criminal psychology when Shakespeare first composed *Macbeth*. Moreover, the gruesome murder-suicide of this crazed Dartmoor native who had been wandering on a heath right before perpetrating these crimes would have contributed to the unsavoury reputation of heaths at this time. Prior to Kant's and Burke's formulation of the sublime as an aesthetic category in the late eighteenth century, Fitz's fate would seem to confirm—as does that of King Lear—that exposure to vast spaces like heaths could incite not an exhilarating dread but a violent madness. Small wonder then that many seventeenth-century agrarian capitalists wanted to eradicate or 'reclaim' them.

Blasting the Heath

As the movement to privatize commons gained momentum in Jacobean England, enclosers and agrarian improvers grew increasingly outspoken in their dismissal of heaths as useless and godless wastelands in need of reclamation. The Jacobean surveyor John Norden asserts that lowland heaths can be 'killed' and brought to 'profitable tillage' through regular doses of manure or marle (1607, 235–6). Similar instructions for 'destroying of heath' can be found in the georgic tracts of the prolific agrarian writer Gervase Markham, who reviles the heath's drab colourscape when he dubs ling or common heather a 'filthie, black-browne weede' and advocates scorching it: 'set every hill on fier, and so burne the very substance of the earth into ashes' (1620, 38–40). This practice of burning heath continues to enkindle controversy in the twenty-first century, but was, as we shall see, already inciting anxiety and environmental regulation around the time *Macbeth* was first written and revised.

Shakespeare's blasted, witch-haunted heath would seem to contradict the assumption that *Macbeth* flatters his patron, since deprecating views of heathlands played into anti-Scottish sentiment (and vice versa) at the English court. Echoing the language of agrarian reformers, a work attributed to James's Master of the Green Cloth sneers that Scotland's 'ground might be fruitfull had [the Scots] the wit to mannure it', and dismisses the country as a treeless wasteland: 'had Christ beene betrayd in this countrey … Judas had sooner found the grace of repentance then a tree to hange himselfe on' (1626, 3). A similarly grim sketch of James's homeland can be found in *A Cat May Look Upon a King*, which snubs Scotland as 'a nasty barren Country, rather a Dunghil then a Kingdome' and emphasizes James's base ancestry by tracing it back to the sordid events of Shakespeare's tragedy, adding the curious detail that Macbeth sought to seduce Banquo's daughter and only slew Banquo (and abducted the girl) after he was refused.[22] Such attacks betray that *Macbeth*'s topography is implicated in early modern ecopolitics. Can a Scotsman accustomed to barren heaths govern the lush terrain of lowland England? An incisive essay on *King Lear* suggests that Lear's wandering amid a 'high grown field' choked with 'furrow weeds' (4.4.7) such as darnel evokes the king's power to remedy dearth while punning on the inauspicious name of James's father, Lord Darnley, and that the tragedy poses a question to England's ruler: 'will he manage the nation's resources in a way that is just, responsible, and above all sustainable?' (Archer et al. 2012, 542). Portraying James's ancestor Banquo as a model for royal husbandry by linking him with seeds and fertility, *Macbeth* asks a similar question and ponders whether its answer should involve eliminating heaths.

Not everyone in early modern Britain regarded heaths as bleak wastes. In *Poly-Olbion*, Michael Drayton depicts 'shaggy heaths' as a habitat for deer herds, recognizes their hydrological role in the landscape, and praises Newmarket Heath, where larksong echoes the poet's blessing: 'therefore deare Heath, live still in prosperous estate' (1612-22, 12.522-40, 21.35). The cartographer John Speed insists that the seemingly 'barren heaths' of Norfolk are 'very profitable' when rightly managed by rotating between pasturing and ploughing (1612, 35), while Henry Peacham ranked the rolling heaths around Royston (of which more soon) among the most beautiful 'lantskips' (1612, 44) in all of England. Heathlands were especially valued by the rural poor where they enjoyed long-standing communal rights of pasturage and turbary (harvesting peat for domestic fuel), the latter of which was vital in these timber-scarce regions. The fact that heath-dwellers tended to be illiterate (low population density discouraged the founding of schools) helps explain why one searches Jacobean literature in vain for anything as effusive as John Clare's valentine to 'Emmonsail's Heath'. Yet the privatizing of heathlands, moors, and mosses by agricultural improvers and tenement builders did not go unprotested in Shakespeare's lifetime. Nearly 50 per cent of the enclosure disputes that flared up during James's reign concerned these so-called wastes.[23] Unable to stop local bigwigs, dispossessed cottagers might take their grievances to the king. Such a scene is recreated in a 1605 text attributed to Robert Armin, who likely played the Porter in *Macbeth*, when a jester complains to Henry VIII about the fate of Terrils Frith:

'Terrils Frith?' sayes the King, 'What is that?'
'Why, the Heath where I was borne, called by the name of Terrils Frith: now a gentleman of that name takes it all in, & makes all the people beleeve it is his; for it tooke the name from him: so that...the poore pine and their cattell are all undon without thy helpe.' (1605, D4^r)

If he heard such complaints, King James would have listened with one sympathetic ear, since converting heaths to farmland, pasture, or housing reduced not only commons for the poor but also hunting grounds for the wealthy. Defending the traditional management of Dartmoor for mining and hunting, the Devonshire chorographer Tristram Risdon bemoans that many parks in the area have been 'disparked and converted from pleasure to profit; from pasturing wild beasts to breeding and feeding of cattle, sheep, and tillage' (1633, 6-7). In other words, some believed the so-called improvements of the heaths and moors were succeeding all too well, and among those concerned over the vanishing of this landscape was no less a personage than King James, who would himself enclose and conserve hundreds of acres of heathland for his own personal recreation.

While travelling to London for his coronation in April 1603, James stopped over at Royston and recognized the nearby Therfield Heath as an ideal habitat for game. The following year he purchased two adjoining inns in Royston, razed them to the ground, and over the next seven years spent a whopping £4,000 on the construction of an opulent hunting lodge. On a visit to Suffolk in February 1605, James was equally smitten with the 'huge uninterrupted heath' (Thurley 2021, 42) around Newmarket and another across the Norfolk border outside Thetford, establishing two more royal hunting lodges. The closest of the three, Royston soon became a favourite retreat, where James could escape from the bustle of London with a few of his closest hunting companions. In the early seventeenth century, the adjacent Therfield Heath would have echoed with the songs, chirps, and caws of now-endangered red-backed shrikes, stone curlews, corncrakes, skylarks, great bustards, and hooded crows (then commonly known as the Royston crow), which made it a popular destination for James's birding expeditions.[24] While much of the once sprawling Therfield Heath was sadly destroyed and converted to arable land in the 1840s (and has since been disfigured by a golf course), the scale of the nineteenth-century enclosures does not mean that it was not under threat in Shakespeare's lifetime. Many people in the early Stuart era, starting with James Stuart himself, expressed anxieties about habitat loss and the decline of England's wildlife. One of his very first edicts after ascending the English throne in 1603 called for the stricter enforcement of anti-poaching laws, and Parliament responded by renewing an Elizabethan Act against unlawful hunting in 1605. Many of James's proclamations to protect wildlife were issued from his hunting lodges at Royston, New Market, and Thetford. Shakespeare's decision to set the encounter between Macbeth and the weird sisters on a heath would have struck a nerve with King James, who disliked being accosted by locals whilst out hunting, regarded prophets with suspicion, and had been returning from Therfield Heath when he received Lord Monteagle's letter full of 'obscure riddles and doubtful mysteries' (226) warning of the Gunpowder Plot. The local communities near the royal hunting lodges, however, resented the shortages triggered by James's visits and his notorious habit of trampling crops while galloping in pursuit of quarry, which seemed to ally him with forces of sterility.[25] In brief, Shakespeare conjured his ominous heath at a time when it had become evident that the Scottish king preferred heaths to the Tudor palaces in and around London, and English courtiers watching *Macbeth* who had never crossed the Tweed may very well have visualized the play's setting as Therfield or Thetford rather than Forres.

Although his detractors complained of James's addiction to the chase, Parliament appears to have shared some of his concerns about the heathlands. Anxiety that the push to reclaim heath would destroy wildlife prompted an important piece of environmental legislation in 1609: an act against the burning of ling and heath. The bill prohibits the burning of heather in spring and summer, alleging the 'great destruction of the Brood of Wild-fowl and Moor-game' by the 'multitude of gross vapors, and Clouds arising from those great fires', which '*blast* [the] fruits of the earth'. Revealingly, this 1609 law applies the verb 'blast' to the effect of anthropogenic pollution: smoke from slash-and-burn agriculture (swiddening) conducted in an unecological manner that harms both fauna and flora.

With this environmental history in mind, it is worth scrutinizing Macbeth's adjective 'blasted'. To modern readers it might suggest bombed, as many heaths and moors (such as Otterburn and Dartmoor) have been requisitioned by the British military for artillery ranges. For Shakespeare's contemporaries, the word most readily implied cursed or blighted, although by whom or what remains murky. According to the *OED*, 'blasted' signifies 'to blow or breathe on balefully or perniciously; to wither, shrivel or arrest vegetation' or 'to be stricken by meteoric or supernatural agency' (7). The term is ambiguous: the blasting is the result of either natural causes (weather) or supernatural (i.e. witchcraft, which might control the weather). However, the 1609 legislation makes it clear that 'blasted' could also imply singed, burnt, or smoke-damaged. Given that burning heath was a subject of parliamentary debate in the early Jacobean period, Shakespeare's 'blasted heath' may glance not merely at some meteorological or supernatural agency but also at the on-going human-induced devastation of this landscape by the fires of agricultural 'improvers'.

Confusingly, however, while agrarian improvers advocated scorching heath in order to destroy it, occasional fires are necessary for their preservation; trees can regenerate and reclaim them if they are not subject to periodic burning. This created friction between farmers, shepherds, foresters, and hunters over the management of heathlands. In his 1592 book on forestry law, John Manwood mentions that swainmotes were expected to monitor the heaths and protect them from arson: 'Item, if there be any man that doth burne any Heathe or Fearne or Ling within the Foreste or townes next adjoyning to the same Forest, you shall present the same' (115). The reasons for this vigilance were twofold and somewhat contradictory: burning heath destroyed the habitat of game animals but also hindered the regeneration of woodlands, thus contributing to the timber crisis of the early seventeenth century. Swiddening, or muirburn as it is known in Scotland, remains a common although controversial practice to this day (see Fig. 1.2). Revealingly, the 1609 legislation does not prohibit the burning of heath tout court; it only outlaws it during breeding season to protect wildfowl. In 1609 King James made another important proclamation while at Royston to stem deforestation, lamenting the 'great spoyles and devastations...committed, both within our Forrests, Chaces, Parks and Wasts', and urging 'the present multiplication and increase of Timber and Wood to all future ages' (*SRP* 207). James's decree that keepers and rangers 'take onely such lops for browse, as the trees which have bene usually lopped shall affoord, and that not in greater proportion then is meete and necessary' (208), has a curious resemblance to Malcolm's command in *Macbeth* that each invading soldier 'hew him down a bough' (5.4.4). In imitating the practice of coppicing or pollarding trees, the assault on Dunsinane evokes sustainable woodlands management, which contrasts pointedly with Macbeth's wishing the 'trees blown down' (4.1.53). If the ending of *Macbeth* dramatizes the victory of light over darkness (see Chapter 8), it also appears to stage a triumph of green over brown. The blasted heath of act 1 gives way to leafy woods in act 5. Such a binary

Fig. 1.2 A Muirburn in Scotland.
Simon Butterworth/Alamy Stock Photo.

reading is complicated, however, by the fact that heaths were not entirely barren but supplied hunting grounds (and hence meat) for the king and commoners, as well as allotments and summer grazing land for the rural poor. In the assault on Dunsinane, the actors on the Globe stage may have toted a leafy prop resembling 'the tree to stalk with' described in Jacobean fowling manuals (Markham 1621, 62–3), giving them the appearance of hunters. Shakespeare's poetic imagery heightening *Macbeth* into a primeval battle between the forces of sterility and fertility is thus entangled in environmental policy disputes in Jacobean Britain over the necessity of preserving a proportion of heathlands alongside woods and fields. These policy disputes also extended to one of the most prominent image clusters in *Macbeth*: birds. The same agrilogistics that drove the reclamation of heathlands justified the protection of some avian species and the eradication of others classified as pests.

Avian Conservation and Reproductive Futurity: Macbeth the Nest-Robber and Macduff's Dovecote

That birds represent a conspicuous motif in *Macbeth* is of course a familiar proposition, the theme of many a grudgingly written high school essay. In her classic monograph on Shakespeare's imagery, Caroline Spurgeon noted the poet's 'intimate knowledge of the life and habits of birds and his intense sympathy with them' (1961, 48). Rebecca Ann Bach (2018, 41) has chided the Formalists for failing to show the same sympathy and treating birds and other animals as mere objects. It must be said, however, that *Macbeth* does not regard all birds kindly, and some rate even worse than objects. Not coincidentally, the murderous Macbeths are associated with rooks, ravens, owls, and kites—species categorized as 'vermin' by early modern law. Under the notorious 1566 Tudor Vermin Act (renewed in 1572 and 1598 in response to meagre harvests), the populace was urged to eliminate these pests, and bounties were placed on the heads of undesirables: the corpses of three crows or three rooks were worth one penny (see Chapter 8), while ravens and kites fetched one penny each (at a time when the average labourer earned five or sixpence a day).[26] Aggravating the problem, the destruction of heath and woodlands meant that animals faced with shrinking habitats were increasingly seen as trespassing upon human domains and pilfering human property. The same concerns over food insecurity that encouraged agrarian improvers to scorch and plough up heathlands also fuelled the drive to exterminate birds that ate seeds or preyed on livestock. In revealing how sovereign power determines which species may live and which must die, *Macbeth* exposes agrilogistics as a form of what Achille Mbembe terms 'necropolitics' (2003).

Due to its tendency to snatch farmyard poultry, the red kite, which Macbeth imagines devouring human corpses—'our monuments / Shall be the maws of kites' (3.4.69–70)—was among the most detested. Although the species once flourished in medieval cities and towns (as the black kite does today in places like Cairo and Kanazawa), they were persecuted so ruthlessly throughout the early modern period that they were extirpated from Britain by the nineteenth century and have only recently been reintroduced by avian conservationists. In the practical part of his brain concerned with managing his farmland around Stratford, Shakespeare would likely have endorsed these egregious vermin laws. A good deal of the avian imagery in the Scottish play—such as Lady Macbeth's croaking raven, her husband's picture of the crow flying toward the 'rooky wood' as he dispatches his assassins, and Macduff's memorable comparison of the child-killer Macbeth to a chick-predating 'hell-kite'—serves to blacken these birds as pests, effectively promoting contemporary campaigns to exterminate them.

Other avian species mentioned in *Macbeth*, however, particularly those valued by the aristocratic classes for the hunt or as food, were granted protected status by Tudor and Stuart lawmakers. It is therefore significant that Macbeth endorses illegal birding in one of the play's celebrated soliloquies when he wishes to 'trammel up the consequence' (1.7.3) of his crime. The brilliance of this line results from its transformation of a common noun into a verb. A trammel is a large and lengthy net deployed to capture ground-nesting fowl in open heathlands, as detailed by Gervase Markham:

> This Nette, when you come into the place where the haunt of Birds are which rest upon the earth...you shall then...traile it along the ground, not suffering

that ende which is borne up to come neere the ground by a full yard or more. Then on each side the Nette shall bee carried great blazing lights of fire... [while] others with long Poles... beate the Birds as they goe, and as they rise under the Netts so to take them. (1621, 97)

Given Macbeth's reference to trammelling his enemies, the Murderer's line 'let it come down' (3.4.15) may not simply be a grim joke about impending rain but a clue that Macbeth's instructions for the ambush called for them to drop a net. The King's Men certainly owned a net among their properties when they staged *Pericles*. If a net were deployed here in *Macbeth*, the presence of torchlight combined with Banquo's repeated command that Fleance 'fly, fly, fly' (3.4.16) may have given this scene a strange resemblance to the nocturnal birding (known as bat-fowling) described above by Markham. Macbeth's wish that he could 'trammel up the consequence' would likely have caught the ear of King James, who sought to restrict such destructive tactics for hunting heathland fowl. His 1603 proclamation explicitly forbids the use of 'Nettes and other Engines' (*SRP* 15) to catch pheasants, partridges, herons, and mallards that 'of late yeeres... have bene more excessively and outrageously spoiled & destroyed then hath bene attempted & practised in former age' (*SRP* 15). The Children of the Chapel may have ridiculed James for swearing when a bird dodged his bullets but a survey of hunting legislation indicates that the king and his gamekeepers blamed his unsuccessful expeditions not on his poor marksmanship but on the scarcity of game due to overhunting out of season and the mass slaughter perpetrated by nets (see Fig. 1.3). Macbeth's ominous reference to the trammel net links a tragic act of regicide to the ecological tragedy of extirpation, supporting James's efforts to preserve healthy wildlife populations and thus better 'sport' for the monarch.

While scholarship on the Scottish play often highlights James's toughening of the witchcraft statutes, Shakespeare likely knew that the king was also cracking down on overhunting and egg-snatching, encouraging Parliament to impose harsher penalties on nest-robbing in 1603 (1 Jac. c. 27) and 1610 (7 Jac. c. 11).[27] Banquo shares his descendant's interest in bird nests when he speaks of the martlet's 'procreant cradle' (1.6.8), while observing that its breeding requires 'delicate' or clean air, not polluted by the swiddening banned in the 1609 statute. The description of the martlet (either the swift or house martin) as the 'guest of summer' places this insectivore on the side of fertility. More shockingly, this dialogue invites us to imagine Macbeth's castle as a nest and his guest Duncan as a bird, thereby priming us to view his murder as a nest-robbing and the violation of the king's conservation laws as tantamount to treason.[28] On the morning after Duncan's assassination, when the Old Man reports that 'a falcon, towering in her pride of place, / Was by a mousing owl hawked at and killed' (2.4.12–13), the cross-species metaphor incriminates Macbeth in the illegal killing of a raptor protected by royal and parliamentary decree. A Jacobean audience would have been

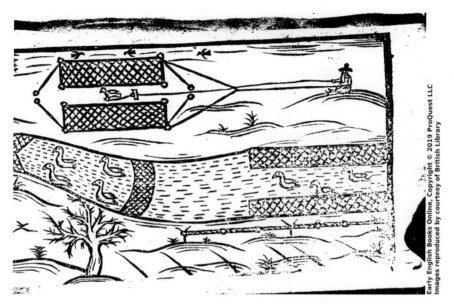

Fig. 1.3 Gervarse Markham, *Hungers Prevention: Or, the whole Arte of Fowling* (1621).
Courtesy of the British Library, digitized by the Google Books project.

all the more likely to twig on to Shakespeare's strange eco-allegory since the name of the Duncan character in Holinshed is Duffe, an early modern spelling of dove, while the name of his son Malcolm signifies 'devotee of St Columba', Scotland's most famous saint, whose name literally means dove in Latin. After his murder, Duncan's body is transported to 'Colmekill' (2.4.33) or Dove-chapel. Both Duncan and Malcolm are depicted as meek and peaceful, qualities synonymous with this bird, and the traditional symbolism of the dove as peace-bringer would have endeared it to peace-loving King James. Macbeth does not simply murder sleep but also peace itself, incarnate in a dove-like king.

Viewed alongside legislative efforts to protect nesting birds, the surprising of Macduff's castle becomes something more than an episode of sensational violence. Lady Macduff's image of the wren defending 'her nest', her refusal to 'fly' from it, and the son's declaration that he will live 'as birds do', to which she retorts by affectionately calling him a 'poor bird' all groom the audience to imagine the sacking of their castle as a nest-robbing. Lady Macduff's concern her naïve child will 'never fear the net nor lime, / The pitfall nor gin' (4.2.36–7) foreshadows his murder while blackening the sinister use of 'Nettes and other Engines' outlawed by royal proclamation. Shakespeare pushes the castle/nest analogy to the cusp of absurdity when one of the cut-throats taunts Macduff's son before stabbing him: 'What, you egg!' (4.2.86). One of the strangest and most lampooned insults in all of Shakespeare, the line can have an awkwardly comic ring, and hence is often cut in modern performance. The dark humour, however, springs from its abrupt collapse of biological taxonomies in rhetorically violent metaphors by which the murderer de-humanizes his victim. That an egg might deserve the same ethical consideration as a full-fledged adult would not have been immediately self-evident in the seventeenth century, and still requires some mental exertion to grasp. The point here is not to lend succour to anti-abortion activists but to observe that a belief in the rights of the newborn or unborn, especially of non-humans, has to be taught, and authorities in Stuart England were striving to inculcate this lesson around the time Shakespeare composed *Macbeth*—albeit selectively. If Macduff's comparison of the child-killer Macbeth to a 'hell-kite' stealing a farmer's chickens sanctions the persecution of the kite as vermin, the raid on Macduff's castle condemns nest-robbing and thus bolsters the conservation efforts of Shakespeare's patron.

Given the three successive references to Macduff's 'flight' in eight lines (4.2.1, 3, 8), Simon Forman's transcription of Macduff as 'Macdove' and 'Mackdove' invites further scrutiny. Early modern pronunciation and the persistence of a late medieval spelling of dove as 'douf' and 'douff' makes it highly plausible that Jacobean audiences heard 'dove' in the stressed syllable of Macduff, which would prime them to imagine the sacking of his mansion as a raid on a dovecote. Shakespeare uses a similar image when Coriolanus compares the havoc of his solo assault on Corioli to that of 'an eagle in a dovecote' (5.6.115). An estimated 24,000 of these structures dotted the English landscape in the seventeenth century when doves and pigeons provided an important meat source in winter.[29] Macduff's county of Fife was particularly renowned for them, and Shakespeare would have been familiar with examples near Stratford-upon-Avon like the ones at Kinwarton and Temple Grafton—where local legend has it that Shakespeare once fell asleep after a drinking contest (see Fig. 1.4). In lean times dovehouses would have been subject to break-ins by the hungry poor but were also plundered by the king's saltpetre men, who impounded the valuable dropping-laden soil to make gunpowder, on which the Crown held a monopoly. When Shakespeare penned this scene, doves (regarded as vermin by farmers since they ate grains) had just been protected by a 1605 law that prohibited killing them within 100 paces of a dovecote, which the invasion of Macduff's manor violates.[30] Dovecotes were also a flashpoint in a high-profile legal battle over the Crown's claim to own all the soil of the realm, eventually decided in the king's favour by Chief Justice Coke in 1606, provided the saltpetre men confined their digging to birdcotes and outhouses and repaired whatever property they damaged.[31] In 1603 James had issued a statement rebuking the 'oppression' and 'wrongs' committed by his saltpetre men, so the king may very well have divined a resemblance between the assault on Macduff's castle and the ransacking of dovecotes by corrupt servants acting in his name (*SRP* 13). It is a testament to Shakespeare's grim humour and

Fig. 1.4 The Dovecote at Temple Grafton, outside Stratford-upon-Avon.
SOTK2011/Alamy Stock Photo.

acute sense of the animal-human continuum that he conceived the ensuing scene in which 'Macdove' and Malcolm (Columba) 'seek out some desolate shade' (4.3.1) to bewail their losses as a dialogue between two bereaved turtledoves. Early moderns interpreted the plaintive coos of this now endangered species, which mates for life, as mourning cries for their dead partners (see *The Winter's Tale*, 5.3.132), a belief on which Shakespeare based his elegy 'The Phoenix and Turtle'.

Sadly, birds were not the only creatures whose breeding cycle was threatened as early modern England sought to make its food supply keep pace with human population growth. Stuart policy-makers were also deeply concerned about the depletion of England's fishing stocks (see Chapter 3). Parliament bolstered legislation to criminalize fishing during spawning season (1 Jac. c. 23) and passed a 1605 'Act for the Better Preservation of Sea-fish' (3 Jac. c. 12), which imposed haul quotas and banned nets with small mesh sizes that prevented fry from wriggling through to spawn the next generation. The murderer's bizarre comparison of Macduff's son to 'young fry' (4.2.86) had a freighted meaning for Jacobean audiences, incriminating Macbeth in yet another environmental violation. Although laws regulating fishing were difficult to enforce, perpetrators might be set in the stocks or subject to public humiliation.[32] Butchers in early modern England could likewise be pilloried for similar offenses: selling meat during Lent, price-gouging, or slaughtering calves out of season. While veal was an expensive delicacy, Tudor legislators seem to have grown alarmed that farmers were killing excessive numbers of newborn calves in a deliberate bid to create scarcity to inflate the price of beef. In 1609, Parliament renewed and strengthened a 1530 Act 'Against Killing of Calves... and Weanlings'. Although Macduff compares Macbeth to a monster or mooncalf (a creature with a genetic abnormality) when he threatens to put him on display 'to be the show and gaze of the time' with the words 'Here you may see the tyrant' (5.8.27), such exhibitions were not reserved for non-humans. When Malcolm brands Macbeth a 'butcher' (5.9.35) and makes a spectacle of his severed head, the tragedy's closing scene mimics the ritualized public shaming of fishers and butchers who transacted their business in an unsustainable fashion and were guilty of what a modern conservationist would call species tyranny.

From a monarch's-eye-view, Shakespeare's tragedy endorses the future-focused governance of James to ensure a reliable supply of natural resources (both grain and game) to buttress the political stability of the realm. In contrast, Macbeth, painfully aware of his 'barren sceptre', prioritizes his temporary power even at the cost of destroying what Cordelia in *King Lear* calls 'our sustaining corn' (4.3.6): 'Though bladed corn be lodged [flattened]' and 'Nature's germens tumble' (4.1.54). To the horror of Shakespeare's contemporaries, Macbeth here wishes for a harvest failure, like the Porter's grain-hoarding farmer who 'hanged himself on th'expectation of plenty' (2.3.4). From the perspective of the agrarian reformers, particularly those from the southern lowland counties, those who wished to protect the barren heaths were allying themselves with forces of sterility that smacked of witchcraft. There is, therefore, something highly fitting in Macbeth's overthrow by what he perceives as an army of trees. Commentators have rightly seen Birnam Wood's assault as ecological vengeance for Macbeth's transgressions against 'natural law' but it would be more accurate to arraign him for violating the laws of King James and certain agricultural interests which presume a false equivalence with nature's.[33] Insofar as the play envisions conservation in terms of maintaining the royal hunt and vilifies other species not categorized as food or game, *Macbeth* remains trapped within the anthropocentric dualisms of an agrarian, monarchical society prone to scarcity: that is, within agrilogistics and the shallow ecology of sustainability.

Is there any way out of this impasse? Could the Scottish tragedy's fascination with equivocation and amphibology also challenge dualism and nudge us towards an apprehension of what Morton calls a 'dark ecology' that accepts contradiction, disequilibrium, and fragility? In a provocative queer reading of *Macbeth*, Heather Love argues that Banquo and his dynasty represent 'reproductive futurity' while the childless Macbeths subvert this ethic (2011, 201–8).[34] Lady Macbeth's wish to purge herself and her husband of the maternal 'milk of human kindness' (1.5.17), her renunciation of motherhood in seeking to stop menstruation—'the compunctious visitings of nature' (1.5.45)—and her fantasy of bashing out the brains of a suckling infant place her firmly on the side of those 'not fighting for the children'.

If Lady Macbeth's disavowal of motherhood would have struck Shakespeare's contemporaries as unnatural, such pledges register differently today as the world population soars toward the 8 billion mark. Lady Macbeth's speech could be construed as a bold assertion of the anti-natalism backed by many queer ecocritics.[35] And yet Shakespeare's tragedy hints at some limitations with this philosophy beyond its potential to cloak insidious race-biased theories of eugenics. Macbeth's fatal misreading of the Bloody Child's prophecy that 'none of woman born / Shall harm Macbeth' (4.1.79–80) suggests how anti-natalism might warp into a hyper-separationist fantasy of transcending the biological cycle of birth, decay, and death. The play also reveals how easily anti-natalism can be caricatured and demonized via Lady Macbeth's murderous ambition and the witches' gleeful involvement in child sacrifice, including the post-partum abortion of 'the birth-strangled babe / Ditch-delivered by a drab' (4.1.30–1). There are, fortunately, other ways—although not all of them uncontroversial (see Chapter 7)—to reduce human overpopulation without glorifying infanticide. But perhaps a more effective tactic would be to uphold the Macbeths not as anti-natalist baby-killers but as opponents of agrilogisitics, allied with crows and wolves, and to read their tragedy against the grain (in a literal sense) as an elegy to a wilder, medieval past.

In summation, *Macbeth* presents two important lessons that reflect Britain's geographic divide and appear at loggerheads but should be complementary: first, the play, in contrast to its protagonists, champions sustainability and the fertility of the southern, lowland farming economy, imagining a reproductive futurity that encompasses other species valued by humans; secondly, the childless Macbeths, in contrast to the tragedy, ally themselves with heaths and persecuted vermin in ways that lionize the inhuman wildness of Scotland and the northern uplands. The play, in other words, has it both ways, just as England's Scottish hunter-king would support policies to protect both woodlands and heaths in keeping with his vision of a unified Great Britain. Perhaps an ecocritical analysis of *Macbeth* might have it both ways too. Insofar as we sympathize with its tragic hero and are thrilled by the heath, our relief at the triumph of fertility over sterility, light over dark, is mingled with regret at the demise of something primal and lawless in nature that Shakespeare's poetry has exalted. Perhaps reading *Macbeth* in the Anthropocene might prompt us to reflect on the need for both shallow and deep ecologies, and to consider the ecological continuities between the medieval past and modern present. The study of early modern literature is particularly well suited to this project of fostering an intergenerational ethic, and ecocritical readings of *Macbeth* should strive to burnish the play into something like a cross between the unborn king's mirror and Macbeth's prophetic letter: the vision of a past that empowers us to feel our future in the instant.

2
Timon of Athens and Scottish Mines
The Folio's Gold as Vibrant Matter

Although it ranks among the most seldom staged and studied of Shakespeare's tragedies, *Timon of Athens* is a play that somehow 'always seems topical' (Billington 2012). Perhaps directors and critics feel obliged to compensate for the play's comparative obscurity and perceived artistic defects by blazoning its relevance. Yet attempts to teleport *Timon* to our moment can also diminish the acuity of insight that comes from historical distance, as Sharon O'Dair maintains: 'in productions of *Timon* we might see ourselves—and the negative effects of capitalism—more clearly if we understand that Timon is not our contemporary' (2007, 470).[1] This chapter seeks to vindicate that paradox, advancing an ecohistoricist reading that brings its applicability to our current environmental predicament into crisper focus. While situating the tragedy in the context of Jacobean prospecting for gold and silver in Scotland, it argues that *Timon of Athens* does not merely anticipate Marx's familiar definition of money as alienated labour but also—with its pre-Cartesian conception of the agency of metals—runs ahead of critical vitalism's efforts to theorize money as 'vibrant matter' par excellence.[2] Insofar as Timon credits gold with a greater-than-human agency that destabilizes the biosphere, Shakespeare and Middleton's post-humanist tragedy envisions early modernity as the onset of a Capitalocene (Moore 2017), and is perhaps even more radical than *King Lear* in implying that humans are not only lower than beasts but even subjugated by metals.

The historical context of *Timon* is hardly terra incognita for Shakespearean critics. Thanks to the path-breaking research of Coppélia Kahn, David Bevington, Michael Chorost, and Andrew Hadfield, it is well known that *Timon* comments on the profligacy of James and his courtiers. Since the new millennium, critics have started to excavate the tragedy's ecological subtext. Frederick Waage has highlighted Timon's scrabbling in the dirt as evidence of the 'terrocentric' (2005, 147) mentality of Shakespeare's agrarian society, while Simon Estok has provocatively read the play as a challenge to 'meat-based models of masculinity' (2015, 92).[3] This chapter follows a trail blazed by John Jowett, who contends that the play engages in contemporary debates over the ethics of mining. The dramatic scene in which a mattock-wielding Timon strikes gold and hauls it up from beneath the stage would put spectators in mind of a miner prospecting for precious ores. Acknowledging that Timon's accidental discovery of gold derives from a satiric

Shakespeare Beyond the Green World: Drama and Ecopolitics in Jacobean Britain. Todd Andrew Borlik,
Oxford University Press. © Todd Andrew Borlik 2023. DOI: 10.1093/oso/9780192866639.003.0003

dialogue by Lucian, Jowett unearths some curious parallels with the episode of Mammon's Cave in Book 2 of Spenser's *Faerie Queene*, and hails this as a 'new minor source for the play' (2004b, 81). While Shakespeare and Middleton were, like Spenser, influenced by anti-mining discourse in classical authors such as Ovid and Pliny, the two playwrights were also stirred by actual mining activities in the early years of King James's reign. Specifically, *Timon of Athens* can be seen as a scorching critique of James's 'plott' with a mining engineer named Sir Bevis Bulmer, whose character and fate bear more than a casual resemblance to those of Shakespeare and Middleton's spendthrift. By further situating *Timon* alongside James's dealings with goldsmith and mining entrepreneur Sir Thomas Foulis and a lost play about a Scottish silver mine, this chapter presents fresh evidence why this mordant satire may never have been staged in Shakespeare's lifetime, and why it deserves greater consideration from ecocritics in our time.

Sir Bevis Bulmer and the 'Knights of the Golden Mines'

In Ben Jonson's comedy *The Staple of News* (1625), modelled on Aristophanes' *Plutus* (to whom Timon is compared in the opening scene), Pennyboy Junior scorns a loan proffered by his disguised father, insisting he has his own supply of inexhaustible wealth:

> Who, sir, I?
> Did I not tell you I was bred i'the mines
> Under Sir Bevis Bullion?
>   (*CWBJ* 6:36.1.3.55–7)

At the play's court performance many would have caught and some winced at the allusion to Sir Bevis Bulmer (whose name Jonson punningly transmutes to gold), the most renowned mining engineer in Jacobean England. The father's sarcastic response would doubtless have provoked some contemptuous snickers from Jonson's audience:

> I quite forgot, you mine-men want no money,
> Your streets are paved with't. There the molten silver
> Runs out like cream on cakes of gold.
>   (1.3.58–60)

Jonson may very well have been aware of Bulmer's mining ventures when he composed *Volpone* and *The Alchemist*; by 1625, it was painfully clear that mining was not always a quick and sure-fire route to riches. Bulmer, reputedly one of the wealthiest subjects in Jacobean Britain, had died in abject poverty twelve years earlier, owing money even for the clothes on his back. When Shakespeare and Middleton composed *Timon of Athens*, however, Bulmer had been dubbed a knight by King James, who naïvely sought to repair Crown finances with fabulous wealth from Bulmer's gold and silver mines in Scotland. If Bulmer's exploits were still well remembered enough for Ben Jonson to mock him in 1625, it is likely that Shakespeare and Middleton would have been aware of the scandal caused by this mining speculator's bankruptcy around 1606–7. Bulmer's life furnishes many striking parallels with Timon's, and a closer consideration of Bulmer's reckless generosity and the ups and downs of his fortunes will be useful for the light it throws on Shakespeare and Middleton's economic satire and its environmental politics.

Although the details of his birth are unknown, Bulmer is believed to be the son of Sir John Bulmer and Margaret Stafford, both of whom were executed for their part in the northern Catholic uprising known as the Pilgrimage of Grace. With the family lands confiscated by the Crown, the young Bulmer must have recognized the need to find other sources of revenue, which would explain why he gravitated toward the mining industry, in which vast fortunes could be made. In the 1570s Bulmer was involved with the ironworks at Rievaulx Abbey in North Yorkshire, and the lead mines at Leadhills in Lanarkshire, which he managed on behalf of an Edinburgh goldsmith. In 1583 Bulmer sunk lead mines in Mendip Hills at Rowpits, and four years later partnered with Adrian Gilbert and John Popplar to smelt the silver ore from their mines at Combe Martin in Devon—a venture that reportedly earned him staggering profits of £20,000 the first two years.[4]

Like Shakespeare and Middleton's Timon, Bulmer had an expensive habit of gifting luxury objects (forged of precious metals from his own mines) to ingratiate himself to influential courtiers. In 1593 he presented the Earl of Bath with a silver porringer, inscribed with verses in which the metal speaks and boasts that Bulmer's 'skill and toyle...Refined mee so pure and cleene' (qtd in Tyson 1996, 50). The following year Bulmer gifted another silver porringer to Sir Richard Martin, Lord Mayor of London and Master of the Mint, engraving it with a picture of himself and more self-congratulatory verses:

> I dydd no service on the earthe,
> And no manne set me free,
> Till Bulmer by his skill and charge,
> Did frame me this to bee.

(qtd in Tyson 1996, 51)

Bulmer here issues a defence of the ethics of mining, employing the classical trope of prosopopoeia so that non-human metals endorse the anthropocentric conviction that they are imprisoned and 'debased' in their natural state, only acquiring purpose and value through human enterprise. By stamping his own portrait on the metal (like the monarch's profile on a coin), Bulmer not only transforms it into an advertisement of his technical ingenuity but also vaunts his (and the Crown's) technological dominion over the mineral wealth of the realm. While these ornate drinking vessels should interest scholars of early modern material culture, they cast a particular glint on *Timon of Athens*. When Lucullus sees Timon's servant approach, he immediately assumes he is about to receive a gift: 'I dreamt of a silver basin and ewer tonight' (3.1.6-7). Later, when Lucius professes himself unable to loan Timon money, one of the Athenian citizens, functioning as a Choric figure, fumes that the ungrateful Lucius 'ne'er drinks / But Timon's silver treads upon his lip' (3.2.73-4). The recurrent cannibalistic imagery of Timon's beneficiaries 'drinking' and 'eating' his body is inspired by exactly the kind of ostentatious gift-giving in which Bulmer indulged. Whether or not Shakespeare and Middleton specifically had Bulmer in mind when re-telling the story of the ancient Athenian misanthrope, Bulmer's silver porringers offer a perfect visual complement to this striking passage in the play.

As this anecdote suggests, Bulmer was a brazen self-publicist. He even penned a memoir, entitled with characteristic immodesty, 'Bulmer's Skill', touting his accomplishments. While it was never printed and the manuscript is now lost, it did pass through the hands of another mining engineer and refiner by the name of Stephen Atkinson, who offers a synopsis of its contents. Much of what we know about Bulmer derives from this source, and its information can be considered reliable since Atkinson had been his protégé and colleague.[5] This is not to say that Atkinson's *Discoverie and Historie of the Gold Mines in Scotland* (1619) is without its own agenda. In recounting Bulmer's exploits, Atkinson strives to prove that gold does exist in the northern clime of Scotland, and to encourage further investment in Scottish gold prospecting by hinting that previous efforts had only failed due to Bulmer's personal shortcomings—namely, his compulsive generosity and over-trusting nature.

Emboldened by his luck with lead and silver, Bulmer began prospecting for gold in Lanarkshire in 1593 after receiving a mining patent from the Scottish Parliament. At Glen Ea's Hill at Windgate, Bulmer struck pay dirt, acquiring, in the words of Atkinson, 'as much gold there as would maintain iii times so many men as he did keepe, royally' (*GMS* 37). Shortly afterwards Bulmer hit a mother lode at Hinderland Moor, where he 'gott the greatest gold, the like to it in no other place before in Scotland' (*GMS* 40). Around 1596 Bulmer journeyed to London and, eager to cut a figure at court, presented the queen with a porringer made of gold from his mines, engraved with the following lines: 'I dare not give, nor yet present / But render part of that's thy own' (qtd in Tyson 1996, 54). This inscription would have been construed by Elizabeth as a reminder of her victory in the notorious Cases of Mines, in which it was decided that the Crown possessed eminent domain over all mines of gold and silver in the realm. This landmark decision led to the creation of the mining duopoly of the Society of Mines Royal and the Company of Mineral and Battery Works, and meant that those who undertook the financially risky enterprise of gold- and silver-mining toiled for the benefit of the Crown in expectation that the monarch would adequately compensate them for their labours. No wonder that Bulmer's verses, despite their disingenuous protestation that the porringer is not a gift, also comprise a paean to the gift economy of the English court, which Shakespeare and Middleton portray so scathingly in *Timon of Athens*.

If Bulmer gifted the golden porringer in expectation of a quid pro quo, his scheme apparently worked. In 1599, the appreciative queen awarded Bulmer a lucrative patent for the impost on all seaborne coal. Over the next few years, Bulmer pocketed five shillings for each chalder of coal exported abroad from England and Wales, and twelve pence for each chalder transported by sea to other English or Welsh haven towns, exacting the money with such doggedness that coal-boat captains at Newcastle lodged a complaint against his 'hard proceeding'.[6] Although he had to pay the Crown a kingly annual fee of £6,200, the coal-trade was so brisk that he still netted profits of £1,000 per year. With the proceeds from his gold and coal, Bulmer constructed a stately home near Glengonnar Water in Scotland, where he, like Timon, kept 'great hospitality... and maintained himself then in great pompe; and thereby he kept open house for all comers and goers...[and] feasted all sorts of people that thither came' (*GMS* 36–7). On the lintel over the front door, Bulmer had the following doggerel inscribed:

> Sir Bevis Bulmer built this bour,
> Who levelled both hill and moor,
> Who got great riches and great honour,
> In Short-cleuch Water and Glengoner.
>
> (qtd in Tyson 1996, 53)

This boast reveals that a form of mountaintop removal mining was occurring on the hills and moors of early modern Scotland. But the hubris of reshaping God's good earth in this way made some people uneasy. What we would call the environmental impact of mining—choked waterways and sterile spoil tips—provoked complaints and even legislative action throughout the sixteenth and seventeenth century, and to this day the Leadhills area and Glengonnar Water, the very spots where Bulmer sunk the first mine and built his opulent country house, remain contaminated by dangerous levels of cadmium, lead, and zinc.[7]

Given his longstanding connections in Scotland, Bulmer's fortunes seemed to be on the upswing in 1603 when King James ascended the English throne. Shortly after his coronation, James summoned Bulmer to London and asked 'to heare more of my gold Mynes in Scotland. What thinke you thereof? Are they to be discovered? May they become profitable to us and our crowne?' (*GMS* 44). When Bulmer responded with guarded optimism, James informed him he had devised a 'plott' to find more Scottish gold: in exchange for an outlay of £300, James would dub twenty-four investors 'Knights of the Golden Mines' (*GMS* 45). As James's proclivity for dispensing knighthoods (particularly to his fellow Scots) in the first few months of his reign had already occasioned resentment, this new scheme did not sit well with the old guard of the English court, many of whom were sceptical of the enterprise. An unpublished epigram, attested by four different manuscript witnesses, expresses wry amusement at the irony of a gold strike in such an impoverished country:

> A Myene of Gold some say their's found
> In Scotland; that's a wonder.
> To see noe money above ground
> And yet to find some under.[8]

Dudley Carleton sounds similarly dubious in a 1604 letter when he dismisses the king's mining surveyor as 'Bulmer the alchemist' and remarks that there is 'little hope of this new discovery, though the Scotchmen compare it at least with the Indies, and the knights of the mine must needs go forward' (DC 57).[9] But the ballyhooed project was soon quashed by the future Lord Treasurer Robert Cecil, who apparently kept a wary eye on Bulmer's mining activities.[10] In the end, only one investor, a Sir John Cleypoole, was actually dubbed a Knight of the Golden Mines, but James did grant Bulmer a knighthood at this time, perhaps as a compensatory gesture after the stymying of their 'plott' to ignite a Scottish gold rush. As it turned out, Cecil's doubts would prove justified. Of the £3,000 James invested in Bulmer's mining operations at Crawford Moor in Scotland, he saw a pitiful return of a mere three ounces of gold (Laing 1800–4, 3:52).

As Atkinson tells it, the problem was not that the Scottish soil was too cold to generate precious metals but that Bulmer had unwittingly sabotaged the venture by destroying his credit due to his perpetual largesse to thankless beneficiaries. Bulmer had found gold at Crawford and intended to set up large-scale mining operations, 'but it is said that his hospitality and [want of] frugality were the theeves that burst in and so robbed his house, and cutt his purse bottom cleane away' (*GMS* 37). In 1606 and 1607, a period contemporaneous with the writing of *Timon of Athens*, Bulmer was scrambling to acquire funds to retain his rights to the coal impost and to carry on refining operations at his gold and silver mines. Understandably, he sought to call in favours and secure loans from those to whom he had been so open-handed. Although King James advanced him £100, Bulmer proved unable to raise the necessary capital and lost the lucrative patent. According to Atkinson, he had 'trusted overmuch to those which deceived both him and themselves' (*GMS* 43) and was ruined by 'too many prodigall wasters hanging on every shoulder of him. And he wasted much himself, and gave liberally to many, *for to be honoured, praised, and magnified*, else he might have bin a rich subject' (*GMS* 40, italics added). Bulmer's compulsion to bestow gifts so freely out of a need to be 'honoured, praised, and magnified', perfectly matches the psychological profile of Shakespeare and Middleton's Timon. Like Timon's servants, Atkinson repeatedly bewails that Bulmer's generosity to courtiers and potential investors was not reciprocated: he gave much 'to unthankfull persons...and such as he was most liberall unto, they were rediest to cut his throate' (*GMS* 39). Although this idiom for betrayal is common enough, it does figure notably in *Timon of Athens*. At Timon's feast in scene 2, the cynic Apemantus transforms the convivial act of carousing with guests into an image of vulnerability:

> If I were a huge man I should fear to drink at meals,
> Lest they should spy my windpipe's dangerous notes;
> Great men should drink with harness [armour] on their throats.
> (1.2.50–2)

Timon himself later implicitly compares his treatment at the hands of his debtors to having his throat cut, fantasizing that other Athenians suffer the same fate:

> Bankrupts, hold fast;
> Rather than render back, out with your knives
> And cut your trusters' throats!
> (4.1.8–10)

Excessive liberality may not be the only trait Bulmer shared with Timon. Atkinson also mentions that Bulmer 'followed other idle veniall vices...that were not allowable of God nor man' (*GMS* 40). In early modern England, such deliberately cryptic phrasing can often be construed as an accusation of sodomy. The festive and conspicuously homoerotic atmosphere of Timon's house may also have prevailed at Bulmer's country estate, and would further suggest why this mining engineer proved to be a favourite of King James.

Although knocked back by the loss of the coal patent, the bankrupt Bulmer still had one hope of vaulting back into the black: the Hilderstone silver mine. The hype surrounding this discovery deserves greater attention, as it became the subject of a scandalous lost play that provoked the fury of the king, and helps elucidate why the King's Men would have been extremely wary of staging *Timon of Athens* during James's reign.

Timon, Thomas Foulis, and the Lost Play of 'The Scottish Mine'

In early 1605 a Scottish collier named Sandy Maund was prospecting for coal in the Bathgate Hills, now known as Hilderstone, and unearthed a heavy piece of reddish metal. He brought a sample of the ore to Bulmer, who discovered that it contained large quantities of silver. At one shaft, which was nicknamed 'God's Blessing', the ore assayed at between £60 and £120 per ton, and Atkinson, who was working for Bulmer at the time, reportedly was able to refine £100 sterling a day. Bulmer quickly notified King James, who was entitled to a tenth of the profits since all silver mines technically belonged to the monarch. However, the cash-strapped Bulmer and the owner of the land, Sir Thomas Hamilton, could not afford the steep set-up costs, and sought to convince the king to invest in an enterprise guaranteed to flood the royal coffers.[11]

Interestingly, another chief investor in the Hilderstone mine was Hamilton's brother-in-law and Bulmer's business associate, Thomas Foulis, a goldsmith and a mining entrepreneur who had a troubled history of financial dealings with King James that mirrors the plot of *Timon of Athens*. As Bulmer's partner in the mines at Leadhills in the 1590s, Foulis, was reputed one of the richest men in Scotland, and became the major financier for the Scottish monarchy in the mid-1590s, borrowing vast sums to bankroll the king's expenditures. When it became apparent that James could not pay him back, the royal secretary, John Lindsay of Balcarres, purchased one of Foulis's outstanding debts in early 1598 and then called it in, a 'hostile move' that hurled Foulis into bankruptcy, despite the fact that 'the real bankruptcy was that of the Crown which refused to pay him' (Goodare 1999, 185–6). King James then endorsed this betrayal by demanding that Foulis return the opulent 'H jewel' he had loaned him as security, effectively destroying Foulis's credit. Outraged by the king's ingratitude, Foulis suffered a nervous breakdown not unlike that of Timon: he 'fell by his wits' according to one observer, while a second reports that Foulis 'fell in a phrenesie, becaus he was not able to satisfie his creditors for the debt he had contracted in furnishing the King'.[12] The fact that Foulis had served as King James's jeweller is also noteworthy, given the prominent appearance of a jeweller in act 1 of *Timon of Athens*. How long Foulis's 'phrensie' lasted is unclear, but by June 1598 the Scottish Parliament granted him a *supersedere* to shield him from his creditors and prevent his arrest, and voted to pay him back in instalments over a six-year period. James's debt to Foulis amounted to the head-spinning figure of £180,000, and the money to cover it was earmarked from the £30,000 per annum subsidy that England was paying to the Scottish monarchy at this time. In other words, England was effectively handing over a considerable slice of its treasury to Thomas Foulis, but the promised payments were not always forthcoming, and this massive bill became England's problem after James's ascension to the throne. The lion's share of the debt was still outstanding in 1606 when Parliament approved a new tax to rectify the king's finances, passing the buck, so to speak, to the English people. Tales of James's dubious treatment of his goldsmith-banker Foulis would thus have been circulating in 1606–8 when *Timon of Athens* was likely composed, as the Crown began collecting taxes to the tune of £81,880 to pay off debts Foulis had incurred on the king's behalf nearly a decade earlier. The plot of *Timon* duplicates many aspects of the Scottish fiscal crisis, and indicates just how searingly topical this play would have been at the time.

Given his personal history with Foulis and Bulmer, James may have felt obligated to underwrite their excavations at the Hilderstone silver mine, but the Privy Council sensibly demanded some proof of Bulmer's grandiose claims. They ordered Bulmer and five commissioners to travel to Hilderstone to collect specimens of the ore and appraise the value of the mine. To ensure there was no fraud involved, the ore was to be shipped to London and refined at the Tower. To Bulmer's dismay, the first ship sank on the journey, but a second arrived in February 1608.[13] While the refining costs were much higher in London (due to the price of coal in the capital), the results were promising enough to convince the money-hungry James. In April 1608 Bulmer was appointed 'Maister and surveyair of the earth werkis of the lait discoverit silver myne' in Hilderstone, and soon after awarded a grant of £2,419 to be 'ymploied about the mines in Scotland' (Tyson 1996, 60).

With these extravagant sums up for grabs, it is no wonder that James's high-risk investments in the Scottish mining industry provoked snipes from satirists in London, who were growing increasingly disenchanted with the new regime. In early 1608, probably not long after word circulated of the sunken lode of silver, the Children of the Blackfriars staged a play that ridiculed James's enthusiasm for his Scottish mines. An account of the furore it unleashed survives in Sir Thomas Lake's letter to Robert Cecil, dated 11 March 1608, which reports that the king was so 'offended in ye matter of ye Mynes' and by unflattering caricatures of the French nobility in Chapman's *Conspiracy and Tragedy of Charles, Duke of Byron* that he 'vowed [the actors] should never play more but should first begg their bred'.[14] Another letter by the irate French ambassador, Antoine Lefèvre de la Boderie, provides further damning evidence of the child company's *lèse majesté*:

> A day or two before, they had slandered their King, *his mine in Scotland*, and all his Favourites in a most pointed fashion [*ilz avoient dépêché leur Roy, sa mine d'Escosse et tous ses Favorits d'une estrange sorte*].[15]

These accounts testify that a play poking fun of James's mining activities was staged at Blackfriars in early 1608.[16] Shakespeare and Middleton must have been aware of this uproar, to which the furious James responded by ordering the playwright (possibly John Marston) imprisoned and threatening to ban all theatrical performances in London indefinitely. Although the king eventually relented, the lost play mocking the Scottish mine at Hilderstone was a major reason why the Children of the Chapel lost their lease at Blackfriars in 1608 to Shakespeare's company.[17]

M. C. Bradbrook speculated the vituperative tenor of *Timon* fits with a 1608 performance at Blackfriars, where audiences relished biting topical satire. If so, perhaps it sought to capitalize on the *succès de scandale* of the Scottish mine play while evading the king's wrath by masking current events in Greek garb. But the absence of act divisions in the Folio text of *Timon* has emboldened one editor to insert the phrase 'for the King's Men at The Globe' under the title (*TMCW* 471) and date the play circa 1606. If Jowett is right in thinking that *Timon* was conceived in 1606 as a companion piece to *Volpone*, it may comment not only on James's fiscal woes in the spring of that year, when Parliament was heatedly debating the new tax to pay off his debts to Foulis, but also on his recent failed 'plott' to raise revenue by dubbing investors Knights of the Golden Mines.[18] A third possibility is that the extant text remains in an unfinished state. The supposition that Shakespeare and Middleton abandoned the overly pessimistic *Timon* for artistic reasons may contain some flecks of truth, but the evidence garnered in this chapter indicates that political pressures against it would have been even more insurmountable. A tragic satire begun in part with an intent to warn James of the unreliability of gambling the Crown's finances on gold and silver prospecting may itself have been too dicey to stage by early 1608, risking a stint at Newgate for the authors and royal displeasure that had gotten the previous acting troupe booted out of the very indoor theatre where the King's Men had at long last acquired permission to perform.

Unfortunately for Bulmer and James, a play about mining and bankruptcy would have remained too sore a topic over the next few years for Shakespeare or Middleton to return to the script. The silver deposits at Hilderstone below twelve fathoms quickly dwindled so that the amount of sterling it produced was well below the costs of extracting and refining it. Despite summoning some German mining engineers to assist the proceedings, James saw little return on the £20,000 Scots he had sunk in the mine, which was effectively closed by 1610, and the bankrupt Bulmer departed for the wilds of Ireland to search for his next big strike. It never happened. He died penniless in 1613, owing his biographer Atkinson £340 and having recently borrowed £10 to purchase the clothes on his back: 'so the man who had mixed with the highest in the land died a pauper, ignored by all who had been so willing to court him in his heyday' (Tyson 1996, 62).

To frame *Timon of Athens* within the history of the Jacobean mining industry and its economic volatility is not to insist that Bulmer or Foulis were the exclusive and immediate inspiration for the tragedy. After all, Bulmer's death occurred several years after the most likely date for the play's composition. Yet this study affirms the paradox that the tragedy's ancient Athenian setting should be construed as a sign of its dangerous topicality. Historicist interpretations of *Timon* have focused on its eponymous protagonist as a stand-in for James, but the economic history presented here indicates that a culture of debt was endemic in

Jacobean London, especially among courtier-miners, and many Renaissance writers, by composing odes in praise of aristocratic largesse, both promoted and benefited from this prodigality. One such offender was Robert Aytoun, a prominent Scottish poet at the Jacobean court, who rose to high office after writing Latin panegyrics to King James and Lord Hay, one of the biggest spenders of the age. Aytoun's 1605 verses to Hay, entitled *Baisa* [Kisses], are fulsome and notably homoerotic. Hay, who introduced the notorious custom of ante-suppers, in which guests were invited to ogle a sumptuous banquet of food that was then whisked away and discarded, was guilty of the wasteful munificence satirized in *Timon* and Aytoun himself may be the sort of mercenary hack Shakespeare and Middleton had in mind in their acidic depiction of the play's sycophantic poet.

It must be said that poets and playwrights not only encouraged liberality but were themselves chronic borrowers. The impecunious Thomas Dekker was twice jailed for debt and Shakespeare's collaborator, Thomas Middleton, owed money in 1606 to a London goldsmith by the name of Robert Keysar.[19] Interestingly, Keysar had recently taken over as the manager of the Children of the Queen's Revels, the company that would stage the scandalous lost play about the Scottish silver mine. Middleton claimed he had given his tragedy *The Viper and Her Brood* to Keysar to satisfy the debt, but this did not prevent Keysar, whose 'career as a goldsmith is riddled with fraudulent dealings' (Corrigan 2004, 84), from suing Middleton for the sum of £16. This goes a long way toward explaining Middleton's caustic portrait of the goldsmith Yellowhammer in *A Chaste Maid in Cheapside*, and may account for some of the harangues against gold in *Timon of Athens*.

Shakespeare, too, would have sensed the tremendous power wielded by goldsmiths in the early modern London theatre world, particularly after his own company had enlisted a goldsmith named Thomas Savage (who, as one of the ten sea-coal meters of London, must have known Bevis Bulmer) as a trustee to purchase their shares in the Globe in 1599. Shakespeare's sense of their influence in London would have sharpened during his residence on Silver Street, an area popular with money-lending goldsmiths, and Charles Nicholl includes *Timon* among Shakespeare's Silver Street plays (2007, 31, 63). In February 1610, the same Keysar who had sued Middleton lodged a formal complaint with King James and the Court of Requests against the King's Men, accusing Richard Burbage, John Heminges, and Henry Condell (but not Shakespeare) of denying his one-sixth share in the Blackfriars (which he claimed to have purchased from John Marston) and suppressing competition by acquiring private playhouses.[20] The above history underscores not only the obvious point that Renaissance show business required risky financing but also that plays like *Timon of Athens* register a pervasive unease at the growing dependence of the theatre industry—epitomized in the appointment of the entrepreneur Keysar as manager of the Blackfriars' children— and the English economy in general on credit supplied by goldsmiths and what might be called the Jacobean mining lobby.[21]

Timon's critique of the 'culture of debt' abetted by the mining industry gives the play an ecocritical edge. First, the impact of excavations on the land could be severe, as illustrated by the woodcuts in Georgius Agricola's *De re metallica* (which undermine the author's defense of the ethics of mining) and the hubristic vaunts of Renaissance miners like Cornelius de Vos, who vowed 'no charges whatsoever should be spared, till mountaines and mosses were turned into vallies and dales, but this treasur[e] house should be discovered' (*GMS* 19), and Bulmer, who similarly boasted of having 'levelled both hill and moor'.[22] Secondly, the play skewers the mining and finance industries for their culture of conspicuous consumption and reckless, magical view of the earth's bounty as boundless. Whether or not Shakespeare and Middleton had Bulmer in mind as an example of a contemporary Timon, it is noteworthy that one of the most Timon-like figures at the Jacobean court was a gold prospector, lead merchant, and coal baron, engaging in environmentally destructive mining practices to finance his luxurious lifestyle.

To peg *Timon of Athens* as little more than an angry tongue-lashing of goldminers and goldsmith-financiers, however, sells the play short. Shakespeare and Middleton's underrated tragedy is much more profound than a topical satire on merchants and profligates at the Jacobean court. What impels much of the play's best poetry is the startling recognition that human agency is circumscribed not only by other humans but also, as Marx famously recognized, by money. Re-examining the tragedy through an eco-materialist lens, the final pages will shift the focus from the acts of historical personages to the agential force of non-human actants—a force more easily registered through what I call the 'typographical rewilding' of early modern texts.

Timon and the Agency of Gold

The word 'gold' recurs in *Timon of Athens* like a neurotic fixation. As Jowett (2004a, 55) notes, of the thirty-six uses of the word in the text (nearly double the amount of any other play), thirty-three appear in sections attributed to Shakespeare. This statistic speaks loudly for Shakespeare's fascination with minting poetry from gold when he wrote this play. One relevant piece of textual history that Jowett understandably neglects to mention in the majestic introduction to his modernized edition is that the 1623 Folio text consistently capitalizes gold. A few random examples will suffice:

> 'Plutus God of Gold / is but his Steward' (TLN 328–39).
> 'Usurers men, Bauds between Gold and want' (726).
> 'Gold? Yellow, glittering, precious Gold?' (1628).
> 'Give us some Gold good Timon' (1747).
> 'Rob one another, there's more Gold' (2095).
> 'And Gold confound you howsoere' (2099).

To be sure, the Folio compositors regularly capitalize substantive nouns, so there is nothing exceptional about gold in this regard. But Timon's habit of apostrophizing gold as if it can hear him activates the capital G, so readers of the original Folio are subliminally reminded of the metal's agency through typographic personification. Moreover, not all early modern texts capitalize in the same fashion. For instance, the word 'gold' appears fourteen times in the 1607 Quarto of *Volpone* and is only capitalized twice, although one of those occasions is the famous opening line of the play in which Volpone salutes his treasure: 'Good morning to the Day, and next my Gold' (1.1.1). Considering that the monologue is an apostrophe, capitalization here seems thematically appropriate, and further underlines the apotheosis of Gold as a deific presence as vital to the human economy as the spring sun is to the earth's vegetation. Similarly, in *Timon of Athens*, the capitalization of Gold gains a greater lustre in contexts that endow it with a phenomenal influence as a 'visible God' (2027) over human affairs. Suggestively, in Timon's rant addressing Gold as a 'valiant Mars' (TLN 2023) that can overmaster Hymen and Diana, the word 'man' is not capitalized but 'Beasts' and 'Gold' are. When Timon later insults the Painter and Poet as 'slaves', the word is not capitalized whereas Gold is twice in the same line: 'there's Gold, you came for Gold, ye slaves' (TLN 2337). Exclamations such as 'What a Gods Gold' (TLN 2255) lose some of their potency in modernized editions. While it would be absurd to claim that all capitalization is rhetorically significant, these nuances often do matter and gain even more weight from the 'material turn' in early modern scholarship. New materialism and material feminism have begun to produce exciting new perspectives on Shakespeare, but taking their Latourian perceptions of non-human actants seriously entails that we rethink how we edit and read early modern texts. Restoring seventeenth-century capitalization may make reading fractionally harder but offers ample compensation by enhancing the sense of poetic estrangement. Rather than impose post-Enlightenment notions of hierarchy and agency on early modern texts (which modernization inscribes), unediting to conserve the original typography can in effect rewild the Shakespearean page.

An unsung text contemporaneous with *Timon* that exhibits the same rhetorical capitalization is Edward Hake's OF GOLDS KINGDOME, which the author attempted to present to King James in 1604 around the time of the short-lived Scottish gold rush. The titular poem likens Gold's subterranean mobility—'Gold can closely creepe / where th'aire could never come'—(A4^v) to its undermining of the moral distinction between virtue and vice. A subsequent poem entitled 'No Gold no Goodness' elaborates on this theme and plays on the resemblance between God and Gold, signalling the latter's apotheosis through capitalization: 'But O our God, O where art thou / That suffrest Gold to conquer now? (1604, 23). Like Apemantus's jeer 'traffic's thy God' (1.1.244), Hake rails against the materialism of the elite as idolatry:

> Your Gold and Goods your God you make:
> For whereas Gold is, you are won,
> But where Gold is not, you have done.
>
> (1604, 24)

In verses echoed by *Timon*, the former MP for Windsor lashes out at supposed friends and relatives who abandoned him during his bankruptcy and fulminates against a 'Liberall man' and 'a Golden Swaggerer' who entertain guests with lavish suppers and late-night banquets. The book concludes with a 'complaint of Gold' that voices the same sentiments, albeit without the same lyrical finesse, as Shakespeare's protagonist:

> And now to Gold I bend my speech againe:
> Goe packe thee hence, Corrupter of our age,
> Enclose thy selfe in Mines, let earth retaine
> Thy tyrant corpse, that so on earth dost rage,
> That makest great ones serve thee as a Page.
>
> (1604, 52)

Whether or not Shakespeare read OF GOLDS KINGDOME, it affords a glimmering example of how a Jacobean poet might deploy capitalization to endow Gold with a tyrannical authority exceeding that of any earthly monarch, as James would discover to his dismay.[23]

The liberal capitalization that prevailed in Shakespeare's England reflects a pre-mechanistic worldview, and Gold is particularly interesting in this regard because of debates in Renaissance natural philosophy over the ambiguous status of minerals and metals. Many sixteenth-century texts (e.g. John Maplet's *Green Forest*) endorse the view of the Roman naturalist Pliny that metals, gems, and stones possess a rudimentary life-force. One of the most prominent defenders of enchanted mineralogy in the Renaissance was the Italian polymath Cardano, whose *De subtilitate rerum* (1550, 106–9) argued that minerals are capable of growth and thus possess what Aristotle terms a 'vegetable soul' and occupy an intermediate position between stones and plants. The niche of minerals and gems in the Scala Natura was, however, coming under assault in refutations of alchemy and in early modern works of mineralogy, which challenged the assumption that an exhausted gold vein could swiftly replenish itself underground.[24] A mid-seventeenth-century text, erroneously attributed to Sir Thomas Browne, poses the question 'Whether Metals Live' and answers with an emphatic negative, presenting a categorical rebuttal of Cardano on several points: (1) the classification of 'imperfect animate' is an oxymoron; (2) to claim that metal is begotten or generated is simply a metaphor; (3) magnetism or attraction is not proof of a soul; (4) the supposed veins or pores of metals differ from human veins and pores; and (5) to attribute growth and age to metals is again a rhetorical sleight of hand, false personification (Anonymous 1657, 24–6). This counterargument is worth rehashing at length because it indicates an epistemological shift—famously theorized by Foucault—in which previous tenets of natural history based on analogy and resemblance were in effect dismissed as mere poetry.[25]

In his meditations on Gold in *Timon of Athens*, Shakespeare checks and reverses the drift towards this Enlightenment episteme, insisting that poetry can distil the true essence and agential force of metals more clearly than a sober, prosaic description. Shakespeare showcases language's power to reveal these profound truths in Timon's pun on metal as the earth's 'Mettle' (TLN 1799), a word which means vigour, life force, but also seminal fluid. The homophone drives home the absurdity of categorizing metal as inanimate by confounding it with the vital principle. Surprisingly, however, the vitality of metal only debases it, as Shakespeare equates the formation of gold with the spontaneous generation of insects, reptiles such as the 'gilded Newt', and other 'abhorred Births' (TLN 1803–4) from sun-warmed slime. Shakespeare follows this salute to Gold as a living creature with a vision of its greater-than-human longevity and mobility: 'Thou[l]'t go (strong Theefe) / When Gowty keepers of thee cannot stand' (TLN 1649–50). While the human body succumbs to infirmities as one ages, timeworn Gold circulates as swiftly as the day it was minted. Hounded out of Athens by his debts, Timon acquires an acute sense of Gold's puppeteer-like power over human bodies. When he grumbles that 'the Learned pate / Duckes to the Golden Foole' (TLN 1619–20), the latter adjective is more operative than the noun it describes; golden nullifies and overrides the foolishness of the fool.[26] Immediately after his accidental discovery of Gold, Timon muses on its magnetic power to 'lugge your Priests and Servants from your sides: / Plucke stout mens pillowes from below their heads' (TLN 1634–5). Gold can make the young and beautiful woo a repulsive leper, and force respectable citizens to kneel before thieves as if they were senators (TLN 1638–40). In this perspicacious rant, a seemingly inert metal dictates the status, comportment, and body language of humans, transfiguring their appearence.

This god-like power of Gold grows even more apparent and menacing during Timon's conversations with Alcibiades and the prostitutes, when Shakespeare attributes a lethal force to it. Gold hires troops to pillage Athens and Timon's harangue underscores its power to steel human hearts against compassion and mercy. Just as Alcibiades' mercenaries kill for money, Phrynia (whose namesake infamously modelled for a golden statue) and Timandra proclaim they will 'do anything for Gold' (TLN 1765). If Gold forces citizens and senators to bend and kneel, it also controls the most intimate parts of the sex worker's body. Shakespeare portrays this with a crude literalism when the Gold Timon tosses in the 'lap' of the prostitutes prompts them to expose themselves by holding up their 'Aprons mountant' (TLN 1749–50). Timon previously referred to Gold as the 'common whore of Mankinde' (TLN 1645), and here traces a parallel between the circulation of Gold and transmission of venereal diseases by paying the prostitutes to spread the latter. The ravages of syphilis result indirectly from Gold's allure, and Shakespeare goes so far as to imagine it triggering a pandemic of s.t.d.-induced impotence that, like war, might eradicate the human race itself by 'quell[ing] / the sourse of all Erection' (TLN 1779–80).

The apostrophe—or direct address of a non-human creature, object, or abstraction—is so commonplace in Renaissance literature that it is easy to underestimate the radical authority with which Shakespeare invests Gold in *Timon*. To be sure, the play draws on a long philosophical and religious tradition that utilizes poetic tropes to decry filthy lucre and the temptations of Mammon. It echoes Ovid, Pliny, and Spenser in disparaging mining as oedipal rape when Timon digs in the 'womb' of our 'common mother' (4.3.177).[27] The play also toys with the Christian maxim *radix malorum est cupiditas* ('desire of money is the root of all evil'), when Timon, after begging for a root, unearths gold, the root of all evil. Anxiety over money's power to confuse ontological categories notoriously informs Aristotle's critique of usury as an 'unnatural breeding' of metals (1964, 1.10), and Shakespeare plays on the generative properties of wealth when the Senator describes how a gift to Timon 'foals me straight / And able horses' (2.1.9–10). Refining Aristotle's critique, Karl Marx discerned how money possesses 'the occult quality of being able to add value to itself. It brings forth living offspring, or, at the least, lays golden eggs' (1867, 149). No wonder that *Timon of Athens* was Marx's favourite Shakespeare play. In his *Economic and Philosophic Manuscripts*, Marx quotes at length from Timon's apostrophe to Gold, and praises Shakespeare for having distilled money's 'real nature' as 'the distorting and confounding of all natural and human qualities' (1844, 60).[28] Insofar as money, according to Marx, 'is *the truly creative power*' (1844, 61), it mimics and rivals the creative power of the poet to transfigure reality.[29] This is precisely why Shakespeare responds to it with such indignant eloquence: in pondering the staggering influence of Gold, Shakespeare was finally confronted with a creative energy that overmatched his own.

Despite its highly topical satire, *Timon* is a parable for our times in that it discerns a correlation between the human economy and what modern parlance would term the greater-than-human ecology. Exiled into the wilderness, Timon no longer views nature as a gift economy but as a violent realm of competition for resources, characterized by perpetual theft: hence his declaration to the three thieves that everyone practises covertly what they perform openly: 'all that you meet are Theeves' (TLN 2096). The Athenians refuse to recognize what Jean-Luc

Marion, building upon Heidegger, calls the 'givenness' (2002) of the earth, and Timon worries that the bounteous housewife nature or the gods above might act in kind. This anxiety that the earth might cease its bounty to an ungrateful species fuels Timon's dark fantasies of human extinction. Instead of an Anthropocene dominated by homo sapiens, the misanthrope Timon foresees a post-apocalyptic future in which the earth reverts to the beasts. So, too, does the ape-man Apemantus, who imagines people devolving into baboons and monkeys and reminds Timon that nature does not obey human behests:

> What think'st
> That the bleake ayre, thy boysterous Chamberlaine
> Will put thy shirt on warme? Will these moyst Trees,
> That have out-liv'd the Eagle, page thy heeles
> And skip when thou point'st out?
>
> (TLN 1842–6)

Re-evaluated from an eco-Marxist perspective, Shakespeare's bleak vision of Gold's power to invert the perceived order of nature appears like a premonition not of an Anthropocene but of a Capitalocene.[30] The advantage of this nomenclature, proposed by the historian J. W. Moore, is that it offers a sobering reminder that humanity is not the telos of history. While it would be absurd to claim that Shakespeare consciously formulated the notion of a Capitalocene centuries before Marx and Moore, the classical tradition of the Iron Age marked by Gold-mining and metallurgy offered him a historiographic parallel to conceptualize the destructive energy and epoch-forging power of metals and money, and his tragedy does imagine the Gold-induced extinction of the human race.

Timon's appraisal of Gold's formidable agency also feels prescient in that it melds neatly with the new materialisms. If critical vitalism has sometimes struggled to reckon with the biological realities of death and extinction, *Timon* seems all the more valuable in its evocation of a menacing vitalism that is defiantly not human-centred: gold controls and outlives us mortals. As a poet, Shakespeare can only combat metal's titanic power, as Ovid did, with the lasting power of ink.[31] Re-examining the play's invectives against Gold in their original capitalization best honours that effort and reaffirms the paradox that a historical approach can make Renaissance plays like *Timon* feel timelier than ever.

3
'Watery Empire' in *Pericles*
British Sea Sovereignty, the Fisheries, and the Eco-material History of Purple

While critics once faulted its haphazard crisscrossings of the Mediterranean as symptomatic of the play's structural problems, *Pericles* is increasingly valued as a luminous porthole onto the maritime culture of Jacobean Britain. It has been dubbed 'the play of the sea par excellence' (Holland 2005, 12), one which 'interrogates the meaning of the maritime more radically than other plays...and integrates it more decisively into its plot' (Klein 2016, 126). Unsurprisingly, *Pericles* has become a favourite springboard for the 'New Thalassalogy' or Blue Cultural Studies. Steve Mentz views Marina as a portrait of 'sea-infused humanity' and the play in general as a challenge to terra-centric conceptions of human-environmental relations (2009b, 69). Lowell Duckert suggests that *Pericles*'s poetry functions as a kind of underwater breathing apparatus that allows us to vicariously venture beneath the waves (2019), while Dan Brayton reads the fishermen's jests alongside Brueghel's 1557 painting *Big Fish Eat Little Fish* (2012, 160) in a chapter that implicates Shakespeare's abundant ichthyological metaphors in the expansion of European fisheries. Riding the wave generated by these critics, this chapter plumbs the significance of the sea in *Pericles* from an eco-historicist viewpoint. More precisely, it situates the play in the milieu of the Jacobean court amid acute concerns regarding the overexploitation of Scottish herring fisheries, and the Stuart dynasty's attempt to compensate through spectacles that enacted imperial dominion over the waters of the Atlantic.

While the 'mouldy tale' of Apollonius on which the plot is based might seem an odd vehicle for such a topical commentary, the poet Gower calls attention to his 'good navie' (8.384), and a number of medieval and early modern writers identify Apollonius as the ruler not only of Tyre but also of the nearby Phoenician city of Sidon (Archibald 1991, 98), which means 'fishery' in Greek, an etymology cited by Shakespeare's collaborator George Wilkins in his *History of Justine* (1606, 71ᵛ).[1] The decision to rechristen the eponymous hero only reinforces this interpretation, as it turns out that the ancient Greek demagogue Pericles was an important name to conjure with in political debates over British sea sovereignty in the early seventeenth century. And yet if *Pericles* caters to the Stuarts' political ambition for a 'watery empire' (2.1.49), it also exposes the human fantasy of owning the sea as a naïve delusion. Indeed, beyond dramatizing the susceptibility of mariners to shipwreck, Shakespeare countermines the legal fiction that Britain owns vast swathes of the sea by playing to contemporary fears that the sea owns Britain. That is, *Pericles*'s recurrent allusions to floods and 'the rapture of the sea' (2.1.151) respond to events like the Bristol Channel Flood of 1607 and anxieties about coastal erosion slowly devouring the kingdom. Ultimately, however, this chapter critiques the trope of hungry seas as a misleading personification, one that disguises human rapacity—a rapacity encouraged by state-sponsored fish days and the mass harvesting of sea-snails or 'Tyrian fish' to produce purple dye for royalty, an industry centred in Pericles's hometown. The chapter then weighs the disturbing correspondence between the fish trade and the sex trade, arguing that Shakespeare's co-author Wilkins, as both a victualler and a pimp, had a wry appreciation of the figurative ties between the two. In the final act, however, the play tilts from viewing the 'creatures' of the sea as a mere commodity towards accepting them as family. In Pericles's embracing of Marina and Thaisa as his long-lost daughter and wife, Shakespeare and Wilkins's romance frames the sea as a place that both undoes and recalibrates kinship. At a time when European powers often sought to resolve resource disputes through marriage alliances designed to foster transnational cooperation, *Pericles* celebrates exogamous marriage and finding kin across the seas, even if it falls short of realizing what Donna Haraway calls 'making kin' across the species line.

Mare Britannicum and the Free Seas Debate

In the wake of the 2016 Brexit referendum, stunned pundits struggled to comprehend that the political order of post-war Europe might be capsized by fish. Yet a driving force behind the Leave campaign was the desire of the UK fishing lobby (in particular the Scottish Fishing Federation) to wriggle free of the European Union's Common Fisheries Policy and its restrictive sustainability initiatives.[2] Readers unfamiliar with early modern maritime history might be surprised to learn that similar geo-political wrangles over fishing rights were already raging in the Tudor and Stuart eras, when overfishing first became a topic of serious public concern.[3] In response, a number of influential figures at the Jacobean court were proclaiming British sea sovereignty around the time that Shakespeare and Wilkins composed *Pericles*. As English access to Scotland's North Sea fisheries was a key incentive for the Union of the realms, King James was particularly protective of them; in 1609 he issued a proclamation staunchly asserting Britain's right to control the fisheries bordering its shores, appointing commissioners at London and Edinburgh to sell licenses to foreigners who wished to trawl them. That same year, however, Britain's jurisdiction over its coastal waters was threatened by the publication of *Mare Liberum* [*The Free Seas*] by the Dutch jurist Hugo Grotius. This landmark work of maritime law insisted on the right of the Dutch to establish trade routes to the East Indies, challenging Portuguese hegemony over the region, but also made ripples in Britain, where it might be read as a pointed rebuke to British prohibitions against foreign fishing vessels entering its territorial waters.

While Grotius's manifesto would receive its most famous rebuttal in John Selden's *Mare Clausum* (1635), other British writers had outlined the case for 'closed seas' decades earlier. Curiously, arguments very similar to those advanced by the pro-Brexit fishing lobby were set forth over four centuries ago by John Dee. Although best known as a magus, the polymath Dee was also the first propagandist for a British empire and believed the swiftest way to establish it was through what he called 'imperial Thalassocracy'. In his *General and Rare Memorials pertayning to the Perfect Arte of Navigation*, Dee repeatedly points to Pericles as a model not only of eloquent leadership but also of maritime power:

> What wold that Noble, Valiant, and Victorious Atheniensien PERICLES say yf now he were lyving, and a Subiect of Authority in this Brytish Kingdom? What Common Contribution, wold his pithy Eloquence perswade, for the mayntenance of this Pety-Navy-Royall? (1577, 11)

Citing extracts from the Life of Pericles in Plutarch, Dee credits Athenian dominance to Pericles's support of the city's naval superiority, which made them 'the lords and maisters of the sea' (12).[4] At several points Dee insists the surest way to secure Britain's prosperity is through imitating the example of this Greek leader:

> O, a Sownd Cownsailor and Couragious Capitain, most mete for the Brytish Sea Royalty recovering. O Pericles, thy life (certainly) may be a pattern and Rule to the higher Magistrats (in very many points) most diligently, of them, to be imitated. (12)

Lamenting the contrast between a heroic Greek past and the degenerate British present, Dee grieves there is no 'Brytish or English Pericles now lyving' to persuade the public of the importance of maritime supremacy.[5] Critics have often puzzled over why Shakespeare (or perhaps his collaborator Wilkins) altered the name of the eponymous protagonist in the well-known tale *Apollonius of Tyre*, proposing that the playwrights intended an homage to Pyrocles from Sidney's *Arcadia*. Dee's encomium to the Athenian statesman Pericles as—in his playful orthography—a 'cownsailor' of maritime expansion offers an alternative rationale for this decision to rechristen the character and the play.[6] This connection between Dee's *Perfect Arte of Navigation* and *Pericles* was spied by Bradin

Cormack, who reads the play alongside decorative compasses and crests on Renaissance maps that stake out Britain's maritime sovereignty over its coastal waters (2007, 256–90). Since *Perfect Arte of Navigation* dates from 1577 it might seem far-fetched to cite it as an influence on a Shakespearean text composed three decades later. However, a survey of Dee's later unpublished writings on 'thalassocracy' supports this conjecture, and provides fresh evidence for the enduring significance of *Pericles* in debates over the fisheries.

Twenty-one years after Dee composed his treatise on navigation, he revisited the topic in a manuscript treatise entitled *'THALATTOKRATIA BRETTANIKI'* [*British Sea Sovereignty*]. Dated 8 September 1597 and addressed to Edward Dyer, the manuscript directs the reader back to Dee's earlier treatise and specifically underlines the passages hailing Pericles as an exemplar for Britain's current rulers.[7] Although Dee died in obscurity in 1608, his dream of a 'Brytish Pericles' must have sounded prophetic at the Jacobean court when Shakespeare composed the most sea-obsessed of all his plays. In the ensuing pages, I would like to expand on Cormack's insight to re-examine *Pericles* with an eye not only to legal disputes over oceanic jurisdiction but also to the ecological consequences of that jurisdiction in restricting overfishing. Importantly, Dee was also a fierce defender of England's sovereignty over its fisheries, and denounces the incursions by 'foreign fishermen overboldly now and too, too injuriously, abusing our rich fishings about England, Wales, and Ireland ... [in] seas appertaining to our ancient bounds and limits' (1577, 7). If Dee sounds uncannily like a Brexiteer when he complains that this maritime trespassing costs England 'many hundred thousand pounds' (7) per annum, he also railed vociferously against overfishing by the English in the Thames during spawning season, accusing English 'trink boats' of destroying 90,000 bushels of fish each year, with a market value of £220,500 (1577, 44)—worth about 45 million today (2018). In other words, at stake in the free-seas debate was not merely bragging rights over the ocean's pathless wastes but also lucrative fishing rights, and Dee stands as one of the first persons in European history to outline a case for both a domestic and international fisheries policy based on quantitative analysis and an ethos of sustainability. Insofar as Shakespeare and Wilkins's romance seems to realize Dee's wish that Pericles be revived as an exemplar for Britain's transmarine empire, the play is complicit in this political campaign to assert and extend Britain's claims to territorial waters and fisheries, and invest in a navy that could enforce them.

There is some reason to believe that Shakespeare was acquainted with the rhetoric of British sea sovereignty well before he composed *Pericles*. During the Christmas season of 1594/5, Gray's Inn hosted an extravagant revel, now generally referred to as the *Gesta Grayorum* but which was then known as the revels of 'Henry, Prince of Purpoole'. The festivities included a performance of *A Comedy of Errors* by the up-and-coming playwright William Shakespeare and a masque featuring a 'Hymn in Praise of Neptune' composed by Thomas Campion:

> Of Neptunes Empyre let us sing,
> At whose command the waves obay:
> To whom the Rivers tribute pay,
> Downe the high mountaines sliding.
> To whom the skaly Nation yeelds
> Homage for the Cristall fields
> Wherein they dwell;
> And every Sea-god paies a Iem,
> Yeerely out of his watry Cell,
> To decke great Neptunes Diadem.
>
> (Davison 1602, K8ʳ)

If Campion grants the fish a degree of autonomy, he construes their relation to humans as a kind of feudal dependence, in which they pay 'homage' with themselves as currency. Considering that this song was sung before Queen Elizabeth and her courtiers, including the Lord Admiral, as well as lawyers steeped in disputes over maritime jurisdiction, it sounds suspiciously like an ode to English thalassocracy.

The controversy over sea sovereignty that exercised Dee and Campion resurfaced during the reign of the Scottish King James, and the fisheries would prove a key focus of Stuart environmental policy. The fact that Scotland contains more rugged uplands made its people far more dependent on fishing for subsistence than the English, and hence 'more protective of their coastal and oceanic fishing grounds' (Armitage 2000, 108). Such was the importance of fishing to the nation's economy that James's marriage to Anna of Denmark had been partially motivated by a desire to secure Scottish claims over valuable herring fisheries in the Orkneys, and Anna became a pivotal figure in these maritime disputes. Although the young James VI might have resented Dee's insistence upon English hegemony over Scottish waters, he wisely chose not to aggravate Elizabeth during her reign by rebuffing such claims. After ascending the English throne, however, James saw the opportunity to unite the northern fisheries, and Dee's treatise must have retained an appeal, as his prescient emphasis on Britain and his bold renaming of the Mare Germanicum as the Mare Britannicum would have jelled with James's agendas both for national unification and maritime jurisdiction. Unfortunately for James, his efforts to expand British fishing operations in the North Atlantic encountered fierce resistance from the Danes. Counting on the goodwill of his brother-in-law, James wrote to Christian IV in 1603 requesting permission for English fishing vessels to trawl through the waters around Iceland, but was rebuffed. Two years later, a diplomatic crisis erupted when the Danes impounded English ships that had entered the Sound without permission, which one historian calls 'essentially a move by Christian to gain leverage over English fishing rights in the North Atlantic' (Murdoch 2010, 144). To help ease tensions, Christian dispatched the ambassador Henry Ramelius to England, and the following year, 1606, travelled himself to London. While this state visit produced high hopes for an Anglo-Danish alliance, the two nations could not agree on a common fisheries policy and the Jacobean government instead sought to regulate the access of the Dutch to the North Sea fisheries. Desperate to raise revenue, James drafted a proposal in 1608 to impose a tax on every tenth fish caught by Dutch vessels (SP 14/32/30–31), a policy denounced by Grotius in his *Mare Liberum* as 'brainsick covetousness' (2004, 33).[8] Undeterred, James issued a royal proclamation on 6 May 1609 censuring the 'over great encroachments' (*SRP* 218) of foreign fishers in British waters, and demanding they pay steep fees for fishing licenses. If Robert Cecil's estimates are reliable, the Stuart government had good reason to be concerned: the number of foreign fishing vessels in British waters reportedly swelled from 200 in the 1590s to 3,000 in the first decade of the seventeenth century.[9]

The task of unfurling the legal case for James's maritime policy fell to a Scottish law professor by the name of William Welwood, whose work echoes the patriotic and proto-ecological arguments sounded by Dee. At a time when *Pericles* was one of the most popular offerings on the London stage, Welwood, like Dee, upholds its titular hero as a spokesperson for Britain's oceanic empire, citing a passage from Thucydides, '*Magna res maris imperium inquit Pericles*' [It is a great thing to rule the seas, said Pericles] (1615, 11).[10] Welwood first waded into this debate with *The Sea-Law of Scotland* (1590), dedicated to King James, and over the next two decades laboured on an expanded version, which finally appeared in print in 1613. *An Abridgement of All Sea Laws* is also dedicated to James, and its counterblast against Grotius argues for maritime jurisdiction based on the need for 'conservacie' of the herring fisheries, 'to the end that not onely a peaceable but also a full and plentifull fishing may be enjoyed' (1613, A3^v). Welwood's plea for 'conservacie' sounds remarkably like modern environmental notions of conservation, and his language makes it clear that early moderns were acutely aware of the devasting impact of overexploiting the fisheries:

> If the uses of the seas may be in any respect forbidden and stayed it should be chiefly for the fishing, as by which the fishes may be said to be *exhaust and wasted*, which daily experience these twenty years past and more hath declared to be overtrue. For wheras aforetime the white fishes daily abounded even into all the shoares on the Easterne coast of Scotland, now forsooth by the neere and daily approaching of the buss-Fishers the shoals of fishes are broken and so farre-scattered away from our shores and coasts that *no fish now can be found* worthy of any paines and travails, to the impoverishing of all the sort of our home fishers and to the great damage of all the Nation. (1613, 71–2, italics added)

In piscatorial verses printed the same year as Welwood's treatise, John Dennys invokes Ovidian historiography to bemoan a decline from a golden age of plentiful fishing:

> The Fish as yet had felt but little smart,
> And were to bite more eager, apt, and bold:
> And plenty still supplied the place again
> Of woeful want, whereof we now complain.
>
> (1613, C1ᵛ)

Overfishing is not a uniquely modern problem, but one that Shakespeare's contemporaries found to be 'overtrue', and deeply enmeshed with questions of political sovereignty.[11]

Seen through the blue prism of the New Thalassology, *Pericles* registers and intervenes in this dispute over the alleged ownership of the seas and fisheries. In the famous beach scene, the shipwrecked prince eavesdrops on some garrulous fishermen and observes:

> How from the finny subject of the sea
> These fishers tell the infirmities of men
> And from their watery empire recollect
> All that may men approve or men detect.
>
> (2.1.47–50)

The striking phrase 'finny subject of the sea' echoes the language of the free seas debate. Pericles here speaks like a prince in identifying the fish as 'subject' to the Crown but it remains ambiguous whether the 'watery empire' belongs to the fish, the fishers, or 'men'. Although Pericles himself never grabs a fishing rod, the portrayal of angling as a royal pastime in *Antony and Cleopatra* (2.5.10–18) affords it a certain prestige, while Pericles's greeting 'Peace be at your labour, honest fishermen' (2.1.51) gains an added resonance from the monarchy's support of the industry, as well as the hostile seizures and violent skirmishes that sometimes occurred during the herring wars of the early Stuart era. The name of the second fisher, Pilch, recalls the fish known as the pilchard but also the leather apron worn by fishers, and possibly derives from Thomas Nashe's *Lenten Stuff*, a work that demonstrates the vital importance of the fishing industry to England's economy and tries to patriate the herring as a distinctly English species:

> On no coast like ours is it caught in such abundance, nowhere drest in his right cue but under our Horizon; hosted, rosted, and tosted here alone it is.... The poorer sort make it three-parts of their sustenance; with it, for his dernier, the patchedest leather *piltche labaratho* may dine like a Spanish Duke.... Her Majesty's tributes and customs this *Semper Augustus* of the sea's finnie freeholders augmenteth and enlargeth uncountably. (1599, 26–7)

The subtle change from Nashe's description of herring as the 'sea's finnie freeholders' and a Caesar among fish to *Pericles*'s 'finny subject of the sea' neatly captures the shift towards a more proprietary closed-seas policy under James.

Evidence for this shift can also be dredged up from *Sicelides*, probably the best example of a piscatorial drama in early modern Britain. Composed by Phineas Fletcher as a royal entertainment for King James's visit to Cambridge in 1615, *Sicelides* endorses state ownership of coastal waters while echoing Shakespeare and Wilkins's romance. Tyrinthus, whose name evokes Tyre, has been away for fifteen years and separated from his two children: a boy named Perindus and a girl, Olinda, whose mother died whilst giving birth to her, much like Marina. To save his lover from being sacrificed to a sea orc, Perindus leaps into the sea, where he is rescued by two comedic fishers reminiscent of the ones who aid the shipwrecked Pericles. When the duo first enters with their boat and nets, one orders the other to help him: 'Will you come Sir, you are yet in my jurisdiction on the water' (D2^v). Fletcher likely devised the joke to appeal to the king's interest in legal disputes over maritime jurisdiction. The fishers later appear to violate such jurisdictions by plucking Perindus from the sacred (i.e. closed) seas outside their fisheries, incurring the wrath of Neptune's priest:

> Thou foolish fisher, thinkst it good to stop
> The course of justice, and breake her sword, the Law?
> By Law thou lie'st: hee justly death deserves,
> Who that destroyes, which him and his preserves.
>
> (K4^v)

Although the priest pardons them when the true culprit is unmasked, the scene recalls debates, stoked by the publication of Welwood's rebuttal to Grotius in 1613, over maritime salvage and the stiff punishments meted out to anglers who violated laws on fishing out of season or allotted catchment zones. The priest's claim that destroying a nation's food supply should be a capital offense is a far more draconian environmental policy than anything proposed in Stuart proclamations, but the desperate plight of the oceans was leading to desperate measures.

A decisive factor behind the Stuart campaign for *mare clausum* was the dawning recognition that herring were no longer quite so abundant or affordable, and *Pericles* hints at a decline in the fisheries when the king and queen of Tarsus bewail a famine that has inflicted their nation, so that:

> These mouths who but of late earth, sea, and air
> Were all too little to content and please,
> Although they gave their creatures in abundance,
> As houses are defiled for want of use.
>
> (1.4.34–7)

In 1607 England had suffered a severe dearth, which sparked an uprising in Shakespeare's own county, so the fisherman's warning that Pericles will starve if he cannot fish (2.1.67) 'echoes a real and present anxiety' (Gossett 2004, 122). Yet Cleon's lament implies a scarcity not only of grain and flesh but also fish. When harvest failures drove up prices for grain and beef, early moderns would have supplemented their diet with more seafood, but the seaside town of Tarsus appears unable to do so. The logical conclusion is that the once abundant fish population has crashed, most likely due to human activity since shoals moved further away from shore when overfished, as Welwood observed. Parliament's passage of a 1605 'Act for the Better Preservation of Sea-fish' (3 Jac. c. 12) attests to an alarming decline in British fisheries shortly before Shakespeare and Wilkins composed *Pericles*. Cleon's warning that London might someday suffer the fate of Tarsus if it fails to curtail its 'superfluous riots' (1.4.54) or feasts thus has an eco-critical undercurrent. The warning must have struck home with Jacobean audiences given that the 1607 dearth would have made many, especially a victualler like Wilkins, conscious of their reliance upon increasingly scarce and expensive fish. In 1587, William Harrison complained that the poor were forced to eat rotten fish during Lent because 'other fish is too dear' (374), for which many blamed incursions by foreign fishers (Sgroi 2003, 17–18), and some on the presence of too many strangers in the realm. When a citizen in the play of *Sir Thomas More* incites all Londoners 'that will not see a red herring at a Harry groat' (6.1) to join in an anti-immigrant riot—with a pun that underscores Nashe's assertion of the herring's intrinsic Englishness—he taps into popular support for British sea sovereignty over the Dutch in Shakespeare's day, while reframing an environmental crisis as an immigration crisis.

Before departing for the court, Pericles acknowledges his indebtedness to the fishers for agreeing to relinquish his armour, 'By your furtherance I am clothed in steel' (2.1.150), and makes a solemn promise to pay them back: 'if that ever my low fortune's better, / I'll pay your bounties, till then rest your debtor' (2.1.138–9). Critics have sometimes faulted Pericles for failing to deliver on this promise (especially since he does reward them in Wilkins's prose account), but the message may not have been lost; James's 1609 proclamation could be seen as the off-stage equivalent of the 'certain condolements, certain vails' (2.1.146) expected by the fisherman in *Pericles*. Such an interpretation is bolstered by the setting of this scene in Pentapolis. Scholars have identified this location with a cluster of Greek settlements in present-day Libya, but an English audience would readily associate the name Pentapolis (i.e. Five Cities) with the Cinque Ports of England, which were hubs of the nation's fishing industry.[12] In April 1609, one month before the royal proclamation, fishermen from the Cinque Ports had petitioned James to impose a tariff of 15 shillings per last (twelve barrels) on all fish imported from Holland (SP 14/45/22). As the royal finances had suffered a figurative shipwreck, James's 'low fortune' prevented him paying back the fishing lobby in actual coin. Nevertheless, his maritime policies not only generated revenue for the Crown but also, by reducing the number of foreign vessels in British waters, would boost the hauls and profits of British fishermen. In requesting 'condolements', the fishers in *Pericles* may be lobbying for some such support from the Crown, reminding James of his obligations to the trade.

The 1609 proclamation was not the first or last time the English monarchy championed the herring and cod industries. Elizabeth's and James's defence of the Lenten fast was motivated not merely by their Anglican faith but by an ulterior belief that aiding commercial fishing would in turn buoy up the English navy. In Shakespeare's England, fasting entailed abstention from beef, chicken, and pork, while fish was the staple fare, and ensuring a supply for the whole nation required a large fleet of fishing vessels. The ostensibly pagan Greek fishers in *Pericles* follow this Christian custom, telling Pericles they will regale him with 'fish for fasting days' (2.1.79–80). Gower's remark in the opening chorus that the tale has been sung on 'ember eves' (1.0.6) would also savour of fish, as ember days comprised four sets of three consecutive days in which flesh was prohibited and fish consumed in its stead. The first of these ember days overlapped with the commencement of Lent, and there is reason to think that fasting was on Shakespeare's mind—and that fish were on his plate—during the composition of *Pericles*. As the play refers to the *Haddington Masque*, staged 9 February 1608, and was entered in the Stationers' Register on 20 May 1608, scholars date it to late winter or early spring of that year. Since Easter fell on 27 March in 1608, Lent would have begun around 15 February. Noting that Shakespeare may have retreated to Stratford to witness the birth of his granddaughter on 21 February 1608, René Weiss concludes it is therefore 'likely that Shakespeare would have used the period of Lent for his part, Acts 3–5, when the theatres were closed' (2015, 124). Shakespeare may have often availed himself of the downtime of Lent to write, but *Pericles* in particular—perhaps because it is a product of collaboration with a victualler—seems redolent of fish.

Prince Henry and Pericles, Prince of Purple

This chapter has anchored *Pericles* in Jacobean maritime policy, but it would be a mistake to regard James alone as the only figure of consequence at the Stuart court. A play featuring a 'Brytish Pericles' would have exerted a particular appeal in 1608 for the followers of James's eldest son, Prince Henry. While the king regarded himself as a peacemaker, Henry's circle subscribed to Dee's vision of a militant Protestant empire in North America, and called for greater investment in the navy to defend and extend British waters. Hopes for the prince as a future mariner-king would have been afloat as early as 1604, when Charles Howard, the Lord High Admiral, presented the 10-year-old Henry with his very own ship, a

Fig. 3.1 Jan Porcellis, *A Storm at Sea* (c.1606–10). RCIN 402633. Royal Collection Trust.
© Queen Elizabeth II 2021.

28-foot-long vessel which the prince christened *The Disdain*. Three years later the shipwright Phineas Pett fashioned a model ship for Henry, and the gift apparently thrilled the young prince so much that he commissioned Pett to produce a full-scale version in 1608, the year in which *Pericles* premiered. Known as the *Prince Royal* (a stunning model replica of it can be seen at the National Maritime Museum in Greenwich), this ship was the English navy's first-ever three-decker (Strong 1986, 57). Henry's enthusiasm for all things nautical also extended to fine art. He employed a small army of artists and wood-carvers to decorate the *Prince Royal*, and Henry at this time also acquired some of the first seascapes ever seen in England, including *A Storm at Sea* by Jan Porcellis, which features a dramatic image of a shipwreck (see Fig. 3.1).

Imagining Prince Henry and his circle as implied spectators of *Pericles* offers another frame through which to reappraise the play, particularly in light of the compelling case for Shakespeare as a 'court dramatist' put forward by Richard Dutton. The decision by the King's Men to stage a play with numerous scenes set at sea and on shipboard might be seen as a gesture comparable to the gifts of Howard and Pett—a deliberate bid to cater to the teenage prince's infatuation with the maritime world. Although there is no evidence to confirm that Henry ever attended a production of *Pericles*, its storm scenes would no doubt have delighted rather than unnerved the owner of Porcellis's painting, who also enjoyed swimming in the Thames. In the year after the founding of Jamestown, many at court would have entertained high hopes that Prince Henry might become the Pericles of whom Dee had dreamt: the fearless champion of British sea sovereignty.

A similar message can be discerned in a court masque composed by Samuel Daniel in 1610, two years after *Pericles*, to celebrate Henry's formal installation as the Prince of Wales. Entitled *Tethys' Festival,* the masque was commissioned by Henry's mother, Queen Anna, who was actively involved in negotiations over the fisheries and later commissioned Welwood to write another treatise on maritime law (Alsop 1980). In a brilliant diplomatic manoeuvre, James had stipulated that the proceeds from foreign fishing licenses would support the maintenance of Anna's household, so that if Christian refused to pay he was effectively depriving his own sister. Daniel was doubtless aware of these quarrels, as the masque flatters the Stuarts as the divinely appointed overlords of an oceanic empire. Neptune appears clutching a trident with Latin mottos derived from Virgil, suggesting that James, by *regendo & retinendo* [reigning over and guarding] the ocean, will achieve a Pax Britannia in the Atlantic.[13] The masque pins its hopes for this peace on Henry, who as the half-Danish heir to the English throne would be in a position to reconcile the European squabbles over the fisheries better than his father. After Neptune places the symbolic trident into James's hands (anticipating William Dyce's 1847 depiction of Britannia), Triton presents Henry with a scarf that is simultaneously a map of 'the spacious empery / That he is borne unto another day' (E1ᵛ). On behalf of Tethys, Triton urges Henry not to venture into the Mediterranean, but to steer towards the Atlantic:

> For there will be within the large extent
> Of these my waves, and wat'ry government
> More treasure, and more certain riches got
> Then all the Indies to Iberus brought,
> For Nereus will by industry unfold
> A chemic secret, and turn fish to gold.
>
> (F1ʳ)

The written account of the masque explicitly mentions that Nereus, the Old Man of the Sea, appeared hauling 'golden fish in a net, with this word *Industria*', so the pageantry fulfils the prophecy of turning fish to gold—a prime example of the Jacobean fantasy of environmental alchemy—a miracle figuratively enacted in Anthony Munday's 1616 civic pageant *Chrysanelia: The Golden Fishing* (see Fig. 3.2).[14]

But Shakespeare's audience would have been aware that certain fish could be transformed into a colour even more valuable than gold. Critics have viewed *Pericles, Prince of Tyre* in relation to the Mediterranean and to maritime trade, but virtually nothing has been made of the fact that the protagonist's hometown was the renowned epicentre of the purple dye industry. Before the synthetic production of mauve in 1859, a truly lustrous, indelible purple could only be produced from the hypobranchial glands of carnivorous sea snails, once found in abundance in the eastern Mediterranean. As it required approximately 10,000 snails to make one gram of dyestuff, enough to stain only the hem of a single toga, purple dye was literally worth 'more than its weight in gold' (Bagnall 2012, 5673), and early modern sumptuary laws dictated that clothing of this hue could only be worn by royalty. Modern readers thus fail to fully grasp the sybaritic splendour of the 'purple sails' adorning Cleopatra's barge: the colour is arguably the most

Fig. 3.2 Henry Shaw, The Fishmongers' pageant, from Anthony Munday, *The Golden Fishing* (1616).
© British Library Board.

luxurious aspect of the whole spectacle, as it was literally stained with the mucus of hundreds of thousands of crushed snails. The process of manufacturing purple from sea snails was well known in Shakespeare's day through its detailed description in Pliny's *Natural History* (9.36–8).[15] The numerous references to 'purple' blood by Renaissance poets like Spenser, Shakespeare, and Donne are not evidence of colour blindness but of an alternate configuration of the colour spectrum dictated in part by the use of an animal-based dye derived from a secretion then regarded as blood, and hence betray that this regal colour involved the violent exploitation of non-human nature.

Due to the labour and expense of making it, purple once radiated an elegance it no longer connotes, and fabrics of this hue were held in high esteem by the Stuart court. During his installation as Prince of Wales, Henry appeared in a surcote of purple velvet followed by twenty-five Knights of the Bath in purple satin, which may well have stirred memories of the 'Henry, Prince of Purpoole' revel in which Campion's hymn to Neptune was sung, and an inventory of Queen Anna's wardrobe reveals that she owned several gowns dyed or lined with purple.[16] It is therefore significant that in *Tethys' Festival*, Queen Anna, Princess Elizabeth, and their ladies in waiting appeared clad in 'a head-tire composed of shells and corral' and 'a great murex shell in form of the crest of a helm' (F2^v). As Daniel would have known, murex was the common name, mentioned by Pliny, for the molluscs harvested for purple dyes. Curiously, Shakespeare's landlady, Marie Mountjoy, had designed the head-tires for Queen Anna's masques in 1604–5 (Nicholl 2007, 143–4), which included the appearance of the goddess Tethys as a personification of 'power by sea' (A3^r). It is tempting to speculate that Mountjoy may have lent a hand with the shell-encrusted headdress in *Tethys' Festival*, and that Shakespeare may even have seen it.[17] Be that as it may, this Stuart masque exalts the state's sovereignty over not only the fish of the Atlantic but also the marine gastropods (then classified as shellfish) of the Mediterranean, which were slaughtered by the thousands since the Hellenistic era to produce the trappings of luxury for the elite.[18]

No stage direction in *Pericles* explicitly calls for a murex-shaped helmet or mollusc to appear, but the distraught Pericles does picture the queen's coffin on the sea-floor 'lying with simple shells' (3.1.64). In anticipation of Ariel's 'full fathom five' song, the image hints that the coffined Thaisa may not be dead so much as metamorphosed into a kind of sea snail.[19] Gower's description of the eponymous hero 'sail[ing] seas in cockles' (4.4.2) likewise nudges the audience to visualize Pericles as a sea snail, as if a transhuman merger with shells can render our species amphibious and naturalize human presence in the sea. Shannon Kelley has observed that the play enacts a fantasy of 'human-shell inhabitation' and likens Pericles's emotional catatonia to withdrawal into an enclosed shell (2015, 169). In support of this perceptive reading, one might add that when he crawls out of the sea 'thronged up with cold' (2.1.71) and recovers his armour, Pericles's behaviour mimics that of shell-dwelling molluscs such as periwinkles, which his name strangely resembles. The resemblance would have been closer in the seventeenth century, as common early modern spellings of the snail indicate a tri-syllabic pronunciation with a voiced e at the end: perwincles, perwinkles, per-wyncles.[20] A popular snack for playgoers at the Globe, periwinkles speckle Britain's shores, dwelling in intertidal zones where they are submerged twice a day, and British dyers used them back in Anglo-Saxon times to create reddish-purple dyes.[21] With their greater awareness of the materiality of colour, Jacobean audiences, especially at court, might well associate shell imagery in a play set in Tyre—in which a Tyrian princess makes money by weaving 'sleided silk' (4.0.21) and 'silk, twin with the rubied cherry' (5.0.7)—with the eco-material traffic for purple in Shakespeare's day, when the king had just renewed the Charter of the Levant Company.[22]

After all, Tyre was so synonymous with the production of this luxurious dye that the play's title conceivably puns on clothing, like the 'rich tire' (3.2.22) worn by Cerimon, and its eponymous hero could be rechristened Pericles, Prince of Purple. It is fitting therefore that in *Pericles*'s prose source, *The Patterne of Painefull Adventures*, Apollonius of Tyre appears at his wedding in 'a gowne of purple Satten embroidred with golde' (Twyne 1607, C2^r). Shakespeare undoubtedly knew of the city's reputation for the dye, as Gremio boasts in *The Taming of the*

Shrew of his 'hangings all of Tyrian tapestry' (2.1.341). So, too, did George Wilkins, whose first published work includes the memorable incident of a banished general who is so offended by his son peacocking in purple robes from Tyre that he sentences him to be crucified in his finery (1606, 74ʳ). The fact that *Pericles* only mentions purple once, and in association with violets (4.1.14), almost seems like a strategic omission, but Marina's 'rubied cherry' silk could be purplish since Renaissance purple encompassed shades moderns would call red. It is, moreover, highly likely that the King's Men acquired some purple or faux-purple (made from madder) costumes for this play like the 'purpell sattin' cloak in Alleyn's inventory (*HD* 291). When Cerimon pries open the chest, he discovers Thaisa's body 'shrouded in cloth of state' (3.2.63), a phrase that would prompt the King's Men to outfit her in a royal colour, probably either gold (as in Gower) or Tyrian purple. If the play followed its source, then Thaisa, after her murex-like immersion in the sea, would have shed her 'vestal livery' (3.4.9) and re-emerged in purple, since in *The Painefull Adventures* she dons 'a purple robe' (K2ʳ) when she reunites with her long-lost husband, thereby reclaiming her identity as queen of Tyre.[23] If so, the emotional climax of Shakespeare's romance would have been as much chromatic as linguistic. Like the purple clothing adorning Henry and Queen Anna, purple-dyed costumes in performances of *Pericles*, especially at Whitehall, would represent a vibrant material symbol of royal dominion over the ocean.

Exposing a purple undertone in the palette of *Pericles* suggests that the play belongs alongside other luxurious art objects produced for or by the Jacobean court, such as the purple-velvet-bound copy of *Basilikon Doron* that James presented to his son, and invites a closer comparison with Daniel's *Tethys' Festival*. Critics have sometimes regarded Daniel's masque as an influence on *The Tempest*, but it is equally conceivable that *Tethys' Festival* owes something to *Pericles*. Daniel's 'wat'ry government' echoes Pericles's 'watery empire', while the festival of the sea-goddess resembles 'Neptune's annual feast' (5.0.17) in Shakespeare's romance. In both cases the involvement of royalty, Lysimachus and Prince Henry, in celebrations of sea deities betrays an ideological drift, the divine conferral of maritime sovereignty. Whether *Pericles*—with its classical pageantry 'honouring of Neptune's triumphs' (5.1.14)—was designed for court performance or is a 'populuxe' (Yachnin 2001) drama, marketing the glamour of the Stuart masque to a mass audience, an ecocritic might smell something rotten in its affinity with *Tethys' Festival*. In response to a worrisome population crash of herring in the North Sea, *Tethys' Festival* advocates what is now known as distant fishing to haul in more cod from off the Newfoundland coast.[24] In 1610, Daniel's sea deities authorize Britain's imperial sovereignty over the Atlantic but in hindsight it is tempting to view them as embodiments of anthropocratic dominion over the global ocean. Fortunately, the representation of 'masked Neptune' (3.3.37) in *Pericles* is much murkier and far more complicated than in Daniel's masque, and the next section will seek to plumb this ambiguity more deeply.

Pericles's Devouring Seas and the Bristol Channel Flood

If Jacobean court culture imagined the sea under royal jurisdiction, it must be stressed that early modern portrayals of the maritime world did not always align with state ideology. While imprisoned on the island of Jersey in a cell overlooking the English Channel, the dissenter William Prynne composed a series of poems variously likening the sea to God's wrath toward the wicked, divine benevolence toward the elect, the torments of hell, and the cleansing force of baptism (1641, 82–3). In effect, Prynne enlists the sea in his on-going battle against the Stuart establishment, transforming it into the poetic correlative of a spiritual realm located outside the earthbound political order, whose vast power bedwarfs secular authority as much as the ocean does a small island. Co-written by a playwright in the employ of the king, *Pericles* is, as the preceding pages have indicated, nowhere near so radical. However, its depiction of the sea as the 'principal symbol of exposure, spatial immensity, and ungrounded contingency' (Gillies 2003, 183) can be seen as tempering the rhetoric of Jacobean thalassocracy. Instead of depicting a stable, halcyon sea that can be sailed and governed with ease, *Pericles* also reminds monarchs of the need to respect and 'obey' its greater-than-human force. The courtier Dudley Carleton would mock the portrayal of the maritime environment in the Stuart masque as 'all Fish and no water', and Shakespeare and Wilkins embed a similar critique in their play, giving the lie to this illusion by forcing the king to enter 'wet' (SD 2.1.0).[25]

The introduction outlined the case that Stuart absolutism had a profound impact on the environmental politics of the late plays in that James's vision of himself as a god-like ruler over his domain spurred Shakespeare to dramatize the limitations imposed on monarchy by the unruliness of the natural world. Lear's exposure in the storm may be the *locus classicus*, but Shakespeare composes variations on this theme in the sea-storms of *Pericles* and *The Tempest*. In contrast to the absolutist fantasy of maritime dominion in *Tethys' Festival*, *The Tempest* opens with a blunt assertion of the impotence of monarchical authority amid a turbulent sea: 'what cares these roarers for the name of king?' (1.1.18). *Pericles* makes this same point not once, but twice, in the two storms that constitute the most dramatic spectacles in the play. In the midst of the first storm, Pericles glosses its fury as evidence that 'earthly man / Is but a substance that must yield' (2.1.2–3) to the elements. Critics generally prefer the second storm, attributed to Shakespeare, over the first, credited to Wilkins, finding the second more poetic and the first more didactic (Jones 2015, 120). Sketching an ekphrastic seascape of a 'vast' that belittles the human and combining it with the hurly-burly of staged storm effects in which 'the seaman's whistle / Is as a whisper in the ears of death, / Unheard' (3.1.8–10), Shakespeare's intervention in *Pericles* constitutes one of the earliest depictions of the oceanic sublime in English literature. An implied moral can be heard in the second storm too, as the futility of Pericles commanding the surges, winds, thunders, and flashes to cease—in accordance with the golden rule of good writing—shows rather than tells of the powerlessness of humans, even monarchs, to control the seas. Insofar as this spectacle, especially in a modern proscenium theatre or cinematic adaptation, enables the audience to watch the storm in safety, it replicates the detachment of Renaissance seascapes like the one by Porcellis owned by Prince Henry. However, Shakespeare's emotive language, particularly in the more immersive Renaissance playhouse, stirs a compassionate reaction like that of Miranda, who suffers along with the shipwrecked. Intervening in the *paragone* debate to exhibit the superiority of drama to painting, *Pericles*'s sea-storm torpedoes the callous ethics of Renaissance seascape, embraced by Francis Bacon via Lucretius as a metaphor for scientific objectivity and by Prince Henry as flattering his imperial pretensions to own the ocean.[26]

To fathom why Shakespeare and Wilkins would risk incurring royal disfavour by depicting sea-storms that shipwreck a king and therefore erode the Stuart rhetoric of maritime sovereignty, one might appeal to the familiar New Historicist dialectic of subversion/containment. When autumn storms in the North Sea hindered his return voyage from Denmark, James penned a complaint in sonnet form against the mutinous winds (*KJSW* 121), declaring Zephyrus's defiance of him the exception that proved the rule of his Orphic authority over the sky, sea, earth, and animals. The incident only reaffirmed his faith in his own cosmic importance: the devil must have suborned witches to conjure the storm. Just as the term Anthropocene re-inscribes the human dominion it critiques, dramatizing the unruliness of the sea might incite a yearning to rule it, or glorify the state's power to withstand its vicissitudes. When the fishers recover his father's armour from the deeps, Pericles exclaims, 'The rough seas, that spares not any man, / Took it in rage, though calmed have given't again' (2.1.127–8). The passage captures the mutability of the sea, its capacity to bereave and restore, which is central to *Pericles*'s plot and also shapes *The Tempest*: 'though the seas threaten, they are merciful' (5.1.181). The subversion/containment dialectic has provoked numerous cavils and objections over the past few decades, but the ocean in *Pericles* issues an ecocritical caveat: humanity and the world-remaking forces of our technology cannot contain nature because we can never be entirely outside it. The argument that a state-subservient drama produces disorder to justify repressive power does not hold water when it comes to the volatility of the sea, for the early modern sea could not be controlled or contained, as a survey of late medieval/Renaissance oceanography and failed hydroengineering projects will illustrate all too well.

Besides the memorable shipwreck scenes, *Pericles* offers several pointed reminders why human claims to rule the inconceivably vast and ungovernable ocean might be greeted with scepticism. During the Little Ice Age, it would have been particularly evident from the congealing of large shelves of sea-ice in the North Sea that the dimensions of a nation like Denmark or Norway could expand and contract drastically between summer and winter and from one year to the next. Ice-flows, silted rivers, tides, and storm surges bedeviled the defenders of *mare clausum*, who sought to stake out a clearly defined 'exclusion zone' extending a designated number of miles from the coast. Even more worrisome was the recognition by Renaissance antiquarians of the geo-morphological havoc wrought by coastal erosion. While European nations were annexing the seas and even reclaiming drowned land (see Chapter 6), such achievements were rendered hollow by the fact that the ocean was actively reclaiming the land. Two of the best-known examples are the drowned villages of Old Winchelsea and Dunwich, which were inundated in the onset of the Little Ice Age, and similar disasters would recur throughout Shakespeare's lifetime.[27] In 1605 the inhabitants of the Norfolk fishing village of Eccles-on-Sea petitioned for a tax reduction on the grounds that it had become in effect Eccles-in-Sea: sixty-six of its eighty houses and over 1,000 acres of it were now 'all eaten upp with ye sea' (qtd in Stannard n.d., 3). Pouring salt in the wound, as it were, the sea flooded the Norfolk coast again in 1608, when *Pericles* was first performed, and the following year Parliament passed new legislation to establish a sea breach commission.[28] While the fishermen in *Pericles* dredge up armour, inadvertent feats of marine archaeology by Renaissance anglers had led to the disconcerting realization—attested in the writings of William Camden, Edmund Spenser, and Michael Drayton—that much of the southern North Sea had once been dry land and that a wide land bridge now known as Doggerland (after Dutch fishing vessels) had connected prehistoric Britain with the continent. It is probably not a coincidence that the person who popularized the 'isthmus hypothesis' (Ferguson 1969, 30) was John Twyne, the father of Lawrence Twyne, author of the chief narrative source for *Pericles*. Play-goers aware of the Twyne family's notorious theory that the sea had swallowed a portion of Britain might well have associated the violent sea storms and flood imagery in Shakespeare's adaptation of Twyne's text with catastrophic sea rise. In brief, 'coastal change' was an environmental anxiety in Shakespeare's time comparable to contemporary fears of climate change and coastal erosion aggravated by global warming.

These anxieties reached their highwater mark with the 1607 Bristol Channel Flood, an event that would have boosted the credibility of Twyne's theory and that seems to have left traces on *Pericles*. In response to the encroaching of the sea, many early modern seaside communities had launched ambitious hydroengineering schemes. In the Welsh town of Aberthaw a massive sea wall was constructed in 1606, spearheaded by Sir Edward Stradling, the former Sheriff of Glamorganshire, and commemorated in an ode written by his second cousin and adopted son John:

What greater than to prescribe laws for Neptune, and impose new limits on his floods?
  Behold, this soil used to be salt, there is a crop were there was a sea,
  Where the fish sported in this field, the sheep goes a-straying. (1607, 152)

A few months later, on 20 January 1607, one of the greatest natural disasters in the history of Britain struck in the form of a tidal bore compounded by a storm surge of such force (scientists have proposed it may have been a tsunami) that it utterly demolished the new sea wall, submerging farms as far as 14 miles inland under 12 feet of water and drowning an estimated 2,000 people. Witnessing the devastation first hand, John Stradling composed what amounts to an authorial retraction of his previous poem. 'Mortals pointlessly strive to restrict the outlaw waters with laws' he exclaims, while denouncing the treachery of Neptune:

> Neptune, there is no faith in your government.
> Boldly you protect the things that are yours,
> And by force you snatch those that belong to others.
>
> (1607, 162)

As the 1607 flood occurred so soon after the completion of the sea wall, the pious-minded may have seen it as an act of divine judgment upon human manipulation of the environment.[29] Stradling's poem voices such misgivings, but skirts the theological problem by placing the blame on pagan sea-gods. Needless to say, Stradling here presents a very different Neptune from Daniel's, and a radically different view of maritime jurisdiction. The second version confesses that humans pointlessly try to impose law on the 'outlaw waters,' for Neptune's 'government' can always reassert its sovereignty over the land. The pattern that emerges from Stradling's poems is containment followed by subversion or rather submersion, not vice versa.

Reports of the 1607 flood soon appeared in the London press, and would have lent a topical frisson to *Pericles*'s references to the 'rapture of the sea' (2.1.151). That the second storm in *Pericles* collapsed part of the Ephesian coast is hinted by the Gentleman, who exclaims that his lodgings:

> standing bleak upon the sea
> Shook as the earth did quake;
> The very principals did seem to rend
> And all to topple.
>
> (3.2.14–17)

A similar disaster struck Tarsus, for the epitaph inscribed on Marina's monument indicates that the same storm had engulfed the coastline.

> At her birth
> Thetis being proud swallowed some part o'th' earth.
> Therefore the earth, fearing to be o'erflowed,
> Hath Thetis' birth-child on the heavens bestowed;

> Wherefore she does, and swears she'll never stint,
> Make raging battery upon shores of flint.
>
> (4.4.38–43)[30]

The epitaph offers an etiological fable for the persistence of the waves towards the pebbled shore: Marina's supposed death instigates an eternal war between the sea and land. While some critics find the verses un-Shakespearean, their alleged awkwardness may instead spring from their insertion as a topical reference to the coastal floods of 1607.[31] Pericles himself evokes a coastal flood when he is reunited with Marina, and weirdly asks Helicanus to strike him:

> Lest this great sea of joys rushing upon me
> O'erbear the shores of my mortality
> And drown me.
>
> (5.1.182–4)

The metaphor channels anxieties about coastal floods on the macrocosmic level and diverts them to the microcosmic, while draining their tragic force in a moment of joyful anagnorisis. Like the casting of Perdita as a Persephone figure whose discovery presages the return of spring in *The Winter's Tale*, the finding of Marina promises a kind of truce in the war waged by the sea upon the land declared in her epitaph. Shakespeare and Wilkins's romance thus assuages fears of coastal erosion and catastrophic deluge, offering a fantasy of recovery from the 1607 flood. Crucially, however, the play appears to predicate this recovery upon a recognition of kinship with the sea through the figure of Marina, whom the play imagines, like Caliban, as a humanoid fish.

Making Kin with the Sea in *Pericles*

In the portion of *Pericles* attributed to Shakespeare (acts 3–5), the play's negotiation with the sea centres on Marina. Her name signals her status as an embodiment of the marine world, and the fact that the playwrights changed it from Thaise, transferring that name to Pericles's wife, indicates that the personification was a deliberate one. In considering the plight of her character—born at sea, abducted on the seacoast, and trafficked like a maritime commodity—Shakespeare sensed an opportunity to comment on disputes over sea sovereignty. Dionyza's scheme to have Marina murdered on the 'sea-margent' (4.1.25) reflects the liminality and relative lawlessness of this space, between sea and land, and potentially mitigates the crime of her kidnapping. Advocates of *mare liberum* argued that free-roaming fish could not be claimed as the exclusive property of any nation, whereas supporters of *mare clausum* regarded fishing in foreign waters as tantamount to piracy: the seizing of goods that belonged to another. Born at sea, Marina is not a citizen of Tarsus, and her abduction on the seashore by pirates resembles the controversial raids by seventeenth-century fishers violating territorial waters.

The play further develops this analogy following Marina's arrival in Mytilene, where her body is hawked and sold like fish in a fish market. Shakespeare's plays often engage in what Brayton terms 'figurative fishmongering' (2012, 145), but *Pericles* in particular revels in the confusion of fish and flesh, perhaps due to the involvement of Shakespeare's co-author, Wilkins. In legal documents, Wilkins gives his profession as 'victualler', but the location of his tavern near the disreputable Turnbull and Cow Cross Streets, and the fact that so many of his eighteen brushes with the law involved violence against women accused of prostitution points to the inescapable conclusion that this was a cover for his illicit activities as a pimp (Prior 1972). In the early modern imagination, these two professions were commonly entwined, as illustrated by paintings of fish markets (see Fig. 3.3) and the brothel scenes in *Pericles*. The Bawd's gripe that their 'creatures' are 'rotten', 'sodden', and 'unwholesome', (4.2.8, 17–18) invokes the lexical field of rotting fish, and the dispatching of Bolt to acquire 'fresh ones' mimics a victualler sending out a factor to the fishmongers.[32] Such vulgar innuendos must have been part of the everyday trade jargon of the victualler/pimp Wilkins; critics have sniffed out his

Fig. 3.3 Joachim Beuckelaer, *Fish Market with Ecce Homo* (1570). Nationalmuseum Stockholm PD.

'coarsening influence' (Duncan-Jones 2001, 209) in these scenes, and rightly deplored Shakespeare's collaboration with a merciless woman-beater. But professional collaboration does not invariably entail mutual admiration, and it is by no means certain that Shakespeare condoned Wilkins's treatment of women. On the contrary, the writing of Marina's dialogue refutes her dehumanization into a 'creature of sale', and could be regarded as an exposé of what Carol J. Adams has called 'the sexual politics of meat' (1990). Instead the final act of the play transforms Marina from a maritime commodity into kin.

To better appreciate the fish-flesh continuum in *Pericles*, it is helpful to recall that Marina's character is modelled on Palaestra in Plautus's *Rudens* [The Rope], the Roman comedy that supplied the most important classical precedent for theatrical representations of fishing and the maritime world in Renaissance drama.[33] What seems to have most struck Shakespeare about *Rudens* is its demonstration of the sea's power to remake identity by dissolving and reconstituting the bonds of citizenship and kinship, a theme found in *The Comedy of Errors*, *Twelfth Night*, and in *Pericles*. Shipwrecked after her abduction by a sex-trafficker, Palaestra falls into the sea an orphaned and stateless slave (whose personal belongings proving her identity are compared to fish), but eventually emerges a free Athenian, finding both a father and a husband. Born at sea, Marina is likewise motherless and stateless, and hence compares the world to 'a lasting storm' (4.1.18). After she is kidnapped from the seashore and sold like a catch of fish, she, too, finds a father and a husband. The romance plot enacts the discovery of kin across class lines in a way that smudges the line between fish and humans, while *Pericles*'s narrative arc, moving from the denunciation of incest to a celebration of exogamous marriage, underscores the benefits of making kin across the ocean.

But whether the play truly succeeds in finding kin across the species divide in the literal sense advocated by Donna Haraway remains questionable. While Haraway's glorification of the octopus-headed Cthulu is a marked improvement on the Renaissance's anthropomorphic Neptune, fish cannot so easily be hauled within the fold of 'companion species' as dogs, as the etymological derivation of companion from 'eating bread with' hints. In the seventeenth century, one did not eat-with fish, one ate them, and the religious sanctioning of their consumption during Lent would have made it even more difficult for Jacobeans to swallow Pythagoras's theory that the soul of a relative might transmigrate into the body of a fish. The Renaissance doctrine of correspondence, which assumed that every land animal had a marine equivalent, helped sustain belief in mermaids or *Homo marinus* (see Pliny 9.10) well into the seventeenth century, but Protestant naturalists like Conrad Gesner and Thomas Browne were gradually establishing the otherness of the sea. Shakespeare's contemporaries might cite the fact that fish spawn without penetration to dehumanize and coerce the sex-averse, but the plight of the sexually harassed mermaid Marina inverts that of the 'woman [who] was turned into a cold fish for she would not exchange flesh with one who loved her' (4.4.277–8) in the ballad peddled by Autolycus. In refuting her denigration to commodified flesh by asserting her high-born status, Marina eventually reinscribes the boundary between humans and marine creatures. As Pericles implies, there are limits to what we may 'detect' in the sea. Even imagining Pericles as a periwinkle only allows us access to the littoral or nearshore region; it is far more difficult for human transcorporeality to extend into the forbidding bathypelagic and abyssopelagic zones (Alaimo 2016, 113), where the ocean is neither blue nor purple but black. Moreover, periwinkles were edible. *Pericles* does toy with the metaphorical equivalence of sea and land so that the fish-eat-fish world resembles the terrestrial world of rich-eat-poor, but the problem with this analogy, Renaissance depictions of sea-monsters, and the trope of the devouring seas is that they cloak the rapacity with which humans prey on the ocean.[34]

What is perhaps understressed in the scholarship on early modern sea sovereignty focusing on law and politics is that fishers were compelled to violate the territorial waters of neighbouring nations in pursuit of ever-shrinking shoals in their own local fisheries. The knee-jerk tendency to blame foreigners for the fisheries' decline disguises the fact that all nations share in the blame. It is not a strictly Danish, Dutch, or English problem but an ecological problem—one that requires a collective solution. The fishermen in *Pericles* jest bitterly how the big fish gobble the little fish, but the class analogy of the predatory rich versus the oppressed poor blinds them (and the reader) to their role in an assemblage or human shoal far more voracious than any fry-devouring whale.

With that in mind, it must be noted that the consumption of seafood was not a remote concern for playgoers in Shakespeare's London. Excavations at the Rose playhouse have uncovered that Elizabethan spectators snacked on oysters, whelks, mussels, periwinkles, and a variety of fish (Bowsher and Miller 2009) such as Sir Toby Belch's 'pickle herring' (1.5.117)—which were unloaded at the nearby pickle-herring district in Southwark (Katritzky 2014)—and cod bones have even been discovered at Shakespeare's New Place (Mitchell and Colls 2016, 168). Neither Shakespeare nor Samuel Daniel could foresee that almost four centuries later, the Atlantic cod fishery would collapse, forcing Canada to declare an indefinite moratorium on the industry (Clover 2004). Abetted by poetic hyperbole imagining the ocean as infinite, Stuart Britain and other European powers struggled to acknowledge limits to their consumption of marine resources.

If Shakespeare's contemporaries found it difficult to make kin with fish, early modern governments did the next best thing: making kin with other nations to promote a collective response to oceanic management. In an era before the European Union, European countries forged alliances through dynastic marriages, which clarifies why *Pericles* touts the benefits of the monarch traversing the seas to find a spouse. Just as Pericles's marriage to the daughter of the king of Pentapolis will enable him to claim its offshore fisheries and regain the 'supremacy' (2.3.40) of his father, King James's wedding to Anna of Denmark secured Britain's rights to the fish-laden waters around the Orkneys. The odd circumstances of Marina's birth might be seen as abetting Tyre's annexation of the Mediterranean, in the same way that Edward I facilitated England's incorporation of Wales by arranging his son's birth to occur at Caernarfon. While modern readers understandably wince at Marina happily marrying a brothel-goer, the dynastic perspective of the Jacobean courtly audience would have discouraged Shakespeare from diverging from Twyne's *Painefull Adventures* on this point. The marriage of Marina and Lysimachus further expands Tyre's maritime empire and would have doubtless pleased James, who reportedly had plans to wed his half-Danish son to a French princess to further solidify British control of the Channel and the North Seas. The play endorses a cosmopolitan, pan-European solution (in which Britain naturally assumes a leading role) to territorial quarrels over the seas, dangling the hope that James would someday bring about an end to the Renaissance herring wars through his heirs. It is therefore highly fitting that a 2018 EU consortium (including English, Scottish, Danish, and Dutch universities) devoted to protecting Europe's maritime cultural heritage—especially its fisheries—was named 'Pericles'.

The violent sea storms in this play may debunk the fantasy of maritime dominion, but Shakespeare's pivot to tragicomedy in *Pericles* heralds the start of his search for a more optimistic view of human-environmental relations after the apocalyptic anxieties voiced in *Timon*, *Lear*, and *Macbeth*. If the play falls short of 'making kin' with fish, it still conveys a 'proto-ecological hope of coming to terms with the sea' (Mentz 2009b) by recognizing the oceans as an international and inter-generational responsibility. In an incisive reading of Shakespearean tragicomedy, Valerie Forman traces its mimicking of mercantilist economics—mixed with Protestant discourse of redemption from sin—in which investment represents a temporary loss or debt that underwrites a future gain (2013, 78). Early modern efforts to impose bans on fishing during spawning season and taxes based on the tonnage of fishing vessels relied on similar logic. King James's motivation may have been economic and self-interested, but the need for 'conservacie' (A3^v), as Welwood terms it, of the fisheries was fostering policies in 1608 that four centuries later would be recognized as ecological. *Pericles* is primarily a tale of human resilience but submersing it in its eco-historical context reveals how the recovery of Marina enacts an environmental ritual for the recovery of the turbulent, overfished seas.

4
Welsh Mountains, Alpine Pastoral, and Eco-Masculinity in *Cymbeline*

Detecting a narrative arc in both Shakespeare's life and oeuvre, the Victorian biographer Edward Dowden labelled the final phase of the playwright's career 'On the Heights' (1878, 60). The phrase captures Dowden's judgement that the late 'romances', a designation he popularized, view the human condition with a lofty, almost olympian detachment. In his 1903 edition of *Cymbeline*, however, Dowden conflates the medieval definition of romance as a literary genre with the word's nineteenth-century connotations by observing that the late plays unfold against a 'beautiful romantic background of sea and mountain' (xi–xii). It is the distance between the figurative philosophical 'heights' and the literal mountain that the following study of *Cymbeline* intends to traverse. It would be anachronistic to presume that Jacobean audiences thrilled at alpine scenery with the same frisson as readers of, say, Shelley's 'Mont Blanc' or Dowden himself, who composed a number of mountain-inspired poems, including one entitled 'On the Heights' (1876, 11–16). Mountains may be emblems of permanence, but the emotional and intellectual responses they provoke are very much historically conditioned. A landmark 1959 study by Marjorie Hope Nicholson (reprinted in 1997 and hailed as a forerunner of ecocriticism) surveyed early modern attitudes towards mountains, documenting the gradual awakening of 'mountain-feeling' in the late seventeenth and eighteenth centuries. In the Tudor and Stuart periods, she argues, writers tend to dismiss mountains as unsightly warts or repulsive, jagged protuberances that clashed with a prevailing taste for symmetry and proportion. High hills may figure in Elizabethan literature as emblems of spiritual struggle (e.g. Donne's Third Satire) or worldly ambition (Spenser's July eclogue), but picturesque mountain scenery is rare. The mountain-dwellers in Thomas More's *Utopia*, the Zapoletes (based on the Swiss), are savage mercenaries, and Shakespeare fittingly has More denounce the 'mountainish inhumanity' (6.155) of a xenophobic mob. Nicholson finds 'no evidence that Shakespeare had any feeling for high hills, which he had probably never seen' (1997, 40), and asserts that, apart from Edgar's vista on the imaginary cusp of Dover Cliff, Shakespeare avoids the 'wild and irregular' in nature. Similar opinions resound in Robert Macfarlane's otherwise excellent *Mountains of the Mind*, which declares that early moderns deemed mountains 'aesthetically repellent' and the idea of climbing them 'tantamount to lunacy' (2004, 14–15). Such sweeping verdicts, however can be easily qualified, and only seem persuasive when weighed against nineteenth-century sensibilities. Rather than working backwards to construct a retrospective genealogy of the Romantic sublime, this chapter instead performs an eco-historical reading of the Welsh scenes in *Cymbeline* as an example of alpine pastoral, a neglected subgenre of this dynamic literary mode. Rather than gape at lofty peaks as sublime spectacles, Shakespeare's contemporaries tended to politicize, moralize, and monetize mountainscape. In *Cymbeline*, the rugged Welsh peaks and bracing alpine air promote physical endurance and vigour, and the upbringing of the kidnapped princes Guiderius and Arviragus affirms early modern medicinal and pedagogical theories regarding the benefits of mountain-living long before Rousseau.

Significantly, the mountains also offer a strategic stronghold for military conquest and an almost cartographic prospect for imperial governance, which helps explain why *Cymbeline* and other royal entertainments are eager to place Welsh mountains under English jurisdiction. Commentators have long recognized that *Cymbeline* caters to James's dream of a unified Britain, as Wales seemed to offer a prototype for an amicable political union.[1] Revisiting this subtext with an eye on the environment, this chapter reads the play alongside the English annexation and exploitation of Welsh natural resources following the Unification Acts of 1536–42, and reveals how this merger was re-legitimized in the 1610 investiture of Henry Frederick as Prince of Wales. If Anglo-Welsh unification appeared to be a fait accompli on paper, it still required the cultural assimilation of Wales's alien topography. Cavilling with Nicholson's post-Romantic fixation upon the sublime, I argue that a more positive view of mountains emerges in the late Tudor and early Stuart periods in Shakespeare and contemporary English writers like Thomas Churchyard, Michael Drayton, and Ben Jonson as the result of redefining alpine spaces as 'British' rather than strictly Welsh or European, and a dawning recognition of mountains not as barren wastelands or wens, but as precious repositories of water, timber, coal, ore, silver, pasture, game, and even British masculinity.

Mountain Gloom? Early Modern Prospects of Mountains

In Nicholson's monograph, the fulcrum at which English views of mountains begin to tip from gloomy to glorious is Thomas Burnet's *Sacred Theory of the Earth*. First published in Latin in 1681 (and in English three years later), Burnet's work does seem to anticipate the formulations of Kant and Burke on the sublimity of mountainous landscapes:

> There is something august and stately in the air of these things that inspires the mind with great thoughts and passions. We do naturally, upon such occasions, think of God and his greatness. And whatsoever hath but the shadow and appearance of [the] INFINITE, as all things have that are too big for our

comprehension, they fill and overbear the mind with their excess, and cast it into a pleasing kind of stupor and admiration. (1684, 95–6)

At other times, however, Burnet sounds much less enthused by mountain prospects, and the overarching argument of his book is that their jagged peaks resulted from the geological violence of Noah's Flood, since God must have created the antediluvian earth as a perfectly round and smooth orb. Issuing an important caveat to Nicholson, Janice Hewlett Koelb observes that sixteenth-century writers often deploy the word 'waste' as a synonym for the Latin *vastus*, and that the modern connotations attached to waste produce a misleading impression that early modern attitudes to mountains were decidedly negative (2009, 460). On the contrary, many early moderns regarded mountains as sites of revelation, as illustrated by Moses on Mount Sinai, or poetic inspiration, such as Parnassus, the mountain home of the Greek muses. Indeed, one of the most popular Elizabethan verse miscellanies was entitled *England's Parnassus* (1600), which is organized by topography and adorns hills and mounts with adjectives such as 'golden', 'sacred', 'pleasant', and 'stately'. Nicholson herself concedes that some Renaissance texts mingle revulsion at their craggy deformity with admiration for their grandeur. In particular, Churchyard's *Worthiness of Wales*, Drayton's *Poly-Olbion*, and the Jonsonian masque present far more nuanced and even approbatory views of mountains than have been acknowledged by environmental historians. This more positive reappraisal of mountains can be broken down into five main points, which are often inter-connected, like peaks in a range: (1) mountains appear majestic and can thus be symbols of a monarch or prince; (2) the panoramic views they afford fostered the new genre of landscape painting on the Continent, which in turn encouraged a reappraisal of British hills and mountains as scenic; (3) mountains offer a transhistorical link to the classical, religious, and ancient British past—sparking a kind of chronological sublime even before a conception of geologic time; (4) mountain-folk may seem coarse, but partake of the toughness of the terrain, so that mountains function (as they still do in modern alpine narratives) as a proving ground for heroic masculinity; (5) finally, mountains furnish unique resources and even habitats, providing economic services that the twenty-first century would deem ecological. Examining these five points in turn will provide a long overdue corrective to Nicholson, and open up new vistas on Shakespeare's *Cymbeline*.

The perception of mountains as majestic did not originate with Burnet or 'America the Beautiful' (originally entitled 'Pikes Peak'), composed by Shakespeare professor Katherine Lee Bates. With their penchant for analogical thinking, many early modern English writers associate the height of mountains with the exalted status of the monarch. In *The Worthiness of Wales*, Churchyard declares, 'You may compare a King to Mountayne hye', and does exactly that for ten lines before repeating the metaphor by dubbing the mountain 'a noble, stately thing…compared unto a King' (1587, M2ᵛ). Drayton likewise views the mountain as regal: 'The Mountaine is the King, and he it is alone / Above the other soyles that Nature doth in-throne' (1612, 103). King James himself spun a sonnet from this same analogy: 'the Cheviott hills doe with my state agree' (*KJSW* 124). Such comparisons of hills to an elevated throne or 'state' cannot be considered ideologically innocent, especially in works penned by or for royalty or dedicated (as *Poly-Olbion* was) to the Prince of Wales.[2] The royal mountain thus might function as a symbol of benign English rule or the princedom itself, a metaphor that gained real purchase in 1610, when Britain acquired a new Prince of Wales for the first time in over six decades. Tellingly, in Jonson's masque celebrating Henry's investiture, the Prince emerges from a mountain—depicted with 'all wildness that could be presented' (3:725.2)—that transforms into a royal palace. His entrance is accompanied by faeries and sylvans singing 'tunes to Arthur's Chair' (3:733.219), revealing this mountain to be the twin peaks in the Brecon Beacons dubbed Cadair Idris, which the English misinterpreted as Cadair Arthur (or 'Arthur's Chair'). Like the 'Arthur's Seat' that towers over Edinburgh, the moniker reflects an urge to see mountains as relics of Britain's mythic past, and their greater-than-human scale as commensurate with the feats of its larger-than-life heroes. The mountain's metamorphosis in Jonson's *Oberon* from a rugged, satyr-haunted wilderness to a throne and stately palace indicates that a transformation in attitudes towards uplands was underway long before Burnet aired his theories on sacred geology. The regal metaphors and legendary associations heaped on mountains in early modern culture bestow a grandeur on them that is difficult to reconcile with the prevailing view that all pre-Romantics abhorred them as hideous blemishes.

The reputations of high hills and mountains were also lifted by the emergence of Dutch landscape painting in the late sixteenth century in the works of artists like Pieter Breughel, Lucas van Valckenborch and Hendrik Goltzius. In a feedback loop, artists sought out high elevations to capture panoramic expanses, which in turn encouraged others to climb hills and mountains to enjoy the picturesque vistas. This love of the picturesque sprung up before William Gilpin popularized the term, as attested by seventeenth-century texts like Joseph Hall's 'Upon a faire Prospect':

> What a pleasing variety is heere of Townes, Rivers, Hills, Dales, Woods, Medowes, each of them striving to set forth other; and all of them to delight the eye? So as this is no other then a naturall and reall Landscip drawne by that Almightie and skillful hand in this table of the Earth for the pleasure of our view. (1630, 12–13)

The phrase 'naturall and reall Landscip' is not a pleonasm, but betrays the fact that landscape originally signifies an artistic rendering of a prospect rather than the terrain per se.[3] A detailed overview of the history of landscape is beyond the scope of this study, but two overlooked points need to be stressed in this context. First, the Renaissance valued high hills and mountains for the 'pleasing variety' of objects (as Hall phrases it) they disclosed rather than their terrifying sublime aspects. As Conrad Gesner declared in 1545, 'all the elements and diversity of nature can be found in the mountains' (qtd in Weber 2003, 18). Instead of barren and forbidding wastelands, British mountains awed the viewer with a sense of copiousness, long hailed as a hallmark of Renaissance aesthetics. Secondly, a growing regard for mountainous landscapes in England coincides with the installation of a new Prince of Wales, and is reflected in the art and drama produced to celebrate that event, including Shakespeare's *Cymbeline*.

Although he enjoyed the title of Prince of Wales for fewer than three years, Henry Frederick's role as both a muse and tastemaker in that brief time would be difficult to overstate. When he obtained his own income at the age of sixteen, Henry began to nurture an artistic court culture distinct from his father. His activities as a patron and collector were commemorated in a 2012 exhibition at the National Portrait Gallery, which included Robert Peake's famous depiction of the teenage prince unsheathing his sword to slice a hunting trophy from a slain deer (see Fig. 4.1). Note how the aptly-named Peake angles the sword to draw the viewer's gaze upwards toward the mount in the middle ground and hilly landscape in the background, which the future Prince of Wales appears poised to conquer.[4] In January 1610, Henry began amassing a collection of almost exclusively Dutch paintings with the aid of Dutch ambassador, Noel Caron, and would have been aware of the new vogue for Dutch 'landtskip'. While no complete inventory of its contents survives, art historians have established that his collection was 'one of the first in Britain not primarily composed of portraits', and included Palma Giovane's *Prometheus Chained to the Caucasus* and *The Devil Sowing Tares*, which both feature mountains in the background, as well as pieces by Hendrik Goltzius and Joos de Momper, famous for their alpine landscapes.[5] Henry's art collectors also had contacts at the court of Emperor Rudolf II, whose official painter, Roelandt Savery produced tableaus of fantastic mountain scenery (Fig. 4.2) inspired by Tyrol but which could proudly hang beside Turner's paintings of Wales.[6] Impressed by the enormous rock grotto nicknamed 'Mount Parnassus' in his mother's gardens at Somerset House, Henry hired the designer Saloman de Caus and Robert Cecil's gardener, 'Mountain' Jennings, to construct a similar faux-mountain in the gardens at Richmond Palace (Thurley 2021, 77) around the time Shakespeare composed *Cymbeline*.

If the evidence for Henry's interest in mountainscape is somewhat circumstantial, one prominent figure at the Stuart court with Welsh connections and a demonstrable enthusiasm for alpine scenery was Inigo Jones. It so happens that Prince Henry was Jones's patron, and it was Jones who collaborated with Ben Jonson on *Oberon*, the masque for Henry's investiture featuring a tableau of the Brecon Beacons. In a keen-eyed analysis of the *Oberon* masque, John Peacock

Fig. 4.1 Robert Peake, Prince Henry and Robert Deveraux, 3rd Earl of Essex, in the Hunting Field (*c.*1605). RCIN 404440. Royal Collection Trust.
© Queen Elizabeth II 2021.

observes that Jones sought to move beyond the rocks and mounts that crop up in civic pageants by incorporating the perspective of the new Dutch landscape art. By good fortune, a sketch by Jones believed to show the mountain scene in *Oberon* survives in the Chatsworth archives (Fig. 4.3). According to Peacock, 'the result looks like a stylized excerpt from one of the mountain landscapes of the Brueghel tradition, or a theatrical adaptation of the rock and mountain prints of Jones's contemporary Goltzius', and indicates how set designs for court entertainments were 'moving tentatively toward the Antwerp landscape style' (2005, 167). Jones's design for *Oberon* offers an inkling of what Shakespeare expected the more sophisticated among his audience to imagine in their mind's eye during the Welsh scenes in *Cymbeline*.

Further proof of Shakespeare's fascination with mountains has been obscured by the loss of *Cardenio*, staged before the Stuart court and the ambassador of the alpine region of Savoy in June 1613. Given the existence of Jones's *mis-en-scène*

Fig. 4.2 Roelandt Savery, *Mountain Landscape with Castle* (1609).
© Fundación Colección Thyssen-Bornemisza, Madrid.

for *Oberon*, it is tempting to speculate it or something similar may have been unfurled for *Cardenio*'s court performance, like the 'prospect of mountains' (4.1.1) twice called for in the stage directions of *Double Falsehood*, Lewis Theobald's adaptation/reconstruction of the lost play. Following the lead of Cervantes, *Cardenio* likely presented Spain's Sierra Morena as a place of melancholy and madness rather than primal masculinity. That mountains loomed large in the original can be inferred from the one fragment of it that seems to have survived unadulterated: the song 'Woods, Rocks, and Mountaynes' set to music by the King's Men's lutenist, Robert Johnson.[7] If the song depicts mountains as a realm of 'bitter cold and hunger', Theobald's rendering of the scene emphasizes that its echo-prone rocky terrain also affords the outcast a consoling, sympathetic landscape.[8] As in *King Lear*, the journey into the wild precipitates a nervous breakdown but one that prompts a radical questioning of human dominion over the earth and other creatures:

> Horsemanship! Hell—riding shall be abolish'd.
> Turn the barb'd steed loose to his native wildness;
> It is a beast too noble to be the property
> Of man's baseness.
>
> (*DF* 4.1.28–31)

94 SHAKESPEARE BEYOND THE GREEN WORLD

Fig. 4.3 Inigo Jones, Mountainscape for *Oberon* (1611).
© Devonshire Collection, Chatsworth. Reproduced with permission of Chatsworth Settlement Trustees.

Whether or not these words were penned by Shakespeare—or Fletcher or Theobald channelling Shakespeare—the decision of the King's Men to adapt the tale of Cardenio, whom Cervantes dubs 'The Knight of the Rock' (1612, 218), is indicative of growing interest in alpine wilderness in early Stuart Britain.[9]

One might assume that the relatively modest size of British peaks in comparison to their European counterparts—Scafell Pike stands 978 metres tall, not even a quarter the height of Mont Blanc—would discourage alpine poetry in Britain, but an incipient nationalism prompted some writers to find other yardsticks to measure their greatness. Enflamed with patriotism, Drayton imagines the Malvern Hills (only 425 metres high) scorning to change their name with Olympus, over six times their size (1612, 102). Jonson pays tribute to the burgeoning regional pride in the Welsh landscape when, in a typical bit of metadramatic schtick, he has a chorus of Welsh characters criticize his *Pleasure Reconciled to Virtue* for depicting the 'outlandis mountain' (5:331.47) of Atlas—the design of which resembles Joos de Momper the Younger's anthropomorphic mountains—when Wales offers a half-dozen homegrown peaks that are just as dramatic. When a

Welsh lawyer rattles off a list of some of the nation's highest peaks, his countryman Jenkins responds, 'Why law you now, is not Penmaen-maur, and Craig-Eryri as good sound as Adlas every whit of him?' (5:331.61–2). For the pre-Romantics, the magnitude of a mountain is rated not so much by its elevation (which could not be pinpointed with accuracy anyway) as by a quality that Jonson jokingly refers to as 'good standing' and 'good descent' (5:331.49)—punning on the Welsh obsession with pedigrees—or what one might call its storiedness. Rather than awe the spectator with sublime heights, the mountain inspires early modern British writers by its ability to monumentalize and mythologize the nation's ancient history.

Although overlooked in Nicholson's Anglocentric and Swisscentric study, a notable shift in English views of mountains was triggered prior to the eighteenth-century Grand Tour by the Cambrophilia of Tudor antiquarians such as William Camden, George Owen, John Dee, and Michael Drayton. As Willy Maley and Philip Schwyzer (2010) have ably demonstrated, Britishness did not emerge full-blown in the eighteenth century as the imposition of Englishness on the Welsh, Irish, and Scots; rather English nationalism in the Tudor and Stuart eras largely consisted of the appropriation of native Welsh history and identity, an appropriation facilitated by the fact that the Tudors originated from Wales (Schwyzer 2004). This appropriation also required claiming the Welsh mountains and redefining them as British rather than exclusively Welsh. Indeed, for Camden the survival of Britishness is predicated upon mountains, to which the ancient Britons retreated before the Anglo-Saxon onslaught:

> Nature hath loftily areared [Wales] up farre and neere with Mountaines standing thicke one by another...and made this part thereof a most sure place of refuge for the Britans in time of adversitie. For there are so many roughes and Rocks, so many vales full of Woods, with Pooles heere and there crossing over them, lying in the way betweene, that no Armie...can finde passage. (1610, 667)

Taking a cue from Camden, Drayton likewise frames the alpine wilderness as a 'refuge' to which the 'oppressed Britans flew' (1622, 111), and in Song 9 Mount Snowdon recalls how the 'poore and scatter'd few of Brutes high linage left, / For succour hither came' (137). Drayton's chorography here captures the crucial interplay between history and natural history, reminding his readers that the mountains which sheltered the Britons permitted Welsh culture—and hence Britishness—to endure.[10] Camden's Cambrophilia and his praise of the Welsh mountains as the 'British Alps', an appellation echoed by John Speed in his *Theatre of the Empire of Great Britaine*, also had a discernible impact on his most famous pupil, Ben Jonson, particularly on the masques he wrote to celebrate the installations of James's heirs as Prince of Wales. In *Oberon*, Prince Henry emerges from a mountain to impose order on the Welsh wilderness, while the Welsh characters in *For the*

Honour of Wales observe that Charles Iames Stuart is an anagram for 'claims Arthurs Seat' (37)—a mistranslation of the Welsh mountain Cadair Idris. In both masques, mountains serve as ideological emblems of antiquity and political authority (embodied in the mythic folk hero King Arthur) that buttress the Stuart dynasty's dominion over all of Great Britain.

The exaltation of a Prince of Wales in 1610 upon a mountain throne entailed a reappraisal of Welsh mountains, just as England's coronation of a Scottish king had encouraged new ways of seeing heath and moorlands (see Chapter 1). In his Elizabethan plays, Shakespeare tends to paint mountains in a pejorative light. Pistol fires an insult at Fluellen in *Henry V* by calling him a 'mountain-squire' (5.1.32), while the Welsh Parson Evans in *Merry Wives* is ridiculed as a 'mountain-foreigner' (1.1.133). Mountains were synonymous with backwardness and a primitive hardscrabble existence. Mountains were un-English. In some Renaissance alpine texts, however, the perceived defects of mountainous terrain make it the perfect testing ground for masculine valour, and mountains play a notable role in poems and dramatic entertainments, including *Cymbeline*, that portray the Stuart prince, who was the son of a Scottish father and Danish mother and less than 1 per cent Welsh, as an incarnation of the heroic virtues of the ancient Britons.

Alpine Pastoral and Welsh Eco-masculinity

In his twelfth-century natural history and travelogue, Gerald of Wales offers a curious explanation for why the Welsh had soundly routed the English during Henry II's failed invasions. Not only did the English lack any understanding of the Welsh people and landscape (a fault that Gerald's topographical survey seeks to remedy) but also the rugged, hilly terrain makes the Welsh more physically robust: 'By marching through the deep recesses of the woods and *climbing mountain-peaks in times of peace*, the young men train themselves to keep on the move both day and night' (1.8, italics added). In his *Britannia*, Camden quotes King Henry's own excuse that the Snowdonians' upbringing in mountain 'caves' renders them more war-like, while the English youth are 'so deintily brought up, love to be housebirds and to live lazie in the shade, being born onely to devour the fruits of the earth' (1610, 668). Similar aetiologies for the valour of the Welsh can be found in the most important Elizabethan work on Welsh mountains, Churchyard's *Worthiness of Wales*. While most English regarded Wales as a place of economic deprivation, Churchyard muses on the paradox that Welsh 'weaklings nurst so harde' can yet be so fierce and resilient. Half the solution to this riddle is that the Welsh must descend from the mythic Brute and the war-like Trojans (nature); the other half has to do with the mountainous landscape and the frugal lifestyle it necessitates (nurture). In Churchyard's view:

> These ragged Rocks brings playnest people foorth,
> On Mountaine wyld the hardest Horse is bred:
> Though grasse thereon be grosse and little worth,
> Sweete is the foode where hunger so is fed.
> On rootes and hearbs our fathers long did feede,
> And neere the Skye growes sweetest fruit in deede.
>
> (1587, M1r)

The simplicity and frugality of the mountain-dwellers make them resemble a relict population of primitive humans from Ovid's Golden Age. Suggesting mountain folk resemble their rocky environs, the poem evokes Ovid's myth of Deucalion and Pyrrha, who regenerate the human race after a global deluge by throwing stones (the bones of their grandmother) over their shoulder in an exemplary illustration of what Jeffrey J. Cohen calls 'lithic enmeshment' (2015, 50–1). To journey up the mountain is to journey back in time to recover human origins, and in Shakespeare's Britain this journey was also tied to the quest for national origins. Tudor antiquarians viewed Wales as a repository of the 'positive qualities of ancient Britain' (Kerrigan 2008, 117), and a chief reason for this is that the pristine ruggedness of the mountain environment enabled the early modern Welsh to retain the spartan virtues of their ancestors. When Innogen wanders into the mountains she soon realizes how 'famine' makes nature 'valiant', and that 'plenty and peace breeds cowards, hardness ever / Of hardiness is mother' (3.6.19–22). In this vein, Churchyard draws a stark contrast between the stoic hardiness of the petromorphic Welsh (conditioned by their stony habitat) and the cushy decadence of England's valleys, where 'Wealth fosters pride, and heaves up haughty heart' (M2v). The opposition between countryside and city is of course a familiar one to students of Renaissance literature. In an important work of Renaissance ecocriticism, Jeffrey Theis mints the phrase 'sylvan pastoral' (2009) to designate a literary sub-genre in which woodlands rather than open pasture serve as an antithesis to the urbane court. As a corollary to Theis's formula, one might propose that Renaissance writers developed an 'alpine pastoral', and that this sub-genre is characteristic of many English texts about Wales, including *Cymbeline*, hinging on the contrast between pastoral uplands and arable lowlands.[11]

Several of the opinions voiced by Churchyard about the virtues of mountain-living are echoed in Shakespeare's play. In his opening monologue, Belarius makes an emphatic distinction between their Welsh mountain-cave and an impious palace, rewriting their distance from court and its 'proud livers' (3.3.9) as closer proximity to heaven. As if taking a page from Gerald of Wales and Churchyard, he sends his adopted sons, Guiderius and Arviragus, to scale the mountains for 'sport' and health. Belarius's instructions make it clear, however, they will gain more than physical stamina:

> Now for our mountain sport. Up to yond hill,
> Your legs are young; I'll tread these flats. Consider,
> When you above perceive me like a crow,
> That it is place which lessens and sets off,
> And you may then revolve what tales I have told you
> Of courts, of princes, of the tricks in war.
>
> (3.3.10–15)

This passage is a sterling example of the alpine pastoral. His claim 'To apprehend thus / Draws us a profit from all things we see' (3.3.17–18) recalls Duke Senior's discovering 'good in everything' in Arden, while the dwindling of the human shape to crow-size sounds like a benign revision of Edgar's grim meditations on the imagined precipice of Dover Cliff.[12] In a quintessentially Shakespearean pun, the mountain is a place that 'lessens' but also 'lessons', as Belarius compares the far-reaching prospect afforded by the mountain heights with the pastoral perspective of critical distance from civilization. It is noteworthy that later in the play Innogen views Milford Haven from a mountaintop and thinks it closer than it is because she lacks familiarity with (besides the longer Welsh mile) the optical distortions of perspective possessed by the Welsh-bred brothers (3.6.5). In another alpine metaphor, Belarius displaces the perils of the mountain onto the court, likening it to a peak 'whose top to climb / Is certain falling, or so slipp'ry that / The fear's as bad as falling' (3.3.47–9). Belarius believes the alpine pastoral will breed contempt for the trivialities and vexations of politics, and keep the brothers from Cymbeline's court. In this regard, mountain-climbing in the Renaissance could be an exercise in detachment from worldly concerns, simulating a divine, far-reaching perspective from which human tribulations appear miniscule, temporary, or insignificant. The alpine pastoral thus offers a platform for the philosophical serenity of the romances that prompted Dowden to situate the post-1608 Shakespeare 'On the Heights'.

This is not to imply that the alpine pastoral is apolitical. Mountains were often hailed as bastions of Welsh liberty and independence, but Churchyard's comparisons of Welsh summits to a 'watch' or watchtower, a 'stately guard' (M2r), and a kingly throne implicate his poem in English surveillance and conquest (Oakley-Brown 2016). Invoking De Certeau's notion of the 'panorama', Garrett Sullivan advances a similar thesis that the mountain vistas in *Cymbeline* unfurl a 'landscape of sovereignty' and participate in 'the conceptual and cultural annexation of Wales, its subsumption into British (or English) monarchical culture' (1998, 146). As this chapter has suggested, however, that annexation also entailed a more positive reappraisal of both Wales and mountains, and, as Sullivan acknowledges, the mountains that invite a sense of territorial dominion also make James's proposed unification of Great Britain problematic as insurmountable signifiers of Welsh difference.

In seeking a way out of this impasse, *Cymbeline* imagines a hybridization of English nature and Welsh nurture for which the British mountains afford a training ground. The play's alpine pastoral is, in keeping with the tenor of the late romances in general, a complex pastoral that resists the impulse to simply trumpet nature over civilization. Importantly, Guiderius and Arviragus push back against Belarius's view of the mountain as a 'safer hold' (3.3.20), and flatly refuse their foster-father's advice to fly 'higher to the mountains' (4.4.8) as the battle commences. In contrast to Shakespeare's early comedies, in which courtiers flee society for the green world, the young protagonists of the late romances are royals raised in the green world. Oblivious of their own status, they are free to enjoy the benefits of a rural childhood, while maintaining an innate nobility derived from their royal blood. Belarius himself avers that the brothers' highborn ancestry and rustic upbringing among the mountains render them an ideal balance of courtesy and ferocity. They can be as gentle as a soft breeze nudging a violet:

> and yet as rough,
> Their royal blood enchafed, as the rud'st wind
> That by the top doth take the mountain pine
> And make him stoop to th' vale.
>
> (4.2.172–5)

This imagery associates the Welsh-bred princes with mountains and alpine air, while metaphorically re-enacting Guiderius's off-stage killing of Cloten. Significantly, Cloten sneers at Belarius and Arviragus as 'villain mountaineers' (4.2.71), and soon after hurls the same epithet at Guiderius, calling him a 'rustic mountaineer' (4.2.100).[13] In early modern usage, the term does not signify a mountain-climber but an ignorant or uncivilized mountain-dweller, equivalent to the American insult 'hillbilly'. Cloten expresses the same contempt for uplands as uncouth wilderness heard in the teasing of Fluellen and Parson Evans. In *Cymbeline*, however, Shakespeare leaves little doubt that the hardy mountaineer will prevail against the pampered courtier, and the intended slur almost has the ring of a compliment, as the play tacitly impugns the masculinity of the English in comparison to the Welsh.

Studies on the vexed relationship between masculinity and nature have focused largely on nineteenth-century American literature, decoding the wilderness as a proving ground for a hypermasculine identity. Long after the closing of the frontier, such plotlines continue to play out in modern mountaineering narratives such as *Into Thin Air* and *Touching the Void*, survival epics about a manly confrontation with the abyss. More scrutiny, however, needs to be given to the construction of masculinity in the wild in other eras and places, including early modern Britain. *Cymbeline* appears, on a far more modest scale, to anticipate the man versus mountain narrative, with one important difference. While 'the prototypical male hero in American literature finds himself constantly fighting against the wilderness but at the same time... aspires to unite with it' (Brandt 2019, 4), *Cymbeline* presents almost the inverse scenario: the brothers' feral upbringing has united them with the Welsh wilderness but they now must leave the hills to mature into civilized manhood. Part of the reason is that the wilderness that tests masculinity also threatens to undermine it. Following the death of their nurse, Belarius and Arviragus (whose name evokes the androgynous virago) must do the cooking and house-keeping until Innogen conveniently arrives just in time to take care of these potentially emasculating domestic duties. Her cutting the food into characters or letters encapsulates the play's synthesis of nature and art, the raw and the cooked, but, in contrast to Renaissance norms, it also re-inscribes the latter as female and the former as male. Hunger makes her valiant, but her first remark on crossing into Wales and traversing its rugged mountain roads is 'a man's life is a tedious one' (3.6.1), and she later exclaims she would 'change [her] sex to be companion' (3.6.85) with the brothers. Qualifying the typical gendering of nature as female in Renaissance pastoral, the play's alpine pastoral construes wilderness as a male domain but in ways that conspire to naturalize men's monopoly on political power.

Although Belarius at one point laments the brothers' 'want of breeding' and 'hard life' (4.4.26–7) amid the mountains, it is precisely their exposure to the elements as 'hot summer's tanlings / and the shrinking slaves of winter' (4.2.29–30) that equips them with the fortitude to repel the Roman invasion. It is therefore significant that Posthumus likewise dons the humble garb of a 'Briton peasant' (5.1.24), making him an honorary mountain-man, before going into battle. His declaration to have 'less without and more within' (5.1.33) neatly captures the ethos of the alpine pastoral. A mountain upbringing not only imparts manly vigour in the play but also confers a strategic advantage in warfare, as implied in Churchyard's comparison of the mountain to a 'warlike Seate' and 'Fortresse'. In the Renaissance, the mountain vista could be as useful as a map in planning a military campaign, and Belarius explicitly urges the brothers to contemplate 'tricks in war' while on the summit. He later reverses the tide of the battle and rallies the British by reminding them they possess the 'advantage of the ground' (5.2.11). In recounting their heroic stand, Posthumous observes how they were 'accommodated by the place' (5.3.32) and his belaboured rhyme about the two boys and a lane credits the landscape with agency in the improbable victory, drawing on their knowledge of wild footpaths in contrast to Roman roads (Sullivan 1998). Randall Martin likewise attributes their triumph to their ability to 'think like a mountain' in that they have imbibed a kind of 'animal intelligence learnt from hunting and scavenging in their Welsh habitat' (2015, 126–7). While Martin borrows the phrase 'think like a mountain' from the twentieth-century environmentalist Aldo Leopold, the early modern writers examined in this chapter attest that Shakespeare's contemporaries were beginning to value a capacity to dwell-with and think-with the mountain as a way to reactivate the primal valour of the ancient Britons.

The connection between the stolen princes and the mountains is even stronger when it is recalled that Guiderius is given the alias 'Paladour' in the First Folio. Mount Paladour was thought to be the ancient British name for the hilltop town of Shaftesbury—of which Shakespeare was almost certainly aware. In 1601 Shakespeare contributed his poem 'The Phoenix and Turtle' to an eccentric book entitled *Love's Martyr*. Dedicated to the Welshman John Salusbury, *Love's Martyr* was largely the work of the self-styled 'Brytish poet' Robert Chester, who writes that the British King Lud 'at Mount Paladour...built his Tent, / That after ages Shaftsburie hath to name' (27). Modern editors have consistently regularized 'Paladour' to 'Polydore' (which he is called on three other occasions in the First Folio), a preference questioned long ago by George Steevens: 'there are some who may ask whether it is not more likely that the Printer should have blundered in the other places than that he should have hit upon such an uncommon name as Paladour in the first instance' (1803, 20:41). They may ask more vociferously given that Mount Paladour was notorious in Tudor chronicles as the place where an eagle predicted the Welsh would regain possession of Britain.

> Concerning the words of the Eagle at the building of Caer Septon in Mount Paladour in the time of Rudhudibras...some thinke that an Eagle did then speake & prophesie...the recoverie of the whole Ile againe by the Brytaines.
> (Lloyd 1584, 5)

As an eagle figures conspicuously in *Cymbeline*'s prophecies concerning Britain, the name Paladour when uttered in the play's finale would have a significant resonance for a Jacobean audience. This crux deserves reconsideration given that the preference for Polydore has bred a confusing association with Polydore Vergil, the historian famous for casting doubt on the Arthurian legends and ancient British history. In other words, Polydore has almost the exact opposite tenor of Paladour. If editors are willing to emend the forty occurrences of 'Imogen' in the Folio text to 'Innogen', then the Folio's initial spelling of the prince's name as Paladour merits equal consideration. It seems far more plausible that Belarius, eager to blend in and conceal their identities, would give his foster son a Welsh name (like Morgan and Cadwall) linked with the heroic British past rather than an anomalously Greek or Italian one.

If the name Paladour hints at the correspondence between the prince's identity and his alpine environment, so too does the name of the pseudo-Welshman Belarius. Playing on the Latin for waging war (*bellare*) and the French for beautiful or good air (*bel air*), it evokes the invigorating power attributed to mountain air in Renaissance geo-humoralism. The Welsh scenes make frequent reference to air and breezes as well as rocks, for the green world in *Cymbeline* is not simply green but a place of grey stone and transparent wind. Whereas the blustery mountain air energizes Guiderius and Arviragus, the Italian Iachimo complains that the British air 'revengingly enfeebles' (5.2.4) him to excuse his defeat in combat by Posthumus. Similarly, the outsider Innogen, associated in the prophecy with the 'tender air' of the lowlands, grows faint in Wales from a kind of altitude sickness.[14] No wonder Churchyard—himself an ex-soldier from the Welsh Marches—believes the Welsh to be natural-born warriors, and the bracing air and hilly terrain of Wales a fit breeding ground for England's warrior princes such as Henry V. Viewed in this light, the mountains in *Cymbeline* seem less like a hideout than the perfect boot camp for the princes, conditioning them for their future role as warrior-kings.

Whether or not *Cymbeline* was conceived as part of the celebration of Henry's investiture, it is widely acknowledged that Guiderius and Arviragus present idealized doubles of Henry and Charles Stuart.[15] When Henry officially assumed the title Prince of Wales in 1610, he was already becoming the darling of the more militant Protestants at court, who saw him as a crusader for the Protestant cause and for a British empire. *Cymbeline*'s mountain idyll is integral to what Jodi Mikalachki has called the 'masculine romance' (1995) of British nationhood promoted by Prince Henry's circle. The play glorifies the noble virtues of the ancient Britons in the all-male family in the Welsh cave while displacing their savagery onto Cymbeline's evil queen. James himself had been separated from his beleaguered mother and raised in the lofty crags of the eyrie-like Stirling Castle and (to Queen Anna's chagrin) wished his son to have a similar childhood. Did this elevated perch in Stirling Castle instil in the boy king a sense not only of security but also of the monarch's exalted, semi-transcendent stature? While Belarius abducts the infant princes without Cymbeline's knowledge, James entrusted Henry's upbringing to the Earl of Mar, who raised Prince Henry at Stirling Castle until 1603, when he was brought to England and placed under the guardianship of Thomas Chaloner, who tutored Henry in the hunt.[16] In his conduct book for Henry, *Basilikon Doron*, James had recommended hunting in particular as a noble pastime that 'resembleth the warres' (*KJSW* 253) and prepares a monarch for the rigours of travelling through his realm. Chaloner apparently took this advice to heart. Although Henry did go up to Oxford briefly in 1605, one pedagogical theorist at the time judged an Oxbridge education far inferior to that of Chaloner's 'Academie' where young nobles might learn how 'to rule in peace, & to commande in warre'.

This tribute appears in John Cleland's *Hero-paideia* (1607), the education of a hero, which supplies an illuminating inter-text for the Welsh scenes in *Cymbeline*. Cleland dedicated it to Prince Charles, hailing his upbringing alongside his brother Henry as the model of a new, distinctly British (as opposed to English) education that rated outdoor pursuits at least equal to rote book-learning.[17] Like James, Cleland extols hunting as a manly exercise that imparts not only courage but also a first-hand knowledge of geography, natural philosophy, and applied zoology: the chase will teach Henry and Charles 'the situation of mountaines, plaines, the courses of brooks and rivers...[and] the nature of beastes' (1607,

223–25). Clearly, Renaissance pedagogues did believe in outdoor education. Whereas Cloten illustrates Cleland's observation that valour is 'mistaken by manie, who thinke it to consist onlie in bragging, beating, threatning, and thundering out of al cruel menace' (230), the princes embody his view that valour consists of action. Belarius's complaint that his wards have been 'trained up meanly' (3.3.82) is therefore at best a half-truth, for their upbringing resembled that of the Stuart princes under Thomas Chaloner. A learned courtier and soldier of Welsh extraction, Chaloner was also an avid naturalist, who 'gained a very deep insight into the operations of nature' (Kippis 1784, 3:419), and whose passion for alchemy sparked an interest in mining and alum-manufacturing.[18] In 1610, Chaloner was appointed Henry's chamberlain, in charge of managing the Prince's expenses, diet, and dress, and thus cut a powerful figure at the Stuart court after an absence of several years overseeing Henry's education.[19] The critical consensus that Shakespeare's contemporaries could detect Henry and Charles beneath Guiderius and Arviragus makes it highly likely the courtly audience of *Cymbeline* would have associated Belarius with Chaloner, while spying in the Welsh scenes a romanticized vision of the princes' youth spent not in Wales but in the Surrey hills and deer parks around Nonsuch.

If Shakespeare's play, like Peake's portrait of Henry and the slain deer, endorses the innovative educational practices of Chaloner's academy for reviving the warrior masculinity of the British past, this is a fortiori true of a contemporaneous play with the almost redundant title *The Valiant Welshman*. Marisa Cull (2014, 120–39) has demonstrated that this play (performed by the Prince's Men) celebrates the manly heroism of the ancient Britons and their defiance of Rome, whereas Shakespeare's romance (written for the King's Men and endorsing James's foreign policy) also acknowledges the need for civility and multilateralism, as Cymbeline agrees to pay tribute to the Romans after defeating them in battle. Although Cull cautions that the brutality of Cloten's beheading 'undermines the glorious ancient past of Wales...as a useful model for the current prince' (2014, 144), adding to the complexity of Shakespeare's alpine pastoral, one should not underrate *Cymbeline*'s flattery of Henry.[20] Observing that Boccaccio's source-text for the wager plot calls for the Innogen-character to be executed at a 'lonely spot, with precipitous crags and trees all around it', Roger Warren (2008, 34) conjectures this may have prompted Shakespeare to shift the action to Wales; however, the wish to please the new Prince of Wales and tap into the Cambrophilia occasioned by the English translation of Camden's *Britannia* (which rebrands the Welsh mountains as the 'British Alps') would have furnished even stronger motives. In the character of Guiderius, Shakespeare's romance peddles the same fantasy as Jonson's masques that acquiring the title Prince of Wales has magically endowed Henry with the robust virility of the ancient Britons and Welsh 'mountaineers'. Henry's unexpected death in November 1612 would prove the hollowness of such claims. Nevertheless, *Cymbeline* remains an important testament to the prominence and allure of mountainscape, for better or worse, in early modern discourses of masculinity and nationhood.

Enclosing the Mountain: Alpine Georgic and the Dewilding of Wales

The glorification of the Welsh mountains as a preserve of ancient British virtues circulated alongside other more pragmatic views that challenge the presumption that all pre-Romantics dismissed mountains as unproductive wastelands. While Belarius claims the alpine vista enables him to draw 'profit from all things' (3.3.17–18), many in Jacobean Britain were drawing literal profits from hills and uplands like never before. In this respect, another sixteenth-century writer on mountains worthy of mention but overlooked in Nicholson's study is the Swiss naturalist Conrad Gesner. In the 1540s, Gesner penned some rapturous praises of the Alps: 'What a delight for the justly moved soul to admire the spectacle presented by the enormity of these mountains, and to lift one's head into the bosom of the clouds?' (16). While Gesner's essay has been reprinted with the title *On the Admiration of Mountains*, and excerpted in a mountaineering anthology, it first appeared as a preface to his *Libellus de lacte et operibus lacctariis* (*Book on Milk and Milk Production*). It is revealing that the aesthetic appreciation of mountains as beautiful emerges in the Renaissance as a tangent to the assertion that mountains are economically valuable, and a consideration of the alpine pastoral should therefore be balanced with an inquiry into the alpine georgic.

In the Elizabethan and Jacobean eras, an alternative view of Wales emerged not as a barren hinterland but as a comparatively unspoiled wilderness whose resources were ripe for the plucking. Prior to the Tudor Unification Acts, the Welsh had traditionally practiced partible inheritance (like gavelkind in Kent), so that lands were divided equally among heirs. After adopting the English custom of primogeniture, Wales experienced a notable shift towards larger farming estates, and the increasing concentration of wealth and lands in fewer hands. Not coincidentally, the decades after the Unification Acts witnessed 'rapid agrarian expansion', as 'pastures were cleared and enclosed from the high waste, which even at these extremes, was being tamed at its edges. Ridding was the order of the day' (Emery 1967, 114, 140). A memorable example of this land clearance in post-Unification Wales can be found in Churchyard's poem:

> They have begun of late to lime their land.
> And plowes the ground where sturdie Okes did stand:
> Converts the meares, and marrish every where,
> Whose barraine earth, begins good fruite to beare.

> They teare up Trees and takes the rootes away,
> Makes stonie fieldes smooth fertile fallowe ground:
> Brings Pastures bare to beare good grasse for Hay,
> By which at length in wealth they will abound.
>
> (1587, F3ʳ)

Churchyard's work registers a tension between the alpine pastoral and alpine georgic, since development brought a prosperity that threatened to erode the spartan virtues of frugality and toughness that made Wales valuable as a repository of atavistic Britishness. Yet in entitling his ode *The Worthiness of Wales*, Churchyard underscores the land's rising financial worth, which he links to its de-wilding: 'Where thornes did growe, sayth now there springs up gold'.

A survey of deeds and property transactions in the archives of the National Library of Wales confirms that during the late sixteenth century the 'frontiers of land use were pushed into the remoter folds and heads of moorland valleys, as high as 1,400 feet' (Emery 1967, 149), and that this mania for enclosure was most pronounced in the Marches and other portions of Wales like Pembrokeshire controlled mostly by the English.[21] High wool prices and the English appetite for beef propelled the conversion of woodlands and uncultivated uplands to pasture for sheep and cattle. Early modern Britain had its own version of the Texas-Oklahoma cattle drive, as Welsh drovers ushered large herds from upland pastures to fairs and meat markets throughout England, from Ludlow to London (Skeel 1926). The Jailer who orders Posthumus to 'graze where you find pasture' (5.4.2) flaunts the dehumanization of prisoners of war, but also glances at Wales's reputation as a breeding ground for sheep, goats, and cows. In Middleton's *A Chaste Maid in Cheapside* (1613), Walter Whorehound plots to arrange a marriage between a goldsmith's son and a whore disguised as a Welsh heiress, dangling mountains as bait: 'They say she has mountains to her marriage; / She's full of cattle, some two thousand runts' (*TMCW* 4.1.93–4). By the Jacobean era, then, mountains could be regarded as valuable assets, not barren warts, and the alpine pastoral should therefore be inspected to avoid the potential mystification of eco-material realities.

This positive attitude towards uplands would have been reinforced by the growing recognition that they were often repositories of mineral wealth (see Chapter 2) and timber. In 1607, Sir John Wynn notified the English Council of the Marches of his mineral prospecting in Parys Mountain on Anglesey, which would become the largest copper mine in Europe in the eighteenth century (NLW MS 465E/45). In 1602, Wynn's son-in-law Roger Mostyn acquired and expanded a large colliery in Flintshire. Coal and lead were mined at Hollywell and Halkyn Mountain in the early 1600s (NLW Bettisfield Estate Records 872). Around this time, the Welsh-born Hugh Myddleton prospected for coal near Chirk and later acquired silver and lead mines in the Cardiganshire hills. The English also erected lucrative ironworks in early modern Wales and the border counties that exploited local ore deposits and woodlands, and which, despite the turn to coppicing, decimated much of the Forest of Dean. In 1611, the Crown leased 330 acres of woodlands near Bradley Hill to the iron-monger Edward Winter at an inflated price and in return waived the legal statutes requiring the preservation of large timber trees and fencing off of coppices to allow them to regenerate.

Such reckless practices were decried in the neglected works of Welsh poets such as Robin Clidro, whose 'Marchan Wood' adopts the perspective of the now endangered red squirrel to protest against the obliteration of the Welsh woodlands. The poem's reference to a 'hill wood' indicates that the English interlopers were pushing into higher elevations left untouched prior to Unification, and forcing the locals to rely on 'peat from the mountain' (due to the scarcity of timber) as domestic fuel. Another Welsh poem, 'Glyn Cynon Wood' bemoans the destruction of a woodland in the hilly region between Aberdare and Llanwonno, and wags an angry finger at the English iron industry:

> Many a birch tree green of cloak
> (I'd like to choke the Saxon!)
> Is now a flaming heap of fire
> Where iron-workers blacken.
> For cutting the branch and bearing away
> The wild bird's habitation
> May misfortune quickly reach
> Rowenna's treacherous children!
>
> (qtd in Borlik 2019, 414–16)

This anonymous poem (which probably dates from the early seventeenth century) explicitly recognizes the value of the wild as a habitat for non-humans: red deer, badgers, stags, and birds are all portrayed as victims. It even imagines an inquest or trial in which birds serve as jurors (the owl acting as hangman) and pronounce the wood-cutting a capital offence. It so happens that one of the main offenders was Shakespeare's patron, the Third Earl of Pembroke, William Herbert. In 1608, Herbert became the Constable of St Briavels, near Tintern, and in 1612 the Warden of the Forest of Dean, and was awarded the right to claim a hefty 12,000 cords of wood per year to fuel his ironworks. While Herbert was expected to comply with the Timber Acts, his commissioners 'were found to have failed to prevent, or connived at, the felling of large timber trees, the embezzlement of wood by the making up of irregularly-sized cords, and the [illicit] sale of wood to coopers, trencher makers, and carpenters' (Baggs and Jurica 1996, 354–77). To circumvent the fierce opposition from the local community, the Earl's wood-cutters tried felling timber on a Sunday morning in 1614 when people were at church, but 'fifteen desperate knaves' later set his heap of cordwood ablaze, and 'dancing about the fire cried, "God save the King"' (qtd in O'Farrell 2011, 146). While scholars have connected the Dean iron industry to Milton's *Masque Presented at Ludlow Castle* (Sanders 2001),

Shakespeareans have made little fuss about the fact that Pembroke, the co-dedicatee of the First Folio and a contender for the Fair Youth of the *Sonnets*, was actively involved in the rapacious extraction of natural resources in the Welsh Marches around the time Shakespeare composed *Cymbeline*.

Shakespeare's presentation in *Cymbeline* of Wales as a lush green world must be seen alongside this history of environmental exploitation. While the play does not articulate anything like the searing eco-critique voiced by some Welsh poets, it radiates an eco-nostalgia that idealizes the Welsh wilderness as a proving ground of a primal masculinity in ways that resist the enclosure movement and the ethos of the alpine georgic. Belarius and his foster-children are able to find refuge in the Welsh mountains precisely because the hills were commons, on which many of the rural poor squatted in *caban unnos*. In reality, however, the life of Henry and Charles Stuart bore little resemblance to that of actual seventeenth-century Welsh mountain-folk, who were 'held in such continual labour in tilling of the land, burning of lime, digging of coals, and other such slaveries' (Owen 1603/1994, 46). Like the 'white Indians' of Fenimore Cooper's Shakespeare-inspired romances, Shakespeare's portrait of the Stuart princes as rugged, faux-Welsh mountaineers living in close intimacy with their surroundings engages in cultural appropriation to protest environmental devastation. *Cymbeline* mythologizes the absorption of Wales within the imperial destiny of Britain while also defiantly asserting the ecological, psychological, and cultural value of its unspoiled wilderness that this same imperial dominion will inevitably degrade. *Cymbeline* thus foreshadows a problematic tendency of the early environmental movement to ventriloquize Indigenous voices rather than listen to them, and more work could be done to place Shakespeare's Welsh play in conversation with Welsh writers.

Mountain as Eyrie and the Endangered Eagle

In setting *Cymbeline* in the ancient past, Shakespeare privileges the alpine pastoral over the georgic, conjuring a wilder Wales that was under threat in his day. The play implicitly recognizes the enduring worthiness (to use Churchyard's phrase) of mountains as an abode of wildlife that enriches human existence and poetry in particular by providing a storehouse of imagery and metaphor. Citing Shakespeare's references to the azured harebell and cinque-spotted cowslip, Jonathan Bate remarks, 'it is perhaps in *Cymbeline* that Shakespeare's art of natural observation is at its most acute' (2009, 48). For Bate the biographer, the cornucopia of natural imagery in the play reflects the likelihood Shakespeare composed it back at Stratford, but the more immediate effect of *Cymbeline*'s botanical language is to insist on the fecundity of the Welsh landscape, counteracting the perception of its uplands as barren crags. Even the 'moss' that grows abundantly on the Welsh mountains in winter serves to 'winter-ground' (4.2.227–8) or preserve Innogen's corpse. Whether or not the scene glances at the rot-defying powers of upland peat moss (or avian funerals in the imagined burial of this 'bird' by the robin), it qualifies the finality of death as 'dust' with a benign vision of ecological reintegration, which miraculously proves true when Innogen revives.[22] The Welsh mountain thus offers a high-altitude counterpoint to the sea-floor in Ariel's song. This brings us to one last important factor conspiring to boost the reputation of mountains in the Renaissance: the rise of natural philosophy. By the early seventeenth century, herbalists understood that many plants grow only at higher elevations, and as these tended to be rare or even unknown, they became highly prized. It is telling that the first recorded ascent of Snowdon, which occurred in 1634, was made by a botanist, Thomas Johnson, who was not seeking sublime views but alpine plants. In addition to botanists, mountains also attracted Renaissance egg-hunters and ornithologists, who knew that some species nest only in alpine cliffs. Significantly, *Cymbeline* presents mountains as the last refuge of an endangered Britishness while gesturing at the threatened nests of actual birds.

Like *Macbeth* (see Chapter 1), *Cymbeline* swarms with avian images—the ruddock or robin, the jay, the wren, the lark, the owl—but its nine explicit references to the eagle (triple the total of any other play) seem especially apt given its mountain setting. Innogen's claim she 'chose an eagle' (1.1.140) when she chose Posthumus captures his inner nobility and foreshadows his transformation into a Welsh mountaineer. Posthumus is also eagle-like in his ability to 'behold the sun with firm eye' (1.4.12). Belarius's 'full-winged eagle' (3.3.21) is a fit symbol for soaring ambition but also helps evoke the mountainous Welsh environment of act 3. Picking up on his foster-father's image, Guiderius compares himself and his brother to mountain-bred eagles when he retorts, 'we poor unfledged, / Have never winged from view o' th' nest' (3.3.27–9), likening their alpine cave to an eyrie (which Shakespeare and his contemporaries often spelled 'aerie' to underline its connection with air). The brothers are again connected to the bird when Posthumus recounts how they transformed the Roman soldiers from 'eagles' into 'chickens' (5.3.42). It also features in the play's most memorable *coup de théâtre*: Postshumus's dream-vision. Discounting Ariel's harpy, *Cymbeline*'s artificial eagle is the only bird brought on stage in Shakespeare. No doubt audiences marvelled at the spectacle of its descent, but some would have been thrilled simply by the glimpse of an endangered raptor rarely seen in England.

In making persistent references to the eagle in his Welsh play, Shakespeare hints at the affinity between a species, a particular habitat, and cultural identity. While Camden proposes an etymology derived from snow, it was widely believed that the ancient Welsh name for Snowdonia, *Eryri*, meant 'land of the eagle'. The eagle was commonly used as a standard for Roman legions and Shakespeare alludes to its associations with the Roman sky-god, but the Welsh also regarded the bird as a national symbol and portent.[23] In naming the prince Paladour, Shakespeare identifies him with the eagle that predicted a Welsh resurgence, and even puns on the Welsh for eagle, '(h)eryr', when in the next line he refers to him as the 'heyre...of Britain' whose 'spirits flye' (TLN 1648, 1651). Perhaps most significantly, eagles were also linked with Wales because it was one of the few places in Britain where they could still be seen in 1610. It is no accident that the greatest literary tribute to the eagle in early modern English literature was composed by the Welsh-born Henry Vaughan. Eagles had once been fairly common throughout England in the Roman and medieval eras (as attested by sixty Anglo-Saxon place-names incorporating the word).[24] There were in fact two native species, the golden and the white-tailed (also known as the sea-eagle or erne). The white-tailed eagle tended to nest on Britain's rugged west coast (including large sections of the Welsh coast), but could also be found in wetlands. Since the golden eagle preferred woodlands, fish-stocked watersheds, and high nesting sites such as mountain cliffs, Wales afforded an ideal habitat for this raptor. Harrison's *The Description of England* reports that the largest and most famous eyrie was at Castell Dinas Brân in Wales (where John Leland had seen it in 1538). This castle had been the stronghold of Llywelyn the Last, the final Welsh ruler of Wales, who assumed the title *Eryr, Eryrod, Eryri* (The Eagle of all Eagles of the place of Eagles) until his defeat, when Edward I appropriated the symbol by christening Caernarfon Castle's tallest battlement Eagle Tower. In early modern Wales, then, the nesting of the figurative king of birds near a royal castle could be regarded as conferring sovereignty. In *Cymbeline*'s final scene, the soothsayer glimpses 'a Roman eagle, / from south to west on wing soaring aloft' (5.5.469) fly into the radiance of the sunset, and glosses this as an omen of the truce between Roman and Britain. Commentators have noted that it also functions a symbol of *translatio imperii et studii*—the transfer of empire and culture from Rome to Great Britain (Hopkins 2010)—but it is worth belabouring the point that Shakespeare predicates this transference on a shared organic heritage or ecological continuity between the two nations.

Sadly, this continuity was jeopardized in the seventeenth century, as many early moderns regarded eagles as vicious pests. Harrison's *Description* reports that farmers complained of their snatching kids and lambs, and even dispenses advice on how to steal eagle eggs—'a thing oft attempted' (1587, 227). Such thefts took their toll. Roger Lovegrove remarks that the golden eagle is surprisingly absent from Tudor inventories of vermin—not because it was unmolested but because it was already extirpated from lowland Britain in Shakespeare's day (Yaldon 2007; Lovegrove 2007, 116). John Ray and Frances Willoughby still observed eagles in Snowdonia in 1656 and 1662, but by then they were already a rarity. As a result of human depredation, by about 1800 the golden eagle had vanished from Wales as well, where plans are currently afoot to reintroduce them as an iconic Welsh species. The white-tailed fared only slightly better. It does appear in 1566 Vermin Act (worth 4 pence a head), but seems to have been confined mainly to Scotland, Wales, the Lake District, and some scattered wetlands. The large-scale draining of the English Fens and Somerset Levels that began in earnest during the reign of King James (see Chapter 6) is believed to have caused a precipitous decline in their numbers, so that Shakespeare's generation may have been one of the last in lowland Britain to glimpse a wild eagle. Some have even questioned if Shakespeare ever set eyes on an eagle himself.[25]

How do we read Shakespeare's recurrent eagle allusions differently knowing that this raptor was being gradually exterminated in the seventeenth century? Belarius's observation that the eagle is not in a 'safer hold' (3.3.20) than the beetle might draw on an Aesopian fable but also calls attention to the vulnerability of eyries to egg-snatching—which the hunter-kings Henry VIII and James I both sought to criminalize. Since hunting with a golden eagle was typically reserved for royalty, James would have been particularly eager to protect the species, once again indicating how environmental conservation grew out of the monarch's hunting privileges and identification with the realm's megafauna. As an emblem of godhood (Jove's bird) and empire (a Roman standard), the eagle in *Cymbeline*, like the tamed peregrine falcon in James's youthful portrait (see Fig. 0.1) or the eagle in the king's menagerie, seems a mascot of royal absolutism, vicariously extending it skywards to the pitch of an eagle's flight.

If *Cymbeline* depicts the Welsh mountains as a preserve of the primal manliness and sovereignty of the ancient Britons, the converse is also true: the perpetuity of Britishness, Tudorness, and royalty in James's own offspring is contingent on the preservation of the Welsh wilderness and its creatures. Gerald of Wales had observed the country's 'mountain-heights abound in horses and wild game' (1.3), but Belarius's order that the princes go 'up to th' mountains' (3.3.73) to hunt also betrays the contemporary reality that animals are already scarce in the deforested lowlands. Many seventeenth-century writers (including Camden and Drayton) knew from Gerald that beavers had once flourished in the Welsh River Teifi but had been extirpated from Britain about a generation before Shakespeare's birth: Shakespeare's seven references to the beaver all refer to the metal face-guard of a helmet. A similar fate had befallen the wolf. When Arviragus complains they are 'warlike as the wolf' (3.3.41), he hints at the reason for their future military victory, while helping to set the story in both Wales and the remote past. Wolves had once been common in pre-modern Wales until an English king, ironically named Edgar the Peaceful (r. 959), targeted them for extermination by demanding the Welsh pay him an annual tribute of 300 wolf pelts. This story was current in Shakespeare's day; it is even retold in one of King James's favourite books, John Caius's *Of English Dogs*. A demand of tribute comprises a major plot-point in *Cymbeline*, and although the Romans expect cold hard coin rather than wolf fur, the play's topicality invites the reading of it as a payment not simply from Britain to Rome but from Wales to England. As this chapter has hopefully demonstrated, the annexation of Wales and diversion of its wealth and resources came at a steep cost in ecological terms.

Criticism on *Cymbeline* and early modern nationhood has rightly harped on fears of the 'eradication of a distinctive Welsh identity' but this might also entail concern at the eradication of Welsh wildlife.[26] The play's use of the eagle for literary foreshadowing evokes and mimics the Roman practice of augury, divining the future from the behaviour of birds. But the future of the 'holy eagle' (5.4.85) in Shakespeare's Britain was itself in doubt. Amalgamating mountainous Wales and England into Britain, *Cymbeline*'s alpine pastoral recognizes the importance of topographical complexity for biodiversity at a time when much of lowland England's wildlife had been depleted. If no man is an island, as in Donne's famous adage, no species is an island either. Each species' disappearance diminishes us. Environmental philosophers have diagnosed modern humans with 'species loneliness', a sense of isolation and deprivation from the paucity of our contact with other life-forms.[27] A wolfless Britain makes the British less capable of being wolflike. An eagleless Britain makes the British less eaglelike. A de-wilded Britain severely curtails the scope and vivacity of its poets' language. Of course, Shakespeare was not openly advocating the reintroduction of the wolf (indeed, his patron sought to exterminate them from Scotland). But his copious nature imagery does offer a temporary antidote to species loneliness and can induce a sense of ecological nostalgia for a wilder past. If *Cymbeline* naturalizes English dominion over Wales, it also seems to capture what the Welsh call *cynefin* (cun-eh-vin), a word for which there is no English equivalent. *Cynefin* can be used as both a noun to mean the habitat of a person or animal and an adjective to mean familiar, but essentially signifies a sense of place: the feeling of being habituated to one's habitat. Even if Shakespeare had a Welsh schoolmaster, it is highly unlikely that his vocabulary, capacious as it was, included *cynefin*. Nevertheless, the word offers a useful tool to gauge the importance of the mountains in *Cymbeline* as a nest of both Welshness and wildness. *Cymbeline* thus stages something that often eludes landscape painting: topophilia or place-attachment. It represents Wales as a vibrant habitat, recognizing that its union with England entails a celebration of greater cultural, topographical, and biological diversity: it is this diversity that makes Great Britain great, as Drayton implies in celebrating the ecological muchness of *Poly-Olbion*.

In a bizarre continuation of the *translatio studii* as *translatio naturae* that concludes *Cymbeline*, Shakespeare bears responsibility for the introduction of starlings to North America, when a misguided ornithologist and Shakespeare-enthusiast named Eugene Schieffelin released thirty pairs in New York City's Central Park in 1890 out of the desire that America possess all the species named in his plays. Perhaps Shakespeare's *Cymbeline* might provide a better argument for reintroducing eagles to rewild the mountains of Wales.

5

Performing *The Winter's Tale* in 'the Open'

Bears, Ermines, Rural Girlhood, and the White Sea Fur Trade

Surely no stage direction in Shakespeare has exercised the ingenuity of scholars and theatre directors more than '*Exit, pursued by a bear*' (3.3.57). Among the myriad ways in which it has been staged over the centuries—with actors in bear-suits, taxidermic specimens on wheels, furry puppets, video projections, bear-shaped shadows, offstage growls, and oversize teddy bears—one in particular seems to neatly illustrate the purview of this chapter. In a 1986 Royal Shakespeare Company production of *The Winter's Tale* directed by Terry Hands, a large polar bearskin rug that had adorned Leontes's palace suddenly sprang up from the floor to chase Antigonus.[1] While the moment elicited laughs from the audience, its humour results from its abrupt collapse of the distinction between inanimate object and animate creature, between the domestic and the wild. The undoing of such tidy dichotomies has become one of the chief tasks of animal studies and the new materialism over the past decade. To date, however, little attention has been paid to the importance of fur in the theatrical culture of Renaissance England, as a performing object with a disturbing provenance—one that potentially troubles the alliance between these critical approaches.

In the narrative of his 1609 voyage to the Arctic, Jonas Poole recounts killing and skinning seven polar bears, including a she-bear accompanied by two cubs 'as big as Lambs of a month old' (Purchas 1625, 561). Realizing the two orphans would make fine additions to the royal menagerie, the opportunistic Poole shipped them back to London. Whereas King Henry III had kept a polar bear (a gift from the king of Norway) in the Tower of London in the 1250s, King James entrusted the cubs to the actor Edward Alleyn and Alleyn's father-in-law Philip Henslowe, who were not only the Masters of the Royal Game but also two of the most influential figures in Jacobean show business. Theatre historians have long speculated about the presence of performing bears on the Renaissance stage. Arthur Quiller-Couch (1931) proposed that Shakespeare's company could have availed themselves of Alleyn's stable of trained bears at Paris Garden in Southwark when staging *The Winter's Tale*, and J. H. P. Pafford (1963) concurred that this was a possibility in the second Arden edition of the play. In an influential article, however, Nevill Coghill (1958) insisted that bears were simply too unpredictable and dangerous to let them run amok, and this verdict more or less prevailed during the second half of the twentieth century.[2] The case was reopened in 2001 when Teresa Grant uncovered new evidence of the polar bear cubs amongst Henslowe and Alleyn's accounts, and she and Barbara Ravelhofer (2002) have argued that since the cubs were young enough to imprint on a human handler they could have been sufficiently tractable to perform on stage. They may very well have been the 'two white bears' (3:733.214) hitched to a chariot in Ben Jonson's *Oberon*; one may have had a cameo in the King's Men revival of *Mucedorus* circa 1610, or possibly even scampered across the boards in the Whitehall production of *The Winter's Tale*.[3] While some remain sceptical that actors would risk their lives by performing alongside real bears (Cooper 2005; Pitcher 2010, 143), it is conceivable that without Poole's slaughter of the cubs' mother Shakespeare may never have written the most famous stage direction in English literature.

The Anthropocene has transformed the polar bear into an environmental martyr, a symbol of the threat climate change poses to the planet and its biodiversity. In 2009, the four hundredth anniversary of Poole's voyage, a sixteen-foot-tall polar bear statue was floated down the Thames right past Shakespeare's Globe to raise public awareness of global warming (Vaughan 2009). Needless to say, seventeenth-century audiences would have perceived the cubs very differently. More than just exotic creatures from the frozen north, they would have been regarded as living advertisements of the fortunes to be gained in the early modern fur trade. After all, Poole's voyage was sponsored by the Muscovy Company, which was heavily invested in importing fur from Russia, and rewarding its shareholders with lucrative dividends from pelts, timber, hemp, and whale oil. When *The Winter's Tale* was performed at court in November 1611, the recently returned Muscovy Company factor and ambassador to Russia John Meyrick may have been in the audience, while other company agents were in Pustozersk to negotiate a deal to boost fur imports, which had been disrupted by the Polish-Muscovite war and incursions by the Swedish and the Dutch.[4] Thanks in part to the profits raked in by the Muscovy Company, Shakespeare's contemporaries were beginning to view the Arctic not as an icy wasteland or abode of fabulous monsters but as a wilderness abounding in natural resources, including whale oil, walrus ivory, and animal fur. Shakespeare himself seems to have taken an interest in tales of polar exploration. Sir Toby's passing reference to 'an icicle on a Dutchman's beard' (*TN* 3.2.26) proves that Shakespeare knew of Willem Barentsz's voyages to the Arctic between 1594–7. Gerrit de Veer's travelogue (published in English in 1598, 1605, and 1609) includes a vivid account of the Dutch crew slaughtering and skinning polar bears (see Fig. 5.1). To Jacobean merchant venturers, such images of the bear-infested Arctic would entice as much as terrify, for the whiteness of the snowy north signified an opportunity to acquire white fur—a luxurious signifier of monarchical power.

Fig. 5.1 The Barentsz expedition killing and skinning polar bears on Novaya Zemlya in 1596, from Gerrit de Veer, *The true and perfect description of three voyages... on the north sides of Norway, Muscovia, and Tartaria* (1609).
Science History Images/Alamy Stock Photo.

It is therefore apt that King James not only blessed the Muscovy Company's ventures but also, in an all but forgotten episode of Jacobean geo-politics, signed on to an audacious scheme for Britain to annex a considerable portion of northwest Russia. Not content with its toehold on 'Bear Island', where Jonas Poole and his crew slaughtered several polar bears and hundreds of walruses, the Muscovy Company sought to expand its influence in the region by dispatching a small expeditionary force in the summer of 1612 to participate in some strong-arm diplomacy on behalf of the nascent British empire (Dunning 1989, 2007). The leaders of this outfit sent James a tempting proposal in which the beleaguered Russians would outsource defence of the region against the Polish and Swedes to an army of mercenaries financed by the Muscovy Company and, in exchange, cede control over what is now Arkhangelsk Oblast to an English 'protectorate' (SPF 91/1 220–1ᵛ). In early 1613, the Privy Council convened twice to debate the plan, while an excited James met repeatedly with Meyrick to hammer out the details before sending him to Moscow to negotiate the deal (Dunning 2007, 295–7). In other words, not long after the performance of *The Winter's Tale* at Whitehall and during its revival at Princess Elizabeth's wedding, the Stuart government was not only anticipating an alliance with the Palatinate and Bohemia but also partnering with a joint-stock company in an ambitious scheme to conquer a swathe of Arctic territory abutting the White Sea, which James desired not because he wished for more human subjects in these frigid, sparsely populated latitudes but because he realized the vast profits to be made from its fur-bearing animals. Shakespeare's decision to insert a bear in his adaptation of Robert Greene's *Pandosto* and rechristen its Russian princess with a name evoking the ermine may be something more than mere coincidence.[5]

In a witty and scintillating essay, Lowell Duckert (2013) examines Shakespeare's bear as 'a transspecies being whose animacy queers ideas of the autonomous human species'. This chapter pursues a similar line of argument to Duckert and other scholars who have charted the interplay between stage and bear-pit, but focuses on the animistic power of animal skin as a performing actant in the networks of both Renaissance drama and the global economy.[6] Interestingly, the same Alleyn and Henslowe who took charge of the polar bear cubs were respectively the chief actor and financier of the Admiral's company, whose 1598 property inventory includes a 'beares skyne' as well as a 'lyone skin' (*HD* 319). While these entries lend credence to the belief that Elizabethan theatre companies (at least prior to 1610) had human actors don fur suits rather than rely on actual bears, this debate has now reached the point of diminishing returns. Worse, it perpetuates the assumption that the species line must be sharply drawn. For too long, theatre historians have approached the equivocal evidence for ursine performance as a problem in need of solution. In contrast, proponents of animal studies might exercise the Shakespearean virtue of negative capability and argue that our inability to determine conclusively who or what played the bear reflects the ontological confusion that prevailed in the Renaissance before the 'invention of the human'. By tolerating uncertainty rather than policing boundaries, critics might instead hail the Renaissance playhouse as dramatizing what philosopher Giorgio Agamben refers to as 'the Open' (2004)—a conceptual space where humans and other species become suspended in 'indistinction'.[7]

Pastoral romances like *The Winter's Tale* delight in indistinction, often embodied in the motif of the feral child who dissolves the boundaries between infant and animal. Supplementing Agamben's theory with some historical context that further establishes Shakespeare's tailoring of his late plays for the Stuart court, this chapter reveals how the idyllic picture of Perdita's Bohemian childhood recalls Princess Elizabeth's upbringing in rural Warwickshire. By adapting a popular Elizabethan romance, *The Winter's Tale* seeks to recapture the epistemological openness that Shakespeare's Jacobean contemporaries associated with childhood and girlhood in particular. Yet the plunge into indistinction is not without its hazards. Framed as a court drama, *The Winter's Tale* resembles an imperial romance, in which the blending of nature and culture, the grafting of the 'gentler scion to the wildest stock' (4.4.93), celebrates the amalgamation of wilderness into empire. Acknowledging that Elizabeth's royal gardens and menagerie enact environmental sovereignty, I argue they constitute a benign despotism in comparison to Skinners' pageants, which trumpet—in Dekker's phrase—the 'glory of furs'. By pitting bear plays and romances against these civic processions, this chapter spotlights the performative power of fur in therianthropic species-crossings while considering how such crossings might threaten the speciesist logic that entitles humans to kill and flay other animals. At the same time, it also aims to demonstrate the limitations of new materialist or object-oriented theory for animal studies, in that erasing the subject/object divide risks colluding with the Skinners' pageant in its refusal to discriminate between an animal and its fur.

Hermione as Ermine: Fur and Monarchy in the Early Anthropocene

Whether or not the polar bear cubs participated in Jacobean theatrical spectacles, evidence overwhelmingly indicates that skin and fur—the reason their mother was slaughtered and flayed—did have a conspicuous supporting role in many Renaissance plays. In addition to the bear- and lion-skin, Henslowe's inventory lists several costumes adorned with fur: 'i short clocke of black vellet, with sleves faced with white fore', 'i mannes gown faced with whitte fore', a 'blak velvett gowne w^t wight fure', and a gown 'fact [faced] w^t ermin' (*HD* 322, 291–2). There is even proof that the leading man of the Admiral's company, Edward Alleyn, wore fur offstage. While most Shakespeareans are familiar with the life-sized painting of Alleyn at the Dulwich Portrait Gallery, few realize that the thick craquelure over his black gown conceals the presence of large bristling furs (Ingamells 2008, 20). Apropos of Renaissance portraiture, Erica Fudge remarks how animals and animal-objects are all too often 'absented from the picture, made to seem unnecessary and inconsequential, with the result that the human emerges as the only necessary and consequential being in the frame' (2012, 88).[8] The painting over of Alleyn's fur perfectly captures this erasure. In contrast, W. B. Morris's copy of the portrait, which depicts the furs clearly, might serve as a visual corollary for this chapter's attempted restoration. The documented presence of fur in the wardrobe of a major Elizabethan acting troupe and upon the body of the era's most celebrated actor should remind us that the entertainment industry in Shakespeare's day was implicated not only in animal-baiting but also in the commercial fur trade.

In stripping away the 'robes and furred gowns' to expose man as a 'poor, bare, forked animal' (3.4.101), *King Lear* debunks, as Laurie Shannon has shown, anthropocentric narcissism by emphasizing that our furless bodies are in fact maladapted to survive in the wild (2012, 165–73). Shannon's thesis is thoroughly convincing, yet ecocriticism should also attend to the consequences of humanity's desire to compensate for its furlessness, since the market for furs was one of the biggest forces behind de-wilding during the medieval and early modern eras.[9] Killed for its pelt, the beaver vanished from English and Welsh rivers during the late Middle Ages, and the last record of any in Scotland dates from the Tudor period.[10] The pine marten, the native species most valued for its fur, proved more tenacious, but overhunting severely depleted its numbers. In the late seventeenth century John Aubrey reports that they were 'utterly destroyed in North Wiltshire'.[11] Badgers, foxes, hare, rabbit, and squirrel would also have been routinely trapped and skinned. The Arctic was not the only region where bears suffered persecution. Brown bears had once prowled the woods of Roman Britannia, and were probably killed off in the Anglo-Saxon era (c.1000) to protect livestock.[12] While Shakespeare's contemporaries also flayed lambs to make budge, sheep were more unwilling accomplices than victims in the de-wilding of Britain. Thomas More's *Utopia* notoriously transmogrifies the meek sheep into a carnivorous, rampaging monster, devouring whole villages, but sheep-farming depopulated the countryside of more than just humans. By rights, Antigonus's exclamation 'I am gone forever!' (3.3.57) should be reassigned to the bear and Shakespeare's legendary stage direction be revised: Exit bear, pursued by sheep and shepherd. The wolf was also gradually extirpated from southern Britain in the late Middle Ages, partially as a result of a tribute of wolf-pelts the English King Edgar I had imposed on the Welsh and the extermination policies of monarchs like Edward I, but also due to the displacement of woodlands by pasture. *The Winter's Tale* celebrates Britain's pastoral economy in its famous sheep-shearing scene, but the zoomorphic depiction of Autolycus as a human wolf-in-peddler's-clothing represents a comic travesty of the threat once posed by the now vanished wolf. Might the same be said of the play's bear? While Shakespeare's romance is set in antiquity, the devouring of Antigonus gives a misleading picture of the seventeenth-century environment in that it casts humans as victims rather than predators. The dwindling or, in some cases, disappearance of native fur-bearers in Britain and Europe due to habitat loss and overhunting led to the development of global trading networks that fuelled the Muscovy Company voyages to Bear Island and Arkhangelsk, and the Russian incursions into the Urals and Western Siberia. In a despicable vicious circle, the growing scarcity of fur is in part what gave it such allure as a fashion accessory affordable only to the rich, and some species may have been more highly persecuted as their numbers declined.

On the Renaissance stage, the mere wearing of animal fur constituted a dramatic spectacle in and of itself. Beyond signifying wintry weather or a scene in a cold climate, furs would convey detailed information to Elizabethan spectators about the status or profession of the characters, as sumptuary laws strictly dictated which social ranks could wear which variety of fur. A 1574 proclamation restricts the wearing of furs 'whereof the kind groweth not in the Queen's dominions' to those with annual incomes in excess of £100, with exceptions made for the pelts of beech marten, grey jennets, and budge or lambskin (*TRP* 2:458–9). Only a king or queen could wear the coveted white fur of the ermine, so the 'ermin' in Alleyn's 1602 inventory and the other 'wight fure'—whatever species it was flayed from—in the Admiral's Men's wardrobe would have been essential co-actants in enabling a common player to project majesty.[13] Do the astronomical prices ermine fetched at European courts help explain why European voyagers were so eager to kill and flay white-furred polar bears?

A survey of the royal wardrobe expenses from the late medieval and early modern periods offers a shocking glimpse of the mass carnage subsidized by the English monarchy. Between 1392–4, the clothes-hound Richard II purchased the fur of 1,634 ermines, 308 pine martens, 18 beavers, and over 200,000 squirrels. Henry IV owned a single robe made from 12,000 squirrels and 80 ermines. In a five-year span between 1413–18, Henry V purchased 625 imported pelts of sable and 20,000 martens. To put this in perspective, the number of pine martens killed by Henry V equals *three times* the number of Frenchmen his army slew at Agincourt. 250 martens were killed to line a velvet gown of Henry VI, while Henry VIII possessed a satin gown adorned with the fur of 350 sables.[14] Look again at the famed Coronation Portrait of Elizabeth I while processing the fact that each black dot on her gown represents a single slaughtered ermine and Good Queen Bess acquires an unfortunate resemblance to a Tudor Cruella de Ville. The hunter-king James sports similar regalia in a 1603 engraving by Pieter de Jode I and a later portrait by Paul von Somer (see Fig. 5.2). If few of Shakespeare's contemporaries batted an eye at these horrific bodycounts, they would have at the eye-watering sums of money the Stuarts spent on furs at a time when the Commons and Treasurer were battling to restrain royal expenditures.

As the son of an alderman and glover—'you fur your gloves with reason,' quips Troilus (2.2.37)—Shakespeare would have grown up around fur, and been personally acquainted with both its ornamental use and ceremonial power. While no costume inventory survives for Chamberlain's or King's Men, it is a virtual certainty that Shakespeare's acting companies also owned fur-lined robes for the roles of the monarchs listed above. Curiously, in the 1603 Quarto of *Hamlet*, the Prince refers to his mourning garb not as an 'inky cloak', but a 'sable suit' (2.33). This variant may not seem particularly noteworthy, since sable can be glossed as black, as the play itself attests: the ghost's beard is 'sable-silvered' (1.2.241), and Pyrrhus wields 'sable arms, black as his purpose' (2.2.455). From an eco-materialist perspective, however, this poetic use of sable as an elegant synonym for black risks obfuscating the violence of the fur trade, transforming an animal into a mere adjective. It is therefore noteworthy that Shakespeare seems to give the same word a different meaning prior to the Mousetrap when Hamlet, jeering at the brevity of Gertrude's mourning, exclaims, 'Nay then let the devil wear black, for I'll have a suit of sables' (3.2.124). This confusing passage only makes sense if Hamlet is talking about the literal fur of the sable (which can also be dark brown), a signifier of luxury and power

Fig. 5.2 Paul van Somer, *James VI & I* (c.1620). RCIN 404446. Royal Collection Trust. © Queen Elizabeth II 2021.

which he deems incompatible with mourning. On stage, as at court, exotic furs generated the aura of kingship, the dominion of the human hunter over the animal world replicating the monarch's dominion over the realm.

The bio-semiotics of lustrous white fur in contrast to dull wool would also help define the ambiance and politics of *The Winter's Tale*. As he toys with the anxious shepherds, Autolycus feigns indignation that the marriage of a lowly shepherdess to the prince would 'Draw our Throne into a Sheep-Coat' (TLN 2661). As Rebecca Ann Bach observes (2018, 149), the editorial tendency to modernize the Folio text to 'sheepcote'—i.e. a sheep hut—cloaks the pun on the woollen coat known as a frieze, commonly worn by rural labourers and which therefore likely featured in the costuming of this scene. Whereas Bohemians with heavy purses might be able to afford the 'Lawn as white as driven snow' (4.4.220) hawked by Autolycus, and 'the white [linen] sheet bleaching on the hedge' (4.3.5) was a common sight in spring, white furs were a sartorial badge of royalty. As a prince, Florizel should be strutting about in the white furs of ermine (the stoat in its winter coat), minever (fur made from the white bellies of red squirrels), or lettice (the snow weasel). There is, therefore, a cruel poetic justice in Autolycus's sentence that the shepherd's son be 'flayed alive' (4.4.788), as it replicates his alleged crime of de-furring the prince while forcing the son to suffer the grisly fate of a fur-bearer. *The Winter's Tale* identifies white with royalty when Hermione's spirit appears to Antigonus in 'pure white robes' (3.3.21). The words pure and robes would alert a Jacobean audience to imagine this garment not as a linen sheet of penance but as ermine, whose white fur was symbolic of purity and hence would have telegraphed Hermione's innocence.

This dressing of Hermione in ermine is especially fitting since the creature is sewn into her very name. Certain readers may shudder at the thought of Shakespeare as an h-dropper but h-dropping at the start of words was commonplace in early modern English and since ermine–still spelled *hermine* in French— was sometimes written and pronounced 'Ermion', Hermione would have sounded uncannily similar to ermine. The 'Ermion' spelling occurs in Sidney's *Arcadia* (1593, 33ʳ), where the beast appears on the impresa of a knight defending the honour of a woman who fell in love with her suitor's best friend, instigating an outbreak of violent jealousy. Moreover, the now accepted pronunciation of Hermione's name is not exclusively accurate: twice in scene 2 and twice in the final scene the iambic pentameter demands that it be pronounced as disyllabic: 'He's beat from his best ward. Well said Hermione' (1.2.34); 'And leave you to your graver steps. Hermione' (1.2.172); 'Thou art Hermione or rather thou art she' (5.3.25); 'Hermione was not so much wrinkled, nothing' (5.3.28). Leontes's verses can become irregular in the throes of jealousy, but his mind is not addled in the above-cited instances. While Antigonus and perhaps the prose-speaking characters say it with four syllables, four of the five times Leontes utters her name the verse clearly calls for two. Only one occurrence is ambiguous and even this could as easily be spoken with two or three syllables as four: 'Hermione my dearest thou never spok'st' (1.2.88). This suggests the original pronunciation was much closer to 'ermion' with a barely audible o. For this to happen five times cannot be coincidental given Shakespeare departed from his source in choosing her name, Hermione's origins in ermine-exporting Russia, the ermine's notoriety as a symbol of purity, and the play's obsession with animal/human boundary crossing. In other words, Leontes uses a diminutive form of Hermione as a term of endearment that betrays his subconscious wish to see her as an impossible paragon of sexual chastity. In Sidney's romance, the ermine impresa bears the motto 'Better dead than spotted' and a similar Latin tag accompanies the ermine emblem in Henry Peacham's *Minerva Britanna* (1612): *Cui candor morte redemptus* [Purity Redeemed by Death] (75, see Fig. 5.3). These mottos derive from bestiary lore that the ermine prized its unsullied coat so much it would rather be slain by hunters than go through muddy terrain to evade them. When Hermione protests she values her honour above her life (3.2.107–08) her behaviour mimics that of her namesake.

Fig. 5.3. The ermine as emblem of purity, from Henry Peacham, *Minerva Britanna* (1612). Beinecke Rare Book and Manuscript Library, Yale University.

The ermine is an apt heraldic mascot for *The Winter's Tale* since early moderns regarded it not only as synonymous with this season (stoats only change their coats in winter in snowy climes such as Scotland and Russia) but also as an emblem of royal chastity, as memorably captured in the 'Ermine Portrait' of Queen Elizabeth (see Fig. 5.4). Incidentally, the portrait's erroneous depiction of a leopard-spotted creature (Peacham's woodcut makes the same mistake) indicates

Fig. 5.4 Nicholas Hilliard, The 'Ermine Portrait' of Queen Elizabeth (1585). Reproduced with permission of the Marquess of Salisbury, Hatfield House.

that Shakespeare's contemporaries no longer knew what an ermine looked like and massively underestimated the number slain to line a monarch's gown. But for queens who were also mothers, like Hermione and Queen Anna, the ermine represents a problematic ideal, epitomizing the double bind of female sexuality. Leontes seems to be conducting a sadistic experiment in which he forces his wife to emulate his pet name for her and regain her chastity after pregnancy by dying like an ermine. Given Shakespeare's interest in geo-humoral psychology and Richard Dyer's observations on hierarchies within whiteness, the ermine pun is particularly charged in the mouth of a Sicilian, betraying his sense of Hermione's otherness. In early modern geo-humoral theory, a marriage between a Sicilian and a Russian would be categorized as a cross-racial relationship almost on the level of Othello and Desdemona.[15] A Christian Eurocentric tendency to construe whiteness as purity infects Leontes with an insecurity about his own whiteness, driving him to 'sully / the purity and whiteness of [his] sheets' (1.2.324–5) and tarnish his wife's reputation so he can remove the ermine furs that act like a dermal prosthesis and magnify her whiteness. Although there is, to my knowledge, no extant portrait of James's Danish queen posing with an ermine like Elizabeth or Da Vinci's *Lady with an Ermine*, it is curious that Anna's wardrobe inventory reveals a marked preference for white and includes an ermine surcoat and ermine-trimmed gown.[16] In the cultural context of the Elizabethan revival at the Stuart court, *The Winter's Tale* seems to warn the audience against judging the current married queen by the virginal purity of her predecessor.[17] A material ecofeminist reading of it might suggest that it dramatizes how an unhealthy obsession with purity harms women, non-whites, and non-humans.

Seeing Hermione as ermine-like changes the optics of the play and helps us perceive whiteness in *The Winter's Tale* as 'a multispecies sensory process' (Yates 2013, 85) derived (in the absence of artificial snow on stage) from the cruel material practices of the fur trade.[18] The transspecies quibble furnishes further proof of the play's investment in 'indistinction' via 'zoomorphic blendings' that elicit 'sympathy for a suffering fellow creature' (Höfele 2011, 38). Valuing hybridity over purity, Shakespearean romance generates an epistemological openness in which the spectacle of treating humans like animals might enable us to recognize our treatment of other animals as inhumane. In light of the entry for an ermine gown in *Henslowe's Diary*, it seems a virtual certainty that the King's Men owned a similar garment—probably a downmarket imitation in which the black spots or 'powders' were actually bodgy shanks cut from the legs of black lambs—and highly likely that Hermione wore it in the opening scenes only to be disrobed during her trial. When combined with repeated references to Hermione as a 'creature' (1.2.448, 3.2.198, 3.3.18) with a 'white hand' (1.2.103) and white robes, and the description of the undressing Florizel as 'half-flayed' (4.4.645), Shakespeare's wordplay invites the audience to imagine the queen as a humanoid ermine and the treason trial 'i'th' open air' (3.2.103) that strips her of her title and hence her exclusive right to wear ermine—as happened to Anne Boleyn—as a figurative skinning.[19] No wonder she supposedly dies as a result. Paulina accuses the tyrannical Leontes of this exact torment while daring him to do the same to her: 'what flaying?' (3.2.173). Like some unfortunate victims of the fur trade, Hermione has been flayed alive.[20]

Playing the Bear

While ermine was a luxurious badge of purity and royalty, furs from other species might bristle instead with sub-human savagery. In adaptations of medieval and early modern romances, fur would help radiate the wildness of the so-called 'wild men'. Bremio wears fur in *Mucedorus*; in the prose tale of *Valentine and Orson* (the basis of a lost play), Orson's skin is said to become hirsute like that of the she-bear who suckles him; and the earliest record of Caliban's costume states he was traditionally clad 'in a large bearskin or the skin of some other animal' (Malone 1821, 15:13). Thanks to the vogue for fine silk and velvet, large fur gowns had declined in popularity in the sixteenth-century (Veale 1966, 156), and would thus have been perceived as a throwback from a less refined, medieval era. On the Renaissance stage, however, that would have contributed to fur's appeal. Donning fur would have helped actors like Alleyn to channel a primal fury, creating spectacles to rival the baiting pit by simulating the charisma and ferocity of an apex predator. Similarly, the furs worn by a hunter would be a badge of prowess and courage. The 'lyone skin' in the Admiral's property inventory, for example, would have been worn by Alleyn in his role as Hercules—'a part to tear a cat in' (1.2.25) in Bottom's recollection—in a lost play that probably re-enacted the human-driven extirpation of the European lion from its once common range in Greece. In Shakespeare's *King John*, the Duke of Austria likewise appears in a lion's skin, but the enraged Constance impugns his courage by heckling him instead to 'hang a calfskin on those recreant limbs' (3.1.55), a taunt gleefully echoed by Philip the Bastard. Furred gowns and animal skins, then, were more than merely passive objects but might exude a bestializing influence, in accordance with the sixteenth-century Swedish writer Olaus Magnus's observation that people who sleep under wolverine-fur blankets 'have dreams that agree with the nature of that creature, and have an insatiable stomach...and seem never to be satisfied' (1555, 180). Strangely, a commodity responsible for de-wilding a large swathe of the planet's remaining wilderness might function on stage as an instrument of psychological rewilding.

Fur's species-blurring power would have been particularly evident in the Renaissance bear play, a genre that enjoyed greater popularity on the Renaissance stage than many theatre historians realize.[21] *Henslowe's Diary* mentions a number of lost plays that almost certainly featured ursine encounters. In the absence of extant texts, any claims about the contents of these plays are perforce speculative. However, an examination of the likely sources for their plots combined with an understanding of repertorial practices does permit some responsible conjectures: in this case, that audiences at the Rose in the late 1590s would have been repeatedly treated to the spectacle of humanoid bears, and that fur functioned in these productions as a vehicle for trans-speciesism, which in some ways is as important for animal studies as transvestism is for gender studies. If cross-dressing in Renaissance drama betrays the performative nature of gender, animal impersonation might enable a fleeting perception of what Erica Fudge calls 'dressing up as human' (2004, 61).

Based on a popular medieval French romance first translated around 1510, *Valentine and Orson* had been the subject of a play staged by the Queen's Men which the Admiral's company either acquired or adapted in 1598 (*HD* 93). It seems a reasonable supposition that the lost play would have included the dramatic episode of the birth of the twin brothers in the woods, and Orson's abduction by a she-bear. Given the bearskin listed in the Admiral's inventory, such a scene would not have been beyond their technical means. It is even possible that the actor playing Orson (whose name means bear in French) would have worn some kind of hirsute suit since the prose romance declares that the abandoned child was naked and, 'by reason of the nutriment it received from the beare, became rough all over like a beast' (1555, L3^r).

A bear may also have lumbered across the Rose stage in *Chinon of England*, performed as a new play by the Admiral's Men on 3 January 1596, and staged fourteen times during that year (*HD* 33–54). Although the text is lost, an extant prose romance with this title from 1597 recounts how a sorceress transformed a character named Bessarian into a bear and hung a parchment around his neck promising to grant the wishes of whoever slays the beast. Despite losing his ability to speak, Bessarian retains the capacity to reason and think. If this episode figured in the lost play, it would have confronted audiences with another ursine-human hybrid.

A person trapped in a bear's body may also have featured in *The Arcadian Virgin*, for which Henry Chettle and William Haughton were paid an advance of 15 shillings by Henslowe in December 1599 (*HD* 128).[22] W. W. Greg speculated that it was based on the tale of Atalanta, who was abandoned as an infant (like Perdita) and suckled by a she-bear (like Orson). However, the eponymous virgin could just as plausibly have been Callisto, whose tale (which reveals the shared etymological derivation of Arcadia and Arctic from the Greek for bear) would have been well known from Ovid's *Metamorphoses*.[23] A maiden devotee of the goddess Phoebe, Callisto is raped by Jove and then transformed by a jealous Juno into a bear. Ovid makes it clear that Callisto retains her human consciousness, and even her fear of other wild beasts: 'for though she were a Bear, / Yet when she spied other Beares she quooke for verie paine' (2.611–12). This play may never have been staged—as Henslowe does not record any additional payments to the two authors—but the advance nevertheless suggests that the Admiral's Men thought ursine impersonation would still make good box office in 1599, and the fact that sexual jealousy imprisons Callisto in bear form for sixteen years before her reunion with her son presents a curious parallel with Hermione's separation from Perdita.

Whether or not *The Arcadian Virgin* was ever performed, a bear of some sort certainly did traipse across the Rose stage in another lost play entitled *Cox of Collumpton*. The astrologer-physician Simon Forman attended a performance of it on 9 March 1600 and jotted down a memorandum of how Cox's two wicked sons Peter and John were driven to suicide:

> For peter being *fronted wth the sight of a bear viz a sprite* apering to Jhon & him when they sate vpon deuisio^n of the land^{es} in *likenes* of a bere & ther wth peter fell out of his wites and way lyed in a darke house & beat out his braines against a post & Jhon stabed him self.   (MS Ashmole 236, f. 77v, italics added)

Forman's notation implies that the performance somehow telegraphed that the bear was not merely a bear. Does 'likenes' mean animal-skin and 'sprite' a human actor?

While Forman's record of *The Winter's Tale* (which he saw at the Globe in May 1611) curiously fails to mention a bear, other evidence proves that Shakespeare's troupe sought to capitalize on this crowd-wowing spectacle. Judging by the number of reprintings, the most popular play in early modern England was not by Shakespeare or Marlowe. It was the anonymous *Mucedorus*, first performed around 1590 and reprinted seventeen times between 1598 and 1668.[24] When the King's Men revived the play around 1610 at Whitehall before King James, the bear scene was expanded, perhaps—if Grant and Ravelhofer are correct—to incorporate one of the polar bear cubs brought back by Poole. In the 1610 Quarto, the bear trots on stage and startles a buffoon named Mouse, whose comic monologue seems to offer tantalizing clues as to how the scene may have been performed:

> Was ever poor gentlemen so scared out of his seven senses? A bear? Nay, sure it cannot be a bear, but some devil in a bear's doublet: for a bear could never have had that agility to have frighted me.   (2.2–3)[25]

Taken literally, this reference to the 'bear's doublet' seems a retrospective hint that the staging involved an actor in a bearskin. As a clown character, however, Mouse must be regarded as an unreliable narrator, and the comedy or dramatic irony would be enhanced if the audience saw an actual bear. The phrase might even conceivably refer to a human garment worn as a twee costume by a performing bear and then fitted over a bearskin concealing a human. In other words, there are no clear-cut answers, and the revisions to *Mucedorus* indicate that Renaissance theatre companies may have staged the same scene a number of different ways, depending on the venue, audience, and properties or animal performers available.[26] Mouse's confusion may be comic, but it also encapsulates the predicament of theatre historians, unable to strip away the fur to determine what lies beneath.

Even when the play-text survives, the performance of the bear is in some ways 'lost'—and this is not necessarily a cause for regret. Theatre historians attempting to establish with certainty how bear scenes must have been staged do so in violation of the moral embedded in Renaissance romance about the inextricable entanglement of nature and art. As Andrew Gurr (1983) shrewdly observes, even 'real' trained bears are not the same thing as wild bears, or the King's Men might need a new Antigonus for every performance. Although some of the evidence is circumstantial, this survey of the Renaissance bear play indicates that the theatre of Shakespeare's day frequently sought to revel in confusion by presenting ursine-human hybrids, and this confusion would encourage Jacobean audiences to perceive the ermine-like Hermione as zoomorphic. With this in mind, modern productions of *The Winter's Tale* in which the actor playing the horn-mad and lion-like Leontes doubles as the bear are faithful to the Renaissance sense of the precariousness of the animal-human boundary.[27] The point is not that there is one 'right way' to stage the bear scene. Rather than presume a bear costume would be comic and a real bear tragic, we might accept hybridity and aporia as inbuilt features of Shakespeare's tragicomedy, since performances in which it is unclear if one is 'supposed' to recognize the actor underneath the animal skin (or perceive a trained bear as a wild bear) can generate a salutary wonder by suspending audiences in Agamben's 'Open'.

In a passage from *The Open* of particular interest to early modernists, Agamben expounds how the 'anthropological machine' of previous eras sought to produce a 'non-man' by imagining the *homo ferus* and the *enfant sauvage* as animals in human form (2004, 37–8). Antigonus invokes this motif of the feral child when he wishes for a wild animal to adopt Perdita:

> Some powerful spirit instruct the kites and ravens
> To be thy nurses. Wolves and bears, they say,
> Casting their savageness aside, have done
> Like offices of pity.
>
> (2.3.184–7)

Adhering to its source, *The Winter's Tale* dramatizes the nature/nurture conflict in terms of social class rather than species. Nevertheless, Shakespeare's introduction of the bear, the shepherd's pronunciation of 'bairn' (3.3.68), and the wrapping of Perdita in a '*bear*ing cloth' (3.3.112, italics added) make her an honorary cub, creating a strange parallel between her and the orphaned polar bears.[28] Cross-species nurture, however, is central to the Valentine and Orson tale staged by the Queen's Men and Admiral's Men since the courtly knight Valentine and wild man Orson do not realize they are brothers. Only after they save one another's lives is it revealed that they were separated at birth, and the recognition scene effectively enacts Donna Haraway's notion of 'making kin' (2016) across species.[29] Of course, Orson is not really a bear but an abandoned human, just as the stage bear who abducts him may be a human dressed in bearskin. But the virtue of Agamben's 'Open' is that it demands we suspend such distinctions. In this regard, it resembles the recovery in early modern romance of an epistemological innocence or poetic faith in which the audience suspends disbelief in the separation of human culture and non-human nature. Long before Agamben and Coleridge, *The Winter's Tale* furnishes evidence that Shakespeare's contemporaries had begun to regard such innocence as the fortunate lot of the child.

Perdita, Princess Elizabeth, and the Ecology of Rural Girlhood

Trained animals and animal skins were not the only inhuman performers on the Renaissance stage. Infants like the abandoned Perdita would have been impersonated by swaddled dolls or cloth bundles (Higginbotham 2013, 104). The overlap is suggestive; since both animals and infants seem devoid of language, realist art and rationalist philosophy relegate them outside of history. On the authority of Aristotle, Renaissance pedagogues regarded children as closer to animals than mature adults.[30] In the vision of young Polixenes and Leontes as 'twinned lambs that did frisk i'th sun' / And bleat (1.2.67–8), *The Winter's Tale* also aligns childhood and child's play with the animal condition. But Shakespeare's romance proves less like Aristotle's and more like Agamben's philosophy in redeeming the child's alleged ignorance as a state of epistemological grace. It turns out the Romantic idealization of the child as closer to nature enshrined by Wordsworth was already emerging at the Stuart court in the figure of James's daughter, the Princess Elizabeth. If Shakespeare pays tribute to young Henry and Charles in *Cymbeline*, it is equally conceivable that Perdita compliments Elizabeth, the intended bride of the future king of Bohemia. Although Frederick was not officially crowned until 1619, rumours that he would obtain this elective monarchy were circulating at least by 1612 (and possibly earlier in order to placate objections that the princess would be marrying beneath her), and there is a distinct possibility that the Folio text of *The Winter's Tale* incorporates revisions for a court performance at the 1613 Palatine wedding.[31] That a play featuring a marriage between a princess and a prince of Bohemia was performed at a wedding between a princess and the presumed prince of Bohemia may be an astonishing coincidence, or it could be further evidence of a marked tendency of the leading playwright of the King's Men to capitalize on public interest in court politics.[32]

A connection between Elizabeth Stuart and Perdita becomes all the more compelling in light of the Princess's bucolic childhood, which appears to have shaped the romance's environmental poetics. After James' accession in 1603, he sent his 7-year-old daughter to live in Shakespeare's home county of Warwickshire at Coombe Abbey, which her custodians, John and Anne Harington of Exton, re-landscaped for her amusement. A vivid portrait of the princess as a young girl can be found in the *Memoirs relating to the Queen of Bohemia*. This undated text attributed to one of Elizabeth's ladies-in-waiting appears to have been written down in the eighteenth-century by Frances Erskine but was 'evidently based on stories and accounts handed down in the Erskine family', intimate associates of James and the Stuart children, and is largely 'confirmed by contemporary accounts' (Lewalski 1993, 17).[33] According to Erskine, the princess took a particular delight in 'a little Wilderness at the End of the Park' (n.d. 112), and an island adorned with trees and plants 'so well mixed and disposed that for nine Months in the Year, they formed a continual Spring' (113). Elizabeth also developed a passion for animals, which her guardians indulged by constructing what was essentially a petting zoo and a giant aviary. The princess 'was extremely fond of all the feathered Tribe…and she now formed the Design of collecting in this little Paradise, all the different Kinds that are in Nature' (113). She also cultivated her own garden and greenhouse 'well stored with Curiosities and exotic Plants' (114), which may have prompted Shakespeare to include Perdita's floral catalogue as it prompted her husband to commission the Hortus Palatinus at Heidelberg as a wedding present. Elizabeth also studied country dancing, which *The Winter's Tale* showcases in the dance between shepherds and shepherdesses (4.4.167). Although her father forbade her to learn Latin, Harington regaled her with lectures in 'natural philosophy' in the vernacular. First printed around the time of Rousseau's *Emile*, the *Memoirs* may be embellished to reflect Rousseau's portrait of the child as noble ecologist (stress on noble), but bears comparison with *The Winter's Tale* in that both texts transfigure the childhood of a Stuart princess into a pastoral romance to glorify the child's pure relation to nature.[34]

Jennifer Munroe (2011) has shown that *The Winter's Tale* draws on the gendered discourses of early modern husbandry and housewifery to pit a macho ethos of dominance against a feminist ethos of care, the latter voiced in Perdita's censure of grafting as a violation of 'great creating Nature' (4.4.88). A similar divide evidently existed in the gender-based education of the Stuart children. Whereas her brothers were schooled in Latin and the bloody ritual of the hunt, Elizabeth's guardian taught her to 'admire the beauties of Creation' in the belief it 'enlarges the Mind and the Heart' (114), encouraging her to tend flowers and care for animals.[35] On one level, this is of course highly objectionable, and the *Memoirs* present a valuable reminder that nature education which discriminates by gender might reinforce inequalities and disqualify women from influential public professions. But insofar as the hunt enacts masculine domination of the wild, Princess Elizabeth's education in natural philosophy seems more aligned with contemporary eco-pedagogy, raising caveats with Chapter 4's reading of the upbringing of the Welsh princes in *Cymbeline*. Furthermore, Erskine was only doing for Elizabeth Stuart what her contemporaries like Thomas Gray were doing for Shakespeare, whose own Warwickshire childhood and supposed lack of classical languages would be hailed as the well-springs of his genius and prompt his admirers to apotheosize him as the 'Poet of Nature'.

More to the point, Shakespeare, himself the father of two daughters raised in the countryside, peddles a similar myth by transforming, like a fairy godmother in reverse, the Stuart princess into something resembling the 'Faire and happy Milke-mayd' in Overbury's *Characters*. Just as the milkmaid rejects artifice such as 'face Physicke' (1616, I4^v) and luxurious dress, preferring the plain dress of 'innocence' and the 'Physicke' afforded by her garden and beehive (I5^v), Perdita dismisses cosmetics, grafted flowers, and her 'borrowed flaunts' (4.4.23). Shakespeare's lively shepherdess who speaks of milking her ewes invites comparison with the milkmaid who, as a result of her rural upbringing amongst animals, owns a 'heart soft with pittie' (I5^r) and a mind unclouded by jealousy. In its vision of a country lass for whom the 'golden eares of corne fall and kiss her feete when she reaps them' (I5^r), this character sketch confirms what *The Winter's Tale* and

The Memoirs relating to the Queen of Bohemia suggest: that Stuart England had begun to revere girlhood as a state of prelapsarian intimacy with nature. Jaded as we are by the excesses of the Victorian child cult, it is easy to sneer at this sentimentality. The Overbury milkmaid represents an urban male fantasy of a 'country wench'. Nevertheless, Shakespeare's Perdita illustrates why some ecofeminists might find the figure of the child shepherdess or eco-girl, despite her drawbacks, too powerful a chess piece not to play. Exemplifying Erskine's balance of mind and heart, Perdita has enough book learning to invoke Proserpina, but her knowledge of herbs, flowers, birds, and the seasons—the 'Daffodils / That come before the swallow dares and take / The winds of March with beauty' (4.4.118–20)—bespeaks an ecological literacy which Munroe and other ecofeminist scholars seek to reclaim.

Putting an ecofeminist twist on Agamben's theorization of childhood as a state of epistemological purity helps to clarify why *The Winter's Tale* disparages the adult male intellect whilst predicating its comic resolution on the recovery of the lost daughter. In *Infancy and History*, Agamben proposes that the fairy tale operates by inverting categorical distinctions to narrativize language acquisition as a 'natural' development of signifying powers human infants share with other creatures rather than a rupture with the animal condition. The bewitched human subject is dumbstruck and plunged 'back into the mute language of nature' while beasts can speak so that 'man [sic] and nature exchange roles before each finds their own place in history' (1993, 61). In the tragic half of *The Winter's Tale*, Paulina appreciates that 'the silence often of pure innocence / Persuades when speaking fails' (2.2.40–1) but Leontes is deaf to the child. Only after his reunion with Perdita does he stop ranting and learn to express 'speech in...dumbness, language in...gesture' (5.2.14–15). The sight of his wife's image leaves him dumbstruck again, restored to 'infancy and grace' (5.3.27), while the seemingly non-human comes to life and speaks. Leontes's experience of 'wonder' (5.3.22) anticipates Agamben's 'open', as the climax of the play hurls him and the audience back into the child's quasi-mystic state described in Thomas Traherne's 'Dumbness', in which the poet finds in 'ev'ry Stone and ev'ry Star a Tongue'.[36]

In Shakespeare's fairy-tale like romance, culture and nature exchange places as Agamben outlines but the play privileges the role of women as mediators. When the shepherd searching for lost sheep discovers a 'child' (and reminds us that child meant 'girl' in early modern rural dialects), the Bohemian scenes begin the recuperation of the lamb-like innocence lost by Polixenes and Leontes. Drawing a correlation between the bear suit and body suit with prosthetic bump that performs Hermione's child-bearing, Maureen Quilligan hints that the play recognizes women as more keenly conscious of the shared embodiment between humans and other species. This makes the labelling of Hermione and Perdita as 'creature[s]' sound less demeaning. The allusions to protracted sleep and post-partum confinement—Hermione's 'childbed privilege' (3.2.10)—evoke ursine hibernation (wintering) and the pun on mammal in Mamillius figures the child's nearness to the animal in terms of maternal nurture. If the rechristening of *Pandosto*'s Bellaria as Hermione transforms her into an ermine, the source's name for the Perdita character, Fawnia, would prime Shakespeare to see her as an epitome of girlhood's doe-eyed innocence.[37] Leontes, in contrast, may be unwittingly lion-like in his attempted infanticide but recoils in terror at the thought of himself as a horned, bestial cuckold. Moreover, his abstruse, Latinate language, the subject of much critical commentary, betrays his Latin education and is appropriately triggered by the male mind's frustrated exclusion from the biological mysteries of pregnancy. Hermione's bafflement—'you speak a language that I understand not' (3.2.78)—is not an indictment of her intelligence but of Leontes's mental estrangement from the phenomenal world that envelops the child and frisking lamb. His exclamations that if he is mistaken, 'then all the world and all that's in't is nothing' (1.2.291) and that the 'centre' or earth 'is not big enough to bear / A schoolboy's top' (2.1.102–3) further illustrate his detachment from both the earth and child's play. While reproving Leontes's desire to probe and control his wife's fertility (associated with gardens and fish ponds), Shakespeare's play also questions the adult male's dream of controlling the environment in Perdita's critique of grafting, instead praising the power of dramatic art to recapture a lost equilibrium between nature and culture. *The Winter's Tale* thus not only attempts to resolve the conflicts of *Othello* but also, through the vicarious recovery of a puerile epistemology, to repair the alienation from nature that vexes *As You Like It* (Watson 2006, 77–107) by temporarily recuperating a state of 'infancy and grace' (5.3.27).

As helpful as Agamben's theories are for illuminating the 'openness' shared by the animal and infant, the preceding pages make it clear why they should be ballasted by a consideration of socio-historical conditions pertaining to gender and class. The girl's proximity to nature is not so much biologically engrained as a side-effect of a patriarchal society that denied women access to Latin education and hence philosophy and logic, which supposedly nurtured the capacity for abstract thought. Adroitly dissecting beliefs about the sexed brain in Shakespeare's day, Caroline Bicks argues that Renaissance culture nonetheless endowed adolescent girls with distinct cognitive abilities (2021, 4), which Shakespeare's youthful heroines like Perdita flex to resist the patriarchal programming of their minds and bodies. The embodied mind of the infant or pre-pubescent girl, however, proves much more difficult to scan on stage by an adult male poet whose medium is words.[38] No wonder the play leaps over Perdita's bairn-hood. Shakespeare, as William Empson notes of Lewis Carroll, 'will only go half-way with the sentiment of the child's unity to nature' (1974, 262) by insisting that it must be outgrown and is less becoming in some than others. Several characters remark that Perdita's noble comportment distinguishes her from the peasantry and the play contrasts her with her simpleton foster brother, whose moniker 'Clown' derives from clod and hence smells of closeness to the soil. Autolycus parodies the patronizing courtier but the play invites us to share in his mockery of the Bohemian peasantry, not least for their child-like credulity in believing preposterous ballads: 'Yet Nature might have made me as these are. Therefore I will not disdain' (4.4.750). Meanwhile, the bickering of the milkmaids Dorcas and Mopsa reveals that the countryside is not void of sexual jealousy: *et in Arcadia ego*. Erskine's *Memoirs* remind us that Coombe Abbey was not the 'real' countryside but a pastoral simulacrum like Marie Antoinette's *hameau de la reine* at Versailles and the same goes for Perdita's Bohemia. Like Spenser's depiction of her namesake Queen Elizabeth as queen of shepherds, Shakespeare's fanciful portrait of James's daughter as 'queen of curds and cream' (4.4.161) has an ideological gleam. Agamben's theories help explain *The Winter's Tale*'s enduring appeal, but situating the play in its courtly context enables us to see Shakespeare's pastoral romance as an imperial romance. Although far less crude than subsequent specimens of the genre like *Tarzan*, it features a feral princess motif that naturalizes the rule of the court over the country, enabling colonial power to gain knowledge of the wild periphery and claim it as a birthright. The imperial romance would have been particularly evident when staged before the Stuart court in 1613, not only binding Warwickshire to London but also promoting favourable views of Bohemia as a future outpost of Great Britain through the marriage of Elizabeth and Frederick. The play pays tribute to Elizabeth's faux wilderness, country dances, botanical garden, and royal menagerie, all of which impose order on nature. Nevertheless, in comparison to *Cymbeline* and the violent masculine ritual of the hunt, *The Winter's Tale* and Elizabeth's 'fairy farm' exhibit a semi-benign mode of environmental sovereignty, and this will become even clearer when juxtaposed with the cruel spectacles of the fur trade, to which I now turn.

The Skinners' Pageant: The Triumph as Anthropological Machine

If pastoral romance dreams of healing the rupture between humans and nature, that rupture was exalted in a peculiar form of urban street theatre in Jacobean London known as the Skinners' pageant, an 'anthropological machine' in which the animal/human distinction is re-forged with a vengeance. All of London's livery companies organized entertainments to celebrate the elevation of one of their members to Lord Mayor, but the Skinners in particular would have relished the occasion since luxurious furs conspicuously adorn the ceremonial gown of office. While the Lord Mayor's show is one of the best-known examples of civic theatre in Renaissance England, there has been little inquiry into the role of fur in these processions or to the distinctive characteristics of the Skinners' pageant in particular. One of the most interesting specimens of this neglected sub-genre is Thomas Middleton's grotesquely mistitled *The Triumphs of Love and Antiquity*, composed for the installation of the skinner Sir William Cockayn as Lord Mayor in 1619. After floating down the Thames, the procession disembarked and marched to the yard around St Paul's Cathedral, where it encountered:

> a Wilderness, most gracefully and artfully furnished with diverse kinds of Beasts bearing Fur, proper to the Fraternity; the Presenter, the Musical Orpheus, Great Master, both in Poesy and Harmony, who by his excellent Music, drew after him wild Beasts, Woods, and Mountains. (*TMCW* l.105–9)

Curiously, Agamben's theory of 'the Open' is derived (via Heidegger) from Rilke's meditations on Orpheus as a posterchild for poetry's 'pure relation' with nature. In contrast, Middleton's Orpheus signifies mastery over the environment. While Middleton likens the Greek musician to a 'wise magistrate' (l.163)—no wonder King James compared himself to Orpheus—and the wilderness to an unruly commonwealth, it is the fur merchant's dominion over animals that the performance brandishes as a qualification and exemplum for his rule as Lord Mayor. In a visual pun, Cockayn is represented in the pageant as an 'artificial cock', who, unlike the fur-bearing beasts over whom he perches, has the power to speak and command. Of course, Middleton, too, possesses this Orphic power. Orpheus's ability to move plants and beasts allies the poet-playwright and set designer with the forces of global commerce, and this conjuring of wilderness to London duplicates the magic of the early modern fur trade to transport the animals' pelts.

A similar scenario unfolds in Thomas Dekker's *Britannia's Honor*, which celebrates the inauguration of the new Lord Mayor of London, Richard Deane, who was both a skinner and an investor in the Muscovy Company.[39] The Muscovy Company's import privileges had just been renewed in 1628 when Dekker composed this puff-piece advertising to a Russian embassy the robust demand for fur in England. A Russian prince and princess actually appear in the pageant, followed by an English Lord, Lady, Judge, University Doctor, Frau, and Skipper, all clad in various animal pelts to illustrate 'the necessary, ancient, and general use of Furs, from the highest to the lowest' (B3^v). Dekker's master of ceremonies is a personification of Fame, who salutes the Russian royalty and proclaims, 'Russia now envies London, seeing here spent / Her richest Furs, in graceful ornament' (B3^v). Like Middleton's pageant, *Britannia's Honor* concludes with a tableau, like a portable diorama from a natural history museum, of a 'wilderness in which are many sorts of such beasts, whose rich skins serve for furs': the lynx, wolf, leopard, fox, sable, rabbits, ferrets, and squirrels, 'some climbing, some standing, some grinning, in lively, natural postures' (C2^r).

In the twenty-first century, when the Lord Mayor and even the queen (as of 2019) have renounced the use of real fur in ceremonial dress, it is hard to imagine a fur-themed fashion show including an exhibition of its victims. What made such a spectacle acceptable to a seventeenth-century audience? One possible explanation is that while modern fur companies might publicize that they have raised the animals humanely, the aim of the Skinners' pageant is to dramatize that the animals are inhuman, and thus ineligible for moral concern. Dekker speaks of the usefulness of various furs in 'distinguishings' (B4[r]) of rank, but the primary distinguishing here is between human and beast. While it would be tempting to compare these furrier pageants to Renaissance fashion shows, both Middleton and Dekker explicitly model them on a far more vicious form of street theatre: the Roman triumph.[40] Middleton includes the word Triumph in the title, while Dekker's fur-clad Russian dignitaries sit like military conquerors in 'a Chariot Triumphant' drawn by two lynxes, a species that features, along with the sable and ermine, on the Skinners' coat of arms. In Roman victory processions, prisoners of war and spoils of conquest—including exotic animals destined for the gladiatorial circus—would be paraded through the streets, and this is precisely the degraded condition of the pageant's fur-bearers, whose abjection recalls that of the Goths in *Titus Andronicus* or the defeated kings hitched to the chariot in Marlowe's *Tamburlaine*. The scene enacts human dominance, a triumph not of love but of absolutist tyranny.

This casts the spectacle of the orphaned polar bear cubs towing Prince Henry's chariot in *Oberon* in a much more sinister light. Musing on the presence of live polar bears in Jonson's masque, Ravelhofer views them as proof that 'Stuart princes and monarchs are demonstrably capable of conjuring up flesh-and-blood fabulous animals and controlling them' (2002, 308), and the same might be said to a lesser extent of Princess Elizabeth's menagerie at Coombe Abbey.[41] In an article on *The Winter's Tale*'s traffic with Russia, Daryl Palmer interprets the bear as a symbol of Russian tyranny, arguing the play invites the audience 'to imagine that courtly capacities for envy and cruelty belonged to old tales from faraway lands of winter' (1995, 33). But the romance's allusions to the fur trade hint that tyranny and cruelty still flourish and much closer to home. Although the imperialist dream of James and the Muscovy Company to establish a British protectorate along the shores of the White Sea failed to materialize, these triumphs provide the next best thing, asserting Britain's hegemony over the region and its wildlife. The Skinners' pageant annexes the wilds of Canada and northwest Russia into the transnational empire of the global fur-trade, which would gradually decimate the very ecosystems here surreally carted down the streets of London in a bizarre spectacle that prefigures the subjugation of the Arctic in the Anthropocene.

The tableau of beasts in 'lively, natural postures' might elicit the same epistemological uncertainty as Hermione's statue in her 'natural posture' (5.3.23). Criticism has tended to view the statue in terms of Pygmalion-inspired erotica, recusant nostalgia for Marian icons, and hydraulic garden statuary.[42] But taxidermy was an emergent art in early modern Europe that inspired awe and longing with its quasi-miraculous power to overcome decay and loss. Renaissance naturalists like

Conrad Gesner, the son of a furrier, experimented with preservation techniques for animal specimens: scraping out their innards, rubbing their skins with salts and oils, and stuffing them with wool.[43] Shakespeare was familiar with these animal-objects; the décor in the apothecary's shop in *Romeo and Juliet* includes a 'tortoise hung, / An alligator stuffed, and other skins / of ill-shaped fishes' (5.1.42–4). When one of the lion cubs at the Tower died in 1605 it was stuffed and presented to the king (Grigson 2016, 44), while a 1607–11 inventory of the royal Wunderkammer of Rudolf II of Bohemia (Queen Anna's brother-in-law) lists a large number of taxidermic sculptures curated by his court painter.[44] The 'many singularities' (5.3.12) Leontes admires in Paulina's gallery before approaching the statue would conceivably have included exotic animal specimens in 'natural postures'.

It seems eerily apt that an ermine surcoat and ermine-trimmed gown were draped on Queen Anna's effigy at her funeral in 1619 (Murray 2020, 30). Did the sight of the dead queen's statue stir uneasy recollections of a certain play performed at court six years earlier? If Jacobean audiences imagined Hermione as ermine-like, or if furs (credited with vivifying powers) adorned her statue on stage, her resurrection might entail the miraculous reanimating of not just marble but a skinned animal that mimics yet upstages the art of early modern taxidermy. *The Winter's Tale*'s ending thus satisfies the yearnings that taxidermy provokes since, to state the obvious, the dramatis personae of the Skinners' triumph do not revive. Like taxidermy and baiting, the triumph only endows animals with what Agamben calls 'bare life'—an existence that has no political or legal status—whereas Renaissance romance revels in 'the Open' and (pardon the unavoidable pun) 'bear life'. Paradoxically, an anthropomorphic ermine or a human dressed in a bearskin may have helped dramatize what contemporary ecocritics would term the 'animacy' and subjecthood of the animal better than a 'real' ermine, tame bear, or fur-clad automaton could.

Whether or not a polar bear had a cameo in *The Winter's Tale*, watching the play did not persuade James to renounce his ermine robes, forswear animal baitings, or oppose the plot to annex northwest Russia. Shakespeare harboured no such specific, activist intentions and probably wore fur himself. Although he often questions the king's proprietary attitude towards the natural world, whatever ecological wisdom his plays afford is defined either within or against the constraints of his time and place. This is a sobering reminder that there are limitations even to Shakespeare's art and that ecocritics should look beyond his work and beyond English literature to understand how other cultures represented and interacted with the environment in the global Renaissance.

In this spirit, it would be illuminating to triangulate the Skinners' pageant and *The Winter's Tale* with the ceremonial use of bearskins by the Indigenous people of the Ural region known as the Khanty, who in the early seventeenth century were themselves being slaughtered by Russian forces (allied with the Muscovy Company) if they refused to pay hefty fur tributes. The Khanty venerated bears and regarded killing them as sinful, something done only in self-defence or with great reluctance, and requiring ritual purification. According to early eye-witness accounts, the Khanty would set out the bearskin on an altar, beg its forgiveness, and disavow responsibility for its death:

> Then the people assemble and hold a great feast and dance around it, declaring in their songs that it was not they who were to blame for its murder... it was the Russians who had forged the iron [of the arrowhead] and the eagle who had provided the feathers. Shouting such songs, they draw nearer and nearer and kiss the extended bearskin. (Novitsky 1715; qtd in Cushing 1977, 147)

Such rituals may have served an ecological purpose in discouraging overhunting, while venting anger at the Russian imposition of outrageous fur tributes that forced them do exactly that, and were performed alongside bear plays mocking braggart hunters (Cushing 1977, 155). Without idealizing these hunters and trappers as noble ecologists, I would argue their reverence for fur as more than a mere commodity bespeaks an animistic epistemology that clashes with the Skinners' pageant (for which they may have reluctantly supplied the pelts) and Western modernity but which Shakespearean romance seeks to recover with its evocation of ancient Greek myth, pastoral childhood, and humanoid animals. Admittedly, *The Winter's Tale* focuses on the husband's atonement for his cruelty to his wife rather than human atonement for animal cruelty. Nor does Shakespeare allow the bear to speak as the Khanty songs do: 'I range the backs of the marten-frequented forests'.[45] But the profound significance of the pun identifying Hermione as an ermine suggests that Khanty ritual and Shakespeare romance may not be as poles apart as they first appear. Acknowledging a ritualistic dimension to *The Winter's Tale* might help us perceive how the play animates fur and stone to goad us into repenting or softening our nature-culture/human-animal dualisms in the radical hope this might restore the vitality of spring to the earth. *The Winter's Tale* contrasts markedly with the Skinners' pageant in that it does not promote the spatial conquest of a far-off snowy wilderness but a temporal abiding of nature's vicissitudes and winter's bleakness, which story-telling, like cruelty-free fur, helps us to bear.

While advancing a new reading of *The Winter's Tale* this chapter has also highlighted a methodological problem with appropriating Agamben's political ontology and Latourian materialism for animal studies. If suturing the animal/human gap risks downplaying the titanic agency homo sapiens possess in the Anthropocene (not to mention the harsh consequences for minority communities demoted to sub-human status), materialist critics must also be wary of effacing the distinction between objects and animal objects, since treating animal skin as simply another material denies the sentience of the creature from which it came, threatening to duplicate the abjection of the living fur-bearer in the

Skinners' pageant. Shakespeare counteracts this abjection by tailoring a lead role in his play not to his company's personnel but to the tailoring of their wardrobe in ways that strangely reanimate and bestow dignified personhood on an ermine. In allowing us to glimpse parallels (for better and worse) between women, children, and non-human creatures, while suggesting their mistreatment by a patriarchal monarch 'something savours / Of tyranny' (2.3.117–18), the play imparts lessons that James may have disregarded but twenty-first-century civilization can no longer ignore. Only by carefully stitching together animal studies and new materialisms in ways that expose and resist the exploitation of other animals, can we do justice to the range of options for staging them in Shakespeare's day, while pursuing more ethical relations with them in our own time.

6
Caliban and the Fen-Demons of Lincolnshire
The Englishness of *The Tempest*

Since Edmond Malone first scented the presence of the Bermuda pamphlets wafting from its pages back in 1808, *The Tempest* has been increasingly framed as a play about the European encounter with the so-called 'New World'. Shakespeare's farewell to the stage was, in a neat coincidence, also 'a prologue to American literature' (1964, 72)—to quote Leo Marx's winning phrase. Aware that Shakespeare wrote the play shortly after England's first serious push to establish a colonial foothold in Virginia, commentators have documented how *The Tempest* shuttles between competing views of Caliban as either a monstrous incarnation of European stereotypes about Native Americans or a sympathetic voice for the dispossessed. By the end of the 1980s, post-colonialist theorists and creative writers had accomplished what Prospero could not: the rehabilitation of Caliban from a comic grotesque into a noble savage of almost tragic stature. It remains a critical commonplace to regard his enslavement by a Milanese Duke as a prescient exposé of the 'victimization of Third World peoples' (Vaughan and Vaughan 1991, 3).[1] So tantalizing and fruitful has this approach proven that critics have been perhaps too eager to wink at some serious caveats levied against it. In a 1989 essay Meredith Skura demonstrated that attempts to claim *The Tempest* as principally about New World colonialism were anachronistic and overblown. Likewise, Jerry Brotton has accused the post-colonial camp of spawning a 'geographically restrictive view of the play [that] overemphasize[s] the scale and significance of English involvement in the colonization of the Americas in the early decades of the seventeenth century' (1998, 24).[2]

During *The Tempest*'s travels throughout the past century of criticism, England itself has been left off the itinerary. Historicist studies have been so fixated on the horizon that they have neglected to attend to relevant developments in Shakespeare's own milieu. Duplicating the mistake of early modern colonialists, modern critics have assumed that barbarism only figures in discourse about cultural Others, thus neglecting its persistence within ostensibly civilized borders. Colonialism, however, is not exclusively an overseas enterprise. A colonial dynamic can also arise within a nation-state when the centre invades the periphery, or an urban elite seizes the communal wilds of the rural poor. What follows is an

Shakespeare Beyond the Green World: Drama and Ecopolitics in Jacobean Britain. Todd Andrew Borlik, Oxford University Press. © Todd Andrew Borlik 2023. DOI: 10.1093/oso/9780192866639.003.0007

attempt at a regional (eco)criticism of Shakespeare that resists the idea of England as a monolithic space, comprised of a single topography or homogenous populace.[3]

In the frame story of *Heart of Darkness*, Joseph Conrad imagines a Roman soldier penetrating the savage backwaters of first-century Britain: 'And this also', his narrator muses, 'has been one of the dark places of the earth' (105). By 1610, England had begun staking out its own overseas empire, but sizeable pockets of the homeland still remained undeveloped and relatively wild. As this chapter will reveal, the push to colonize Virginia was accompanied by a corresponding drive to salvage the ostensibly desolate fens of eastern England. News of the latest undertakings in the fens and rumours about the region's eerie folklore may have weighed just as much on the minds of Shakespeare's audience as the occasional sailor's tale that trickled back from halfway across the globe. Indeed, Shakespeare may have been struck by the uncanny similarities between the two.[4] If the playwright cast one eye across the Atlantic when he sketched his servant monster, his gaze also fixed upon creatures much closer to home. Specifically, I will argue that the chimera known as Caliban is in part inspired by legends of Lincolnshire fen-spirits, and that his plight comments on the displacement of local cottagers by land reclamation projects. To buttress that argument, this chapter proposes that Shakespeare drew upon colourful legends of the Anglo-Saxon hermit and fen-dweller St Guthlac, who may have featured in a lost play staged by the Admiral's Men, Shakespeare's chief rivals. In this hagiography, a learned hermit travels to a remote island surrounded by fens where he is tormented by misshapen demons, dragged through stinking pools and briars, and confronted by a murderous servant, but overcomes them with the aid of his supernatural powers.

The recovery of this neglected context for *The Tempest* does not invalidate earlier post-colonial readings of the play. On the contrary, such readings might be enriched by these findings, which also point to the play's implications for the earth-shaking projects of seventeenth-century English colonists in Ireland to drain bogs and destroy crannogs, and of Spanish conquistadors to fill in Lake Texcoco and its nearby wetlands (Giblett 2016, 19–22). Jamestown itself was surrounded by wetlands, salt marshes, and swamps, which the English settlers loathed as breeding grounds for diseases and mosquitos, and an obstacle to civilization, despite the native Algonquin co-existing with the wetlands for centuries. No less a figure than George Washington invested in the scheme to drain the revealingly named Great Dismal Swamp, and swamp-draining remains a powerful rhetorical trope in right-wing politics to this day. Colonization all too often entails—in the words of the Uruguayan author Eduardo Galeano—'the dry world wag[ing] war on the wet world' (2009, 131), and the obliteration of the English fens glanced at in *The Tempest* marks another key battle in this misguided crusade.

While recognizing the insightful contributions of post-colonial ecocritics, this chapter nonetheless suggests that Shakespeareans have for too long been mesmerized by the play's exotic allusions.[5] Although Shakespeare's global imagination could with the nimbleness of Ariel encompass Tunis, Naples, Algiers, Patagonia, and the 'still-vexed Bermudas' (1.2.229), the figurative eye of *The Tempest* swirls over England. The play does list perceptibly to the east and west, but England remains its centre of gravity. Shakespearean drama has long been regarded as a philosophical laboratory for examining the socio-political and religious conflicts of early modern culture. When Shakespeare's company staged *The Tempest* before the king in 1611, influential parties close to James were seeking his support for lucrative schemes to drain and enclose England's fens. Expanding the merely human purview of historicist and post-colonial approaches to *The Tempest* reveals that Shakespeare was also mindful of what we would now label the environmental issues of his era. In addition to re-orienting the play geographically, this chapter carves out a via media for early modern ecocriticism, balancing its presentist agenda with due attention to the environmental matrix of Shakespeare's Britain.

The historical evidence presented in this chapter may appear, admittedly, somewhat obscure or recherché. If the dots had been bunched closer together, they would have been connected long ago. Yet some degree of conjecture is, I think, warranted due to the vagaries of the documentary record. It is unavoidable when one seeks to recover material about which that record is silent or murmurs only faintly: the folk beliefs of the (largely illiterate) rural poor; the discountenanced and repressed legends of Catholic saints; the ephemeral nature of much early modern theatre (recall that approximately 80 per cent of the plays performed in Shakespeare's day never reached print). Since so much of history dissolves and leaves not a wrack behind, there are bound to be lacuna in the archive. *The Tempest* is often hailed as one of the rare instances in which Shakespeare's imagination worked free of any received plot-structures.[6] From the vista opened up by this essay, however, Prospero's famed meditation on the evanescence of things looks like a nod that Shakespeare was drawing upon sources that he sensed would not survive—and wondering in the process if his plays might suffer the same fate. To steer *The Tempest* back from the far-flung horizons where it has been moored will require some detailed exposition and speculative reconstruction. Nonetheless, when the flotsam of accrued evidence from several distant sources converges on a narrative, that narrative gathers rhetorical force. In this case, the evidence points to *The Tempest* as a confluence for several different cultural texts that have their source, as it were, in the English fens.

Into the Fens

The fen country consists of a sprawling checkerboard of low-lying wetlands in eastern England. Occupying roughly 1,300 square miles around the Wash estuary, it stretches from Hatfield Chase in Yorkshire down through Lincolnshire as far

Fig. 6.1 The Lincolnshire fens in the nineteenth century.
De Luan/Alamy Stock Photo.

south as the outskirts of Cambridge. In breadth, it extends from Peterborough and the limestone hills of the East Midlands to Boston and King's Lynn. In the early seventeenth century, the fens comprised a vast network of shallow lakes, meres, carrs, mudflats, sodden peat, and sludgy tidal creeks oozing through an archipelago of uplands called 'edges' and 'islands', which were often cut off by water in winter (see Fig. 6.1). To outsiders the fens appeared a disease-infested, brackish brown morass, peopled by uncouth cottagers and—according to local legend—grotesque bogeys. With the prices for farmland soaring in the midst of a population boom, it seemed remiss to let so much nutrient-rich land lie 'idle'. In Shakespeare's lifetime, developers (known as 'projectors' or 'undertakers') proposed a number of ambitious but controversial hydro-engineering projects to 'reclaim' and enclose these wetlands. To the thousands of cottagers whose families had lived there for centuries, however, the fens were home. Its stores of thatch and sedge provided a modest livelihood; its peat offered a ready supply of fuel; its grasslands, when dry, were ideal for seasonal grazing; and its lakes and streams teemed with fish, eel, and waterfowl.

From Anglo-Saxon to Victorian times, the fens were also the habitat of far more exotic fauna: goblins, water-sprites, and demons galore. Wild landscapes are the favourite abodes of such beings in part because these inhuman creatures incarnate the inhospitality of the land itself to human dwelling. Just as medieval and Renaissance cartographers doodled serpentine sea-beasts in the uncharted expanses of the ocean, their contemporaries imagined the fens as inhabited by a host of ungodly boggards. Monsters breed in the blank spaces of the map. In *Waterland*, Graham Swift's 1983 novel set in this region, the narrator's observation that 'the bare and empty Fens yield so readily to the imaginary—and the supernatural' (18) is borne out by his father claiming to have seen 'marsh sprites' and 'will-o'-the-wisps'—in 1922. Although *Waterland* is a work of historical fiction, reports of similar sightings recur in the lore of the fenlands, and can be found among the earliest written records of them.

Not all monsters of course are indiscriminately vicious. If newcomers to the fens heard the howls of demons in the cries of waterfowl like the bittern's boom or the cacophonous honks (known as 'gabble ratchets') of wild geese passing overhead at night, residents who learned to co-exist with this environment might imagine it as inhabited by benign spirits of place. A grotesque *genius loci* can sometimes act as a kind of Bakhtinian mascot of the populace, a figure of resistance. In Lincolnshire folklore, the fen-spirits would not take kindly to the projectors' efforts to evict them. Jeffrey J. Cohen's insight that 'the monster's very existence is a rebuke to boundary and enclosure' (1996, 7) has a very literal application in the context of the enclosure of the English fens. Since the monster's function is to scramble and evade categories of human knowing, Cohen stipulates that 'the monster always escapes' (1996, 4). This evasiveness makes them slippery game for the historian. Written accounts of pagan spirits are especially scarce. Consequently, a study of such creatures 'must content itself with fragments: footprints, bones, talismans, teeth, shadows, obscured glimpses' (Cohen 1996, 6). To one such obscured glimpse, which casts a revealing backlight on Shakespeare's *Tempest*, we will now turn.

Caliban and Tiddy Mun's Curse

In 1887 a Scottish folklorist named Marie Clothilde Balfour travelled to the rural Ancholme valley in northern Lincolnshire. She would remain there for the greater part of two years. Her purpose: to gather and preserve the oral legends from remote backwaters that had then been only lightly grazed by modernity. 'I do not think,' she would later write, 'that elsewhere in England one could nowadays find such a childlike certainty of unseen things or such an unquestioning belief in supernatural powers' (1891, 148). Wandering through the rural hamlets near the inland Isle of Axholme, she encountered the folklorist's favourite quarry: an uneducated, loquacious, and elderly woman, a life-long inhabitant of the area. When her grandchildren step out of earshot, the old woman regales Balfour with a colourful yarn about an ancient fen-goblin known as Tiddy Mun. In 1891 Balfour published the story in the newly founded journal *Folklore*. Many an overzealous ethnographer has been fed fantastical whoppers by a quick-witted local eager for a laugh at the naïve outlander's expense. But another fen-dweller interviewed by Balfour confirms that his grandparents had believed in such water spirits. It is, of course, impossible to verify the man's claim that these legends were passed down from time immemorial. Yet the historical record does suggest that pagan beliefs persisted in the area at least two centuries earlier. In 1698, a Yorkshire antiquarian paid a visit to the same Isle of Axholme and referred to it in his diary as 'a mighty rude place before the drainage, the people little better than heathens' (Pryme 1870, 173). While Balfour's veracity has (inevitably) been called into question, there are compelling reasons for treating her stories seriously.[7] Her tale of Lincolnshire fen-spirits is, as this essay will unfold, corroborated in part by other medieval and early modern sources with which Shakespeare seems to have been acquainted.

To bolster the tale's authenticity, Balfour transcribes it in the first person as the old woman told it, complete with a phonetic approximation of her local dialect:

> For thee know'st, Tiddy Mun dwelt in tha watter-holes doun deep i'tha green still watter, an' a comed out nobbut of evens, whan tha mists rose. Than comed crappelin out itha darklins, limpelty lobelty, like a dearie wee au'd gran'ther. Avi'lang white hair, an' a lang white beardie, all cotted an' tangled together; limpelty-lobelty, an' a gowned i'gray, while tha could scarce see un thruff tha mist, an 'a come wi'a sound of rinnin' watter, an' a sough o' wind, an' laughin' like tha pyewipe screech. (1891, 150–1)

As with the several early modern portraits of Shakespeare, certain features of 'Tiny Man' and Caliban do not perfectly align.[8] The differences should be enough to warn us that Tiddy Mun was not the single or even primary source for Shakespeare's monster. The potential prototypes—ranging from the medieval wodewose, to the mooncalf (or prodigious birth), to exotic marine fauna, to Native Americans in early modern travel narratives, or even the recalcitrant Irish—are far too numerous to pretend otherwise.[9] Adding another suspect to this line-up might seem to confuse rather than clarify Caliban's origins. Yet Caliban's hybridity—that is, the diverse cultural referents Shakespeare spliced together to create him—is an index not only of his monstrosity but also of his enticingly complex character. Despite their differences, Caliban and Tiddy Mun share five fairly unique characteristics that suggest a common ancestry in English folklore: (1) both Tiddy Mun and Caliban are associated with fens and stagnant water; (2) both become enraged when their island habitats are violated by outsiders; (3) both are implicated with moon-worship; (4) both are linked with the power to control floods; and (5) both Caliban and Tiddy Mun curse humans by conjuring noxious mists, considered vectors for agues or malaria (literally 'bad air').[10]

Like Caliban, Tiddy Mun's wrath had to be propitiated by magic. According to Balfour's *raconteuse*, in the years when the fens flooded people's homes, families would trudge outside on the night of the first new moon and intone a chant in the direction of the water: 'Tiddy Mun, wi'out a name, / Tha watter's thruff! [through]' (151). The people would repeat the chant until they heard a pyewipe (a lapwing) screech from fens, which was interpreted as 'Mun's holla'. When they woke the next morning, the floodwaters would have receded. In *The Tempest*, Caliban's mother, Sycorax, possesses this same power to 'make flows and ebbs' (5.1.273) here attributed to Tiddy Mun and, by extension, the Lincolnshire fen-dwellers who knew how to placate him.

Although he was normally benign, Tiddy Mun could become malicious, particularly if anyone tampered with the wetlands. In the words of an old rhyme recited by the old woman, 'While tha watter teems tha fen / Tiddy Mun'll harm nane' (152). The woman tells Balfour that 'when the Dutchies delved, an' tha' Dutchies drawd tha water off' Tiddy Mun 'wor sore fratched wi iverbody'. Enraged by the draining, the genius loci summons pestilent mists from what remains of the black-pools. Blight ravages the crops, the cows and pigs fall ill, and infants sicken in their mothers' arms. Calamity is averted when a group of concerned locals devise a ceremony to appease the fen-imp: they pour libations of water in a dyke, disclaim responsibility for the draining, and ask his forgiveness. Miraculously, the cattle and children recover.

Just as Tiddy Mun becomes 'sore fratched' with the Dutch, Caliban becomes infuriated with Prospero. On two separate occasions the play credits Caliban with Tiddy Mun's power to conjure diseases from the fens. In his first appearance, he curses Prospero and Miranda:

> As wicked dew as e'er my mother brushed
> With raven's feather from unwholesome fen
> Drop on you both! A southwest blow on ye
> And blister you all o'er!
>
> (1.2.322–5)

Caliban utters a similar malediction at the start of Act 2:

> All the infections that the sun sucks up
> From bogs, fens, flats, on Prosper fall, and make him
> By inchmeal a disease!
>
> (2.2.1–3)

The similarities outlined here, although conspicuous, are not sufficient to argue that Caliban is Tiddy Mun. But the two may share a common ancestor in the ecological imagination of pre-industrial England. Residents of the fens tended to be short (even by seventeenth-century standards), and were rumoured to have webbed feet and hands, as well other deformities. Modern physicians would probably credit this to malnutrition, but in Shakespeare's era many still believed prodigious births to be the preternatural result of a witch's fornication with a devil or incubus (Latham 1992, 151–8). Prospero informs us that Caliban's mother was a 'witch' (5.1.272) and his father a 'devil' (1.2.321), and the other characters never miss an opportunity to comment on his monstrosity. Most critics view the sorceress Sycorax as a literary descendent of Circe and Medea.[11] However, taking a cue from Arthur Golding, who metamorphoses Ovid's Latin nymphs and naiads into 'elves' of 'standing lakes' in a famous passage pilfered by Prospero in *The Tempest*, Shakespeare may have expected his audience to delight in the conflation of Greco-Roman and English folklore. From this vantage point, the supposed Algerian witch looks much like a Lincolnshire peasant-woman who practiced ritual magic (an ancestor of Balfour's storyteller) while Caliban's father resembles a swamp demon like Tiddy Mun. Since the Yorkshire antiquarian informs us that heathen beliefs were widespread in the Isle of Axholme 'before the drainage', which took place in this region in the late 1620s, such beliefs must still have been circulating a decade earlier when Shakespeare wrote *The Tempest*. In 1611, Caliban's dark invocations of the 'fens', and his use of the word 'flats', a fenland term for flood-prone lowlands, would have primed a Jacobean audience to regard him as a disgruntled, deformed, and superstitious fen-dweller.

For a modern reader, it is tempting to gloss the Tiddy Mun legend as a spectral manifestation of the anxieties of fenland cottagers subsisting in such a daunting and volatile environment. Although intended to make the fens more hospitable and fertile, the draining of the English wetlands in the seventeenth century would, ironically, have amplified these anxieties. Over the centuries, fenland communities had learned to adapt to the vicissitudes of living in a floodplain and developed a regional economy based on the management of its natural resources. Rather than a utopian pipedream, Gonzalo's vision of a place without 'bourn, bound of land, tilth' (2.1.158) evokes the unenclosed English wetlands where cottagers could subsist without intensive agriculture. Constructing dykes allowed the rural gentry to slice up the floodplains into neat segments and create more arable land. Fen draining, in effect, was a means of facilitating enclosure. During an assembly in 1619, locals complained that if the draining were approved, 'the commoner shall be in danger to lose his common by the incroaching Lords' (H.C. 1629, B2r). Powerless to oppose the destruction of the ecosystem upon which their livelihood depended, the cottagers of Axholme invented a supernatural ally.[12] Shakespeare, in essence, does something similar when he creates Caliban. A local reading of *The Tempest* reveals that the creature's execrations channel some of the resentment and hostility of fen-dwellers whose aquatic commons were confiscated by the projectors. Caliban, then, is not only a fen-goblin or caricature of a Native American; he also shares the grievances of the Lincolnshire peasantry, some of whom may have still believed in such spirits and whose communal wetlands were being taken from them by an educated elite wielding a foreign technoscience that gave them a quasi-magical power to control the elements of earth and water.

It is striking that Caliban's chief tasks, collecting wood and trapping fish and fowl, were mainstays of the fenland economy. In the medieval and early modern periods, the fenland cottagers supplied sedge, small timber, and turf (for fires), and boatloads of fish to markets and fairs throughout the region. Just as Caliban must 'fetch...in fuel' (1.2.368) for Prospero, the rural poor around Crowland piloted the skiffs that brought wood, turf, and coal to warm the scholars at nearby Cambridge.[13] Sixteenth- and seventeenth-century sources speak of the fen-dwellers' 'old privilege' to gather wood, sedge, and turf, albeit one under threat by 'covetousness' (Harrison 1577, 440); of the 'great plenty of Turfe and sedge for the maintenance of fire' (Camden 1610, 491), and of 'many thousand cottagers' (SPD Charles I 1636, 339) scouring the wetlands to collect them. The poet Michael Drayton's vignette of rural laborers in the fens is evocative of Caliban's chores of weir-building, snare-setting, and stick-gathering:

> The toyling Fisher here is tewing of his Net:
> The Fowler is imployed his lymed twigs to set.
> ....
> And others from their Carres are busily about,
> To draw out Sedge and Reed, for thatch and Stover fit.
>
> (1622, 2:108)

No wonder Caliban boasts of the 'qualities of the isle' (1.2.339–40) and its abundant natural resources, such as 'pig nuts' (wild tubers), jay eggs, and 'filberts' (hazel nuts). It should be noted that, apart from the marmoset or monkey, the species Caliban subsists upon are native to England, and the isle's mysterious 'scamels' (2.2.166)—often presumptuously emended to sea-mews—likely refers to the fenland bird now known as the bar-tailed godwit.[14] His use of a regional term for a wading bird would further enhance the impression of Caliban as a dispossessed fen-dweller.

The debate over the reclamation of the fens throws light on another textual crux in Shakespeare's play. During the wedding masque, Iris summons Ceres from 'flat meads thatched with stover' bisected by 'banks with peonied and twillèd brims' (4.1.63–4). The Oxford Shakespeare here emends the Folio's 'pioned' to 'peonied,' assuming that Shakespeare must have intended to strew the banks with flowers; some overzealous editors have even changed twilled to 'tulip'd' or 'lilied'. But the Folio reading requires no alteration. 'Pioned' is a verb that means to dig an embankment, while 'twilled' is a dialect word for 'plaited osiers used to prevent bank erosion'.[15] The line may allude not merely to problems with soil erosion, as Gabriel Egan has plausibly suggested (2006, 166), but to the dykes and embankments constructed to drain or divert water from the fens. Flat meads (characteristic of the fens) thatched (thatch was a major export of the region) with stover and crisscrossed with embanked streams sound reminiscent of the marshy terrain of eastern England. Arguably, Ceres' presence there celebrates the fertility of these supposed wastelands. Yet the wedding masque summons the goddess from such sites to indulge in an aristocratic fantasy of a hyper-fecund landscape improved through technological intervention. The food riots dramatized in *Coriolanus* will become a thing of the past, as modern agronomy conjures a world of 'barns and garners never empty' (4.1.111).[16]

Characteristically, Shakespeare stages both sides of the controversy. As a court playwright, he also voices the frustrations of the Jacobean elite with popular resistance to the drainage. Such frustrations are audible in Shakespeare's *Coriolanus*, written about two years prior to *The Tempest* when a severe dearth made agricultural reclamation a national priority. When the people's tribunes pronounce his banishment, Coriolanus rails against the 'common cry of curs, whose breath I hate / As reek o'th' rotten fens' (3.3.119–20). In the next scene, Coriolanus indulges in a surprising simile when he compares himself to 'a lonely dragon that his fen / Makes feared' (4.1.30–1). These speeches befit an anti-populist, pro-drainage sympathizer in that they serve to further blacken the fens as a foul, heathenish backwater. Moreover, his scoffing assurance that such fen-monsters are 'talked of more than seen' (4.1.31) signals Coriolanus's contempt for the superstitious peasantry. This odd allusion to tales of a fen-dragon proves beyond a doubt that Shakespeare had some knowledge of fen folklore by 1608, and would have tickled the ears of Jacobean courtiers who were investing in wetlands reclamation projects despite the stubborn opposition of locals.

If Caliban expresses a profound affection for his watery environment that echoes that of fowlers and fishers who made their home and living in the fens, *The Tempest* also portrays these wetlands as a putrid, disease-ridden morass. Caliban curses Prospero with the malaria once endemic in the fens, to which outsiders lacking immunity were particularly susceptible. Stephano later misdiagnoses Caliban's trembling as a symptom of an 'ague' (2.2.65), a common term for malarial fever, the prevalence of which in wetlands was cited as proof that their drainage would be a public health service. King Lear's allusion to 'fen-sucked fogs' (2.2.356) and the 'fenny snake' (4.1.12) in *Macbeth*'s hell-broth would cast this environment in a similarly ominous light. Shakespeare paints another conflicting diptych of the island in 2.1 when Gonzalo admires its fecundity while Antonio views it as a wasteland, 'perfumed by a fen' (2.1.51). Such divergent responses occur often in early modern descriptions of the American wilderness, but are also a hallmark of contemporary debates about whether to preserve or reclaim England's wetlands. Shakespeare implicitly compares Sebastian to a fen when calls him 'standing water' and the villainous Antonio to a fen-drainer when he promises to 'teach [Sebastian] how to flow' (2.1.221–2). While this appears to advocate the aristocratic enterprise of fen-draining, it also equates it with murderous ambition. In a play staged twice before King James and the court, Shakespeare's complex representation of fens as both fertile and noisome, and of fen-dwellers as both dispossessed victims and treacherous heathens, has ecocritical import, demanding more considered policy decisions from the government on one of the most pressing environmental issues in Stuart Britain.

King James and the Draining of the Fens

Surprisingly little has been said about the submerged presence of the fens in *The Tempest*. Peter Hulme and William H. Sherman refer in passing to the 'domestic colonization' of the fens and the 'play's almost obsessive concern with dirty and stagnant water' (2000, 4–5). Christy Anderson (2000) compares Prospero's magic with hydraulic garden statuary but does not address the use of hydraulics in fen-draining. The long overdue arrival of ecocriticism in Shakespeare studies has already begun to recover some of the playwright's astonishing responsiveness to the natural world. Gabriel Egan has discussed *The Tempest* in connection with anxieties about climate change and timber shortages (2006, 145–51), while Simon Estok has shown how the imperialist gaze categorizes Caliban alongside the savage exotica of the New World (2011, 104).[17] Turning their gaze seaward, Steve Mentz (2009b, 1–13) and Dan Brayton (2012, 166–95) have highlighted the play's fascination with the marine environment and nautical culture. Yet the brown and sodden English wetlands remain something of a lacuna.[18] By shifting the early modern environment (in this case, the fens) into the foreground, this study further demonstrates how ecocriticism can bring unsuspected dimensions of Shakespearean drama into focus.

While the dream of 'reclaiming' the English fens had been percolating at least as far back as 1258 when Henry III established the first Commission of Sewers, it gained new momentum in 1600/01 following Parliament's passage of a General Drainage Act. In 1608, the Privy Council received an optimistic letter on the prospect of draining fens near Boston and began to advocate for more state involvement. But not everyone was convinced or even pleased by these proposals. Drainage bills brought before Parliament in 1606, 1607, and 1610 all floundered amid public outcry. Opposition to the drainage was not only vocal. As early as 1530, certain 'evil-disposed persons' destroyed dykes in Norfolk and Cambridgeshire, and acts of sabotage would continue throughout the seventeenth-century, flaring up again in the first decade of James's reign, and off and on even after the outbreak of the Civil War (see Lindley 1982; Ash 2017). In brief, when Shakespeare composed his play featuring a rebellious fen-creature, the Jacobean court and Parliament were in the midst of a heated debate about the logistics and the ethics of draining wetlands.[19]

The first objection raised against the undertakers was that God created the fens and presuming to tamper with them and destroy the habitat they provided for other living creatures was sacrilegious. The author of an anonymous letter

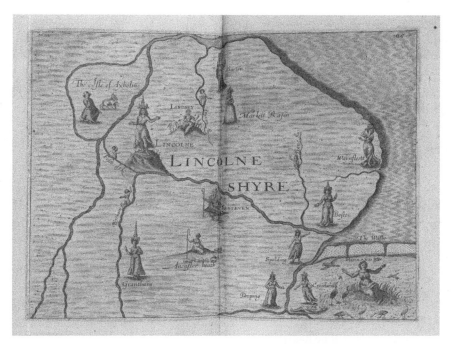

Fig. 6.2 William Hole, The Lincolnshire fens, from Michael Drayton, *Poly-Olbion* (c.1622).
Royal Geographic Society.

reporting on a 1622 session of sewers in Peterborough protests that 'the beautifull order of Nature...in disposeinge of Rivers, Meeres, plaines, &c., soe as *every thing helpeth other in his Kinde*...by theis Undertakers (if they can) is like to bee destroyed' (SPD James I 14/128 f. 150). At the same Peterborough session the locals declared 'fens were made fens and must ever continue such, and are useful in multiplying fowl and fish, producing turf, etc.' (SPD James I 128/105; qtd in Ravensdale 1974, 31). Although often couched in religious language, such arguments sound similar to those forwarded by modern supporters of conservation: one should respect the environment simply because it is there and other creatures depend upon it for their survival. Drayton's poetic catalogue of waterfowl in Holland Fen lists twenty-eight different species, and William Hole's accompanying engraving, in the absence of human settlements, makes it resemble a bird sanctuary (see Fig. 6.2). A second more pragmatic objection voiced in the Peterborough letter is that the fens produce a number of natural resources that would be greatly diminished if the wetlands were drained. In a 1629 pro-drainage pamphlet, the author tries to assuage locals who were understandably concerned that diverting water from the region would 'decay Fishing and Fowling' (H.C. B2[r]). A third objection was the impracticality of the scheme. Opponents of the fen-draining cited the numerous failures to reclaim the Pontine Marshes near Naples, one of the two

Italian dukedoms featured in *The Tempest*.[20] Antonio's jest that the island reeks as if "twere perfumed by a fen' (2.1.51) is well-calculated to amuse the Neapolitan Sebastian, who would be familiar with such marshy terrain. But Antonio's term 'fen' technically refers to the flood-prone lowlands in eastern England, not the alluvial marshes near Naples. In a fifteenth-century document, a Cambridge historian speculated that if the Lincolnshire fens were drained at great expense, they would no doubt 'quickly revert to their old condition, like the Pontaine [sic] Marshes in Italy' (qtd in Fuller 1840, 107).[21] Paradoxically, drawing off water from the fens caused the peat to dry out, contract, and sink further, making the newly drained land more vulnerable to floods, thus requiring even more laborious hydro-engineering works to divert the water again. Remarking on this tendency in his *Britannia*, William Camden concludes 'many think it the wisest and best course according to the sage admonition in like case of Apollo his Oracle, *Not to intermeddle at all with that which God hath ordained*' (1610, 492). In this light, the intractability of Caliban can be viewed as symbolic of nature's obstinacy in opposing human designs to improve or reclaim it.

The year Shakespeare died, Camden's former pupil Ben Jonson invited Jacobean playgoers to scoff at wetlands reclamation projects in *The Devil Is an Ass* (1616). Although such schemes have failed in the past, the wily project Merecraft assures a gullible citizen that he has a new foolproof method:

> I'll begin at the pan,
> Not at the skirts—as some ha' done, and lost
> All that they wrought, their timber-work, their trench,
> Their banks all borne away, or else filled up
> By the next winter.
>
> (*CWBJ* 4:512.2.1.53–7)

Merecraft catches his gull, Fitzdotrrel, with the bait of an 18-million-pound profit and the promise of a patently ludicrous title: the Duke of Drowned Land. Intoxicated by the prospect of fabulous riches and a promotion to the peerage, Fitzdottrell shares the overconfidence of the actual investors:

> All Crowland
> Is ours, wife; and the fens, from us in Norfolk
> To the utmost bound of Lincolnshire! We have viewed it
> And measured it within, all by the scale!
>
> (4:523.2.3.49–52)

The Devil Is an Ass thus belongs in the tradition of other Jonsonian satires on the vanity and greed-fuelled credulity of Jacobean social climbers. The play portrays the transformation of the wetlands into farmland as a massive con equivalent to the transmutation of charcoal into gold in *The Alchemist*, but also hints at the ecological damage it could inflict in its pun on Fitzdottrel's name, which evokes the easy-to-catch wading bird known as the dotterel, whose habitat was destroyed by the drainage.[22]

It is significant that the devil-obsessed Fitzdottrel mentions Crowland as the seat of his new dukedom; as the second half of this essay will unfold, this section of Lincolnshire was not only a target of reclamation projections but also notorious as the abode of devilish fen-spirits. Mistress Fitzdottrel herself worries that Merecraft's project will involve the supernatural soliciting of 'spirits'. Her husband attempts to reassure her:

> Spirits? Oh, no such thing, wife! Wit, mere wit!
> This man defies the devil and all his works!
> He does't by engine and devices he.
>
> (4:523.2.3.44–6)

Before the invention of advanced wind- and steam-powered hydraulic pumps, many early moderns shared Mistress Fitzdottrel's concern that the draining could only succeed through the hubristic assumption of god-like powers over the natural world. In the words of the 1622 report from Peterborough cited earlier, '*the people think the Undertakers will work by witchcraft*, no persons of experience supposing their designs possible' (SPD James I 1622, 128/105, italics added). In this context, Shakespeare's portrait of a magus commanding earth and water spirits would resonate powerfully with contemporary suspicions that fen-draining smacked of the occult. Frances Yates (1979, 186–92) has argued that Prospero practices a white magic allied with Christianity and that Shakespeare modelled him on the famed Elizabethan magus John Dee. Yet it is not widely known that Dee himself took an interest in fenland reclamation, scribbling down notes on the logistics of hydroengineering in a manuscript headed 'Questions and observations about the draining and imbanking the Fens'.[23] At certain moments in *The Tempest*, Prospero's supernatural power over 'elves' of 'standing lakes'—in which category one might place Tiddy Mun—and others that 'chase the ebbing Neptune' (5.1.33, 35) appears almost indistinguishable from the dark arts by which Sycorax controls 'ebbs and flows'. Likewise, in the eyes of a Lincolnshire cottager, the hydrological projects of the Commission of Sewers to 'control ebbs and flows' in a seasonal flood plain might seem tantamount to sorcery. Perhaps it is not a coincidence that a mob attacked Dee's house and, realizing Caliban's scheme, burned his books.

Historians have amply documented the explosive synthesis of Neo-platonic magic and Baconian science in the early modern period.[24] With the rise of ecocriticism in early modern studies, we are slowly becoming aware of the ecological consequences of this synthesis, which threatens to fulfil Prospero's prediction of the apocalyptic demise of the great Globe itself. In *The Tempest*, Prospero experiences an *anagnorisis* that such powers are unlawful and abjures them. In the brave new world of the Anthropocene, the long-term survival of our hyper-industrialized civilization may require a similar abjuration. At least in the matter of the English fens our species has made some progress. In 2000, the UK Environmental Agency launched a fifty-year, multi-million-pound Great Fen Project to restore 3,700 hectares of wetlands.[25]

The question remains of what King James thought of *The Tempest* when he saw it in 1611 and again in 1612/3. Would he have registered its oblique commentary on the fens or been swayed by it? In the first years of his reign James had been hesitant to support drainage schemes on the grounds that it was tantamount to sanctioning the theft of commons, reportedly telling Parliament: 'It is just the same cause, my Lords, as though a pack of thieves should give me £20,000 to give them a patent under my broad seal to rob my loyal subjects, by the which I should perjure myself and become a tyrant' (Maynard 1646, 2). But James eventually succumbed to the pro-drainage lobby under the weight of his own financial pressures and the persuasions of his favourites. On 11 August 1614, James granted a patent to drain and enclose fenlands owned by the Crown to Robert Carr (the identically named cousin of his favourite, the Earl of Somerset) and Thomas Reade. This much-hyped deal provoked Jonson to pen *The Devil Is an Ass* (1616), which the king reportedly 'desired him to conceal' (Herford and Simpson 1:143–4). Yet Jonson's satire did not stop the king from commissioning 'an exact survey' of Hatfield Level in 1617 to determine how much land could be reclaimed (Ash 2017, 149); four years later James launched a campaign to drain the Great Level—a 500-square-mile region of wetlands between the rivers Nene and Ouse—as the Dutch engineer Cornelius Vermuyden reported: 'for the Honour of this kingdom (as his Majesty told me at the time), [he] would not suffer any longer the said Land to bee abandoned to the will of the waters, nor to let it lye wast and unprofitable' (1642, 1). In July 1621, James established a new and more pliable Commission of Sewers, informed them he would personally be the sole undertaker and proprietor of 120,000 acres, and insisted they brush aside any misguided resistance to his plans:

> The King and his Privy Council manipulated and browbeat the Commissions of Sewers; co-opted their formidable statutory powers, placing them at the disposal of the drainage projectors; and worked to suppress any fenland opposition, viewing it as the product of ignorance, intransigence, and private interest.
> (Ash 2017, 134)

In his dispatches, James resorts to the absolustist logic of his political tracts—proposing that 'the King...might take the land from his lieges, as overlord of the whole' (1598, 270)—to promote what is in essence the doctrine of eminent domain.[26] Although legal wrangles and logistical problems stymied James's drainage projects until after his death, this royal support threw more weight and money behind Vermuyden and the Earl of Bedford, who would gradually over the next two decades destroy some of England's most biodiverse wetlands, including Hatfield Chase in the Isle of Axholme, the home of Tiddy Mun. For this service, Vermuyden was knighted by Charles I in 1629.[27]

By the time *The Tempest* appeared in print in the 1623 Folio, King James would have been less sympathetic to dispossessed fen-dwellers than when the play premiered. Had Shakespeare's portrayal of 'the savage and deformed' Caliban reinforced the metropolitan prejudice of the court against the surly bumpkins of the Lincolnshire backwaters? Shakespeare's romance is not so persistently critical as Jonson's comedy, and the masque of Ceres even seems to support the cornucopianism of the drainers. Yet Caliban's protests lodge a minority report. His pained insistence 'this island's mine' (1.2.332) eloquently captures the fen-folk's grievances, stinging Jacobean audiences with the realization that royal projects were bound to encounter opposition and that bending the non-human environment to the ruler's will would require a dubious magic he did not possess.

Guthlac and the Fen Demons of Crowland

Admittedly, the evidence presented thus far linking Caliban with oral legends about the genius loci of the fens is somewhat tenuous. Even the former doyenne of early English folklore, K. M. Briggs, denied Caliban a place in the pantheon of native spirits on the grounds that 'he is at least half human, not a hobgoblin or devil' (1959, 59). In the same book, however, she fudges this point by conceding that Caliban's father may have been an aquatic demon (179–80), which W. C. Curry (1959, 148–55) first proposed and this chapter has revived. Briggs's oversight in failing to connect Caliban with fen-spirits is perhaps not all that surprising. The fact that there are no extant references to Tiddy Mun until 1891, two hundred and eighty years after *The Tempest* was written, presents a daunting hurdle. Few historians today would credit Balfour's claim that this tale is pre-historic in origin. It would, therefore, be irresponsible to assert that Tiddy Mun is *the* model for Caliban. In the other pan of the scale, however, one must set the fact that prior to the founding of the English Folklore Society in 1878 there were very few avenues by which voices like that of Balfour's storyteller could reach print. The date of the tale, in other words, does not prove its belated nineteenth-century origins so much as attest to the historical marginalization of the oral culture of the rural underclass. Moreover, just as faint impressions of Native American culture were preserved in European travel narratives, the folklore of the fens left traces in the records of the dominant metropolitan culture. Abundant evidence suggests that the Lincolnshire fens were notoriously regarded as the home of devilish phantoms long before Shakespeare's lifetime. If Caliban was not directly inspired by

Tiddy Mun, Tiddy Mun may at least be a descendent of the fen-spirits known to Shakespeare and his contemporaries.

An Elizabethan account of the fens and fen-demons can be found in William Camden's influential chorography, *Britannia*. His survey of Lincolnshire dwells in detail on large wetlands in the south known as Crowland (or Croyland)—which Camden depicts as 'a raw and muddy land' pocked with 'foule and slabby quavemires, yea, and most troublesome fennes' (1610, 529–30). Like the Ancholme valley to its north, this sliver of Lincolnshire was, he informs us, 'much haunted in times past with I wot not what sprites, and fearefull apparitions' (530). In a memorable passage, Camden spices up his narrative with a comic interlude about the ludicrous demons that allegedly stalked the region:

> If I should exemplifie unto you...the Devils of Crowland, with their blabber lips, fire-spitting mouths, rough and skaly visages, beetle heads, terrible teeth, sharpe chins, hoarse throats, blacke skins, crump-shoulders, side and gorbellies, burning loins, crooked and hawm'd legs, long tailed buttockes, and ugly misshapes, which heretofore walked and wandered up and downe in these places...you would laugh full merily. (530)

First published in Latin in 1586 (and reprinted seven times by 1607), Camden's *Britannia* was translated into English by Philemon Holland in 1610, the year before *The Tempest* premiered. If Shakespeare chanced upon this passage, it would have furnished him with a sketch for a grotesque fen-monster that would make his audience 'laugh full merily' as well.

The understandable interest in Caliban as aboriginal has obscured Prospero's references to him as a 'Devil, a born devil' (4.1.188) and a 'demi-devil' (5.1.275).[28] While it is not uncommon for early modern travel narratives to demonize non-Europeans, these lines may also signal Caliban's kinship with Lincolnshire swamp-demons anatomized by Camden. Both Caliban and the Crowland devils share a number of physical features that betray their otherness: scaly skin and 'long tailed buttocks' would account for the several references to Caliban as a fish; one of Trinculo's jokes could imply that Caliban has a 'tail' (3.2.11); if we take Prospero's branding him a 'thing of darkness' as pointing to the monster's swarthy complexion, he would be dark-skinned like these fen-spirits. In the passage Camden is translating here, the author adds that the demons had singed hair, which would explain Trinculo's diagnosis that Caliban has 'suffered by a thunderbolt' (2.2.36). This bemused anecdote from Camden might furnish some vital clues as to Caliban's appearance on the early modern stage.[29] Yet the devil here may *not* be in the details. That is, the cumulative effect of Camden's list of anatomical deformities is not so much to single out specific ones as to generate a generalized impression of monstrosity. Shakespeare's insistent yet imprecise descriptions of the 'misshapen' Caliban seem, I would argue, similarly designed.[30]

Camden's source for these grotesques is the medieval *Life of Saint Guthlac*—a hagiographical narrative that has astonishing parallels with Shakespeare's play. A learned hermit travels to a remote island surrounded by fens where he battles against the native demons that inhabit the soggy wilderness. Endowed with supernatural powers of foresight by an angelic familiar, he also thwarts his attempted murder by one of his own servants. There is a strong possibility that Shakespeare may have known the legends of this Saxon saint through Camden, or perhaps even from a lost Elizabethan play. Uncovering the analogues between Guthlac and Prospero will point us toward a new source for *The Tempest* that further elucidates the play's imperial, religious, and ecological dimensions.

Our knowledge of Guthlac derives from an Anglo-Saxon monk named Felix, who compiled his hagiography sometime between 730–40 CE, not long after the saint's death. The text contains many of the conventional trappings of the saint's life, which is not surprising since Guthlac himself was a professed admirer of the genre. Born into a noble family in the Kingdom of Mercia around 674 CE, Guthlac became a fearsome warrior and took part in numerous battles against the native Britons before he eventually grew weary of bloodshed. He entered Repton monastery, where he became enflamed with the desire to emulate the ascetic devotions of Saint Anthony. Seeking isolation, he journeyed to the fens of southern Lincolnshire and persuaded a local to guide him in a small skiff through 'trackless bogs within the confines of the dismal marsh' (Colgrave 1956, 89) until he arrived at a remote 'island' called Crowland. But Guthlac, it turns out, was not alone.

Like Prospero, Guthlac settles on a fenny island infested with 'mysterious unknown monsters [*incognita heremi monstra*]' and 'phantom-demons [*fantasias demonum*]' (88–9). In one account of his life, Guthlac enslaves the demons and forces them to carry out menial tasks.[31] Like Prospero, Guthlac possesses 'prophetic powers' (149) and converses with an angelic familiar spirit who, like Ariel, performs chores for him and informs him of events far-off in space and time (157). In chapter 35, a devil tempts one of Guthlac's human servants named Beccel to kill his master with a knife while tonsuring him. Before the traitorous servant can strike, Guthlac through his prescience knows of his plan and confronts him. When Beccel confesses that a fen-demon had tempted him and begs forgiveness, Guthlac 'granted him pardon for the fault' (113). The episode is reminiscent of Prospero's foreknowledge of the 'foul conspiracy' of the devilish servant Caliban and his Neapolitan accomplices. Prospero's pardoning him and the other traitors in the play could thus be construed as an act of *imitatio Guthlaci*. Guthlac also employs his foresight on less serious occasions. When two clerics come to visit him, he chastises them for having stashed flasks full of beer in the gravel of the marsh (137), just as Prospero knows of the antics and intentions of the drunken Trinculo and Stephano who have hidden wine in a rock by the seashore. Like Prospero's cloak, Guthlac's garment is credited with magical powers. Alone on the island Guthlac often hears disembodied cries of wildlife—which he envisions as demons in the shapes of a 'roaring lion' and a 'bellowing bull' (115)—similar to the aural hallucinations experienced by several characters in *The Tempest*. Felix reports that a jackdaw once stole one of Guthlac's holy parchments and dropped it in a pool, which a thirteenth-century source apparently spun into a yarn that fen-demons tried to steal Guthlac's psalter and hurl it in the marsh, an act reminiscent of both the devilish Caliban's plan to destroy Prospero's magic books and Prospero's vow to 'drown' them.[32]

Perhaps the most interesting of Guthlac's Prospero-like accomplishments is his magical ability to control other creatures and the elements:

> *Not only did the creatures of the earth and sky obey his commands, but also even the very water and the air obeyed the true servant of the true God.* For if a man faithfully and wholeheartedly serves the Maker of all created things, it is no wonder though all creation should minister to his commands and wishes. But for the most part we lose *dominion over the creation* which was made subject to us because we ourselves neglect to serve the Lord and Creator of all things.
>
> (121, italics added)

In commanding the air and water, Guthlac appropriates the powers credited to native genii loci such as Tiddy Mun, while simultaneously slandering such spirits as demons. The *Vita Guthlaci* thus stands as a representative chapter in the saga of Christianity's triumph over Celtic animism in the British Isles. *The Tempest* hints that this process was still on-going in the early modern period, not only in the Americas but also in the fen country of England, where traditional lore and a system of communal management promoting coexistence with wetlands were displaced by technoscience seeking proprietary dominion. And yet, if the wizard-saint Prospero smears the propitiatory environmental magic of Sycorax and fenland communities as witchcraft, he performs similar magic feats himself: controlling the moon and seas, infecting his enemies with the cramps, bone-aches, and fevers caused by malaria, as well as subjugating the elements in his enslavement of Caliban and Ariel, who respectively embody the low and high elemental dyads of earth/water and air/fire. Significantly, Guthlac's and Prospero's power over the elements anticipates that of seventeenth-century projectors who sought to divert the winter floods from the fens.

As Lynn White and others have famously charged, the Judeo-Christian scriptures enshrined an anthropocentric worldview and thus helped underpin Europe's quest for scientific mastery over nature.[33] The legend of Guthlac posits that human 'dominion' can be restored through faith rather than, as Francis Bacon proposed, applied technology. But the Anglo-Saxon saint and his followers did not exist entirely on an immaterial plane. Later sources report that Guthlac engaged in several building projects while at Crowland. As Alfred Siewers (2006) has cogently argued, Guthlac's occupation of a *tumulus* (funeral mound or barrow) on his island in the fens savours of both exorcism and a colonialist act of Anglo-Saxon nation building. This process intensified following Guthlac's canonization, when the Mercian king Aethelbald chose the lowlands around Guthlac's cell as the site for what would become Crowland Abbey. In a poem cited by Camden, Aethelbald fells oak trees to fill in the sodden fenland: 'Of rotten earth good solide ground was rought' (530). Due to the vagaries of early modern orthography, Guthlac's Anglo-Saxon name was also sometimes modernized as 'Cutlake', which may have contributed to stories of his role as a pioneer in the channelling of the Crowland fens. With his power to command the water, Guthlac would have provided a religious precedent for fen-draining, characterizing it as godly work. It is perhaps telling that one of the best-preserved hagiographies of Guthlac (along with the Guthlac scroll) belonged to Robert Cotton, who was also involved in efforts to convert the fens into arable farmland (Summit 2008, 172–7; Darby 1940, 20). Since the isolation of the miry wilderness is precisely what attracts Guthlac to it as a site for holy dwelling, it is ironic that his cult would conspire to literally demonize this ecosystem. Indeed, the author of a seventeenth-century history celebrating the drainage cites this saint's life as a lively illustration of 'the horror of the place' (Dugdale 1662, 179). Just as the word heathen derives from heath (see Chapter 1), Felix's narrative portrays the wetlands as a breeding ground for paganism and thus sanctions their 'reclamation' as the ecological equivalent of grace.

Since Guthlac was a Christian Saxon from Mercia dwelling in territory once inhabited by pagan Britons, his life stands as a rare chronicle of the colonial settlement of England itself. In Chapter 34 of the hagiography, Felix describes how a mob of angry Britons besieged the saint's dwelling and set fire to it. Having lived in exile among them when he was young, Guthlac can understand their barbarous speech. But he soon discerns that his tormentors are not actually Britons but demons disguised as Britons. When they encircle him with their spears, Guthlac dispels them by reciting the first verse of Psalm 67. No episode in Felix's biography has garnered more attention than Guthlac's battle with Welsh-speaking demons. While Victorian historians would dismiss the whole thing as a fever-induced hallucination, early modern antiquarians seem to have believed that the demons were simply British brigands, who used the fenlands as a hideout.[34] The *Life of Guthlac* thus stages a colonial encounter not unlike the one Shakespeare depicts in *The Tempest*. In a comic reversal of this moment, the native Caliban mistakes the foreign Trinculo for 'a spirit' come to torment him (2.2.15); Stephano, in turn, twice mistakes Caliban for a devil (2.2.57, 2.2.97). More importantly, so does Prospero. In the early seventeenth century, England's imperial aspirations would have revived interest in the history of the island nation's own colonization by the Angles and Saxons. This musty saint's life would have offered a domestic precedent for both the colonial project across the Atlantic as well as land reclamation projects in Lincolnshire that this saint himself had helped inaugurate.

Prospero, Guthlac, Cutlack: *The Tempest* as Crypto-Saint's Play

Taken singly, the parallels outlined above might be dismissed as coincidence. Cumulatively, however, they point to the possibility Shakespeare may have known the legend of Guthlac, and that *The Tempest* has elements in common with the genre of the medieval saint's life. As Darryll Grantley has written, 'the saints' legend was one of the most important and enduring of literary forms from the Conquest to the Renaissance in England, despite the fact so little attention is paid to it' (1994, 267). Could Shakespeare, living in post-Reformation England, have been familiar with this Saxon saint?

The cult of Guthlac flourished in Lincolnshire and greater East Anglia throughout the Middle Ages, and he was arguably the second most popular Anglo-Saxon saint after Cuthbert. Crowland Abbey, which housed his relics in a shrine, was a major pilgrimage destination, just up the road from the cathedral town of Peterborough, and its well-preserved ruins continued to attract visitors after the dissolution: a quartefoil carving of Guthlac can still be discerned to this day over the abbey's west entrance. No fewer than nine churches throughout the East and West Midlands were dedicated to the saint. There was also a College of Grey Friars named after Guthlac in Hereford. Although Henry VIII dissolved this priory, it was acquired by the Welsh antiquarian Sir John Prise, who, like Shakespeare, had connections with the Earls of Pembroke, and it is not inconceivable that local legends about its patron saint may have rippled outward to Stratford, only forty miles away.

Felix's Latin *Vita Guthlaci* would be translated into Anglo-Saxon around the turn of the first millennium, and two Anglo-Saxon poems based on his life are preserved in the Exeter Book. The British Library houses a stunning roll from the late twelfth or early thirteenth century that features eighteen roundel illustrations (perhaps intended for stain glass windows) of episodes from Guthlac's *Life* (see Figs 6.3 and 6.4). There are also three Middle English redactions of Felix's hagiography in verse from the fourteenth and fifteenth century. One of these would be included in *The South English Legendary*, the most extensive compendium of saint's lives in medieval England after *The Golden Legend*.

While Guthlac's star appears to have waned in the late medieval era, there are flickering signs of interest in his cult well after the Reformation. In *The Three Laws* (1538), John Bale's Protestant satire on the miracle play, the character Idolatry advises pilgrims 'To give onions to Saint Cutlake' as a remedy for migraines (20). This same power to cure headaches is credited to 'the bell of Saint Guthlac' by a seventeenth-century source (qtd in Fuller 1840, 192). A 1570 edition of the popular almanac *The Shephards Kalendar* records a feast for the saint, celebrated on the day of his death, 11 April. The renowned Dutch artist Maerten de Vos executed a remarkable drawing of Guthlac, which features in *Sylvae sacrae monumentum anachoretium*, an illustrated history of hermits and anchorites published in 1594

CALIBAN AND THE FEN-DEMONS OF LINCOLNSHIRE 159

Fig. 6.3 Guthlac journeys to the island of Crowland, from Harley Roll Y.6. (*c.*1200).
© British Library Board.

Fig. 6.4 Guthlac tormented by bestial demons, from Harley Roll Y.6. (*c.*1200).
© British Library Board.

Fig. 6.5 Marcus Sadler (after Maerten de Vos), Saint Guthlacus of Crowland, from *Sylvae sacrae monumentum anachoretium* (1594).
Rijksmuseum, Amsterdam.

that attests to the enduring renown of this English saint (see Fig. 6.5). Although Protestant reformers regarded post-biblical saints with suspicion, revisionist scholarship has shown that pride in homegrown saints simmered on long after the dissolution.[35] Michael Drayton's *Poly-Olbion* features a lengthy roll-call of English saints, including a passing salute to 'Guthlake', who:

> The mad tumultuous world contemptibly forsook
> And to his quiet Cell by Crowland him betooke,
> Free from all publique crowds in that low Fenny ground.
> (1622, 2:94)

Drayton's fascination with Anglo-Saxon hermits was shared by a number of early modern antiquarians including Robert Cotton, Robert Lumley, and even Prince Henry. It was in Cotton's collection of medieval saints' lives that Camden came across a copy of Felix's *Life of Guthlac*. Cotton's habit of binding saints' lives such as Guthlac's to works of Protestant-inflected history is an apt cultural analogue for Shakespeare's fusing of a medieval miracle play with early modern romance. If Cotton's aim was to 'desanctify hagiography' (Summit 2008, 172),

Shakespeare's synthesis of sacred and profane arguably conspires to sanctify secular theatre.[36]

Another important manuscript of the *Life of Guthlac* belonged to the prominent recusant and book collector Lord Lumley. When Lumley died in 1609, Prince Henry acquired his massive library, the second largest in early modern England. To accommodate its 3,000 volumes, Henry had to construct a new library at St James in 1609 and 1610 (Strong 1986, 209–11). Shakespeare's portrait of a biblioholic Duke whose love of learning distracts him from his princely duties could be conceived as a polite warning to Henry. The royal acquisition of the Lumley library is another unrecognized topical influence on *The Tempest*. Lumley's collection concentrated on science and geography, subjects that must have occupied a large number of shelves in Prospero's library, and it is revealing that the Protestant prince's catalogue of the books lists Felix's *Life of Guthlac* under History rather than Theology. Interest in this hermit would also have been rekindled by the on-going efforts to drain the fens, of which Henry was no doubt aware. During his summer progress of 1609, Henry went hunting in the fens at the royal manor of Hatfield Chase (*PPMF* xxi–xxii), which borders the Isle of Axholme, the stomping grounds of Tiddy Mun. On Twelfth Night, 1610 Ben Jonson catered to the prince's antiquarian tastes with an Arthurian entertainment featuring a shrine to St George and a water-spirit better known as the Lady of the Lake. Jonson's masque may have inspired Shakespeare to dredge up other fabulous stories of saints and aquatic spirits when he composed *The Tempest* for a court performance the following year.

Shakespeare's last plays are generally categorized as late romances. This genre, invented by the Victorian scholar Edward Dowden, did not exist in 1611 when Shakespeare wrote *The Tempest* or in 1623 when Heminges and Condell compiled the First Folio. While Shakespeare's first editors lumped *The Tempest* in with the comedies, Jacobean audiences may have recognized that it shares certain stylistic and thematic features with those divine comedies known as medieval saints' plays. Inhibited by a now discredited belief in the Reformation's swift triumph over Catholic idolatry, critics have shown only mild interest in Shakespeare's knowledge of miracle plays.[37] New Historicist studies have made much of the fact that *The Tempest* was revived for the celebration of the political marriage of Princess Elizabeth in 1612/3, which has obscured the fact that the first recorded performance of *The Tempest* occurred at Whitehall in 1611 on Hallowmas Night, or All Saints Day.[38] Traditionally, Hallowmas was 'a solemn day for praising all of the Saints [as] tangible presentments of God's power on earth' (Bender 1980, 236–7). If Shakespeare wrote the play with foreknowledge of this impending court performance, it may have encouraged him to seek out a saint's life as a template for the plot. Gonzalo's reference to their preservation from the shipwreck as a 'miracle' (2.1.6) may be something of a tip-off as to the play's literary origins.[39] John Wasson has argued that the saint play maintained a clandestine, vestigial after-life even on the Elizabethan commercial stage. Saintly maidens star in *The Commody of the moste vertuous and Godlye Susanna*, the Admiral's Men's *Diocletian* (*HD* 25), Philip Massinger's *The Virgin Martyr*, and of course Shakespeare's *Measure for Measure* and *Pericles*. As late as 1609 a neo-miracle play based on the life of St Christopher was performed alongside *Pericles* in Yorkshire and a St Andrew play was produced in Edinburgh in 1617. In other words, presenting saints on the post-Reformation stage, particularly English saints such as Dunstan, was not so taboo as one might think.

Although the scholar-sleuths of REED have not uncovered evidence of a Guthlac play, a reference to it may be hiding in plain sight in Philip Henslowe's *Diary*. In his ledgers, the impresario of the Admiral's Men records several performances of a play entitled *Cutlack* (*HD* 21–4). While one cannot be absolutely certain, it is a reasonable hypothesis that this play was based on the life of the Saxon hermit. Henslowe's accounts reveal that *Cutlack* was revived (since it is not marked new) in 1594, the same year in which the Admiral's Men staged what appear to be secularized saint plays featuring St Dorothea and St Silvester, as well as a neo-mystery play entitled *Abraham and Isaac*. Robert Boies Sharpe first proposed that *Cutlack* was a play about Guthlac back in 1935 (35–6); Alfred Harbage and Samuel Schoenbaum seconded the identification in their *Annals of English Drama* (1989, 100–1), which was also accepted by Andrew Gurr (1987, 189–200). The Cutlack surname is widespread throughout Greater East Anglia, southern Lincolnshire, and Cambridgeshire, the epicentre of the saint's cult. A Victorian contributor to *Notes & Queries* professes 'little doubt that Cutlack and Guthlac are identical'.[40] Henslowe's papers also indicate that Shakespeare would have known this play. Significantly, the first performances of *Cutlack* took place during the turbulent month of June 1594, when the Rose was closed and the newly formed acting companies of The Admiral's Men and the Lord Chamberlain's Men shared the stage at Newington Butts. During this run, Shakespeare would have ample time to familiarize himself with the rival company's play. When tragicomedies with protracted, improbable plots and supernatural devices came into vogue near the end of his career, Shakespeare may have looked to the now-quaint literature of the Elizabethan period for a source, as he did in 1610 when he based *The Winter's Tale* on Robert Greene's *Pandosto*.

Instead of a straightforward saint's life, however, an Elizabethan drama based on the life of Guthlac would have savoured strongly of the magus and devil play tradition, a specialty of the Admiral's company. Given the unflagging popularity of Marlowe's tragedy, a play about Guthlac combating Welsh-speaking devils could be another *Faustus* spin-off in the vein of Greene's *Friar Bacon and Friar Bungay*. We know that Edward Alleyn, who had played Faustus, discharged the title role. In the only contemporary reference to the lost play, an Elizabethan satirist mocks a swaggering braggart for his feeble imitation of Saint Dunstan's brows and 'Alleyns Cutlacks gait' (Guilpin 1598, 18). The same poem also compares the braggart to a roaring devil in another Admiral's play based on the life of Job. The

Dunstan mentioned here by the satirist in the same line that he alludes to Cutlack was another English saint famous for defying the devil. He has a prominent role in the Elizabethan comedy *A Knack to Know a Knave* (performed in 1592 and published in 1594), and also appears in *Grim the Collier of Croydon*. If a Catholic bishop battling demons in these plays was not considered beyond the pale, it is entirely possible that the Admiral's Men would mount a similar play about a Saxon warrior turned demon-quelling hermit. Admittedly, this identification of Cutlack as Guthlac is not watertight and other viable candidates have been put forward.[41] The argument that *The Tempest* draws on the Guthlac legend does not depend on the saint being the subject of the lost play, but the overlap is, nonetheless, suggestive and the evidence outlined above considerable enough that the case is at least worth reopening.

Although this chapter has proposed that Shakespeare loosely based aspects of *The Tempest* upon the legend of Guthlac, Shakespeare's late masterpiece may be just as notable for twisting rather than subscribing to the conventions of the medieval saint's life. Many miracle plays, such as the Digby *St Paul* and *The Croxton Play of the Sacrament*, focus on the conversion of nonbelievers, but Prospero's conversion of Caliban is far from successful. Only after his coup d'état is thwarted does Caliban promise to 'seek for grace' (5.1.296). Even then, this remains a promise extracted under the threat of torture rather than a fait accompli. Despite all the resemblances between Prospero and Guthlac outlined earlier, it is Caliban who undergoes a number of punishments identical to the trials of the Saxon saint. For instance, Felix recounts Guthlac's ordeals at night alone in his hovel on the fens, frighted by the outcries of animal spirits:

> A grunting boar, a howling wolf, a whinnying horse, a bellowing stag, a hissing snake, a lowing ox, a croaking raven, all raised an ear-splitting din of horrible noises to craze the true soldier of the true God.   (Albertson 1967, 195)

To a Shakespearean, these passages recall Caliban's description of the legions of beastly demons Prospero conjures to plague him, who appear:

> Sometime like apes that mow and chatter at me
> And after bite me, then like hedgehogs which
> Lie tumbling in my barefoot way and mount
> Their pricks at my footfall. Sometime am I
> All wound with adders, who with cloven tongues
> Do hiss me into madness.
>   (2.2.9–14)

At one point, the demons abduct Guthlac and 'plunge him into the foul mire of the murky swamp' (190). Caliban, likewise complains that Prospero's spirits 'pitch me i'th' mire' (2.2.5). We again hear of Caliban suffering this fate, along with Trinculo and Stephano in Act 4, when Ariel leads them through 'toothed briars, sharp furzes, pricking gorse and thorns' and dunks them:

> I'th' filthy-mantled pool beyond [Prospero's] cell,
> There dancing up to th' chins, that the foul lake
> O'erstunk their feet.
>
> (4.1.180, 182–4)

Compare this passage with Guthlac's torment at the hands of demons: 'They took him to the wild parts of the fen, dragging him through the most tangled thickets of thorn bushes, lacerating all parts of his body' (191). In such moments, the demonic Caliban assumes the aura of the tortured saint and martyr while Prospero's magic would be implicitly seen as diabolical.[42] The Guthlac story thus affords another remarkable example of Shakespeare's sophisticated handling of his sources to amplify his play's moral complexity.

Prospero's army of animal torturers illustrates that the penchant in medieval texts to demonize the wildlife of the fens persisted in early modern England. Another demon-sighting occurred in Crowland in 1586 when some fowlers captured seven strange birds with a ring of raised feathers around their necks resembling the Elizabethan ruff. The anonymous author of a pamphlet announcing their discovery construes these birds as 'frilled and ruffed devils' sent as a warning to our 'frilled and over-ruffed dames' (1586, 7). The pamphlet is a salutary reminder not only that Shakespeare's contemporaries moralized natural history and regarded exotic wildlife with as much horror as fascination but also that the fenlands were much more biodiverse in the past. Sadly, the ruff (as it came to be known) has been designated a red list species by the RSPB, largely due to the destruction of its wetland habitat in the seventeenth century.[43]

The relation between Tiddy Mun of Axholme, examined in the first half of this essay, and the Devils of Crowland has yet to be thoroughly parsed. Balfour's story attests that country-folk in Lincolnshire believed that angered fen-bogeys could infect people with agues. Shakespeare's Caliban yearns for this exact same power, and Ariel possesses a similar ability when he afflicts Prospero's betrayers with a 'fever of the mad' (1.2.210). Although Guthlac's demons could be malaria-induced hallucinations, Felix never explicitly mentions demons summoning infections from the bogs. Could Shakespeare have known some of the early modern folklore of the fens? Catherine Belsey (2007) has established that Shakespearean drama is far more indebted to oral folklore than literary scholars care to admit, but since Balfour's transcription of this legend dates from the late nineteenth century it would be rash to hail it as a 'source' for *The Tempest*. Nevertheless, situating the tale of Tiddy Mun alongside Felix's *Vita Guthlaci* is,

I believe, enlightening. While there is likely some degree of ventriloquism in Balfour's transcription, it records an echo, however garbled, of a voice that was all too often suppressed or ignored in Shakespeare's England: that of the rural and largely illiterate underclass. One of the great achievements of *The Tempest* is that it allows this voice to be heard. Although Caliban never gets to speak in his native language or dialect, his harangues bear comparison with the wrath of Tiddy Mun, or—to cite a text assuredly closer to the play's historical moment—a little-known Jacobean protest ballad entitled 'The Powte's Complaint'. Composed in 1619, it adopts the point of view of an indignant fish, who conjures the moon, wind, floods, and blasts to curse the fen drainers: 'O let the Frogs and Miry Bogs destroy where they do enter'.[44] Whereas Prospero's masque summons Ceres to a 'grass plot' (4.1.73) to bestow the blessings of fertility, the ballad implores Neptune to preserve the wetlands from being converted to pasture. It praises the fens as home to a local economy that works with the wider ecological community. If *The Tempest* does not speak out for the fens as bluntly as the pout does, the fish-like Caliban who curses or (punning on his name) 'bans' his master and whose 'conspiracy' interrupts the masque defends his habitat with a similar ferocity.

From an ecological viewpoint, the complexity of Caliban (portrayed as both demon and saint) also extends to the fenland environment he inhabits. A demon-haunted and disease-infested mire or a divinely created nursery for fish and fowl, a flood-prone wasteland crying out for human reclamation or a pristine wilderness best left alone, the English fens could be perceived in diametrically opposed ways. During the periodic harvest failures of the Little Ice Age, rising agricultural prices made the temptation to put uncultivated land under the plough hard to resist. Yet profit-minded farmers would in fact sow much of the reclaimed Lincolnshire wetlands with woad (for blue and green dyes) rather than grain (Thirsk 1997, 87). By the mid-twentieth century, much of the fenlands had become (and still remain) vast monocultures of cash crops: cereals, potatoes, beets, or rapeseed. At a time when efforts are underway to restore these wetlands, the sympathy Caliban now engenders can also encompass his habitat, one of the last bastions of wilderness in Shakespeare's England. Alongside the Irish, Caribbean, and African Calibans we have come to admire, criticism of *The Tempest* needs to make room on the boat for Caliban the pagan genius loci and rebellious fen-dweller protesting the theft of his commons. Rather than diminish these previous readings, this eco-historicist interpretation of Shakespeare's romance clarifies why it lends itself so readily to adaptation as both an anti-colonial and pro-ecological text.

Appropriately, in Aimé Césaire's post-colonial rewrite of *The Tempest*, Caliban is an animist and environmentalist who upbraids the arid rationalism of Prospero:

> You think the earth itself is dead.... It's so much simpler that way! Dead, you can walk on it, pollute it, you can tread upon it with the steps of a conqueror. I respect the earth because I know that it is alive. (1969, 12)

The play ends with Prospero alone in his cell fretting about the island's changing climate.[45] Césaire's critique chimes perfectly with the one advanced in this chapter. This study has unmoored *The Tempest* from its global, post-colonial contexts so that we might ultimately return to them with an enriched understanding of their continuity with local, environmental concerns. In addition to being an honorary prologue to American literature, *The Tempest* is an important document in the history of the Plantationocene. It registers a profound uneasiness not only about the colonization of peoples but also about the colonization of the natural world by an anthropocentric science that is Eurocentric and elitist rather than representative of all humanity, much less the earth's myriad species. In a world threatened by increasingly ferocious tempests, rising sea levels, and toxins in our water supply, Caliban's curse reads like a premonition of ecological blowback.

7

'Purple Plagues or Crimson War'

Population Control in *Measure for Measure*, *Coriolanus*, London, and Ulster

In the classic account of the genesis of the Renaissance, the Swiss historian Jacob Burckhardt attributed it to the 'rebirth' of classical culture, the cult of individualism, the rediscovery of nature, and the rise of civic humanism. A more prosaic factor glossed over by the Burckhardtian tradition is how these various developments were abetted by urbanization and population surges before the advent of the Little Ice Age and the Black Death, demographic trends that resumed apace in the fifteenth and sixteenth centuries.[1] Although the period label early modern has gained greater traction in recent decades, the term Renaissance retains some value insofar as it provides a subliminal etymological reminder that the era's cultural achievements were predicated on a sharp rise in human birth rates. In this literal sense, the flowering of commercial drama in late Elizabethan London at a time when the city's population had quadrupled from approximately 50,000 in 1500 to 200,000 by the century's end—and may have reached 350,000 by 1650 (Finlay and Shearer 1986)—very much qualifies as a Renaissance phenomenon. The Stratford native Shakespeare must have recognized that 'the growth in London's population was a crucial element in [the] theatre's success' (Howard 2007, 15). But he would also have been acutely aware of the negative consequences of unchecked growth. The need to feed England's ballooning population drove the enclosure of commons, heaths, and fens documented elsewhere in this study, forcing the landless poor to trudge their way to London, where they in turn fomented perceptions that the metropolis had become overcrowded. As the following pages will reveal, the plague and harvest failures that rocked England in the first decade of the seventeenth century crystalized apprehensions that the city and possibly the island nation as a whole had exceeded their carrying capacity. These demographic anxieties are particularly audible in *Measure for Measure* and *Coriolanus*, two of the most overtly political dramas Shakespeare ever wrote. Once again, it will become apparent that Shakespeare shares many of the concerns of King James and his Privy Council, while also expressing doubts about the ethics and practicality of state dominion over, in this case, sexuality and the city. Shakespeare's problem comedy and Roman tragedy confront the cruel necessity and callous hypocrisy of population management in Jacobean Britain in ways that presage

Shakespeare Beyond the Green World: Drama and Ecopolitics in Jacobean Britain. Todd Andrew Borlik,
Oxford University Press. © Todd Andrew Borlik 2023. DOI: 10.1093/oso/9780192866639.003.0008

and elucidate some of the fractious debates about demographics in contemporary ecocriticism.

When he assumes control of Vienna in *Measure for Measure*, Angelo vaunts the prognostic power of the law, which:

> like a prophet
> Looks in a glass that shows what future evils
> Either now, or by remissness new conceived,
> And so in progress to be hatched and born,
> Are now to have no successive degrees.
>
> (2.2.98–102)

Angelo here imagines the ruler equipped with a conjuror's magic mirror, like the one in the popular Elizabethan comedy *Friar Bacon and Friar Bungay*. In Renaissance statecraft, however, the magical objects of medieval romance would give way to the projections of realpolitik, and Angelo's glass serves as a proleptic metaphor for what William Petty would call 'political arithmetic'. Angelo's attention to 'future evils' that will be 'hatched and born' identifies sexual reproduction as a problem in need of oversight, while his verbs further degrade it by evoking the oviparous birth of birds and reptiles. Meanwhile, the reference to ending 'successive degrees' recalls the royal prerogative to extinguish heredity titles, offering a legal precedent for population control. In short, the play not only extends the city's spatial jurisdiction into the suburbs (and, more invasively, the bedroom, as the bed trick demonstrates) but also assigns the state a temporal jurisdiction over the future. This dovetails with James's pronouncements that monarchs must not only enforce old laws but also devise new ones, striving 'to *foresee and prevent* all dangers that are likely to fall upon them' (*KJSW* 262, italics added). In reassessing the 'King James Version' of *Measure for Measure* with an ecocritical eye, this chapter cavils with both Foucauldian biopolitics and the lingering tendency to denigrate the monarch as an agoraphobe with a sinister penchant for surveillance. Instead it submits that royal edicts echoed in *Measure for Measure* sprang in part from legitimate concerns about public health and overpopulation, despite the peculiar fact that protecting the former exacerbated the latter. Shakespeare's contemporaries would have been painfully conscious of this paradox in 1603 when a virulent plague outbreak decimated London's population even as its communicable nature simultaneously heightened fears of urban overcrowding.

The population question rears its hydra-heads again in *Coriolanus*, which experiments with theatre's capacity to represent both visually and verbally the unrepresentable vastness of the city. Henry Turner has theorized city comedy as a 'process of coming to knowledge about the consequences of urbanization, [which] depended on generating artificial models and projections' (2006, 187), and the same might be said of Shakespeare's urban tragedy. Menenius's parable of the body politic constitutes one such artificial model but the cluster of bodies rioting for affordable food at the play's start makes the 'consequences of urbanization' disconcertingly apparent. Situating *Coriolanus* and its crowds in their ecopolitical context, I argue that the play advances a trenchant critique of the *Pax Jacobus* from a demographic point of view, while voicing a certain ambivalence about James's plan to curtail overpopulation by providing an outlet for it in the Ulster Plantation. Reviving the Roman past on the Globe stage portrays the Jacobean present as cold, flat, and crowded, and Shakespeare's unruly crowds seem to embody not so much the dangers of mob-rule nor the wisdom of the collective as a demographic crisis, one reflected in miniature in the press of the Globe audience.[2]

Plague and Sprawl in *Measure for Measure*

When Shakespeare's Globe on London's Bankside closed its doors in March 2020 due to the Covid-19 pandemic, theatre historians experienced a mild case of déjà vu, for Shakespeare's own company had faced a similar predicament, shuttering the theatre when the monthly toll of plague deaths topped thirty. In a magisterial op-ed in the *New York Times* entitled 'What Shakespeare Teaches Us about Living with Pandemics', Emma Smith (2020) considers how the plague impinges on his dramatic artistry:

> Shakespeare is not interested in the statistics—what in his time were called the bills of mortality. His fictions reimagine the macro-narrative of epidemic as the micro-narrative of tragedy, setting humane uniqueness against the disease's obliterating ravages. His work is a cultural prophylactic against understanding disease solely in quantitative terms, a narrative vaccine.

This rings true: Shakespeare was a playwright not an epidemiologist. Yet his mixed feelings about the ruthlessly quantitative language of urban governance in the midst of a health crisis call for further scrutiny. His plays are not interested in statistics per se but they are interested in the state's interest in statistics. Since fatal outbreaks threatened the commercial viability of the theatre industry, it is almost inevitable that Shakespeare would be preoccupied with the problem of urban population management and represent it in his fiction. While Shakespeare, as Smith observantly notes, never brings a plague victim on stage, *Measure for Measure* and *Coriolanus* dwell on overcrowding, disease, and famine to game out the demographic projections and policies of Jacobean authorities, including the king himself.

As King James VI of Scotland wended his way towards London in the spring of 1603 to become James I of England, he soon realized that his new realm was far more populous than his former one. Throngs of well-wishers and office-seekers lined his route south, forcing the king and his entourage either to thread their way through them or to skirt around them. In Newcastle, the locust-like swarm converging on his train consumed so much of the available food supply that James had to issue warnings to other local authorities along the way to stockpile extra provisions for his arrival and discourage further admirers from flocking to him (*SRP* 1:8).[3] Few heeded the message. When his procession entered London on 7 May, 'the multitudes of people in highwayes, fieldes, medowes, closes and on trees were such that they covered the beautie of the fieldes, and so greedy were they to behold the countenance of the King, that with much unrulinesse they injured and hurt one another' (*PPMF* 1:113). Overwhelmed by such crowds, James must have been struck by the lopsided demographic differences between the Scottish and English capitals, for London's population exceeded Edinburgh's by a factor of ten.[4] His progress through the crowds would have been accompanied by the constant refrain, 'Make room, make room' (incidentally the title of Harry Harrison's 1966 demo-dystopian classic), which eventually rang in the monarch's ears like a policy proposition.

If they at first posed little more than a logistical inconvenience, London's crowds soon acquired an aura of menace when the number of plague deaths spiked alarmingly in late May and June in what would prove the worst outbreak to ravage England between 1563 and 1665. Acting swiftly, James issued a proclamation on 29 May ordering the rural gentry to leave the city (*SRP* 1:21), and the following week postponed his own coronation, along with the 'Shewes and Ornaments' arranged to celebrate it, on the grounds that 'the great Concourse of people' (*SRP* 1:37) might spread the pestilence. It seems probable that Shakespeare, who may have been involved in preparations for these 'Shewes and Ornaments', would have been impacted by this evacuation order, and returned to Stratford because of it. Indeed, he may have begun *Measure for Measure* in de facto quarantine during this time.

When the plague subsided, James was able to hold his coronation procession in March 1604, but a fear of its resurgence meant that crowd management still remained a priority. One contemporary eyewitness rebuked the overzealous bystanders: '[if you will] in love prease uppon your Soveraigne thereby to offend him, your Soveraigne perchance [may] mistake your love and punnish it as an offence' (Dugdale 1604, B2[r]). Shakespeare himself was almost certainly among this press of spectators, which left traces of its form and pressure on *Measure for Measure*. In a curious metaphor, Angelo likens the sudden influx of blood to his heart to the way

> The general subject to a well-wished king
> Quit their own part and in obsequious fondness
> Crowd to his presence, where their untaught love
> Must needs appear offence.
>
> (2.4.27–30)

The passage has long been recognized as a topical allusion to England's newly crowned monarch.[5] While some commentators have been overhasty in treating Duke Vincentio as an exact doppelgänger for James, there remains a widespread consensus that the king imprinted his stamp on the play.[6] The only real question concerns the depth and likeness of the impression.

Swayed by the anti-Stuart bias of Parliamentarian and Whig historians, critics sometimes cite *Measure for Measure* to caricature James as an aloof agoraphobe, irked by the great unwashed that thronged the streets to gawp at him.[7] While it is true James did not relish the adulation of the masses, the wording of the royal edicts displays an admirable concern with the impact of urban overcrowding on public health, not on the king's psyche. The fact that James's arrival in London coincided with the worst plague outbreak in a century surely must mitigate these accusations that he lacked the common touch. If James did feel somewhat uneasy amid the London crowds, that reaction might spring less from some irrational phobia than a combination of culture shock as he adjusted to life in one of the most populous cities in the world and the advice of his physicians to practice royal distancing in the midst of a virulent plague outbreak. No wonder James preferred to spend his time hunting in the countryside.

To his credit, the king did not simply abandon the people, but consistently took steps to reduce urban density, a recognized accelerant for plague. Attempts to redress this problem had begun during his predecessor's reign. In June 1602 Elizabeth had issued a proclamation (modelled on one from 1580) to destroy all new buildings within three miles of London, ordering the demolition crews to sell off the timber and donate the proceeds to the poor. This policy was motivated in part by concerns over what we would now call urban sprawl and in part by an anxiety that the building spree was contributing to deforestation. But the political will to enforce the Elizabethan edict was lacking. The 1603 outbreak, however, supplied James with the political momentum to clamp down on offenders in accordance with Foucault's recognition of the plague as a catalyst for 'disciplinary projects' (1979, 198). As the sickness hit its peak, killing 3,037 people in the London area in one week (Creighton 1965, 1:476), the king issued a proclamation demanding strict enforcement of this law to prevent landlords from cramming too many people in squalid tenements, and ordering all such buildings to be demolished.

As Shakespeare scholars have noted, *Measure for Measure* explicitly references this policy:

> POMPEY You have not heard of the proclamation, have you?
> MISTRESS OVERDONE What proclamation, man?
> POMPEY All the houses in the suburbs of Vienna must be
>   plucked down.

MISTRESS OVERONE And what shall become of those in
  the city?
POMPEY They shall stand for seed.

(1.2.90-95)

While some editions annotate the passage with a cursory reference to the proclamation, it is worth citing at length to highlight what it does and does not contain:

> it falleth out by wofull experience that *the great confluence and accesse of excessive numbers of idle, indigent, dissolute and dangerous persons*, and the *pestering* of many of them in small and strait rooms and habitations in the Citie of London, and in and about the Suburbes of the same, have bene one of the chief occasions of the great Plague and mortality.   (*SRP* 1:47, italics added)

The proclamation forbids new residents within four miles of the city or any infected suburb, and orders civic authorities 'to take special care, that none of the foresaid Roomes, Houses, or places be hereafter *pestered* with multitudes of dwellers', and that any tenement violating the law 'shall forthwith...be rased and pulled down' (*SRP* 1:48).

What is perhaps most striking about this document and others like it is how the repeated use of the verb 'pester' conflates population with pestilence. The proclamation also specifies that responsibility for enforcement will fall on the Aldermen of the wards, their Deputies, and local Justices of the Peace. In the previous proclamation of 29 May ordering the gentry to vacate the city, James observes 'that heretofore there hath bene a great neglect in obeying Proclamations', and warns his reign will be different: offenders now may find themselves made 'an example of contempt' (22). The parallels with *Measure for Measure* are easily spied. Enforcement of Vienna's 'strict statutes and most biting laws' (1.3.19) has been lax, and the Duke appoints a deputy Angelo to solve the problem. Insisting 'we must not make a scarecrow of the law' (2.1.1), Angelo punishes Claudio as an example. But the parallels are not exact, given that the Duke's proclamation against suburban 'houses' implies 'brothels', whereas the Jacobean edict is not explicitly targeting prostitution but plague and population density. By adhering to his chief source, George Whetstone's *Promos and Cassandra*, in which there is no mention of a plague outbreak, Shakespeare misleadingly represents a public health and demographic crisis as a moral one.

Or does he? While plague, population, and prostitution might seem like three distinct phenomena, that was not quite the case in Shakespeare's London. First and foremost, higher population density correlates with a higher rate of infection and mortality during an epidemic. Bills of mortality made it clear that the plague disproportionately affected the poor in crowded slums and suburbs, and these areas inevitably overlapped with red light districts.[8] Secondly, in the absence of modern germ theory, many in the seventeenth century interpreted pestilence as a divine punishment for sin, especially for civic tolerance of prostitution. Since brothels housed many women under one roof, 'some dozen or fourteen' (2.1.30) in Mistress Quickly's establishment, with numerous customers coming and going in the closest of physical contact, it is easy to see why they would be accused of incubating outbreaks. As Catherine Cox argues, *Measure for Measure*'s imagery of a diseased city reflects early modern understandings of pox and pestilence as 'causally linked' (2008, 432). Thirdly, many in Jacobean London blamed prostitution for inflating birth rates in already overcrowded parishes. Reverberations of this 'bastard bomb' (Geisweidt 2015) can be heard in *Pericles*, when the Bawd speaks of 'bringing up of poor bastards—as I think I have brought up some eleven' (4.2.12–13). In recounting the Duke's willingness to wink at prostitution, Lucio describes a nation speeding towards a demographic disaster: 'ere he would have hanged a man for the getting a hundred bastards, he would have paid for the nursing a thousand' (3.1.380–2). Hardly a neutral judge, Lucio himself has fathered an illegitimate child with Kate Keepdown, and the name of the executioner Abhorson insinuates that he, too, is a prostitute's son. The fact that Elbow's 'great bellied' (2.1.94) wife has been caught in a brothel furnishes grounds for suspecting her husband is not the father. The name of the nine-times married Mistress Overdone suggests a body worn out from frequent copulation but also perhaps regular childbirth. In his snarky parody of character criticism, L. C. Knights asked 'how many children had Lady Macbeth?', but Jacobean authorities watching *Measure for Measure* would have pondered a far more pressing question: how many children had Mistress Overdone?

In a seminal essay, Jonathan Dollimore took critics to task for consenting with the play's assumption that 'unrestrained sexuality is ostensibly subverting social order; anarchy threatens to engulf the State unless sexuality is subjected to renewed and severe regulation' (1985, 72). While there is much to admire in Dollimore's piercing critique, he also concedes that insofar as 'fornication *did* produce charity-dependent bastards...there were real grounds for anxiety' (1985, 80). Benjamin Bertram, meanwhile, has demonstrated that the play applies the discourse of state husbandry to an urban context, remarking that the Duke and Angelo impose an 'instrumental control over natural resources and human behaviour' that spoils an 'eros of natural fertility'.[9] One could refine these arguments further by noting that the state's target in *Measure for Measure* is not so much sexuality per se as its biological output in an era before reliable birth control: more bodies to house in a crowded, plague-infested city, and mouths to feed in an era prone to harvest failures. In this light, Angelo seems less like a Puritan killjoy, and the Duke 'may just be doing his job in the face of daunting demographics' (Braunmuller and Watson 2020, 8). After all, Escalus, a reliable voice of moral authority, concurs that the law is 'needful' (2.1.272). Even as she pleads for her brother's life, Isabella agrees his transgression should be censured and 'meet the blow of justice' (2.2.32). While few readers in the modern West would categorize adultery or premarital sex as a crime, much less a capital one, an eco-demographic interpretation of this problem comedy makes it much more relatable to a twenty-first-century audience.

Measure for Measure's lexical field projects a great deal of negative energy towards sexual reproduction, which is informed by but not limited to a Calvinist sense of original sin. Angelo speaks of the 'swelling evil of my conception' (2.4.6–7), which might refer to sexual arousal but also evokes the distended belly of his pregnant mother, tarnishing conception as an evil not a blessing, as Hamlet does when he likens it to the sun breeding maggots in a dead dog. Breeding again has a pejorative charge when Angelo fantasizes of sleeping with Isabella: 'my sense breeds with it' (2.2.145). In the play's opening speech, the Duke praises Escalus as 'pregnant' (1.1.11) in the art of just governance, and asks 'what figure of us' Angelo 'will bear' (1.1.16), like a father-to-be wondering if his unborn child will resemble him. Hence Angelo's subsequent confession that he is 'unpregnant' (4.4.18), an odd Shakespeare coinage, suggests a male miscarriage. The Duke's hasty flight from the city in 'quick condition' (1.1.53) again evokes couvade syndrome, as if he were an unwed woman sneaking away to deliver her child in secret, implicating him in the problem he wishes to redress. The Duke's condescending rebuke to Juliet that her 'sin [is] of heavier kind' (2.3.28) than Claudio's betrays the sexual double standard of a patriarchal era, but also has a double meaning in the literal heaviness of pregnancy, equating the foetus with the burden of sin. Much of the discomfort this play incites in audiences and critics emanates from its disgust with human fertility. But this disgust can be reframed as unease about a baby boom leading to a demographic imbalance, as figured in the Duke's picture of Vienna as a chaotic nursery where 'the baby beats the nurse' (1.3.30).

As Buell (2016, 6–8) remarks, population faded from the environmentalist agenda since the 1970s for three chief reasons: (1) the doomsday predictions of the late '60s failed to materialize; (2) the intervening decades have witnessed a stark decline in the birth rate in industrialized countries; and (3) imposing strict birth control measures on economically underprivileged countries seems to smack of neo-imperialism and racism.[10] The third factor is a real sticking point, since it effectively prevents poorer countries from modernizing as early modern England did on its way to becoming the world's first industrial superpower. On a smaller scale, Shakespeare confronts a similar problem in *Measure for Measure*: an attempt by the metropolitan elite to curtail population growth by flattening the birth rate and discouraging unwanted pregnancies among the poor. Although the Jacobean policies sprang from concern over public health, the governmental edicts confound population itself with plague.

By downplaying the pestilence, however, Shakespeare raises disturbing questions regarding the justice of population control, contesting the royal proclamations with voices of popular resistance. While Angelo equates siring a bastard with murder or counterfeiting, Lucio sees it as no more serious than a game of 'ticktack' (1.2.186), 'filling a bottle' (3.1.430), or 'untrussing' (3.1.437), that is undressing. He dismisses it as an inevitable part of human nature, 'impossible to extirp...till eating and drinking be put down' (3.1.366–7). Pompey is likewise sceptical: 'Does your worship mean to geld and splay all the youth of the city?' (2.1.220). As his verbs insinuate, such a law dehumanizes the populace as cattle. Moreover, if a law penalizing fornication as a capital offense were enforced for a decade, Pompey warns Vienna will need a 'commission for more heads' (2.1.230). Lucio likewise jests that Angelo's example might 'unpeople the province with continency' (3.1.432). Overdone's complaint that the pox, war, and executions have left her 'custom shrunk' (1.2.80) implies that Vienna has already bled population. The play thus raises the spectre of depopulation, and considers that sexual license might benefit the state, as in Lear's cynical outburst, 'to it luxury, pell-mell, for I lack soldiers' (4.6.115). The Viennese exemption permitting some brothels to remain in the city 'for seed' (1.2.95) reveals that the state's goal is not to outlaw prostitution or illegitimacy tout court but merely to limit the reproductive rate. In 1604, some of Shakespeare's contemporaries may have argued for re-seeding the capital to offset the decline due to plague. After all, an estimated 30,000 Londoners, nearly one-sixth of the city's population, lost their lives in the outbreak. Such alarming figures clarify why *Measure for Measure* 'seems poised between the idea that sex is like the plague...and the contradictory idea that human sexuality is the very thing that triumphs over disease and death through procreation' (Kamps and Raber 2004, 268–9).

Viewing Shakespeare's problem play through a demographic prism also throws a curious sidelight on a neglected aspect of the Reformation: the impact of the dissolution of the religious houses on population levels. Monasteries and nunneries helped to counteract urbanization and population growth by raising many unwanted children and adopting them into the clergy, where they would be less likely to have offspring. Despite popular satires of randy nuns and philandering friars, the official abandonment of clerical celibacy would create the perception of a spike in the numbers of procreative marriages. *Measure for Measure* replicates this demographic trend in having the Duke shed his friar's robes and propose marriage to the novice Isabella, a plot twist that has understandably annoyed many actresses and feminist critics. Reversing Hamlet's 'get thee to a nunnery' speech, the proposal seems a concession to human frailty and the irrepressible nature of sexuality, but reactivates the play's problematic exploration of both consent and reproduction. The Duke's 'motion' that Isabella not return to the convent but marry forces her back into the sexual economy, so that she, too, may have to deal with an unexpected pregnancy. While critics sometimes proffer artistic or biographical explanations for the darkness of *Measure for Measure* by speculating that a middle-aged Shakespeare had outgrown the exuberant comedies of his youth, a more decisive factor might be that the lethally cramped living conditions in plague-stricken London made the conventional ending of comedy, heterosexual marriage and the prospect of children, untenable, for it reproduces the problem that instigated the conflict in the first place.

If *Measure for Measure*'s claim to artistic greatness rests on its eschewing easy answers, for ecocritics this notably includes answers to the question of how to simultaneously accommodate and limit reproductive sexuality. To enforce a law criminalizing sex, Shakespeare implies, requires one to stand outside the biological parameters of the human condition. Hence Lucio jokes that Angelo was not of woman born but 'spawned' by a mermaid or stockfishes. When he mocks Angelo as a 'motion generative' (3.1.375) he is calling him a puppet that is anatomically correct but sterile, and he later dubs him an 'ungenitured agent' (3.1.432), which could likewise mean that he was not conceived through sex or is himself incapable of begetting offspring. Implementing laws against population growth seems to require that authority neuter itself and renounce reproduction, but Angelo's language betrays his own drives and his ironic arousal by Isabella's chastity. Modern eco-sceptics often accuse environmentalists of failing to abide by their own professed values (calling for population reduction while having children), and Shakespeare's portrayal of Angelo as a fallen angel presents a similar case study in hypocritical authority that proves all too human and cannot obey its own behests. *Measure for Measure*'s title is thus doubly apposite: it echoes Christ's warning that hypocritical judges condemn themselves while also evoking the quantitative metrics of demographic policies, whose enforcers cannot exempt themselves from the headcount.

For Freudian criticism, *Measure for Measure* is a tour de force illustration of the proximity of Eros and Thanatos, the entwined drives of sex and death. From a Malthusian perspective, however, the linking of sex and death, epitomized in Pompey's career change from bawd to hangman, captures the paradox that a baby boom must eventually trigger a dieback. Even Claudio's famous metaphor likening desire to rat poison condemns unrestrained libido as a toxic force that brings about its own demise. Given that the play misrepresents Jacobean legislation, which did not criminalize fornication as a capital offense, could we instead view the Duke's proclamation not so much as a political law, which would be manifestly cruel and unenforceable, but as an allegorical restatement of a demographic principle?

Although Shakespeare composed *Measure for Measure* nearly two centuries before Thomas Malthus published his earth-shaking 1798 *Essay on the Principle of Population*, the basic concept of a population check was intuitively understood by many Jacobeans, including a writer personally known to Shakespeare, and who may even have revised *Measure for Measure*: Thomas Middleton.[11] A poem

Middleton co-wrote with Thomas Dekker in response to the 1603 plague considers whether the epidemic might be a kind of demographic emetic:

> For if our thoughts sit truly trying
> The just necessity of dying,
> How needful (though how dreadful) are
> Purple plagues or crimson war,
> We would conclude (still urging pity)
> A plague's the purge to cleanse a city.[12]

When plague struck again two decades later, Dekker would deny this principle: 'we flatter ourselves that the Pestilence serves but as a Broome, to sweepe Kingdomes of people, when thy grow ranke and too full' (1625, 143). Even as he seeks to refute this idea, however, Dekker attests that Malthusian calculus was thinkable in the early seventeenth century.

It is customary to speak of the plague, especially the mid-fourteenth-century pandemic, as the 'Black Death' (an idiom first recorded in 1755), but the phrase 'purple plague' combines a physiological allusion to purpura's blotches and livid, purplish boils with a hue synonymous with majesty. As documented in Chapter 3, vibrant purple clothing was reserved for the monarch, so Dekker and Middleton's colour adjective endows what we now recognize as lowly bacteria (*yersina pestis*) with an imperial authority—as in iconography of the plague as the triumph of King Death—far greater than the vaunted absolutism of James: a point made all too clear when an outbreak forced the king to postpone his coronation. *Measure for Measure* thus hints at the inability of the physician-monarch to control the pestilence and hence at James's feeble authority over the city that his coronation procession ostensibly celebrates.[13] Disease, however, was not the only factor to stymy population growth in the Renaissance. Many recognized that famine and 'crimson war' could also cull human numbers, for proof of which one need look no further than Shakespeare's *Coriolanus*.

Coriolanus and War as Demographic Blood-Letting

> It is to be foreseene that the Population of a Kingdom (especially if it be not mowen downe by warres) do not exceed the Stock of the Kingdom which should maintaine them.
> (Bacon 1625, 83)

The importance of dearth to *Coriolanus* would be difficult to overstate. Inclement weather in 1606 led to a pitiful harvest, which triggered an uprising the following spring against enclosures, blamed for compounding the problem by inflating grain prices. The Midlands Rising began in Northamptonshire before quickly spreading to Shakespeare's home county of Warwickshire, and critics have long recognized these protests as a decisive context for Shakespeare's tragedy, one that likely inspired the playwright to return to his well-thumbed copy of Plutarch to dramatize this particular moment in Roman history when bread riots shook Rome.[14] Shakespeare's engagement with these issues in *Coriolanus* has earned him praise as 'the poet of Jacobean London's food supply' (Boehrer 2013, 80) and the play evinces a similarly keen interest in London's water supply (Martin 2020). But *Coriolanus* might be read even more broadly as a political treatise on the related, overarching topic of population management. Whereas Thomas More's *Utopia* imaginatively blames the decline of enclosed villages on people-eating sheep, the reality was more prosaic: the rural poor simply left the countryside for the city, congregating in overcrowded, unsanitary tenements. The riot that opens *Coriolanus* is therefore not a representation of the Midlands Rising, but a premonition that its dispossessed might overrun London. In his 1607 proclamation suppressing the unrest, James asserts that the 'glorie and strength of all Kings consisteth in the multitude of Subjects' (*SRP* 155), and therefore promises he will order 'the abuses of Depopulation and unlawfull Inclosures to be further looked into' (*SRP* 157). Yet even as he sought to reverse the decline of rural communities, James would, like Coriolanus, take steps to 'depopulate the city' (3.1.266), and Shakespeare's haughty general would have possessed a discernible appeal to the Jacobean ruling classes who were bent on averting a demographic crisis through war, emigration, or both.

It turns out that Thomas Malthus is not the iconoclastic thinker he is reputed to be, for many Renaissance writers on politics had divined the notion of population checks.[15] As England's population climbed in the centuries after the Black Death, and London in particular grew disproportionately large in comparison to the rest of the kingdom, some began to suspect whether the nation could sustain such a rise in human numbers and corresponding decline of other species. In a tract that prefaces Holinshed's *Chronicles*, one of Shakespeare's favourite books, William Harrison observes that many

> doo grudge at the great increase of people in these daies, thinking a necessarie brood of cattell farre better than a superfluous augmentation of mankind... [and] affirming that we have alreadie too great store of people in England.
>
> (1587, 183, 205)

Such opinions cannot be completely dismissed as the grumblings of eccentric cranks. Theories of population growth and control had been floated by Niccolo Machiavelli and Thomas More and reiterated in Shakespeare's lifetime by Giovanni Botero, Walter Ralegh, and Francis Bacon. Ralegh's musings on demographics can be found in his *Discourse of the Original and Fundamental Cause of... War* (*c*.1615), where he formulates an early instance of the 'just war' or 'necessary war' doctrine: 'Suffice it that when any Country is overlaid by the multitude which live upon it, there is a natural necessity compelling it to disburden itself and lay the Load upon other, by right or wrong' (1650, 9). Although Ralegh's *Discourse* was not yet printed when Shakespeare wrote *Coriolanus*, works by Jean Bodin and Botero were Englished in 1606 and would have sparked debate about the politics of population at the Jacobean court at this time; indeed, the translation of Botero was dedicated to Sir Thomas Egerton, a member of James's Privy Council.[16]

Acclaimed as the first modern demographer, Botero recognized that population growth must have limits: 'Let no man thinke... that a Citie may go on in increase without ceassing' (1606, 86), he warns. To illustrate his theories, Botero selects Rome as his case-study, describing how the fledging city-state destroyed nearby regional powers to inflate its own population, expanding in a fifty-mile radius before reaching what modern demographers would call its carrying capacity but what Botero terms its 'compleate number' (94). In a passage echoed by Ralegh and Francis Bacon, Botero predicts that when civilizations exceed the capacity of their 'vertue nutritive' (94), war will erupt: for 'what is there under the Sunne, that doth make man, with more horrible effusion of blood to fight for, and with more cruelty, than the earth, foode, and commodity of habitacion?' (95).

Given the circulation of Botero's writing in London in 1606, it is not anachronistic to propose an affinity between the population theory synonymous with Malthus and Shakespeare's Martius. His opposition to the distribution of corn to the poor, the comparison of him to a grim reaper-like 'harvestman' (1.3.38), and his name evocative of the god Mars and hence lethal warfare all make him an embodiment of demographic backlash. Speaking like a Machiavellian demographer, Coriolanus welcomes the outbreak of war with the Volscians as an opportunity to 'vent / Our musty superfluity' (1.1.220–1). The curious phrase could imply selling excess grain past its best-before date to provision the troops, but also signifies a die-off of surplus population.[17] Anxiety that the city has reached the limits of its 'vertue nutritive' explains why Coriolanus supports dispatching the army to pillage resources from abroad: 'The Volsces have much corn. Take these rats thither / To gnaw their garners' (1.1.244–5). Shortly after relaying the parable of the belly, Plutarch reports 'it liked [Martius] nothing to see the greatnes of the people thus increased' (240), and Martius voices the same complaint in another passage from Plutarch quoted by Shakespeare in which he compares sedition to the weed 'cockle... which had bene sowed and scattered abroade emongest the people, whom they should have cut of[f]... and have prevented their greatnes' (245). In both instances, 'greatnes' primarily signifies political power but carries a secondary connotation of numbers, as the two are of course interlinked. This would have been apparent to Jacobean readers of Botero, whose 1588 work was translated in 1606 as *A Treatise concerning the causes of the magnificence and greatness of cities*, where greatness means population size. The metaphor of the cockle is also charged in this context, as it shifts the blame for the dearth onto the people's ever-increasing demand for food by oddly equating them with an agricultural weed that diminished the harvest. As Martius sees it, Rome's problem springs not from a shortage of food but a surplus of mouths, which war will conveniently reduce.[18] Coriolanus again sounds like a proto-Malthusian when, echoing the misanthrope Timon of Athens, he conjures plague as a fitting punishment for the populace's ingratitude, and even wishes an epidemic slay his fellow citizens. 'Boils and plagues / Plaster you o'er' (1.4.32-3) he barks at his retreating troops. His mother later repeats the curse, evoking the economic impact of the outbreak on livelihoods: 'Now the red pestilence strike all trades in Rome / And occupations perish' (4.1.13-14). The Roman tragedy also conflates crowds and plague when the Tribunes recall the 'dissentious *numbers pestering* streets' (4.6.7). As in the 1603 royal proclamation, pester smacks of pestilence, while the substitution of people for numbers or statistics is a common if deeply troubling metonymy in eco-demography and demo-dystopian fiction.

Unbeknownst to most commentators on the play, the historical Coriolanus cast a shadow over Renaissance debates on population control, as evident from a remarkable but underappreciated inter-text for Shakespeare's tragedy: Thomas and Dudley Digges's *Four Paradoxes... Concerning Military Discipline* (1604). Saving the most scandalous paradox for last, Dudley proposes 'that warre is sometimes lesse hurtfull, and more to be wisht in a well governd State than peace' (96). To defend this radical proposition, he urges a classical precedent:

> The generall daunger [of foreign war] will soone withdraw mens mindes from intestine garboiles to resist the generall mischief, both which appeared in that wise proceeding of the Senate of Rome in Coriolanus time that by this means appeased all divisions.... *For the populousnesse of that Citie, by reason of their peace occasioning a dearth and famine*, and their idlenesse stirring up lewd felowes to exasperate the desperate need and envious malice of the meaner sort against the nobility... in the end the fire brake forth hard to be quenched, and then the Senate... were at length enforced to flie to this medicine, which wisely applied before, had well prevented all those causes, and their unhappie effectes.
>
> (104, italics added)

Digges's reasoning is recognizably Malthusian: prolonged peace triggers a population boom, which eventually breeds famine and conflict. The Roman Senate, Digges argues, followed a similar cruel logic and 'resolved on a warre with the Volsces to ease their City of that dearth, by diminishing their number' (104-5). In 1600, Dudley Digges had become the stepson of Shakespeare's friend and executor Thomas Russell, which makes it a tempting conjecture that Shakespeare was familiar with this provocative work.[19]

Shakespeare also seems to have been acquainted with the similar pro-war apologies of Barnaby Rich, *The Souldiers wish to Britons welfare* (1604) and *Roome for a gentleman* (1609), the latter of which declares: 'Peace breedes Cowards, it effeminates our mindes, it pampers our wanton wils, and it runs headlong into all sorts of sinne' (1609, B1ʳ). Opinions identical to those of Digges and Rich are endorsed in a memorable scene in *Coriolanus* by a chorus of Volscian servants. 'Peace is a very apoplexy', declares the First Servingman, 'a getter of more bastard children than war's a destroyer of men' (4.5.226–28). The Second Servingman agrees that peace only serves to 'increase tailors and breed ballad-makers' (4.5.223), occupations these soldiers dismiss as gratuitous in a virile warrior society. In praising war as 'full of vent' (4.5.226), the First Servingman echoes Coriolanus's declaration that war releases excess population, acting as a safety valve for pent-up energy (including libido, which spawns more unwanted children), while his avowal that peace 'makes men hate one another' (4.5.232) sounds like one of Digges's military paradoxes. Of course the audience need not assent to these cold-hearted opinions. But it seems significant that Shakespeare neglects to assign the servants proper names, and the high incidence of unnamed characters in the play has a dehumanizing effect that conforms with the protagonist's view of the cheapness of human life.[20] When he charges solo into Corioli and leads a horde to sack Rome, Coriolanus appears to be waging war against the very concept of the city, against urban density itself.

In a play concerned with overpopulation, the representation of the protagonist as homosocial, more invested in his relationship with men than his heterosexual nuclear family, has an ideological charge. Coriolanus opposes what queer theorists term 'reproductive futurity' (Edelman 2004) when his wife and mother threaten he will extinguish the tribune's bloodlines—'he'd make an end of thy posterity. / Bastards and all' (4.2.26). The play is even more scathing in its contempt for the excessive fertility of the masses, who are repeatedly dehumanized as breeding animals. Menenius dismisses the plebeians as 'multiplying spawn' (2.2.76), in accordance with the Latin term for the people, *prole*, which simply meant reproducer. Whereas Coriolanus is compared to solitary apex predators, such as the osprey, eagle, wolf, tiger, and dragon, the Roman populace appear as dogs, hares, rats, mice, geese, jackdaws, kites, crows, minnows, flies—species that tend to be gregarious, noisome, or breed prolifically. To deny the populace their birth-right as citizens, Coriolanus sneers—with verbs smelling of the barnyard— they were only 'littered' and 'calved i'th' porch o'th capital' (3.1.240–1).[21] Recalling young Martius shredding the butterfly, the tragedy even likens the Roman populace to insects: Coriolanus and the Volscians will destroy them, Cominius warns, like 'boys pursuing summer butterflies, butchers killing flies' (4.6.95–6). The play's animal imagery suggests how the Great Chain of Being can reinforce sociopolitical inequalities even as it collapses the existential hierarchy between humans and other species.

Appropriately in a play with the most famous exposition of the body politic in Renaissance literature, *Coriolanus* imagines excess population as a disease treated through medicinal procedures. In a 1604 pamphlet, Middleton had compared the crimson ghost of War to 'a barber surgeon that lets blood' (*TMCW* 187), and *Coriolanus* similarly depicts war as a bloodletting. Referring to the common practice of phlebotomy, Coriolanus dismisses the severity of his own wounds by stating 'the blood I drop is rather physical / Than dangerous to me' (1.5.18–19). The phlebotomy motif recurs when the watchmen threaten Menenius to 'let forth [his] half-pint of blood' (5.2.56). The Servingman's diagnosis of peace as 'an apoplexy' is also germane here since Renaissance physicians, following the prescription of Galen, treated this condition by bloodletting. That is, the First Servingman advocates war as a phlebotomizing of the commonwealth. Coriolanus pictures himself as a barber surgeon when he crows before a Volscian that he has 'drawn tuns of blood out of thy country's breast' (4.5.101). In a speech before Parliament in March 1610, James would invoke the same metaphor, comparing the king to the 'head of the natural body', which therefore has the right to 'let blood in what proportion it thinks fit' (*KJSW* 328) and to carefully 'phlebotomize the body' (329) of the realm. If tragedy induces a feeling of purgation, as Aristotle theorized, then perhaps Shakespeare's Roman tragedy, with its numerous references to blood (variations of the word occur thirty times in the play) and exhibitions of bleeding bodies, triggers a sense of emotional-physiological release through the audience's vicarious participation in a simulated blood-letting.[22] Staging the venesection of the body politic, *Coriolanus* is the preeminent example in Renaissance drama of 'crimson war' as a population check.

For all its reactionary anti-populism, however, *Coriolanus* ultimately recoils from the extremes of hard-hearted demographics. If the need to purge Rome of blood spurs Coriolanus to declare war on his own city, blood, in the sense of blood-ties, also eventually compels him to renounce its destruction. Shakespeare's tragedy is acutely aware of the Roman virtue of *pietas*, and the sometimes-conflicting demands of civic piety versus filial piety. Speaking in favour of the former, Volumnia avers that she 'had rather had eleven [of her children] die nobly for their country than one voluptuously surfeit out of action' (1.3.24–5). The mother has imparted these values to her son, who appeals in battle to those for whom 'his country's dearer than himself' (1.6.72). General Cominius likewise privileges civic duty over paternal devotion:

> I do love
> My country's good with a respect more tender,
> More holy and profound, than my own life,
> My dear wife's estimate, her womb's increase
> And treasure of my loins.
>
> (3.3.110–14)

By leading the Volscians to sack Rome, Coriolanus puts this principle to the test. Before meeting his mother, wife, and child, he steels himself by exclaiming he will not 'be such a gosling to obey instinct' (5.3.35), a metaphor that suggests overriding what ethologists call imprinting. Despite his wish to act 'as if man were author of himself / And knew no other kin' (5.3.36–7), Coriolanus fears his son 'hath an aspect of intercession which / Great Nature cries "Deny not"' (5.3.32–3). When Volumnia confronts him with the prospect of 'having bravely shed / Thy wife and children's blood' (5.3.117–18) and the sight of his kneeling son, Coriolanus relents. He achieves tragic grandeur in that he proves ultimately unable to suppress impulses that a modern biologist would attribute to kinship altruism but which early moderns would have considered the natural ties of familial piety.

A similar predicament was confronting the Jacobean state around the time Shakespeare composed *Coriolanus*. Although aware a monarch's greatness was measured by the number of his subjects, James and his Privy Council renewed policies they had implemented during the 1603 plague to curtail suburban sprawl. Grumbling that 'soon London will be all England' (qtd in Porter 1995, 42), James issued a proclamation on 12 October 1607 outlawing new builds near the city so as to stop 'the population increasing to such great numbers' (*SRP* 171–2). The king released a second proclamation on 25 July 1608 calling for stricter enforcement of this policy, complaining that a construction spree of cheap tenements 'doeth draw together such *an overflow of people*, specially of the meaner sort, as can hardly be either fed and sustained or preserved in health or governed' (*SRP* 193). *Coriolanus* can be performed as a power-to-the-people critique of the authoritarian big man, but James Kuzner (2007) contends that the patricians' vision of the citizenry as expendable—or in what Agamben terms 'a state of exception' (2005)—troubles pro-democratic interpretations of the play. If spectators at the Globe might regard the play's 'motif of war as a devourer' (Charney 1961, 143) as an exposé of the brutality of the state's anti-growth policies, some members of the courtly audience would smile on Coriolanus's plan to 'depopulate the city' (3.1.266). But debates over the best means to reduce urban growth also divided opinion within the Stuart court. Arguments defending the expediency of war had been put forth by some of Prince Henry's military advisors, but this jeopardized James's dream of a *Pax Jacobus*.[23] As a self-proclaimed peacemaker, James would instead favour a preventative check on demographic pressure: colonization.

'Take These Rats Hither': Coriolanus, Sir Cahir O'Doherty, and the Ulster Plantation

By 1607, overpopulation had become such an urgent problem that it threatened to derail James's cherished scheme for the Union of England and Scotland. In February of that year, MP Nicholas Fuller delivered a speech in the House of

Commons staunchly rejecting the measure on the grounds that England was suffering from 'a surcharge of people', and the Union would unleash an influx of poor Scots who would gobble up their already depleted resources (Notestein 1971, 222–3). The speech so rattled James that in March he addressed Parliament directly to quash Fuller's objections: 'the Scots are a populous Nation; they shall be harboured in our nests, they shall be planted and flourish in our good Soile, they shall eat our commons beare and make us leane' (*KJSW* 316). Dismissing fears of a tartan invasion as 'idle and vain surmises', James played demographer, insisting that since England was far too crowded the population should instead flow the other way: 'there is roumth in Scotland to plant your idle people that swarme in London streets and other Townes' (*KJSW* 313). *Coriolanus* has rightly been seen as intervening in parliamentary debates over the Union (Garganigo 2002), but this also encompasses the tangential issue of population flow. Like most political disputes in seventeenth-century Europe, commentators adjudicated it by referring back to the history of ancient Rome. It is therefore worth highlighting James's spelling 'roumth', as it offers a reminder that the early modern pronunciation of the word would have sounded like a near homophone for Rome. Shakespeare makes this exact pun in *Julius Caesar*, when Cassius fumes, 'Now is it Rome indeed, and Roome enough' (TLN 255). Each time that Coriolanus and Comenius declare they have fought for 'Rome' the audience would register at least on a subliminal level a conflict over population density. The pun would reverberate throughout this play in particular because Rome's population problem reached a flashpoint during Coriolanus's lifetime.

As Plutarch recounts, the Roman authorities in Coriolanus's day did not suppress the grain riot with an eloquent fable but with an emigration initiative. In the midst of the crisis, ambassadors arrived from Velitres with the grim news that a plague had killed 90 per cent of the population. Sensing an opportunity to 'disburden Rome of a great number of citizens' (1579, 243), the Senate passed a resolution to draft people for compulsory relocation to Velitres or into the army to fight the Volscians.[24] This cunning plan did not unfold without a snag, however, for the Tribunes saw through it and encouraged the people to defy the order. When the conscripts dragged their heels, it was none other than Coriolanus who organized a press gang to round them up and scourge them on their way: 'for the replenishing of the cittie of VELITRES, he dyd compell those that were chosen to goe thither' (1579, 244). Shakespeare glances at this scene from Plutarch when Sicinius denounces Coriolanus as 'this viper / That would depopulate the city' (3.1.265–6). For Shakespeare's contemporaries, then, *Coriolanus* would have been an extremely topical play, not only because of the grain riots but also because of the Jacobean state's response to it: viewing the dearth as a population problem, they launched an ambitious re-settlement scheme, one with far-reaching consequences. In September 1607, the king and his councillors proposed to divert Scots flocking south and ease overcrowding in London by establishing a colony in the 'escheated' lands of Ulster.[25]

Despite the abundant historicist scholarship on *Coriolanus*, little attention has been paid to the play's interest in Ireland.[26] Following the Plutarchan formula of parallel lives, critics sometimes compare Coriolanus to Walter Ralegh or the Earl of Essex, but it should be noted that both these alleged prototypes had strong ties to Ireland.[27] Ralegh held large estates in Munster while Essex notoriously led an ill-fated campaign (saluted in *Henry V*) to suppress the Tyrone rebellion. While the English were also dispatching colonists to Jamestown, Ulster would have been the more attractive option in conformity with Botero's advice that colonies be planted in proximity to the imperial homeland.[28] A leading spokesperson for the plan was none other than Botero's admirer Francis Bacon. In February 1607, Bacon refuted Fuller's speech in Parliament by denying that England was overcrowded and instead contending that its resources were simply underexploited.[29] Hence the Baconian dream of enlarging human empery over the earth, driving the expansion into heaths, commons, mountains, and fens documented in this book, was fuelled in large part by population pressure. This empery was not only metaphoric, however, since Bacon supported alleviating this pressure by deporting London's unemployed vagrants to Ulster:

> Never any Kingdome in this world had, I think, so faire and happy means to issue and discharge the multitude of their people, as this kingdom hath, in regard of *that desolate and wasted Kingdome of Ireland*; which (being a country blessed with almost all the dowryes of nature, as Rivers, Havens, Woods, Quarries, good Soile, and temperate climate, and now at last under his majesty blessed also with obedience) doth, as it were, continually call unto us for our Colonies and Plantations.   (1641, 11, italics added)

While Ulster contained few large towns, this image of it as uninhabited whitewashes over two important facts. First, many rural Irish communities practised transhumance, moving to different locations with their flocks in different seasons of the year, a custom that reduced ecological impact but which the English regarded as barbaric. Secondly, the low population density in the region was a direct result of the Nine Years War, during which the English conducted ruthless scorched earth tactics in Ulster, triggering a calamitous famine in 1602–3 in which an estimated 60,000 Irish died. The county was 'desolate and wasted' and obedient not by any 'faire and happy' coincidence but because a foreign occupation killed tens of thousands and scattered many others as war refugees. Such scruples would not have deterred Bacon, who, like Thomas More and Walter Ralegh, classed wars to enlarge dominions to accommodate population growth as 'Just and Honourable'.[30] Coriolanus clearly shares such views; the play's contempt for the 'multiplying spawn' and his exclamation 'Take these rats hither to gnaw their garners' would have struck many in the audience in 1608 as an endorsement of the Ulster Plantation as a demographic outlet.[31]

Audiences at the Globe would have been attuned to these resonances since the Ulster Plantation was not only an important plank in the court's plan for the Union (binding England, Scotland, and Ireland more tightly together) but the City of London itself was deeply concerned in the venture. To finance the construction of an English settlement at Londonderry, the cash-strapped Crown turned to London's livery guilds.[32] While the Jacobean state was prohibiting new buildings in and around England's capital, they were encouraging such construction in Ulster with London footing the bill.[33] In return for an annual payment of 6 s 8 d per 60 acres (Irish natives were taxed double), the king granted vast stretches of land between County Coleraine and Ballinderry to London investors in perpetuity, along with rights to the natural resources, including a concession on salmon and eel fishing in the River Bann. Despite the agreement's proviso that Irish timber only be used for building projects in the colony, the English overexploited woodlands to export pipestaves, 'a lucrative, albeit very destructive manner of merchandizing the woods entrusted to them' (Orr 2019, 90), which Shakespeare may have glanced at later in Caliban's transporting logs for Prospero (Egan 2006). A leading critic of the City's management of the Ulster colony was the soldier-planter Sir Thomas Phillips, whom one historian has compared to Coriolanus.[34] Phillips's chief grievance was that London investors, motivated more by profits than their patriotic duty to Anglicize the region, had failed to drum up anywhere near the requisite number of settlers to supplant the native Irish. In April 1611, a frustrated James issued a proclamation ordering all undertakers who had received land grants in Ulster to relocate there by May (*SRP* 259). In other words, London experienced the same problem that Rome had when Coriolanus came to the rescue and rounded up conscripts for the colony at Velites. While the parallel is curious, Phillips's quarrel with the City occurred after 1608, so it is unlikely he influenced Shakespeare's portrayal of the Roman general.

A more promising contender would be the last Gaelic warlord Cathaoir Ó Dochartaigh (Cahir O'Doherty). One of the most renowned Irish loyalists during Tyrone's Rebellion, he had earned the nickname the 'Queen's O'Doherty' and was knighted in 1602 for his valour in battle against his fellow Irish in taking the town of Augher.[35] Although a Catholic, O'Doherty adopted English dress and spoke English proudly. In 1603, he accompanied Lord Mountjoy to London to meet the newly crowned King James, who confirmed him in his claims to his ancestral lands. Upon his return, O'Doherty was elected a JP and alderman of Derry and in 1607 served as foreman of the jury that condemned the exiled Irish earls as traitors, rendering Ulster escheated and thereby forfeit to the English Crown. O'Doherty's fortunes soured, however, when Sir George Paulet replaced Henry Dowcra as Ulster's governor. Paulet baited O'Doherty for his Catholicism and openly coveted his lands. When O'Doherty assembled a large group of men for a wood-cutting expedition in the Canmoyre woods, Paulet accused him of plotting a rebellion and insisted O'Doherty provide sureties to guarantee his allegiance or have his estates confiscated.[36] Having shed his blood for England in numerous battles, O'Doherty found the insinuation deeply insulting. When Paulet then called him a boy and slapped him in the face, the enraged O'Doherty organized a revolt in which he sacked and burned Derry down on 19 April 1608, executing Paulet. The assault on Derry soon escalated into outright rebellion, one that generated shockwaves in London, as it jeopardized the court's plan for the Ulster Plantation and the considerable capital invested in it by London's merchants. Between early April 1608 and the suppression of the revolt on 8 July, London would have buzzed with news of O'Doherty's betrayal, chronicled in a pamphlet entitled *Newes from Ireland Concerning the late treacherous action and rebellion of Sir Carey Adoughterie* (1608), which may very well have coloured the writing and/or reception of Shakespeare's Roman tragedy. It is curious that O'Doherty's rebellion was sparked by Paulet belittling him as a 'boy', just as Aufidius taunts Coriolanus as a 'boy of tears' (5.6.103)—an insult that so infuriates Coriolanus that he repeats it three times—an incident that does not occur in Plutarch. While these similarities should not be urged too vociferously since Shakespeare's Martius adheres closely to Plutarch's portrait of him in many respects, O'Doherty deserves to be considered alongside Ralegh and Essex as a historical figure that establishes the scorching relevance of Shakespeare's tragedy. After all, in 1608 Ralegh was locked away in the Tower and Essex had been dead for seven years, but one of Essex's Irish ex-allies noted for the 'pride and highness of his spirit' (1608, B2^r) was on a rampage that threatened to overthrow the colony that he had helped found by fighting for the country that now accused him of treason. No wonder John Osborne's *Coriolanus* spin-off *A Place Calling itself Rome* (1971) so seamlessly transports the Volscian scenes to a Northern Irish town modelled on Derry, an epicentre of the Troubles and the very city burned to the ground by Cahir O'Doherty.

Whereas the maps of Ulster made by the royal cartographer Richard Bartlett (who was beheaded for his presumption) promote the fantasy of it as underpopulated and easily governed (see Fig. 7.1), Shakespeare's tragedy depicts the land of the Volscians as a site of steely opposition to imperial rule.[37] But if *Coriolanus* is not a pro-imperialist apology like Edmund Spenser's *A View of the Present State of Ireland*, neither does it provide an Irish perspective on their displacement, much less that of the non-human population. An intriguing counterpoint to the play in this regard can be heard in a little-known Gaelic text 'A Poem on the Downfall of the Gaoidhil'. Variously attributed to Lochlann Óg Ó Dálaigh or Fearflatha Ó Gnímh, it exists in several seventeenth-century manuscript witnesses and was likely composed around the same time as *Coriolanus*, not long

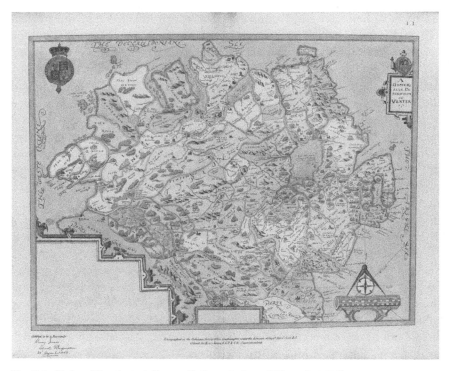

Fig. 7.1 Richard Bartlett, *A Generalle Description of Ulster* (c.1603).
Special Collections, The Library, Queen's University Belfast.

after the establishment of the Ulster Plantation. Its elegiac lament, 'Where have the Gaels gone?' sadly confirms the ideologically fraught reports of the country as depopulated. Bemoaning the 1607 Flight of the Earls, the Irish bard grieves that 'the sons of kings from the pleasant green house / of Breagh are being made into exiles' and denounces the greed of the Anglo-Scots interlopers:

> They divide it up amongst themselves,
> this territory of the children of noble Niall,
> [there's not] a jot of Flann's milky plain
> that we don't find becoming (mere) acres.[38]

The poem deserves recognition as a key text for archipelagic and post-colonial ecocriticism, for it also chronicles the damage the occupiers inflict on the Irish environment:

> We have witnessed egregious changes upon Ireland—
> it is right to enumerate them (or to bewail them)—

> which would have been wondrous at any previous
> time upon the sparkling-watered land of Laoghaire.
> Heavy is the shame! We have come to see
> seats of government being made desolate,
> the produce wasting in a stream, dark thickets
> of the chase become thoroughfares,
> ....
> the hillside is wrenched into fields.
> Assemblies (are held) in places of hunting,
> [man-?] hunts upon illustrious streets, belts of the hedges
> of cultivation over the plain's face,
> without a meet for racing over its cheeks.
> They destroy the hostels of noblemen,
> they build with despotic vigour
> a line of white(washed) multi-pillared courts
> all about the deer-bereft flank of Ireland.

When the poem's opening cry 'Where have the Gaels gone?' repeats in the final line, it now seems to mourn not only the diaspora of the Irish nobility and their followers but also the eviction of Ireland's non-human inhabitants by English de-wilding. The Plantation proves devastating for Ulster's woods, thickets, deer, hills, and streams.[39] *Coriolanus* gives an inkling of the situation in Ulster (spelled Vlster) when the Romans send some of the defeated Volscians 'to exile' (1.6.36) and Coriolanus boasts his wars have emptied Antium of its husbands and heirs (4.1.2). But this play written for a London audience dwells more on a claustrophobic urban ecology, where the 'stalls, bulks, windows, / Are smothered up' by the 'popular throngs' (2.1.204–5, 208), to convey a sense of overcrowding that encouraged British expansion into Ireland rather than on the environmental degradation this expansion would cause. The Volscians never get to speak of 'those maims / Of shame seen through [their] country' (4.5.88-89).

Criticism on *Coriolanus* has rooted it in the Midlands or London suburbs, thereby linking the play to debates over enclosure and food supply.[40] But recovering the Irish context of Shakespeare's Roman tragedy reveals it is also concerned with the ethics and pragmatics of demographic policies based on colonizing and exploiting land cleared for settlement by a quasi-genocidal war. The scene in which the Volscian Servingmen denounce peace seems all the more chilling given that it parrots the opinions of the soldier Barnaby Rich, who had participated first-hand in the brutal depopulation of Ulster, published in a work 'collected and gathered for the true meridian of Dublin' and dedicated to the Treasurer of the Irish Wars, Sir Thomas Ridgeway, whose forces slew O'Doherty. Does Shakespeare's play endorse the views of military men disaffected with James's pacifism who rallied around Prince Henry? Or does it caricature them?

The anonymous author of *Overthrow of an Irish Rebell* gleans this moral from O'Doherty's death: 'God never suffers a hand that takes a pride to be embrewed in slaughter, to scape unpunished' (1608, B3ʳ). Stamping such a moral on *Coriolanus* would align it with James's dislike of military hawks and endorse his programme to subdue Ireland through peaceful settlement rather than by the sword. Yet by evoking O'Doherty's uprising Shakespeare's tragedy admonishes the Stuart government that their grand plan to 'civilize' Ireland while diverting population from London and Scotland would not be so easy as they dreamed.[41] O'Doherty's defeat accelerated the expropriation of Ulster's natural resources—after his head was impaled on a spike in Dublin (see Fig. 7.2) the Crown parcelled out his attainted lands—but the environmental mismanagement of the settler colonists bred resentment and instability in the region. The Gaelic poem reminds us that the Plantationocene did not arise only in the Americas but was also under way within the Anglo-Celtic archipelago. The English occupation devastated the Irish wilderness, felling thousands of great oaks, reducing the ancient woods of Glenconkeyne (to the dismay of the Jacobean Privy Council) to a 'timber yard' to rebuild Derry and export pipe staves, killing the squirrels and pine marten for fur, converting meadows and hunting grounds to tillage, seizing Ulster's fisheries, and starving the Irish into submission.[42] The bard's dirge echoes the accusation of the Caledonian chieftain Calgacus against the Romans: 'they make a desolation and call it peace'.[43]

Immodest Proposals

Viewing *Coriolanus* as an Irish tragedy as well as a Roman one enables us to see how it prefigures the political tragedies that would rock Ireland in the decades and centuries ahead, during which Ireland would play an inglorious role in the development of demographic thinking in Britain. In the 1660s, a member of the Royal Society named Sir William Petty would pioneer a new sub-field of political science he termed 'political arithmetic'. Collating birth and mortality rates, Petty concluded London's exponential population growth would have to halt by the year 1800 or the agricultural workforce would not be capable of feeding the city-dwellers. Tellingly, Petty had developed these theories while working as a surveyor and map-maker for Oliver Cromwell in his ruthless subjugation of Ireland, for which he was rewarded with a vast Irish estate. During Cromwell's campaign, Petty estimated that over a half million Irish died or were displaced, 'wasted by the Sword, Plague, Famine, Hardship and Banishment' (1691, 18), and characterizes this less as a genocidal tragedy than an opportunity. Although Petty denounces as 'impious and inhumane' the Coriolanus-like 'furious Spirits [who] have wished that the Irish would rebel again, that they might be put to the Sword' (26), he himself puts forward the immodest proposal that authorities deport 200,000 Irish and replace them with the same number of Anglo-Scots settlers,

'PURPLE PLAGUES OR CRIMSON WAR' 191

Fig. 7.2 Anonymous, *The Over-throw of an Irish Rebell… Carey Adoughterie* (1608). Reproduced with permission of the Master and Fellows of Trinity College, Cambridge.

while distributing an additional 10,000 young Irish women throughout English parishes and arranging for them to intermarry (29–30). Petty's writings had a tremendous influence in reframing the colonization of Ireland as a demographic challenge, and would in turn inspire the greatest piece of political satire in British literature.[44] Doubtless Shakespeare would have relished Jonathan Swift's 'Modest Proposal' that Ireland solve its population crisis by having Irish mothers eat their own babies, as it is strangely foreshadowed in the cannibalistic imagery in *Coriolanus*. Menenius compares Rome to an 'unnatural dam / that should eat up her own' (3.1.294–5), and Coriolanus is eventually 'devoured' by the wars as a result of the intercession of his cannibal-like mother who sacrifices her own child for the good of the city.

If it seems surprising that the evidence presented in this chapter has not been unearthed before, it is perhaps because few critics wish to dig too close to the third rail of population, or picture Shakespeare intervening in demographic debates. Population control has an ugly history, all too easily co-opted by eugenicists and right-wing opponents of immigration, and is implicated, as this chapter has underlined, in imperialist conquest. Nevertheless, as Greg Garrard contends, 'problems with crude neo-Malthusianism should not be used as an excuse to ignore the ways in which population growth acts as a multiplier of other causes of environmental degradation' (2012, 106). As a Warwickshire native who had himself migrated to London for work, Shakespeare both witnessed and himself participated in the rapid urbanization of Renaissance England, and his writings exhibit a recurrent preoccupation with the politics of sexual reproduction beyond these two plays. Disputes over marriageable age in *Romeo and Juliet* and Benedick's declaration, in a play that might be retitled much ado about compulsory heterosexuality, that 'the world must be peopled' (2.3.233) may resonate differently in the Anthropocene but were still problematic in Shakespeare's day. Shakespeare's *Sonnets* (first printed in 1609) are another case in point, and the opening line 'From fairest creatures we desire increase' has a disturbingly eugenicist undertone in the context of government crackdowns on birth rates among the undesirable poor of London's suburbs. In his coterie poetry and plays staged before court, Shakespeare voices the population management policies of Jacobean elites. As a commercial playwright, however, his livelihood depended on pleasing the urban crowds these policies sought to limit. If the sense of claustrophobia in his simulations of Vienna and Rome would have been mirrored by the crush in the yard of the Globe, Shakespeare is equally cognizant of the practical and ethical difficulties of regulating desire and treating humans like mere numbers. The complexity of his drama in sustaining conflicting views of the population conundrum springs in no small part from his writing for both courtly and public audiences, and his ability to foresee that many solutions, like the Ulster Plantation, only create more problems.

8
Staging Darkness at Whitehall and Blackfriars

Nocturnalization in the Stuart Masque and Shakespeare's Late Tragedies

Night is not what it once was. Whereas most pre-moderns perceived darkness as a source of danger, the Anthropocene has endangered darkness. Two-thirds of the world's human population—and 99 per cent of those in the United States and Europe—no longer experience a truly dark night.[1] No wonder urban ecocritics tend to frame habitat in purely spatial terms and pay scant attention to the night as a spatiotemporal habitat or 'chronotope', despite the fact 30 per cent of vertebrates and 60 per cent of invertebrates have evolved to live in a crepuscular or darkened environment that modern humans have been dissipating at a worrisome rate.[2] Eco-theorists such as Timothy Morton (2016) and Levi Bryant (2013) have conjured a dark or black ecology to signify the opacity of the non-human and the melancholy apprehension of the relationship between objects as chaotic and precarious rather than stable and harmonious, but cultural historians of the early modern era might make an equally valuable contribution to ecocriticism by attending to the literally dark ecologies of the pre-electrified past.[3] Darkness stained the texture of life in Stuart Britain; it impacted human affairs as powerfully as class, race, and gender, and was not only (as we shall see) bound up with ideological constructions of these categories but also invoked to constrict the mobility of the disempowered as well as the differently abled. Informed by recent work in Night Studies—such as Matthew Beaumont's *Nightwalking* (2016), Elizabeth Bronfen's *Night Passages* (2013), Craig Koslofsky's *Evening's Empire* (2011), and E. Roger Ekirch's *At Day's Close* (2005)—this chapter considers the anxiety aroused by darkness in texts written at a time when humans possessed only a flickering dominion over the earth. Whereas previous chapters have surveyed civilization's encroachments upon heath, moor, ocean, mountain, fur country, and fen, the so-called Anthropocene also needs be conceived as a temporal conquest of the planet. A vital but underappreciated aspect of this epochal shift is the phenomenon of human 'nocturnalization', which Koslofsky defines as 'the ongoing expansion of the legitimate social and symbolic uses of the night' (2011, 2). Since this definition encompasses the symbolic, and a sense of what constitutes a 'legitimate' use of night is culturally determined, literature played an integral role in nocturnalization—a phenomenon almost as momentous in some respects as homo sapiens' primordial mastery of fire, which it recapitulates. Historians sometimes point to the 1684 installation of public street lighting in London as a pivotal moment, but Edmund Heming's foil-backed glass-box lanterns should be seen less as a miraculous technological fiat that abruptly endowed London with nightlife than as a socially driven invention necessitated by the gradual human colonization of night that was already well under way at the dawn of the seventeenth century.[4]

One of the great archives of the traumatic onset of modernity, Shakespearean tragedy derives some of this sense of historical discontinuity from shifting attitudes towards night in the late Elizabethan and early Jacobean eras. While Shakespeare's nocturnal worlds have been illuminated by, among others, Elizabeth Bronfen, Simon Estok, and Laurie Shannon, this chapter expands on this research by spotlighting the profound impact of the Stuart court on perceptions of darkness, arguing that Shakespeare's chiaroscuro poetics betray an ambivalence about the King's Men's role in nocturnalization in early modern London.[5] That is, early modern theatre does not simply dramatize nocturnalization; theatre was itself one of the chief cultural attractions that lured people outdoors at night. As the leading playwright of the King's Men, Shakespeare was acutely conscious of the likelihood of his plays being staged at night at Whitehall, where hyper-illuminated court masques exalted the absolute monarch as an all-seeing night watchman and sun-like deity. Juxtaposing the nocturnal carnivalesque in *Antony and Cleopatra* with nocturnal terror in *Macbeth* and *King Lear* will reveal how these plays unavoidably comment upon the scandal of the late hours kept by the Stuart court, and the monarch's grandiose claim to rule the night. Yet this chapter also urges theatre historians to consider how the same play might glisten differently before different audiences, arguing that Shakespeare's Jacobean tragedies reflect a metatheatrical awareness of drastic variations in ambient light levels at different performance venues. In writing night-scenes for afternoon performances at the outdoor Globe, Shakespeare had perfected verbal techniques that function like neutral density filters in film to persuade audiences to take day for night. In court performances at Whitehall, however, these same 'darkling' tactics conspired to dim or blot out the luminous torchlight that signified monarchical power. When the King's Men acquired Blackfriars late in his career, Shakespeare also experimented with baroque effects by incorporating the darkness of this more dimly lit indoor theatre as an intra-diegetic element of the action. If the overlit stage enables spectators to indulge in the absolutist state's fantasy of seeing in the dark, plays like *Macbeth* and *Lear* challenge the putative sovereignty of the monarch over the night by insisting on the epistemological limits of human sightedness. In doing so, early modern tragedy threatens to demonize nocturnal ecologies and foment a nyctophobia that undercuts the idealization of the pre-industrial era as a time of environmental harmony. Yet by situating Shakespeare's late tragedies in their original performance conditions and in a tradition of counter-nocturnalization writing, this chapter also advances a claim for the importance of pre-Enlightenment literature as a means of reactivating the ecological mystique of the unelectrified night and relearning how to dwell within it rather than obliterate it.

'Bright Nights': Nocturnalization in the Court Masque

For most of human history, the majority of people, like Proust's Swann, went to bed early. Curfews of 8 p.m. in winter and 9 p.m. in summer had been imposed on medieval English towns since the time of William the Conqueror, and municipal ordinances to criminalize night-walking were commonplace by the reign of Edward I. Medieval representations of the night, broadly speaking, tend to be pejorative, thus encouraging compliance with curfew, and such attitudes lingered well into the early modern era. In his 1594 *Terrors of the Night*, Thomas Nashe offers a handy crib sheet of grim epithets and foreboding metaphors that night could elicit in Elizabethan literature: the 'Devil's black book', 'the nurse of cares', 'the mother of despaire', and 'the daughter of hell'. Night imprisons human subjects in its 'rustie dungeon' (B1^{r-v}) or, less dramatically, confines them to the bed or fireside. In 1608, however, Thomas Dekker would complain of London's bustling night-life in *Lanthorne and Candlelight*. What had changed? While this fourteen-year gap did not witness a technological innovation as momentous as the advent of gas lamps or electricity, a 'considerable advance' occurred in 1599 when an Act of Common Council obliged every London household on a main thoroughfare to hang a lantern outside on moonless nights from 1 October to 1 March.[6] If the 1599 Act was not quite a flipping of the switch, Dekker's title exposes the brightening of the urban nightscape by artificial light in the first decade of the seventeenth century.[7] This Act appears to have provided a spark for Dekker's lost play of January 1600, *Truth's Supplication to Candlelight*, and it is worth considering how this urban lighting ordinance may have contributed to Shakespeare's representations of the night and night-walking from *Julius Caesar* onward.[8] Two other notable factors in this equation would be the reopening of the indoor Blackfriars playhouse and the involvement of the King's Men in latenight revels for the Stuart court. Curiously, Shakespeare's turn toward tragedy around 1600 coincides with evidence of increasing nocturnalization in the late Elizabethan and early Jacobean eras, when illuminated playhouses helped endow London with reputable night life and Stuart court culture sought to dispel the darkness of the night.

If the 1599 Act signals a push for greater mobility and visibility at night, this process intensified during the reign of King James. In contrast to the more retiring habits of the elderly Queen Elizabeth in the last decade of her rule, James often stayed awake into the wee hours, carousing with Scottish favourites or visiting dignitaries, a habit he acquired during his sojourn in Denmark. Hamlet's complaint that Claudius 'doth wake tonight and takes his rouse' (1.4.8) after midnight would be echoed by critics of the court's new routine under its Scottish king and Danish queen. In accordance with geo-humoral ethnography (the belief climate influences character), the Stuarts' nocturnal regimen would have reinforced dim views of these supposedly uncouth northerners as more acclimated to darkness. Indeed, some early modern writers like Richard Stanihurst and Edmund Spenser speculated that the Latin name for the Scots, *Scotos*, derived from the Greek for darkness, σκότος (*skotos*), a spurious etymology that would have fuelled prejudice against the Scots as quasi-racialized Others.

In point of fact, the Stuarts actually drove nocturnalization by conspicuously increasing the artificial lighting at court, creating a fashion that the Jacobean beau monde strove to imitate. A peek into his biography reveals that James harboured a number of psychological and political motives for banishing darkness from the royal presence: his own father, Lord Darnley, had been assassinated in the dead of night; at the tender age of five James had watched his grandfather die during a traumatic night raid on Stirling Castle; James himself survived a midnight assault on Falkland Palace in 1592; and his interrogation of the alleged coven at Berwick verified his belief that witches gathered at midnight masses to perform acts of *maleficium* against the king.[9] Anxieties over nocturnal mobility only heightened in the aftermath of the Gunpowder Plot, when it emerged that Guy Fawkes and the conspirators had operated under the cover of darkness with the aid of a 'dark lantern' (now on display at the Ashmolean Museum). This device aroused concern because its sliding panel could shield the flame and hence enable one to move about in the dark undetected; one appears as a stage prop in John Fletcher's 1613 play *The Night-walker*.[10] Following Fawkes's arrest, Jacobean authorities immediately upped the number of night watchmen to twenty at Moorgate and thirty-five at Newgate, reaffirming their power to halt night-walkers in the king's name.

Since the state relied on the watch to maintain its authority after sundown, it is easy to see why James would depict the absolute monarch as an ever-vigilant night watchman. In his political writings, James compares God and the state to an 'all-seeing eye and penetrant light', advises Prince Henry to be a 'watchman over your servants that they obey your lawes precisely' (*KJSW* 202, 235), and likens the king to 'a great watchman...[who] must never slumber nor sleep' (1994, 239). Such passages help account for the interest in the royal watchman in Jacobean city comedy. In Samuel Rowley's *If You See Me, You Know Me* (1604), a kind of Renaissance version of *Undercover Boss*, Henry VIII patrols London incognito to inspect the night watch. Predictably, the king discovers an inept constable and his drowsy sidekick Dormouse and must take it upon himself to apprehend night-walking cutthroats and restore order to the night. First performed in 1604, Rowley's comedy bears a notable resemblance to *Measure for Measure* (staged before James at Whitehall on the night of 26 December 1604), which also subjects the night to royal surveillance at a time when the extension of court hours after dark provided an impetus for clamping down on nocturnal crime. It is surely no coincidence that Lucio's name means 'light', a comment on not only his moral lightness but its reliance upon artificial lighting, and that he slanders Duke Vincentio as the 'duke of dark corners' (4.3.154), claiming the Duke 'would have dark deeds darkly answered; he would never bring them to light' (3.1.435). In contrast, the Duke's orchestrating the bed trick exemplifies the power of the state to spy upon and control its subjects in the dark, and Lucio's exposure verifies James's scriptural citation in *Basilikon Doron* that 'whatsoever they have spoken in darknesse should be heard in the light' (*KJSW* 202). Like the ornamental crown-capped dark lantern King James received from John Harington on New Year's 1603 (1804, 324–9), *If You See Me* and *Measure for Measure* are gifts to the author of *The King's Gift* that imagine the ruler as a national watchman, whose authority remains undimmed despite his bumbling underlings and who possesses a quasi-omniscient ability to see in the dark that was duplicated by the optics of court performance by torchlight.

The ideological celebration of the monarch's night-rule would find its most spectacular expression in the Stuart masque, which was as much a light-show as a play, ballet, or opera. With its dazzling array of candles, torches, and fireworks, the masque's lighting conspired 'to stage the monarchy's brilliant authority against a background of darkness and ignorance' (Koslofsky 2011, 52). In an important article, Chris Fitter (1997) links the vogue for chiaroscuro techniques in baroque art to the rise of the literary nocturne in works such as George Chapman's *The Shadow of Night*, John Donne's 'A Nocturnal upon St. Lucy's Day', Henry Vaughan's 'The Night', Robert Herrick's 'Night-piece to Julia', and John Norris's 'Hymn to Darkness'.[11] But it should be emphasized that credit for introducing and cultivating this taste for nightscapes in England belongs to Inigo Jones and his elaborate scene-painting and lighting design for the Stuart court revels. Ben Jonson's *The Masque of Blackness* was performed on Twelfth Night 1605 against the backdrop of '*an obscure and cloudy night-piece*' (2:514.55), and Jones later copied Adam Elsheimer's 1609 painting *The Flight into Egypt*, the first naturalistic depiction of the night in European art, to adorn the set of *Luminalia* (see Fig. 8.1; Orgel and Strong 1973, 711). Jones's designs cast a spell on Jacobean playwrights, as evident from the finale of John Webster's *The White Devil*, when the avenger amid the tableau of corpses boasts that he 'limned this night-piece' (5.6.297). It would be a mistake to regard darkness simply as an inert backdrop, however. Beyond employing torches and chiaroscuro effects as extraneous visual spectacle, the Stuart masque often integrated illumination into the storyline to enact the monarchy's temporal jurisdiction over the night, the failure of which, as we shall see, becomes a significant leitmotif in Shakespeare's Jacobean tragedies.

Following the pioneering work of Stephen Orgel (1975), New Historicists seized on the court masque as a paradigmatic example of the theatricality of state

Fig. 8.1 Inigo Jones, Nightscape for *Luminalia* (1636).
© Devonshire Collection, Chatsworth. Reproduced with permission of Chatsworth Settlement Trustees.

power in Renaissance England.[12] Critics have rightly lambasted the anti-masque's exoticized depictions of Amazons, Africans, and Romani as part of an imperialist agenda but less has been said about the ways in which this imperial project involves the colonization of the chronotope of night itself and the Othering of nocturnal wildlife.[13] Through its spectacular command of lighting effects and pyrotechnics, the Stuart masque repeatedly constructs an image of the monarch as light-bringer, possessing an absolutist dominion over the night and ecologies steeped in darkness. Such fulsome rhetoric resounds in *The Masque of Blackness* (1605), which flatters James as a 'greater light' (*CWBJ* 2:518.154) than the sun-god Sol, in part because his 'beams shine day *and* night (2:520.208, italics added). Drawing on geo-humoral theory, Jonson imagines the 'intemperate fires' of the equatorial sun have scorched and darkened the skin of the African nymphs, played by the Danish Queen Anna and her ladies in waiting in blackface, whereas the artificial light of Britain's *roi soleil* can 'blanch an Ethiop' (2:520). The unveiling of a bright moon 'crowned with a luminary or sphere of light' (2:519) when the nymphs arrive in 'Albion' configures it—as Kim Hall (1995, 133-4) has brilliantly elucidated—as a realm of whiteness and perpetual light in contrast to Niger's realm of extreme light and dark, anticipating the colonial trope of 'darkest Africa', while removing, I would add, such smears from Scotland and Denmark.[14]

The state's jurisdiction over the dark is also glaringly apparent in *Lord Hay's Masque* (1607), in which Night is racialized by its appearance in blackface with a retinue consisting of the nine evening Hours, also in blackface, acting as torchbearers.[15] Composed by Thomas Campion and staged in the late hours of Twelfth Night 1607, this masque simulated night by having the actors perform behind a semi-translucent curtain painted with 'darke cloudes' (A4^v). Flora's brightly coloured bower stood on one side of the stage while on the other loomed the House of Night, about which 'were plac't on wyer artificial Battes, and Owles, continually moving' (B1^r). Night's devotion to chastity recalls Queen Elizabeth in her guise as Cynthia, but courtiers who attended the previous masque may also have found the black-skinned Night reminiscent of Niger, and pondered whether Britain after sundown could be as wild as Africa. Night eventually bows to the authority of the sun-god Phoebus, a stand-in for King James, in a romance plot that allegorizes the planned unification of Britain, abetted by the Anglo-Scottish marriage the masque celebrates (Curran 2009, 69–71) while reversing the conventional association of Scotland with wintry darkness and England with spring's fertility. The Crown's dominion over Britain and the vassal state of black-faced Night (who resembles a rival African monarch) is mirrored by theatre's mimetic dominion over nocturnal creatures, as the ersatz bats and owls flitting across the stage on a zip-line in effect perform their submission to royal authority and human empery. Bats and owls often haunt the enchanter's lair in early modern romance, but these stage props, here vivified by Inigo Jones's dramaturgical magic, might be regarded alongside the taxidermic displays of arctic furbearers in the Skinners' pageant (see Chapter 5), the eagle-owl in Prince Henry's menagerie, or the specimens and illustrations of Renaissance natural history, which sought to transform nocturnal beasts from sources of fear and ignorance into subjects of wonder and knowledge.[16]

The victory of a diurnal order over the nocturnal wild also constitutes a defining theme in Jonson's *The Masque of Queens* (1609), the most vociferous defence of nocturnalization in Stuart literature. Complementing Jones's set design, Jonson's poetry sketches a nightscape in which a coven of hags emerges alongside a supporting cast of nocturnal creatures: owls, bats, toads, and the cat-a-mountain. Fittingly, many of these same creatures furnish the ingredients of the hags' hell broth, which includes 'wolves' hairs', 'adders' ears', 'the screech-owl's egg and the feathers black', the 'blood of the frog', the 'brain of a black cat', 'the eyes of the owl', and 'the bat's wing' (*CWBJ* 3:310–12.134–73). Distilling the dark essence of these animals, the hags conjure a stinking fog with which they hope to smother the resplendent light-show of the court revels. While Campion's masque had insisted on the propriety of the court's night-time entertainments—'Who shold grace mirth, & revels but the night? / Next love she should be goddesse of delight' (C1^v)—Jonson goes even further in demonizing the critics of the Stuart masque as witches: 'Let not these bright nights / Of honour blaze thus to offend our eyes' (3:309.109–10), exclaims the Dame, who orders her followers to 'blast the light'

(3:310.122). In a bid to sabotage the performance, she later invokes Hecate to 'darken all this roof / With present fogs' and 'strike a blindness through these blazing tapers' (3:314.214–6), while the hags raise a storm that will make 'all be black' (3:315.263), 'till the mist arise and the lights fly out' (3:317.302). Unsurprisingly, the smoke dissipates, the witches vanish, and the nightscape is swiftly changed to reveal a luminous pyramid, from which Perseus, or Heroic Virtue, intones: 'All dark and envious witchcraft fly the light' (3:318.328). The abundant candles deployed in this masque shone with an added aura from the performance's coinciding with the midwinter festival of Candlemas, which early modern congregations celebrated with candle-lit processions—a form of sympathetic magic harnessing the lengthening hours of sunlight—and sermons that meditated on Christ's power to expel the darkness of sin. According to residual Catholic beliefs, candles blessed by a priest during Candlemas radiated a special apotropaic power to frighten away demons (Duffy 2005, 16), a power the Catholic convert Jonson transfers to the absolutist state. Illumination in this masque does not merely serve to render the action visible. Instead the masque commandeers extradiegetic lighting as part of the intradiegetic spectacle to dramatize a metatheatrical debate over the ethics of its own artificial visibility, justifying the court's nocturnal revels by disentangling night from darkness and its primeval associations with evil.

On an eco-material level, the witches' sulfuric fog—cf. *Macbeth*'s 'filthy air' (1.1.10)—might evoke heath-burning (see Chapter 1) or the coal-smog that began to vitiate London's air quality at this time. But the dispersal of the foul smoke conjured from animal parts also mirrors the replacing of 'stinking tallow' (*Cymbeline* 1.6.109)—made from animal fat or broiled suet—by beeswax candles at the Stuart court theatricals. Just as Middleton's 'Mist of Error' encourages the Lord Mayor to support clean heat, *The Masque of Queens* extols the court's use of clean light.[17] Unfortunately, clean is not a perfect synonym for eco-friendly, as harvesting beeswax damages hives and the olfactory prejudice against tallow would lead to the adoption of whale-oil as an alternative fuel.[18] Moreover, to produce a single kilogram of beeswax, 'bees must suck approximately 60 million flowers and travel about 1.5 million kilometres—equivalent to circling the globe 37.5 times' (Guerzoni 2012, 49). Such jaw-dropping figures might enable us to perceive Prospero's control over the bee-like Ariel, who 'sucks' (5.1.88) flowers and 'flames amazement' (1.2.198), as an analogue for the monarch's requisition of valuable beeswax. Viewed through the lens of the energy humanities, the overlit court masque instantiates the state's dominion over not only the nightscape but also the eco-material resources from which light was enkindled.

Counter-nocturnalization

While one might assume that all inhabitants of the seventeenth century, and playwrights in particular, would be thrilled by the extension of human leisure hours after sunset, not everyone approved. The playwright and future Parliamentarian Arthur Wilson griped that Queen Anna's dramatics had transformed the court into 'a continued Maskarado', and noted James himself was 'delighted with such fluent elegancies as made the nights more glorious than the days' (1653, 53–4). Among the accusations levelled against Vittoria in *The White Devil* by John Webster, a scathing critic of the Jacobean court, is that

> her rooms
> Outbraved the stars with several kind of lights
> When she did counterfeit a prince's court.
>
> (3.2.72–4)

By blotting out the stars, artificial lighting impairs the humbling perception of humanity's cosmic insignificance. This aggrandizement of human and royal dominion explains why some writers turned to Aesopian satire to pen what might be called counter-nocturnalization texts.

An early Jacobean example of this genre is Michael Drayton's *The Owl*, whose titular bird likewise rails against the stars' erasure by the hyper-illuminated court: 'Where I beheld so many Candles light, / As they had mock'd the Tapers o' the Night' (1604, 363–4). Published a year after James's coronation, Drayton's poem invites a contrast between the diurnal order of Elizabeth's court and the nocturnal debauchery of the new regime. Whereas Campion and Jonson would portray the owl as an ominous emblem of ignorance and witchcraft, Drayton's bird embodies wisdom and prudence.[19] When 'it grew upon the Time of rest' the naïve owl expects everyone to retire to bed and to prayers. Instead he sees the Sparrow feasting and 'billing' his female; the Cormorant scheming to 'compass strange Monopolies' (378); and the Vulture devising cabals to disgrace his enemies. The owl surveys this extension of recreational, financial, and political activities into the night with a scornful eye: 'O God, thought I, what's here by Light within, / Where some in Darkenesse should have fear'd to sin?' (375–6).

Similar tirades echo in the work of John Milton, who conceived of his *Masque Presented at Ludlow Castle* (1634) as a stark riposte to the drunken revels of the Caroline court. While the virtuous brothers find themselves 'night-foundered' in the 'double night of darkness and of shades' (335), the night-loving Comus ventures out with his 'midnight torches' to pursue his nocturnal sport. Comus's rhetorical question—'what hath night to do with sleep?' (1957, l.122)—shocks precisely because of its glib defiance of the circadian rhythms. In *Paradise Lost*, Milton again demonizes night-walking drunkards in 'luxurious cities' like London: 'when night / Darkens the streets, then wander forth the sons / Of Belial, flown with insolence and wine' (1.502–4). Such lines voice Milton's 'contempt for the ascendant nocturnal culture of the aristocracy, which flared into light like the artificial lights of a court masque' (Koslofsky 2011, 51). Is it a coincidence Drayton also composed some of the earliest poetry denouncing human exploitation of the environment, and that Milton's masque censures Comus's rapacious consumerism of the earth's resources?

For ecocritics, one the most interesting counter-nocturnalization texts is Thomas Dekker's *Lanthorne and Candlelight* (1608), which imagines nightfall transforming London 'into a Wildernesse' (A3^v). Whereas some early moderns hailed the extermination of England's dangerous predators as a sign of its civility, Dekker condemns the urban night as a restoration of primal savagery: 'our Country breedes no Wolves nor Serpents, yet these ingender here and are either Serpents or Wolves, or worse then both' (A3^v). In Chapter 12 Sir Lancelot braces himself for a twilight tour of the capital, for he 'knew he should meet with other strange birds and beasts fluttering from their nests and crawling out of their dens' (L1^{r-v}), which includes bankrupts, murderers, and thieves in the shape of owls; lechers resembling glowworms; and cuckolds transformed into horned snails (L1^v–L2^r). In Dekker's Aesopian satire, night triggers a rewilding of humans at the margins of the social order, but one that masks the displacement of other species from the urban environment.

Rather than betray an innate dread of the dark, these texts suggest that perceptions of it in the seventeenth century begin to fissure in conformity with sociopolitical sensibilities. Whereas Cavalier culture celebrates monarchical empery over the illuminated night and sees it as a time of revelry, the more Protestant-minded writers cherish darkness as a time of poetic inspiration and philosophical or spiritual meditation on human mortality and the cosmic sublime.[20] The early modern theatre industry could not avoid entangling itself in this debate, particularly as it invested more capital in candlelit playhouses and night-time performances that Protestant-leaning civic authorities had long sought to restrict. In 1584 the Corporation of London had proclaimed that 'no playeing be in the dark, nor continue in any such time but as any of the auditorie may returne to their dwellings in London before sonne set, or at least before it is dark' (Chambers 1923, 4:302). Such a policy would have been difficult to enforce, however, and evidence suggests that it was widely flouted in the early seventeenth century. A moral treatise entitled *Vertues Commonwealth* inveighs against 'these nocturnall and night Playes, at unseasonable and undue times' (Crosse 1603, Q1^v). The trigger for this screed was likely the growing regularity of evening performances at Blackfriars by the Children of the Chapel in the first years of the seventeenth century. The King's Men's professional rivalry with the Chapel Children at this time, as attested by *Hamlet*, furnishes grounds for supposing that Shakespeare harboured some misgivings about the new fashion for night-time plays. A study of nocturnal environments in Shakespeare's Jacobean tragedies, however, indicates that a bigger factor was Shakespeare's misgivings about the court masque and its campaign for royal jurisdiction over the night—a campaign in which he himself, as the king's chief playwright, was inescapably conscripted.

Of the various responses to the quandary posed by the exceptional length of some of Shakespeare's play-texts beyond the 'two hours traffic' of the public stage, Richard Dutton's answer has an elegant simplicity: Shakespeare's company adapted several of them for court revels 'expressly instituted to fill the cold, dark hours of midwinter' (2016, 37). This task would have weighed more heavily on Shakespeare in the Jacobean era when the King's Men averaged fourteen court performances per year, four times as often as they performed before Elizabeth in the final decade of her reign (Kernan 1995, xvi–xvii). More to the point, court performances under James extended much later into the evening. In 1604, the Venetian ambassador reported that a performance at Whitehall could not start until the king arrived around 10 p.m. An entertainment at Oxford the following year commenced at nine at night and ended after one in the morning (*PPMF* 552). During the marriage festivities for his daughter, Princess Elizabeth, James reportedly had been 'sitting up almost two whole nights' (DC 13 February 1613); no wonder he sometimes nodded off. As the 1613 celebrations included revivals of *The Winter's Tale* and *The Tempest*, one could reasonably infer that some court performances of Shakespeare's plays wound up well after midnight. In our post-Edisonian culture, it is easy to overlook the fact that the lateness of court revels was an integral element of their carnival atmosphere and luxuriousness—a pointed defiance of the diurnal rhythms of the mercantile and labouring classes. In his capacity as court dramatist, Shakespeare was inevitably swept up in this temporal shift, so it is appropriate that his Jacobean plays slyly comment on his patron's routines that forced the King's Men to work such late hours. The duty to alleviate the king's boredom in the murk of winter when James could not indulge in his favourite pastime of hunting may help account for the length of some of Shakespeare's texts, but this only partly explains why so many of his Jacobean plays have an adversarial relationship to darkness. To further elucidate the dark's signifying power in Shakespeare it is vital to locate his Jacobean plays within the indoor playhouses at Blackfriars and especially Whitehall, where the court masque would both instantiate and celebrate nocturnalization.

Nocturnal Carnivalesque in *Timon of Athens* and *Antony and Cleopatra*

This book has projected an image of Shakespeare as an unobsequious court dramatist, who devised plays catering to the monarch's interests while peppering them with critiques of absolutism. The late plays puncture fantasies of environmental sovereignty, and Shakespeare conveys a similar ambivalence about the human conquest of the night as epitomized in the illuminated revels of James. A surprisingly relevant play in this context is *Timon of Athens*, whose eponymous protagonist flaunts his wealth in extravagant displays of artificial lightning at feasts that defy the supposedly natural rhythm of nightly rest:

> 1 LORD We are so virtuously bound—
> TIMON And so am I to you.
> 2 LORD So infinitely endeared—
> TIMON All to you. Lights, more lights!
>
> (1.2.232–5)

This seemingly banal dialogue flickers with dramatic irony. Even with a retinue of torchbearers, Timon cannot discern the stark flattery in front of his nose. It also implies that Timon hosts his dinner, which in early modern usage typically signified a mid-day meal, in a darkened interior space, and that the feast extends late into the evening. Such a suspicion is confirmed when Flavius later bewails the parasites that have 'this night englutted' (2.2.166) Timon's bounty and rebukes his master's excessive lighting as a symptom of his prodigality: 'when every room / Hath blazed with light' (2.2.160–1).[21] This line occurs after the masque of lute-strumming Amazons, an interlude that would have uncomfortably recalled the revels of Queen Anna and her lady courtiers. Timon's remark that the masque has added 'lustre' (1.2.148) to his feast further insinuates that the Amazons' entrance was accompanied by artificial lighting, yet Timon's call for more renders a stage property so familiar as to be almost (paradoxically) invisible into a source of moral queasiness. Although most scholars attribute the masque scene to Middleton, Flavius's speech in 2.2 is probably Shakespeare's, and echoes the critiques voiced by Drayton's owl against the nocturnal regime of the Stuart court and the urban elite.

Critics have long deciphered *Antony and Cleopatra* as a barbed commentary on the decadence of the Stuart court (Kernan 1995, 106–31) and mulled over its representations of blackness (Hall 1995, 153–60; Loomba 2002, 112–34), but synthesizing these approaches indicates how both are tethered to nocturnalization. Antony's ordering his captains to join in a nocturnal feast and 'mock the midnight bell' (3.13.190) chimes with invitations to the court revels of James and Anna, which made a mockery of curfew, as well as medicinal theories that prescribed nocturnal sleep for health.[22] The couple plan to wander the streets after dark in violation of curfew for the joy of people-watching (1.1.55) and then spend the night carousing and staging drunken theatricals. Enobarbus quips that they often 'made the night light with drinking' (2.2.188), punning on artificial light and licentiousness, while a dejected Antony later orders his servants 'to burn this night with torches' (4.2.41), a phrase that suggests a pyrotechnic assault on night itself.

The motif of illumination in the play likely took its spark from Plutarch, who claims that Cleopatra's artificial lighting astounded Antony more than anything in Egypt, including her luxurious barge:

But amongst all other things, he most wondered at the infinite number of lights and torches hanged on the top of the house, giving light in every place, and so artificially set and ordered by devices—some round, some square—that it was the rarest thing to behold that eye could discern or that ever books could mention. (1579, 1690)

Even the sober historian Plutarch cannot conceal his wonder at the radiance of Cleopatra's eye-popping light show. Encountering this passage, Shakespeare would likely have recalled the elaborate lighting at court performances, which provoked similar feelings of awe in spectators at Whitehall. For some, however, this awe was tempered by disapproval of the extravagance, and Octavius speaks for this faction when he grumbles—in tones reminiscent of Webster, Drayton, Milton, and Timon's steward—that Antony 'wastes / The lamps of night in revel' (1.4.4–5). Such a rebuke may have sounded less priggish in a pre-Edisonian culture more keenly aware of the expense and grimy materiality of domestic lighting, and indicates Shakespeare's familiarity with social critics opposed to nocturnalization in Jacobean Britain.

On a more disturbing note, early modern opponents of nocturnalization might harness xenophobic and racist attitudes to condemn nocturnal wakefulness as uncivilized or un-English, an analogical pattern central to Jonson's *Masque of Blackness* and which also casts a shadow across *Antony and Cleopatra*. For Plutarch, Cleopatra's illuminated revels are part of the exotic, sybaritic splendour of the East in contrast to the diurnal order of Rome, and Shakespeare develops this binary by making the night-time sports of 'tawny' (1.1.6) Cleopatra symptomatic of hedonistic misrule. Although Cleopatra subscribes to early modern geo-humoral theories of racial difference when she attributes her 'black' complexion to 'Phoebus' amorous pinches' (1.5.29), the play persistently associates her with images of darkness, moonlight, shadow, and artificial lamplight. Critical Race Studies has often decried the subliminal prejudice in such Eurocentric representations of darker skin tones in terms of 'blackness, shadow, shades, night' (Fanon 1967, 188; Pfeifer 2009), an impulse bolstered by the metaphysical dualisms of Plato, Judeo-Christianity, and Descartes. In Judeo-Christian culture the exception that proves the rule is the Song of Solomon, whose bride Sheba famously declares, 'I am black…but comelie'. The Canticles echo in Jonson's 1605 *Masque of Blackness* and also presumably inspired the court entertainment of Solomon and Sheba staged during the state visit of King Christian IV in 1606, which provides a suggestive inter-text for *Antony and Cleopatra*. The pageant dramatized the Ethiopian-Egyptian queen paying homage to a king synonymous with wisdom (to whom James was often compared), but it descended into a shambolic bacchanal. The actress playing Sheba was so drunk she tripped and showered the Danish king with a tray full of wine and cakes. Too intoxicated to care, Christian brushed himself off and leapt from his chair to dance with her, with the predictable result that both toppled over and had to be carted off to bed. Personifications of Hope and Faith had likewise imbibed to the point of incapacity; unable to deliver their lines, they beat a shameful retreat and were later found vomiting in a hallway (1804, 348–52). Since a letter by John Harington remains the sole witness of this masque (which sounds simply too good to be true), scholars have questioned its authenticity. Whether it is 'a brilliant work of epistolary fiction' (Shapiro 2016, 308) or an embellished report of an actual court performance gone wrong that no participant cared to (or could) remember, the letter invites a reading of *Antony and Cleopatra* as a warning against illicit nocturnalization. It seems fitting that the Solomon and Sheba debacle was reported by Harington, the very courtier who had previously gifted James an ornate lantern as a symbol of royal governance over the night. Harington's letter seems to lament James's shirking of that duty by succumbing to nocturnal misgovernment. In choosing to retell the story of Antony, whose nocturnal dalliances with Cleopatra bring about his downfall, Shakespeare may be politely urging James to eschew the midnight revels of his Danish queen, who had recently performed in blackface as an 'Ethiope', and her hard-drinking brother.[23]

While such an interpretation would deepen the stigma of Cleopatra's blackness, insofar as it signifies her intimacy with the night, Shakespeare's tragedy is more complex and less didactic than Harington's satire. Antony and Cleopatra transform their nocturnal lifestyle into a heroic defiance of the mundane world. Exalting the power of the human imagination over nature, they not only glorify theatre itself but also naturalize artificial lighting as a metaphor for the human condition. This same trope features memorably in *Othello*—'put out the light' (5.2.7)—and *Macbeth*—'out, brief candle' (5.5.22)—but gains added poignancy here due to the transgressive nature of lighting as spectacle at Cleopatra's court, which itself duplicates the stage illumination in indoor performances at Whitehall. After his defeat, Antony mutters 'the torch is out, / Lie down' (4.14.47–8). Gazing upon his corpse, Cleopatra equates him with the proverbial light of her life: 'Look, our lamp is spent, it's out' (4.15.89). Prima facie, these speeches suggest the limits of nocturnalization, which depended—more obviously in a pre-electrified era and in indoor playhouses whose expensive candles needed constant tending—upon finite and quickly consumed resources for fuel. In suicide, however, Antony and Cleopatra transfigure death into an endless night in which they evade the diurnal order of Octavius. Iras makes the point succinctly when she declares, 'The bright day is done / And we are for the dark' (5.2.192–3). Reading the play alongside conflicting depictions of sleep in romance and epic, Garrett Sullivan shrewdly argues that it 'transvalues the association of sleep with sexual excess and hedonism, and it transforms what is within epic a threat to masculinity into something that lies at its very core' (2005, 259). To reframe this argument in relation to the masque, *Antony and Cleopatra* condemns the nocturnalization of the overlit court revels while also extolling such spectacle as integral to the aura of majesty.

Its depictions of the ecstasy and excess of the nocturnal carnivalesque relay a court dramatist's torn feelings about demands for 'princely parsimony' (Cramsie 2002, 81) by Julius Caesar, the suggestively named Chancellor of the Exchequer, who in 1607 drafted a draconian or rather Octavian budget insisting James slash expenses to Elizabethan levels to avoid financial ruin. An understanding of *Antony of Cleopatra* is greatly enriched by juxtaposing it with the efforts of Caesar and the so-called 'New Octavians' to impose a moratorium on late-night masques and feasts at the Stuart court.[24] Like these fiscal reformers, Octavius Caesar reimposes diurnal order, but rather than submit to Roman authority and the humiliation of a Roman triumph the titular pair retreat into an eternal darkness the state cannot dispel or control. Abjuring a simplistic Manichean division of light and dark into good and evil, *Antony and Cleopatra* instead reflects a broader spectrum of attitudes towards night, nocturnalization, and otherness in Jacobean Britain.

'Left Darkling': Tragedy and Counter-nocturnalization in *Macbeth* and *King Lear*

While the Shakespearean night can be a time for love-making and revelry, many early modern tragedies imply that to venture out into the pre-electrified night is to invite misfortune and possibly death. Tragedy's nyctophobic prejudice is memorably captured in Thomas Nashe's *Terrors of the Night*:

> When anie Poet would describe a horrible Tragicall accident, to adde the more probability and credence unto it, he dismally beginneth to tell how it was darke night when it was done, and cheerfull daylight had quite abandoned the firmament. (1594, H2^v)

A data-driven approach backs up Nashe's claim. Dividing Shakespeare's night-scenes according to genre, Jean-Marie Maguin found that only 2 per cent of the romances occur at night, 12 per cent of the histories, and 16 per cent of the comedies, while 25 per cent of the scenes in Shakespeare's tragedies unfold in the dark (1995, 248). Maguin understands this as an 'anthropological feature' of drama, but the following pages will clarify how Shakespeare's Jacobean tragedies *Macbeth* and *King Lear* (especially when encountered in their original spelling and performance conditions) exploit an anthropological/cultural aversion to darkness to transform the dream of royal jurisdiction over the dark into a nightmare.

From a geographic perspective, it is highly appropriate that the Scottish play dramatizes the 'night's predominance' (2.4.8). At 56.5° N, Dunsinane stands 5° farther north than London, 16° higher than New York City, and a half degree closer to the pole than Elsinore. The sense of night encroaching on day after Duncan's murder not only poeticizes the lengthening of darkness during the onset of winter but also captures how this seasonal phenomenon is more pronounced in northern climes. While the 5° difference between London and Edinburgh may seem relatively modest, national pride and geo-humoralism would have amplified it in the early modern English mind. Mary Floyd-Wilson has shown how *Macbeth* effectively 'demonizes the far north' (2006, 161) by insinuating that the harsh environment rendered the Scots more susceptible to witchcraft, and Jeffrey Griswold has refined this argument by observing that Scottish darkness 'detaches the Macbeths from bonds of kinship, nation, and hospitality' (2019, 36).

Looking at darkness in *Macbeth* through ecocritical goggles reveals how it taps not only into anxiety about night-walkers in the wake of the Gunpowder Plot but also into resentment of so-called vermin to vilify nocturnal wildlife. The weird sisters find companion species in the wild cat (*felix sylvestris*) or 'brinded cat' (4.1.1) and the hedgehog or 'hedgepig' (4.1.2), while Macbeth conscripts the wolf, bat, beetle, and owl as accomplices in murder. The same agrilogistics that fed hatred for the 'detested kite' (*Lear* 1.4.254) contributes to *Macbeth*'s tarring of corvids:

> Light thickens,
> And the crow makes wing to th'rooky wood.
> Good things of day begin to droop and drowse,
> Whiles night's black agents to their preys do rouse.
>
> (3.2.51–4)

The image of a crow's flight at dusk into a seething mass of black-feathered rooks—which do in fact roost en masse at twilight—beautifully and powerfully animates the encroaching darkness.[25] While this is undoubtedly poetry of the highest order, Macbeth's ominous references to crows and rooks have troubling implications in light of the Tudor Vermin Acts (discussed in Chapter 1) which specifically targeted these seed-eating species as pests.[26] Chapter 1 compared the ambush of Banquo to illegal birding, but an alternative reading of the scene might ponder the coincidence of a character who worries about which seeds will grow and which will not, and whose name smacks of culinary abundance, falling victim to murderers that Macbeth implicitly likens to seed-devouring birds. Despite the fact crows and rooks are diurnal and crepuscular, their black plumage aligns them with the 'night's black agents' in a passage that connives with campaigns to enforce legislation criminalizing so-called 'vermin' by equating them with night-walking thieves.[27]

In transporting its audience to a benighted and wilder medieval Scottish past, *Macbeth* reverses the trajectory of modernity, in which humans in Western Europe gradually extended their dominion over the night and nocturnal species regarded as radically Other. Picking up on this anachronism, Matthew Beaumont interprets the play as a warning about 'the limits of Enlightenment' (2016, 87), the inability of state power or human reason to completely subjugate the night. In support of this reading one might note that whereas Jacobean authorities encouraged compliance with curfew through ringing bells, Shakespeare compares a beetle's droning flight to bells summoning the worshippers of Hecate, the animal-headed Greek goddess of the night, to venture out into the darkness. Like the sinister Dame in Jonson's *Masque of Queens*, Hecate represents a rebellious counter-authority opposing the sun-king James, whom royal propaganda (as we have seen) invested with the power to transform night into day. While Hecate's parachuting into the play may be an awkward, poetically inferior interpolation by Thomas Middleton, it nevertheless captures a truth about 'night's predominance' in *Macbeth* as a greater-than-human force. An ecocritical reading might reappraise her onstage presence as Middleton's crude attempt to embody—in a form that is both female and animalistic—Shakespeare's representation of the Scottish night as a domain that resists patriarchal and anthropocratic control.

Even when this scene is cut from performance, Hecate still haunts the play in its frequent personifications of Night, which are less accessible to twenty-first-century readers due to the editing of Shakespeare's texts in conformity with modern capitalization. In the shelves of criticism on this tragedy, only—to my knowledge—a single study (Smith 2013, 23–4) remarks on the Folio's consistent capitalization of Night in *Macbeth*. Lady Macbeth summons 'thick Night', Ross speaks of 'Nights predominance', the beetle sounds 'Nights yawning Peale' (TLN 401, 933, 1201), etc. The Folio does not always capitalize Night in other plays, such as *Lear*, and Compositors A and B (or whoever prepared the transcript or prompt-book they worked from) evidently felt preserving this pattern was so important that they even sever the word 'tonight' to accomplish it: Banquo's murder 'must be done to Night', as if it were a sacrifice to Hecate, and his soul, if it can soar to heaven in the dark, 'must find it out to Night' (TLN 1137, 1149). The capitalization of this word has genuine thematic significance. Elevating it to a proper noun honours Night as if it were a separate spatiotemporal realm comparable to Scotland, and a goddess whose dominion rivals that of the monarch. *Macbeth*'s nocturnal animals (Wolfe, Owle, Bat) also glisten differently in the Folio's capitals, which bestow greater agency on 'Nights black Agents' (TLN 1212). Insofar as it better captures an enchanted cosmology that the play itself revives, restoring the original capitalization might be regarded as a typographical rewilding of the Shakespearean text.

Darkness, Startle, and Disability in *Macbeth* and *King Lear*

While Duncan's murder exposes the ruler's vulnerability in the night, the ultimate defeat of Macbeth, paving the way for Stuart succession, aligns the play with modernity. Beaumont's reading of the play as a warning about the 'limits of Enlightenment' holds true for much of the performance, but Malcolm's assertion 'the Night is long that never findes the Day' (TLN 2091) at the fourth act's close foreshadows the restoration of diurnal order. This message would have shone forth more brightly in an illuminated performance before the Stuart king at Whitehall, where the Macbeths' reign of darkness could be perceived as a kind of extended anti-masque. It is by no means certain, however, that audiences at other venues with different expectations and different levels of ambient lighting would experience the tragedy the same way. If reading *Macbeth* in original capitalization produces a rewilding effect, could the same be said of viewing the play in its original performance conditions?

Although first composed before the King's Men acquired their own indoor playhouse, *Macbeth* seems acutely self-conscious of the affective power of darkness on early modern audiences, which lends credence to the theory that the 1623 Folio text represents a retrofitting of the play for Blackfriars. Regarding lighting design from the playing company's perspective, theatre historians detect 'surprisingly little difference' (Gurr 2009a, 228) in the staging of night-scenes at indoor versus outdoor venues, noting that both relied on the same verbal cues and stage props—candlesticks or stagehands carrying torches—to signify darkness. However, experiments with recreating original performance conditions at indoor theatres, aided by the 2014 opening of the Sam Wanamaker Playhouse, indicate that the play-goer's experience might differ in meaningful ways. For instance, Martin White contends that a Globe audience would see the cruel pranks played on the Duchess of Malfi in the dark with a touch of ironic detachment, whereas the audience in the dimly lit Blackfriars would experience it 'from the Duchess's point of view' (2014, 136). A similar argument could be made about the ambush of Banquo. In an indoor theatre, the First Murderer striking out Banquo's torch amounts to a moment of scripted lighting design that more thoroughly enmeshes the spectators in the on-stage confusion.

Another under-examined aspect of candlelit performance is the players' strategic exploitation of darkness to heighten what film theorists refer to as the 'startle effect.' *Macbeth* is a recognizable precursor of the horror film in its consistent inducing of the jump-scare—on no fewer than ten occasions—both to terrify the characters and titillate the audience.[28] Lady Macbeth experiences it when she hears a noise as she awaits the news of Duncan's murder and soon after is discomfited by the entrance of her husband, whose face she cannot perceive in the dark. The same sound had alarmed Macbeth, and apparently recurs in the midst of their conversation, as Macbeth repeats her command to 'Hark' (2.2.19), creating a tense silence. Macduff's knocking at the gate represents the most notorious example, and its discombobulating effect on Macbeth can be inferred from his rhetorical question: 'how is't with me when every noise appals me?' (2.2.59). The sleeping guests suffer it in the ensuing scene when the bell rings and a 'hideous trumpet' (2.3.82) rouses them, while the unexpected news that Macbeth has slain Duncan's grooms startles Lady Macbeth so much she faints, which itself catches characters and spectators off-guard. The sudden appearance of Banquo's ghost induces it (twice) in Macbeth, which prompts Lady Macbeth to upbraid her husband for his 'flaws and starts' (3.4.60). Another memorable instance would be the off-stage 'night shriek' of Lady Macbeth's women when they discover her corpse. Interestingly, this cry spooks the audience but does not faze the now desensitized Macbeth, which allows Shakespeare to comment on the psychodynamics of startle. Psychologists have discovered that the startle response is greater following exposure to negative images, such as corpses, snakes, or wounds (Baird 2000), and Shakespeare's macabre imagery would conspire with the dim lighting at Blackfriars to assault the audience's nerves. Indeed, Shakespeare even attempts to trigger a startle response in his imagery when Lady Macbeth instructs her husband to 'looke like th'innocent flower, / But be the Serpent under't' (TLN 421–2), a phrase that recalls paintings of startle like Caravaggio's *Boy Bitten by a Lizard* (c.1600).

Startle has long been dismissed as a vulgar ploy and seems resistant to theory because of its biological determinism but it can deliver an ecocritical jolt by reactivating primal fear of nocturnal predators.[29] In the context of state-sponsored nocturnalization under James, the triggering of a startle effect has ideological significance in that it overrides the rational faculties to issue a jarring reminder of the limitations of the human sensorium and, by extension, the limitations of human empery over the night.[30] From this angle one can hear in Macduff's knocking a meaning that differs markedly from De Quincey's famous interpretation of it as signalling the abrupt return of normalcy. Instead of sensing how the 'world of darkness passes away like a pageantry' (1949, 1095) the sudden knocks arguably intensify awareness of the dark and its cognitive impairment of humans. To an ecocritic, it is particularly noteworthy that the couple's nerves are rattled by an owl's hoot. Given Lennox's remark 'the obscure Bird clamour'd the live-long Night' (TLN 809), it is tempting to decipher the voice that cried 'sleep no more' (2.2.36) as Macbeth's auditory distortion of the same tawny owl's 'tu-whit tu-whoo' (*LLL* 5.2.915). If Shakespeare incriminates the owl in Duncan's murder, the owl also incriminates the Macbeths, or startles them into incriminating themselves. The play's ending seems to reject an enchanted worldview, but Macbeth's claim that 'understood relations have / By maggot-pies and choughs and rooks brought forth / The secret'st man of blood' (3.4.122–4) is not entirely absurd: such superstitions seem to attribute supernatural wisdom to other creatures but in fact betray humanity's own sense of epistemological frailty, stemming from a recognition that some species—like the heavenly avenger peeping through the blanket of the dark—perceive more clearly in the night than we do.

Rather than resist critical theory, the startle response invites consideration of some common ground shared by ecocriticism and disability studies. Traversing these crossroads, Matthew Cella challenges the 'ableist premise' of much ecophenomenology, which presupposes an abled body's experience of landscape as normative, and questions 'the primacy of vision' (2013, 575–7) in environmental writing. Cella directs our gaze to the ash-grey wastelands of Cormac McCarthy's *The Road*, but similar lessons can be learned from Shakespeare's representations of black night as a realm of visual and cognitive impairment. After arranging Banquo's murder, Macbeth apostrophizes in the gloaming, 'Come, seeling Night, / Skarfe up the tender Eye of pittifull Day' (TLN 1205–6). The second line envisions night as a scarf wrapped over the eyes like a blindfold, but Shakespeare borrows the peculiar adjective 'seeling' from the falconer's practice of sewing a bird's eyelids close together to render it docile. It is an incredibly visceral image of the enfeebled epistemology of humans in the pre-modern night, on par with Thomas Nashe's comparison of night to a 'cursed raven [that] pecks out men's eyes' (1594, B2r). When the First Murderer knocks out Banquo's torch, the stunt—rarely attempted today due to modern health and safety regulations—constitutes another startle effect, one that replicates the verbal images of blindfolds and eye-seeing by hurling spectators into the metonymic blindness of night.

Shakespeare's most piercing exploration of night blindness is of course *King Lear*, a play performed before King James at Whitehall in 1606 on 'St Stephen's Night' in darkest December. Several studies have examined the play's eye imagery and its poignant depictions of disability, but more could be done to link these to its early performance history and cultural histories of the night.[31] In our unfolding climate emergency Shakespeareans have been understandably mesmerized by the storm, but *King Lear* betrays an almost equal concern with exposure to the dark.[32] Tellingly, the word 'night' occurs in the tragedy twenty-nine times, second only to *A Midsummer Night's Dream*. Although neither the Quarto nor Folio text capitalize it, which makes night's consistent capitalization in *Macbeth* all the more curious, *Lear* does endow night with a god-like, tyrannical authority over the king and all humanity. In the opening scene, Lear invokes 'the mysteries of Hecate and the night' when he banishes Cordelia, as if night obeys his commands, but Goneril's cruelty leaves him at the mercy of 'darkness and devils' (1.4.243). After Lear's departure at dusk, Gloucester protests 'alack, the night comes on' (2.2.490) before noticing the rising winds; Cornwall forecasts a 'wild night' (2.2.498) rather than a wild tempest; and Cordelia is appalled by both: 'What, i'the storm, i'th night?' (4.3.29). In one of the play's most unforgettable lines, the Fool credits night with the power to inflict cognitive impairment: 'This cold night will turn us all to fools and madmen' (3.4.77), a self-deprecating quip which diagnoses the cause of Tom's madness and foreshadows Lear's.[33] Lear's noctivagation is also foreshadowed in Regan's 'threading dark-eyed night' (F 2.1.121), which captures the constricted sight and mobility of humans after sundown. Gloucester's epithet 'hell-black night' (3.7.59) equates the visual impairment of humans in a colour-drained nightscape with damnation, and primes us to regard his own blinding as the onset of a perpetual night.[34]

While reminding the Jacobean audience that blindness was intermittently universal, Shakespeare's tragedy leans on disability as a 'narrative prosthesis' (Mitchell and Snyder 2013) to overcome complacent assumptions that sight imparts knowledge or that the monarch possesses an all-seeing and omnitemporal authority. It is a critical commonplace that the imaginary Dover Cliff scene has a metatheatrical sub-text, beguiling spectators to envision a flat stage as a steep precipice, but *King Lear* also conspires to make viewers perceive artificial light as a referent for darkness in a kind of negative exposure of the ideological lighting design in the Stuart masque. Two stage directions unique to the Folio text call for Gloucester to enter 'with a torch' (2.1.37, 3.4.107); in both instances the torches ironically denote the murk of night, serving, like Gloucester's spectacles, to supplement and hence illuminate the limitations of what Edgar calls 'the deficient sight' (4.6.23). While torches could signify night both in outdoor and indoor playhouses, Gloucester's blinding might be even more powerful in the latter, as the absence or extinguishing of his torch could also function metonymically to simulate ocular impairment, reducing the visibility of the action on stage to the spectators. After gouging out his eyeballs, Cornwall makes a sadistic pun on Gloucester's name, 'where is thy lustre now?' (3.7.83), which further darkens the indoor stage by zooming in on the extinguishing of the actor's eyeshine by torchlight. Shakespeare achieves a similar dimming effect with his verbal imagery, such as Gloucester's recollection of 'eclipses in the sun and moon' (1.2.103), and the Fool's extinguished light: 'so out went the candle and we were left darkling' (1.4.208). Shakespeare's use of the now archaic word 'darkling' suggests the experience of being plunged in darkness, and its orthographic resemblance to the participial verb form conveys the seemingly hostile agency of pre-Edisonian darkness.[35] Moreover, the Fool's line would possess a metatheatrical frisson in an indoor performance where extradiegetic lighting was provided by torches or candles that could sputter out.

Situating *Lear* in a performance environment usually ablaze with artificial light makes its descent into darkness even more pronounced and reveals that a Whitehall production would be haunted by 'environmental irony' (Jones 2015, 9) —a mismatch between stage conditions and the world conjured by the play. King James would have watched the play surrounded by a legion of torches and beeswax candles but Shakespeare's darkling poetics subvert the royal gaze. Simulating the ocular deterioration of old age or the onset of glaucoma, the tragedy's end stages an agonizingly slow fade to black: Lear confesses his 'eyes are not o' the best' (5.3.277), Cordelia's corpse presents 'a dull [i.e. dim] sight' (5.3.280), and Kent exclaims 'all's cheerless, dark and deadly' (5.3.288). To a Jacobean audience, this reversal of the court masque's gathering brightness would make the tragedy's critique of anthropocratic absolutism even more searing. Tom's mistaking Gloucester for the night-walking demon Flibertigibbet and his declaration that the 'prince of darkness is a gentleman' (3.4.140) contrive to demonize the colonization of the dark by the elite, while his report that 'Nero is an angler in the lake of darkness' (3.6.6) hints that even god-like emperors might find themselves plunged into an eternal murk. When Kent complains of the 'tyrannous night' (3.4.147) and 'the tyranny of the open night' (3.4.2), the political rhetoric hammers home the once mighty Lear's abjection and invests night with his ruthless authority. In a performance at Whitehall, the very site of the nocturnal revels celebrating royal dominion over the night, *Lear* would deliver an even more sobering check on nocturnalization than either *Macbeth* or *Antony and Cleopatra*.

This is not to argue that Shakespeare devised *Lear* exclusively as a site-specific play for Whitehall. The shorter Folio text and its insertion of stage directions for torches might indicate a revision for Blackfriars, where Shakespeare's company had more control over the lighting design and the stage would have been considerably dimmer than at the palace. Perhaps the acquisition of Blackfriars emboldened Shakespeare to experiment with fades and startle effects and (like Rembrandt) to compose with darkness. With the opening of the Sam Wanamaker Playhouse alongside the Globe, it is now more evident than ever how the professional demand to write plays adaptable for both outdoor and indoor playhouses added to the complexity of Shakespeare's art. It would also have contributed to his sense of modern humans as, for better and worse, cathemeral creatures, active at day and night. Just as an open-air production might stage Lear's exposure in unpredictable ways, theatre historians might wish to explore whether a candlelit theatre could better convey the wildness of darkness. Modern productions may introduce an occasional torch, but their understandable aversion to open flame means that electric lighting effects are far more common, and the darkness of the modern theatre tends to generate scopophilic pleasure rather than dread or epistemological humility. Hence directors and critics might consider how original performance conditions could achieve a theatrical rewilding of familiar plays by returning us to a time when the stage, like the great globe it purported to represent, was less subject to technological control.

Copernican Darkness, the Cosmic Sublime, and Counter-Enlightenment

While the effort to regulate and dispel darkness in Jacobean Britain underpropped royal ideology, I would like to conclude this chapter by exploring the scientific and psychological dimensions of nocturnalization. Even as technological improvements in public lighting and Protestant scepticism towards the supernatural diminished the terrors of the night, the night sky may have acquired a new aura of menace from the dissemination of Copernican cosmology. By proposing a boundless universe, Copernicans such as Thomas Digges and Giordano Bruno made the darkness of the night more substantial and daunting, as star-gazing confronted one with an infinite abyss. Copernican darkness would be qualitatively different than Ptolemaic darkness, more intimidating and oppressive. But literary texts might provoke divergent responses to this new cosmology, ranging from *horror vacui* and a compensatory drive to eliminate darkness to awe and intimations of a cosmic sublime.[36]

Digges had introduced Copernican theory to the English public in his 1576 *Perfit Description of the Celestiall Orbes* (reprinted seven times by 1605), but Shakespeare's interest in it seems to grow more acute in his Jacobean plays, perhaps due to the fact that Queen Anna's home country was a hotbed of Renaissance astronomy. King James had in fact visited Tycho Brahe's observatory during his visit to Denmark and it seems plausible that much of *Hamlet*'s Copernican imagery dates from a 1603 revision to the play for a performance before the Stuart court.[37] Whereas Lorenzo's nocturne in *A Merchant of Venice* depicts a Christianized vision of a neo-Platonic/Ptolemaic universe defined by harmony and bounded by benevolent cherubs, the post-1600 tragedies ponder 'infinite space' and a universe indifferent to human striving.

The ecocritical implications of the cosmic sublime would be difficult to overstate, as it results from the literal de-centring of humans as the cynosure of the universe, dealing the strongest blow to anthropocentric narcissism prior to Darwin. On the flip side, heliocentrism also eroded the credibility of astrology, the belief that the zodiac infused bestial qualities into human bodies via starlight, while attributing greater agency to humans in shaping their destiny. It is noteworthy that James's credulity about witchcraft was counterbalanced by his scepticism towards judicial astrology, which he denounced as 'the Divels schoole' (*KJSW* 157). Shakespeare expresses a similar disbelief about astrology in the speeches of Cassius, Helena, and Edmund, although an eclipse does foretell Caesar's assassination, Helena concedes the stars exert some sway, and Edmund's deeds confirm the accuracy of his horoscope. These caveats and ironies suggest the poet's reluctance to abandon the sympathetic universe for the emergent mechanistic one, as Mary Thomas Crane has argued. Rather than unctuously endorse King James's views, Shakespeare's ambivalence towards astrology matches his ambivalence about nocturnalization. His plays register with a mix of elation and dismay the traumatic change from pre-modern conceptions of humans as passive victims of darkness and the 'fated sky' to self-fashioning individuals defying cosmo-biological constraints on the human condition, and hence foreshadow our collective transformation into geological agents whose rough technomagic remakes our planet and its climate.

While it would be unwise to posit a correlation between opposition to astrology and climate change denial, since the former is predicated on empirical science that the latter rejects, nocturnalization and the debunking of astrology would both contribute to disenchantment and the great 'severing' of the Enlightenment. The triumph of light over dark not only powered the ideological defence of absolutist monarchy and early modern empire-building but proved the defining metaphor in Enlightenment narratives of progress, a narrative about which many ecocritics have profound misgivings. Yet others caution that 'environmentalism is inconceivable without the Enlightenment's legacy' and are rightly wary of 'sinister tendencies' in counter-Enlightenment environmentalism (Hinchman and Hinchman 2001). Attending to the representation of darkness in Shakespearean drama offers a platform to debate the proto- and anti-Enlightenment tendencies in both his writing and in contemporary environmental discourse, and to negotiate between them rather than reject one in favour of the other. Insofar as the Anthropocene recapitulates the early modern conquest of the night writ large, Shakespeare's ambivalence towards nocturnalization might inform our efforts to 'see better' by confronting us with the limitations of both human vision and human empire.

Conclusion

King-Man and the Anthropocene as Species Tyranny

> Kings are justly called Gods, for that they exercise a manner or resemblance of divine power upon earth.
>
> King James, 'A Speach to the Lords and Commons of Parliament' (*KJSW* 1610, 327)

> We humans are the god species, the creators and destroyers of life on this planet.
>
> Mark Lynas, *The God Species* (2010, 1)

This study has primarily concerned itself with the entwining of environmental, political, and literary history in the decade from 1603 to 1613, when James's reign overlapped with the career of England's greatest playwright. The Anthropocene, however, has made the shortcomings of micro-history and periodization starkly apparent, which begs the question of the long-term ramifications of the developments charted in this book. For a Shakespearean ecocritic, it seems strangely fortuitous that the final bow of the playwright allegedly responsible for 'the invention of the human' coincides with an event some palaeo-climatologists regard as signalling human possession of the earth: the 1610 Orbis Spike.

The term spike is slightly misleading, as it was not an isolated, one-off event. 1610 simply marks the nadir of a conspicuous dip in atmospheric CO_2 levels that began in the late sixteenth century and triggered the most intense period of global cooling during the Little Ice Age between 1594–1677. In a brutal irony, this drop appears to have been driven by forest recovery due to tragic population crashes among Native American communities that had practised slash-and-burn agriculture (Lewis and Maslin 2018, 182–5). In other words, the inclement weather and harvest failures that rocked Britain in Shakespeare's lifetime, notably in 1594–6 and again in 1607, and perhaps even the hurricane that wrecked the *Sea-Venture* in 1609, were at least in some small part the result of anthropogenic climate change—or rather Eurogenic, since European diseases and genocidal violence instigated this mass mortality.

While a human-conjured storm restores Prospero's heirs to the dukedom, making *The Tempest* a royalist romance insofar as it upholds the fantasy that natural law strives to preserve the reigning dynasty, the actual climate would prove much less tractable. The Orbis Spike can be linked to the increasing frequency of dearth in Europe in the seventeenth century and Geoffrey Parker has assembled a compelling dossier of evidence that this meteorological turbulence contributed to the eruption of the Thirty Years' War that ousted James's daughter Elizabeth from Bohemia as well as the English Civil War that would dethrone and behead his son (2013, 213–17; 324–47). Although historians agree the Civil War had multiple causes, no doubt many Roundheads would have shared the opinion of the feline narrator of *A Cat May Look upon a King*, who blamed James for placing the administration of the realm in the grasping hands of advisors and favourites, chosen not for their public spirit but their knack for devising 'projecting tricks, and cozening devices to fill a Tyrant's Coffers, to the enslaving of a gallant free Nation' (1652, 66). It is telling that much of the rank and file of the New Model Army were drawn from the landless poor in the very places exploited by Jacobean improvement schemes: the moorlanders of Staffordshire, Pendle, and Rossendale, 'the notorious foresters of Dean', the fen tigers of Holland and Ely, the latter being Oliver Cromwell's hometown (Hill 1972, 36). In brief, one of the powder-trails that ignited the Civil War can be traced back to resentment at the mismanagement of the country's natural resources while they were threatened by climatic instability during the reign of James.[1]

This does not imply that the parliamentary forces can be cast as noble crusaders for environmental justice. They despoiled many sequestered parks and forests; revolutionary groups like the Diggers put heathlands to the plough; Cromwell flip-flopped on fen-draining; and some of the most impassioned environmental writing from the interregnum and its aftermath came from the quills of royalists such as Margaret Cavendish, Abraham Cowley, and John Evelyn. In a magisterial survey, Robert Watson (2006, 137–65) establishes that Cavalier poetry celebrates the countryside and the natural order whereas Puritan writing tends to be introspective and advocate the improvement of nature, but no political faction had a monopoly on environmentalism in early modern Britain in part because the concept itself was not yet coherent or distinct. As Bruce Boehrer warns, seventeenth-century protests against enclosure and fen-draining 'figure within a broader complex of religious, social, and political grievances' to which the rights of the non-human are subordinate (2013, 167). Pre-romantic 'nature writing' is seldom concerned exclusively with nature per se and the same holds true of the Shakespearean topographies charted in this book. But to acknowledge that Shakespeare's representations of wild environs have a political slant does not annul their environmental message. Written by a Warwickshire land-owner in London and pitched to an audience ranging from courtiers and to commoners, his plays stage an ecopolitics in which monarchy and hierarchy must negotiate with the messy realities of local experience and the autonomy of the non-human, with what Bruno Latour has termed the 'parliament of things' (2004). Shakespeare's late plays even fantasize that an encounter with untamed nature might force the powerful to rethink their complacent policies or conceited worldviews.

In a perceptive if badly dated study of Shakespeare's late plays, G. Wilson Knight observed 'through royalistic conventions, the poetry touches some truth concerning man [sic], his high worth in the creative chain' (1947, 116). That truth, I would counter, is at best a half-truth and Shakespeare knew it. His plays also take a cynic's delight in puncturing the eco-hubris of the mortal man-king and entangling him in that chain. An overarching thesis of *Shakespeare Beyond the Green World* has been that his Jacobean plays both weave and unpick the triple analogy of god/king/man, thereby enabling audiences to perceive a troubling correlation between royal and anthropocratic absolutism. It is suggestive that James proclaimed kings gods on earth while justifying British expansionism before a dubious Parliament in 1610, the very year that Lewis and Maslin have proposed as the start-date for the Anthropocene, a new epoch marking the elevation of homo sapiens to the level of a god species, homo deus.[2] Ecocriticism and animal studies have devoted considerable brain power to dissolving the human-animal binary but attending to the human-god binary might be an equally urgent task—one early modernists are well positioned to tackle. Hamlet seems to sum up the Renaissance as evolutionary leap when he declares 'man' to be 'like a god' (2.2.272) but Shakespeare is simultaneously queasy that humans are arrogating a power too great to be entrusted to dust, to a species more ape than angel.

Although absolute monarchs might boast of a semi-divine status more vociferously than others, in reality James was happy to delegate his god-like authority. He farmed out the patents and other material perquisites of the throne to courtiers, who reaped the fruits of an imperial kingship extending its grasp beyond England's borders. As this book has shown, a defining objective of the early Stuart state was territorial aggrandizement: the unification of England with Scotland; assimilating Wales through the figure of the prince; asserting sovereignty over the fisheries of the North Sea and Atlantic; annexing northwest Russia for its timber and fur; and colonizing Ulster and Virginia to ease overpopulation and extract resources. In hindsight, christening the first permanent English colony in North America after James is exceedingly apt: a nod to his role as a figurehead for the Plantationocene. In the Crown's bid to unify the realms and its support of transnational joint-stock companies that laid the foundations for the British empire, James's reign marks a stepping stone on the path from feudalism to the New Pangea forged by global capitalism. It is a commonplace of Global Shakespeare studies that his worldwide popularity owes much to the nascent British empire; but it also owes something to the King's Men proximity to the court and these companies, which obliged Shakespeare to take a keen interest in Britain's widening horizons.

Without scapegoating James, one might nonetheless contend that his polarizing rhetoric of royal absolutism would paradoxically midwife the antithetical ideal of the 'sovereignty of the people'. In his *Trew Law of Free Monarchies*, James pronounced the king '*Dominus directus totius dominii*' [direct lord of the entire dominions] (*KJSW* 269), wielding a Latin term that echoes ominously in environmental history. Beginning the Anthropocene in 1610 lends an added significance to the 1611 publication of the King James Version of the Bible and its rendering of the Hebrew *radah* (trample) in Genesis 1:26 as 'dominion', a translation overseen by Lancelot Andrewes, the very man who placed the royal sceptre in James's hands at his coronation. In trumpeting Adam's 'dominion', Andrewes placed a figurative sceptre in the hand of every Christian farmer, colonist, scientist, and consumer. In his own translation of Du Bartas, James persuades readers to accept him as a divine monarch by enabling ordinary citizens to imagine themselves as dispossessed Adams and rightful kings over nature. Such metaphors had real eco-material impact. Royal patronage emboldened the Muscovy, Levant, Virginia, East India, and Guinea Companies to commandeer resources with the surrogate authority of a king, whilst Francis Bacon and the Royal Society would justify the technological subjugation of nature as the restoration of anthropocratic Adam's rule over paradise. From the historiographic longue durée of the Anthropocene, the subsequent revolutions overthrowing monarchy in England, America, and continental Europe may not be the drastic ruptures they appear. In the ensuing centuries, capitalist democracies appropriated the monarch's 'legitimate exercise of extractive power' (Fremaux 2019, 2), and effectively crowned *homo economicus* as planetary emperor. Hence some ecopolitical philosophers call for a 'green republicanism' to break with the 'tyranny of economic growth' (Barry 2019). While I would cavil with the reductive label green more so than with small-r republicanism, the revival of classical vocabulary to reformulate environmental policy today indicates Shakespeare's relevance to contemporary ecopolitics. One advantage of backdating the Anthropocene to seventeenth-century Britain rather than, say, 1945 is that it might help us to perceive it as a form of ecological tyranny or anthropocratic absolutism, originating not simply from the bomb or some evolutionary advantage like the oversized brain or opposable thumb but from a distinctly European court culture espousing a doctrine of imperial kingship. James exonerated himself from charges of tyranny by insisting he only claimed these absolute powers in theory and did not wield them in practice. Democratic industrialized societies repudiate the claim but collectively exert it in reality. In the so-called first world, we are all petty despots now. The King is dead; long live the kings.

By this reckoning, one secret for the enduring appeal of Shakespearean drama in capitalist democracies stems from something that now seems rather dangerous: its lulling individual egos into subconscious identification with monarchs like Lear, a *méconnaissance* whose consequences have unleashed 'the terrors of the earth' (2.2.471). Pace Eliot's Prufrock and Stoppard's Rosencrantz and Guildenstern, we moderns still glimpse ourselves in the Danish prince thanks in part to the privileges of the autocratic consumer: 'phantom monarchy lives on...in the way we nurse our own sense of entitlement to what were once the prerogatives of royalty' (Charnes 2000, 207). When American writers like Whitman and Twain feared that Shakespeare's high-born heroes might foster a reactionary nostalgia they were only half-wrong, just as Knight was half-right. Due to this transfusion of power from monarchy to capitalist technocracy in early modernity, simply praising Shakespeare as a constitutionalist thinker does not go far enough. We need to see ourselves reflected in Shakespeare's mirror for magistrates, judge ourselves implicated in the delusional absolutism of his flawed protagonists, and hear ourselves named in the royal we.

As a court and commercial dramatist appealing to both king and commoners, Shakespeare was well placed to perceive and dissect the ideological trifecta of god/king/man. If his Elizabethan plays respond to the vogue for republican thinking in the 1590s, his later plays, thanks to James, 'show an absorbing interest in the question of the prerogative of the monarch and the problem of creeping tyranny' (Hadfield 2005, 205). To interrogate this problem, Shakespeare often introduces the fourth category of the beast, equating despotism with cruelty towards animals in ways that anticipate the concept of species tyranny. In *As You Like It*, Jaques denounces the Duke and his followers as 'tyrants and what's worse' (2.1.60) for killing off the deer and thus replicating the Duke's overthrow by his tyrant brother. Gloucester's lament that tyrannical gods treat humans like insects raises the question of whether human suffering is karmic retribution for the wanton cruelty of fly-swatting boys. Although Pericles concedes that 'kings are the earth's gods', he implies this notion permits them to abuse their power, while accusing humans of acting like tyrants when they slay the mole who complained to heaven that 'the earth is thronged / By man's oppression' (1.1.101–4).[3] Such metaphors invite us to tread more softly. As Shakespeare's culture knew, tyranny is not confined to palaces. It begins at home, not only in the husband's mistreatment of his wife or servants but also in the husbandman's lack of care for the other species of which wealth consists. 'The ox is the poor man's slave' (1964, 1.2) as Aristotle declares in a work that enshrined the household (*oikos*) as a microcosm of the state. But while Aristotle believes hierarchy and the 'royal rule' of the husband/father are natural, Shakespeare emphasizes their propensity to degenerate into tyranny. His empathy with outsiders and women in a xenophobic, patriarchal society is matched by his notable concern for the victimization of non-humans in an anthropocentric culture.[4] Macbeth and Leontes, for instance, manifest their tyranny in acts of cruelty against women and children who are, I have argued, figured as animals. Just as Shakespeare circumvents the prohibition on female actresses through cross-dressing, he overcomes the communication barrier between species through poetic techniques that lend other creatures a human voice to contest human kingship. *Shakespeare Beyond the Green World* has sketched only a small number of these humanimal hybrids: doves, apes, eagles, snails, fish, sheep, bears, ermines, owls, wolves, dotterels, bees—to which one could add flies, nightingales, snakes, dogs, deer, donkeys, horses, ostriches (see Q2's spelling of Osric as 'Ostricke'), etc., as well as his splicing of humans with plants. These transcorporeal creatures in turn often embody the environments in which they live: not only farmyards, pasture, and woodlands but also unruly places that resist both dramatic representation and annexation into human empire as mere 'territory' (Elden 2018), such as heaths, seas, mountains, skies, fens, the icy north and the night. The Shakespearean stage is a much wilder place than has been dreamt of in our criticism.

Along with Ovidian hybridity, another dramatic tactic Shakespeare employed to simultaneously undermine monarchical godhood and human exceptionalism is the trope of the bewildered king-in-the-storm, for which he found a scriptural precedent in the tale of Nebuchadnezzar, the subject of a lost play at the Rose starring Edward Alleyn that likely supplied a formative inter-text for *King Lear* (*HD* 55–7). Lear involves us all in his plight by construing pleas to relinquish the luxurious trappings of power as an act of *lèse majesté* against all humanity: without 'more than nature needs, / Man's life is cheap as beast's' (2.2.455–6). But this argument reductio ad absurdum proves not so absurd. The 'cruelentious storm' (Q 3.4.6) sparks in Lear the tragic anagnorisis of his own finitude and animality as he cedes his absolute authority to the elements and the 'tyranny of the open night' (3.4.2). The storms that immerse Pericles in the sea force him to recognize the Mediterranean is not *mare nostrum* but a fluid hyper-object that defies human efforts to fully fathom it much less control it. Only by honouring Neptune rather than presuming to incarnate him as James did does Pericles recover his family and his throne. Out in the wilderness, Timon discovers Plutus is not his steward and the natural world is not his confectionary. The earth rebuffs his command for food and purveys him gold instead, prompting Timon's wish the metal might overthrow human empire and restore the planet to the beasts. After venturing into the thin alpine air, Innogen experiences a ritual death and metamorphosis into organic muck that 'removes the transcendent, superhuman qualities of royalty' (MacFaul 2015, 75). The Welsh mountains resist imperial conquest and Cymbeline in turn acknowledges the limitations on his authority by paying respect to the world beyond his borders and to the higher power of Jove. If *The Tempest* entertains the Baconian fantasy that the state might control the weather, seizing Jove's bolt and commanding the rainbow, Prospero ultimately renounces the technomagic that Marlowe's Faustus equates with 'dominion'. Deeming it wiser to ponder his mortality than his demi-godhood, he boasts of the latter only to clarify what he is relinquishing. In brief, Shakespeare's late plays consistently spotlight the convergences between god/king/man in order to illuminate the fault-lines of the analogy. Philip IV of Spain (with whom James pursued an alliance) would nurture a court culture that flattered him as *rey planeta*, and the poetics of the Stuart masque encouraged James to picture himself in similarly colossal terms, but Shakespearean drama exposes the planetary king as an idol of brittle clay.

James projected himself as an absolute monarch on paper but Shakespearean drama reminds its audience of the wide gap between theory and reality. The king of Scotland could not defend heaths and moors from burning, enclosure, or illegal birding. The owner of the realm's mines and mineral wealth could not compel metals to regenerate, was dogged by insolvency, and suffered a panic attack when he actually entered a coal mine at Culross. James was a would-be Neptune who could not control the sea and a Phoebus who was frightened of the dark. Claiming a supernatural ability to cure the king's evil (aka scrofula), he could do nothing against the plague that delayed his coronation. The turbulent weather of the Little Ice Age did not obey his behests, the fens reflooded, Ireland rebelled, and even London's suburbs flouted his orders. Is the powerless king in Shakespeare a sly insinuation that James's edicts were unenforceable? If royal proclamations were often well intentioned and not entirely toothless gestures, Shakespeare enables us to see them as literary performances, an imperfect Orphic poetry. Whereas James's youthful dabbling in Orphic poetry galvanized his royal absolutism and Francis Bacon deciphered the Orpheus myth as a prophecy of scientific civilization imposing order on nature, Shakespeare's Orphic verses restore agency to nature and marshal it, like Birnam wood, to assault human mastery. His poetry draws much of its vitality from a latent vitalism in nature, anticipating Verlaine's and Rilke's sense of the poet's vocation as *l'explication Orphique de la Terre*.[5] Shakespeare's lasting power derives not simply from his phenomenal command of language but from how he deployed it to question political and scientific schemes for commanding nature that would define modernity. Shakespearean drama would not enjoy such enduring renown if it were nothing more than a series of ad hominem critiques of the king and his courtiers, and this book has affirmed the paradox that literature achieves the universal through the topical. By inviting the audience to identify with the royal protagonist while utilizing theatre to unmask royalty as performative and fallible, Shakespeare prods us to consider our own susceptibility to delusions of grandeur. In tying the 'crisis of authority' in Jacobean politics to both the volatility of the natural world in the Little Ice Age and the dethroning of 'man' by Copernican and Lucretian cosmology, Shakespearean drama enacts a 'deconsecration of sovereignty' that prefigures the crisis of human sovereignty in the Anthropocene.[6]

The environmental degradation chronicled in this book would only accelerate in the four intervening centuries. Much of Britain's mineral wealth has now been extracted, its heaths destroyed, its wetlands drained, its seas overfished, its darkness expunged, and myriad species like wolves, boar, red deer, pine marten, stoat, eel, burbot, sturgeon, kite, eagle, osprey either have vanished or survive in almost negligible relict populations. From this perspective it might seem naïve to downplay the titanic agency humans wield to reshape the planet. Yet many ecocritics understandably worry that the label Anthropocene is ironically anthropocentric, re-inscribing the 'same kind of hubris that led to our ecological crisis in the first place' (Raber 2018, 13).[7] The term can also unfairly imply that all humans bear equal blame for this predicament, 'a claim to universalism that fails to notice its subjugations' (Yusoff 2019, 12). Claims for Shakespeare's universalism can be equally problematic but this study has underlined two reasons his plays still command attention in this new geologic era: first, they force us to notice Britain's subjugations of its own marginalized communities and colonies at the dawn of the 'Anglocene' (Bonneuil and Fressoz 2016, 117); secondly, the Jacobean god-king riled and inspired Shakespeare to illuminate our mortal limits with a lucidity that might help us discern the ecological limits of human empire.

Writing at a time when an emergent proto-industrial civilization was only beginning to tame and colonize the earth, Shakespeare voices the ambitions of the Anglo-Anthropocene but also exposes their recklessness. Our technology may make our species, as Freud declared, a 'prosthetic God' (1930, 66), but the thunder does not peace at our bidding; we cannot command the elements to silence nor bid the flood bate its height; the mossy oaks will not page our heels. We can affect the environment but cannot control it completely. Tragedy has been seen as anti-ecological, but developments in eco-theory suggest ways we might assign value to its failed transcendence.[8] Anna Tsing's promotion of 'disturbance-based ecologies' (2015, 5), Donna Haraway's call to 'stay with the trouble' (2016), and Timothy Morton's embrace of 'dark ecology' (2016) all suggest that wading through the tumult and negativity of co-existence might eventually enable us to arrive at a recognition—what Morton terms 'ecognosis'—of this interconnectivity that is not dispiriting but calmly joyful in its sense of being enmeshed in something greater than ourselves. Tragedies like *Hamlet* still have so much to teach us.

This book has charted a similar course through Shakespeare's Jacobean oeuvre in its shift from tragedy to tragicomic romance. Shakespeare's late plays confront a chaotic and inhospitable nature to repudiate absolutism and carve out an ethics of resilience.[9] Buoyed by the knowledge that Prince Henry and Princess Elizabeth did not share their father's mania for autocratic dominion, Shakespeare's late romances voice a hard-won faith in the regenerative capacity of nature and a radical hope the next generation, adopting a humbler view of the human animal as anatomized by his plays, will prove better stewards. Teaching Shakespeare and environmental literature for the past fifteen years, I, too, find cause for optimism in the growing awareness of the young about the gravity of our predicament and their eagerness to do something about it. In the twenty-first century, can we leverage Shakespeare's global prestige on the world stage, a legacy of the empire that burgeoned in Stuart Britain, to spark cross-cultural dialogues, amplify voices outside the Anglosphere as well as across the species line, and redefine ourselves as planetary citizens rather than caesars? Taking heart from Sidney's claim that Renaissance tragedy 'maketh kings fear to be tyrants', this book has offered up eco-historicist interpretations that might embolden us to read and perform Shakespearean tragedies as ritual abdications of human tyranny and his tragicomedies as fables of resilience and radical hope. Whether or not Shakespeare's plays have an immediate, decisive impact on policy, either at the Stuart court or at modern climate summits, this book has shown that they speak to issues of environmental injustice in ways that continue to catch our conscience, nudging us guilty creatures to dwell more gently on the earth.

Endnotes

Introduction

1. In the Induction to *Bartholomew Fair*, Ben Jonson condemns the improbabilities of romance that 'make Nature afraid' (4:281); the phrase 'maketh Kings feare to be Tyrants' comes from Philip Sidney's *The Defence of Poesy* (1595, E4^v). Eco-historicist methodology has been outlined by Wood (2008) and defended by Watson (2015).
2. Hawkins (1967) noted an important variation on the green world pattern in plays such as *The Comedy of Errors* and *Love's Labour's Lost*, where the setting does not shift but the action remains more or less rooted in a 'closed world'. Berger, meanwhile, prefers the phrase 'second world' or 'second nature', arguing that the 'significant mark of the Renaissance imagination derives less from the idea of the green world per se than from the tendency first to separate, then interrelate different fields of experience' (1990, 14). Forker (1985) illuminates the green world's darker shades in Shakespeare's early tragedies such as *Titus Andronicus*, while Grady calls for an exploration of the green world not as a mythic pattern but as a space produced by 'socio-material conditions' (2009, 76). On how Frye's concept might be adapted for ecocriticism, see Siewers (2013); Merkley (2018); and Mentz (2018).
3. That is, English speakers perceive green more readily in some shades that other language speakers tend to identify as yellow, blue, or green-blue, aka 'grue' (Davidoff et al. 1999).
4. See Pastoureau (2014) and Constantini-Cornède (2015). Citing Gonzalo's outburst in *The Tempest*, Oki-Siekierczak (2015) suggests green's association with fertility might provoke an urge to control and enclose.
5. The Jacobean poet Henry Peacham, for instance, compares the sylvan environment to chaos or the underworld (1612, 182). On the blackness of the forest, see Pastoureau (2014, 106) and Barton (2017, 3).
6. Even the effort to represent wild places as outside history can be regarded as a backlash against their conscription within and transformation by the human economy, as captured by Theodor Adorno's paradox: 'the image of undistorted nature always emerges as its opposite in distortion' (1978, 95).
7. Smith (2009) and Knight (2014) both offer informative studies of early modern encounters with green but sidestep ecocriticism. Watson's piercing study examines the green as a metaphor for the 'real' (2006), while the title of Egan's *Green Shakespeare* (2006) employs it in the broad sense of non-human environment. On Shakespeare and woodlands, see Theis (2009); Nardizzi (2013); and Barton (2017).
8. See Heise (2008); Chakrabarty (2009); and Nixon (2011).
9. This approach follows trailblazing studies by Helgerson (1992) on chorography and Sullivan (1998) on landscapes of sovereignty and stewardship. Other landmark works on the spatial dynamics of the Shakespearean stage include Mullaney on the 'symbolic topography' of its location in the Liberties (1988, vii); West (2002), who looks at

representations of social mobility, enclosure, and sea travel in Jacobean drama; Turner on the 'topographic stage' (2006, 186–215); Dillon (2010) on negotiations of space and place in court revels; Sanders on 'cultural geography' (2011) in Caroline drama; and Elden on the 'tensions, ambiguities, and limits' of Shakespearean 'territory' (2018, 5). McRae (2009) surveys rivers, roads, and inns in non-dramatic texts. With the exception of Sanders, much of this research focuses on space (as theorized by Foucault, Lefebvre, and Bachelard) rather than the more-than-human environment.

10. On the need for an archipelagic framework, see Kerrigan (2008).
11. Anyone who knew the basic formula for the famous dyes of Lincoln or Kendall (a mixture of woad and dyer's broom) would be primed to believe that green was real; one could dip one's hand in a vat of it. While Descartes has long been vilified in animal studies for his mechanistic philosophy denying the sentience of non-humans, it is also telling that he was a pioneer of eliminativism, stripping away colour as a primary material component of the natural world. See Cottingham (1990) and Baker et al. (2015).
12. In a 1593 letter, written while on a tour with Strange's company, Edward Alleyn instructs his wife, the daughter of the dyer and theatre entrepreneur Philip Henslowe, to 'lett my orayng tawny stokins of wolen be dyed a very good blak against I com hom to wear in the winter' (*HD* 277).
13. Cardinal Wolsey's gown derived its crimson sheen from the scale insect kermes, and the 'scarlet' in which he struts about (and Shakespeare wore during James's coronation) was extracted from another type of scale insect harvested by the Spanish on lands seized from the Aztecs. Malvolio's yellow stockings probably took their colour from the saffron crocus grown around the Puritan hotbed Saffron Walden, although starch was also used in the early seventeenth century to create yellows, reds, and greens. Yellow starch was not only stigmatized by Anne Turner's involvement in the murder of Thomas Overbuy (Jones and Stallybrass 2000, 57–85), but also because starch-makers, whose ranks included the dyer Henlsowe and his leading actor Edward Alleyn (*HD* 244), were egregious polluters. In 1608, the Lord Mayor of London petitioned the Privy Council to outlaw starch manufacture in England. Around this time, a former starch-maker denounced the trade for polluting waterways with 'sour waters [that]...empoisoneth and killeth all the fish' and nearby trees, and accused them of 'daily empoisoning with insufferable savours' (Cotton MS Titus BV/113 f. 315). Despite King James's efforts to ban 'noisome' starch manufacturing in January 1610 (*SRP* 237), the trade continued. Thomas Middleton and William Rowley satirized it in *The World Tossed at Tennis* (1620), in which personifications of five coloured starches appear and are unmasked as the daughters of the foul-smelling Deceit. Woad growing also took a toll on the environment. Locals living along the River Somer filed a complaint against dyers in 1556, accusing them of having 'caste into the said river all the soil, woad, water, and filth [of the] said dye-house...[which] hath so corrupted the water of the same river or brook that thereby is...the fish within the same [and] the great fish ponds...destroyed but also is the same water become so unwholesome that your said orator nor any of his men or tenants...can use the same for dressing of their meat, making of their drink, as for any other necessaries' (TNA, Chancery Records C1/1474/26–7). Another versatile dye used to colour ribbons, caps, hats,

leather points, cushions, sewing threads, book covers, and gloves came from logwood, a tree native to the Yucatan. Before chemical fixatives, however, logwood dyes did not stay fast—Shakespeare alludes to the falsity of 'o'erdyed blacks' (1.2.132)—which ignited a scandal in Parliament when it emerged James had granted exemptions to his favourites to import it illegally in exchange for a country house and a slice of the profits (Bowyer 1930, 111). In the following decades, demand for the contraband dye-stuff only grew, prompting British colonists to virtually obliterate the tropical jungles in Belize and Jamaica to replace them with logwood plantations in the belief they were 'improving nature' (Botella-Ordinas 2010).

14. 'Mastery over colour phenomena' was a 'driving force' in the development of alchemy and chemistry in early modern Europe (Baker et al. 2015, 4). For more on the early modern colourscape, see Chiari, who notes Puritan disapproval of bright colours but cautions that the 'iconoclastic fever that swept across early modern England never really put an end to the use of polychromy' (2015, 6).
15. Qtd in Matusiak (2015, 185).
16. The Admiral's Company's property inventory includes a 'raynbowe' (*HD* 320) and the King's Men must have devised something similar when they staged *The Tempest*.
17. Goldberg (1983) unfurled how Shakespeare appropriates the monarch's absolutist powers of representation. Bergeron (1985) demonstrated that Shakespearean romance speaks to dynastic politics at the Stuart court. In contrast, Barroll (1991) downplayed claims for James's shaping influence on Shakespeare as overblown. Kernan (1995) set forth the opposing case for Shakespeare as the 'King's playwright' and liveried servant. Jordan (1997) instead aligned Shakespeare with constitutionalist critics of Jacobean absolutism, while Perry (1997) stressed how James's image and politics were defined by others, most notably his predecessor Elizabeth. Over the last decade, studies by Kurland (2013); Rickard (2015); Shapiro (2016); and Chiari and Mucciolo (2019) have gravitated toward the middle ground that Shakespeare consciously sought to entertain the king without shying away from challenging his policies.
18. Wortham notes that after James's accession Shakespeare's attention pivots from England to Britain (1996, 97).
19. On the king's projects to replenish his coffers, see Cramsie (2002).
20. Gurr acknowledges that court performance represented the acme of success for a playing company, yet cautions that whether or not 'they consciously shaped their stage presentations to match what they understood to be the court fashion remains an open question' (2009a, 35). Recent scholarship has shown that the match is much closer than Barroll contended but less pro-Jacobean than Kernan proposed and a view of certain play-texts as 'occasional' is resurfacing. Dutton (2016), for instance, argues that Shakespeare often revised or expanded works for court performance while Lawrence posits that the King's Men 'became acutely aware of the possibility of premiering new plays at court on key dates in the revels season, particularly 1 November and 26 December' (2019, 95).
21. O'Malley (2021, 186–93) offers a lively account of the anti-BP protests in Stratford in 2018.
22. These phrases appear in John Chamberlain's letter of 24 May 1610 (JC 42).

23. Butler (1998) outlined the need to shift from thinking in terms of a Jacobean court to Stuart courts. For more on Anna's influence on Stuart drama, see the valuable study by McManus (2002).
24. Whether Shakespeare rejected a commission from the king to compose a masque or was simply never asked, this negative evidence 'tells us as much about him as a writer as the plays he left behind' (Shapiro 2016, 5). On Shakespeare as a critic of the House of Commons and its pretence to represent the people, see Arnold (2008).
25. For more on purveyance, see Notestein (1971, 96–106).
26. On Shakespeare and the legal humanities, see Jordan and Cunningham (2006); Cormack (2007); Cormack et al. (2013); Strain (2015); and Hutson (2017).
27. See Maguire's study on Shakespeare's names as 'onomastic predestination' (2009, 13).
28. Berry offers a balanced appraisal of James the hunter as both an 'early conservationist' and an environmental 'tyrant' (2001, 208). For more on the royal hunt, see MacGregor (2000) and Griffin (2007); on hunting and masculinity, see Bates (2013).
29. On husbandry and mastery, see Munroe (2011, 144) and Scott (2014).
30. The animals in Spring Garden were placed under the care (or neglect rather) of his favourite Robert Carr. Manuscript accounts record various payments for feed, sometimes improperly matched to the animals' natural diets (Grigson 2016, 47). Further information on royal menageries can be found in MacGregor (2000) and Hengerer and Weber (2020).
31. See, for instance, Dickey (1991); Gurr (2004); and Höfele (2011, 3–12).
32. James did shield some of his beasts from the 'vulgar gaze' by shipping them to his private menagerie at Theobalds, but visitors could gain access to the Spring Gardens before they were formally opened to the public after the Restoration (Grigson 2016).
33. In a corrective to top-down historiography, Harkness critiques Bacon's Saloman's House as wresting scientific authority away from urban artisans (symbolized by Hugh Plat's 'Jewel House') and investing it in the social elite as the 'appropriate custodians and arbiters of natural knowledge' (2007, 214). While expertise was siphoned upward, James's knighting of Plat signals how royal authority and objectivity might flow back down and incite research prior to the formation of the Royal Society.
34. Sir John Popham (c.1531–1607) served as Speaker of the House of Commons, Attorney General, and Chief Justice of the King's Bench. His sentencing of Ben Jonson may have contributed to the playwright's satire on fen-draining in *The Devil Is an Ass* (see Chapter 6).
35. Hindle (2008) vividly outlines the grievances that sparked the Midlands Rising, to which I will return in Chapter 7.
36. For more on economy as a forerunner of ecology, see Remien (2019).
37. In 1611 James sent a missive to halt the felling of trees by ironmongers in the Forest of Dean on the grounds it disturbed the nesting of hawks (Matusiak 2015, 266).
38. For more on environmental governance in early modern Europe, see Miglietti and Morgan (2017).
39. As early as March 1606, the influential MP Edward Sandys proposed the best strategy to solve the king's financial woes was for the state to become the chief investor in the fen drainage schemes around the Isle of Ely, with all proceeds to go to the king, which he estimated would be worth more than £40,000 per annum.
40. For more on James's writing and authorial personae, see the edited collection by Fischlin and Fortier (2002).

Chapter 1

1. While Brooke (1990, 72–6), and Barroll (1991, 150–2) question the Hampton Court premiere, it seems highly plausible that Scottish play was staged before the Scottish king at some point. Orgel (1999) sees the Folio text as a 'patron-centered' adaptation that adds more song, dance, and special effects to bring it closer to the Jacobean masque of the 1610s, whereas Dutton (2016) frames *Macbeth* as a Blackfriars play, but one that brings the glamour of the court to a wider public.
2. The homophone 'moor' may have mutually reinforced English antipathy to places and peoples (in particular the Romani) perceived as dark or 'tawny'. On Shakespeare and Scotland, see Maley and Murphy (2004).
3. In his *Survey of Cornwall*, for instance, Richard Carew describes how Dartmoor 'lieth waste and open, sheweth a blackish colour, beareth Heath and spirie Grasse, and serveth in a maner, onely to Summer Cattel' (1602, 5^v). When furze or heather bloom, however, heaths can pop with yellows or purples.
4. Confusingly, moor in early modern usage could refer not only to 'uncultivated ground covered with heather; a heath' (*OED* 2a) but also low-lying marshlands or fens, as its etymological link with mire suggests.
5. On the distinction between heath and moor, see Rackham (1986, 282–3).
6. A 1550 statute had allowed cottagers to build on heaths and wastes, where they eked out an existence 'cliff-hanging in semi-legal insecurity' (Hill 1972, 26).
7. Burning strips of heather supposedly increases grouse numbers. In contrast to their modern counterparts, Jacobean foresters and gamekeepers viewed the torching of these shrublands as a holocaust for wildlife, since seventeenth-century hunters pursued a wider variety of quarry besides grouse.
8. Davenant precedes Macbeth's first line with what amounts to an intradiegetic stage direction: 'Command they make a halt upon the heath' (1674, 4). Davenant also interpolates an entire scene in which Lady Macduff meets her husband upon the heath and remarks how 'the darkness of the day / Makes the heath seem the gloomy walks of death' (26). The witches appear shortly afterwards and chant, 'Let's have a dance upon the heath; / We gain more life by Duncan's death' (27). As in Shakespeare, the rhymed couplet evokes conjuring, while Davenant's pairing of heath and death underscores its hostility to human life. Rather than decry Davenant's version as meddling, it could be read as evidence of contemporary fascination with heathlands and a tribute to the power of Shakespeare's scene-painting.
9. Unfortunately, the frontispiece to *Macbeth* in Rowe's 1709 edition depicts act 4, scene 1 rather than the heath from act 1.
10. A 1530 French-English dictionary does record 'lande' as a French equivalent for the English 'Hethe' (Palsgrave 1530, 231).
11. Quotations from Forman are taken from the transcription in Schoenbaum (1981, 7–20).
12. 'Heath in the drie and desolate wildernesse, where no habitation is, is apt and good for nothing, and yet easie to bee consumed with fire: So also the man that putteth his trust in man, and maketh fleshe and bloud his strangth and defence, and passeth not on the Lord, shall not see any good, but shal perish together with his Helpes' (Cawdry 1600, 394).
13. There may be a correlation between increased persecution of witches in the early seventeenth century and the recurrent harvest failures of the Little Ice Age (Behringer 1999).

14. For more on the Hoghton estate, see Honigmann (1985, 13).
15. The fact that Forman refers to the weird sisters as 'feiries or Nimphes' even raises the possibility that their transformation into 'filthy hags' dates from a revision to the play after the trial of the Pendle witches.
16. For more on the Romani in early modern Britain, see Cressy (2016) and Netzloff (2001).
17. 22 Henry VIII c. 12.
18. On Cleopatra and the gypsies, see Hopkins (2004) and LePerle (2017).
19. See MacRithcie (1894, 72–3); Hopkins (2004, 232–3); and McPhee (2017). Verdi's operatic adaptation of *Macbeth*, which recasts the witches as Romani fortune-tellers, may not be as cavalier as it would first appear.
20. See Malay (2010, 96–120).
21. The lost ballads are recorded in Hazlitt (1882, 220).
22. Anonymous (1652, 42–7). The attribution of both these texts to Anthony Weldon is now regarded as dubious.
23. See Manning (1988, 84–5), who uncovers abundant evidence that the 'reclamation of moors, wastes, marshes, and mosses' (118) incited lawsuits and riots throughout the early seventeenth century.
24. In a letter dated 24 October 1605, John Chamberlain reports that the king could not bring himself to leave Royston because of its 'varietie of sports' [i.e. game animals], and had 'now fallen into a great humor of catching larkes' (McClure 1939, 1:212). The king's mania for blood sports was even ridiculed on the stage in a lost play from 1608 in which an actor mimicking James cursed loudly when a bird eluded his aim (Bibliothèque Nationale, MS Fr. 15984).
25. On James's clashes with locals at Royston and Thetford, see Stewart (2003, 178–9).
26. See Lovegrove (2007, 82, 118–27).
27. In 1608, James ordered Dame Katherine Corbet of Woodbastwick, Norfolk, to preserve an eyrie of hawks breeding in her woods. Nevertheless, James had no compunction about hunting certain species of ground-nesting birds, and was delighted when the keeper of Theobalds Park presented him with thrushes' and blackbirds' nests (Matusiak 2015, 182).
28. Daly (1978, 29) notes that destroying a martin nest was believed to bring bad luck.
29. The 24,000 estimate is taken from Hartlib (1655, 227).
30. 2 James c. 27. Evans (1836, 7:221). Since these birds devoured crops, agrarian reformers like Standish called for the banning of 'pigeon-houses' (1611, 33–5) and authorities sought to restrict the right to erect dovecotes to the landed elite but this feudal privilege was increasingly contested in early modern law courts and exercised by wealthy freeholders.
31. Cressy (2011, 91). Martin discusses saltpetre in connection with *Macbeth* but does not mention dovehouses (2015, 88).
32. In 1605, for instance, one Robert Ashwell was 'set openly in the stocks in Cheapside with a paper over his head containing these words: viz. "for destroying of roaches great with spawn in the river of Thames at unseasonable times"' (*Repertory of the London Court of Aldermen*, vol. 26.2, f. 343). I am grateful to Rose Hadshar for calling my attention to this document.

33. See Watson (1984, 107) and Harrison (1992, 104).
34. Love borrows the phrase 'reproductive futurity' from Edelman (2004). On children in *Macbeth*'s performance history, see Miller (2017).
35. See Ensor (2012); for a commentary on the problematic racial implications of anti-natalism, see Seymour (2013).

Chapter 2

1. In her ecocritical work, however, O'Dair favours a more presentist approach (2011).
2. On 'metal as the exemplar of a vital materiality', see Bennett (2010, 55). For a contrast between Marx and Bennett, see Yuran (2014, 63–4). Santer views the 'contemporary efflorescence of new materialisms' as reflecting 'not only a new ethical sensitivity to the liveliness and agency of non-human animals, things, "actants," and environments…[but] the vibrancies of capital' (2016, 44).
3. Also see Grossman (2014) and Borlik (2015).
4. The biographical information on Bulmer is derived from Tyson (1996; 2004).
5. All citations from Atkinson's manuscript, Harl. MSS 4621, come from the 1825 edition by Gilbert Meason.
6. See Lansdowne 156/105 f. 419; Lansdowne MS 169/62 f. 166.
7. On concerns over mining's impact on waterways, see Badcoe (2017, 52–6) and Borlik (2019, 565). The pollution in Leadhills is detailed in a report of the Scottish Environmental Protection Agency (2011).
8. The libel appears in BL Add MS 22118 f. 9^v; Bodleian MS Douce f. 34^v; Bodleian MS Malone 23 p. 120; Folger MS V.a. 319 f. 26^r, and is reprinted in Bellany and McRae (2005, E4). Although undated, it was most likely composed in 1604–5, when James was promoting this scheme with Bulmer to sell knighthoods to mining entrepreneurs.
9. Also see Kurland (1992).
10. A 1605 letter to Cecil in the archives of Hatfield House lists the names of 102 men Bulmer employed in his Scottish gold mines.
11. Hamilton would have had some leverage with the king because he had been a member of the Octavians—a group of eight financial reformers who had sought to rein in the Crown's expenses in the 1590s.
12. See Calderwood (1842–9, 5:673), and Ashton to Hudson 20 January 1598, *CSP Scot.*, xiii. I, 155; qtd in Goodare (1999, 185).
13. In the *Timon* comedy, Timon's wealth is lost at sea when his gem-laden ships sink. The same disaster befell Bulmer's ship transporting his Scottish silver. Is it possible this unpublished comedy (*c.*1605–08) could be the lost play that mocked James's Scottish mine?
14. TNA, SP 14/31 f. 166^v.
15. Bibliothèque Nationale, MS Fr. 15984; qtd in Teramura (2015).
16. Chambers (1923, 2:53n) long ago recognized that the *mine d'Escosse* mentioned by La Boderie was a topical allusion to the Hilderstone silver mine.
17. On the lost play, see Teramura (2015); on the company in general, see Munro (2005).
18. Chambers placed *Timon* in 1608, in between *Coriolanus* and *Pericles*. Jowett's case for an earlier date rests mainly on stylometric tests and the absence of act divisions. But if

the script remained incomplete, the act divisions may not yet have been inserted, while the linguistic analyses are merely suggestive rather than conclusive.
19. See Giesekes (2007, 116).
20. TNA REQ 4/1/1. See Ingram (1986).
21. On Henslowe's financial woes as an analogue for those of Timon, see Bailey (2011).
22. Interestingly, Atkinson identifies De Vosse as a painter in league with the English artist Nicholas Hilliard in a gold-mining venture in Scotland around 1580 (*GMS* 33–5). A Cornelis de Vos is listed among the shareholders of the Society of Mines Royal in 1568, but the artist named Cornelis de Vos associated with Rubens was born in 1584 and active in the first decades of the seventeenth century. Atkinson appears to have conflated two different individuals, although it is possible they may have been related. On Hilliard's mining investments, see Strong (1975, 4–7, 17).
23. The capitalization of Gold trails off in the final pages, possibly because Hake's incessant tirades against it exhausted the typesetter's supply of upper-case Gs. A classic but still relevant defence of original typography can be found in Riding and Graves (1927).
24. The German mining engineer Georgius Agricola advocated a more empirical mineralogy in his *De natura fossilum* (1546), and the Swiss naturalist Conrad Gesner also sought to scrape away some of the encrusted lore of Pliny in his work *De rerum fossilium, lapidum, et gemmarum* (1565).
25. For an application of Foucauldian theory to Renaissance mineralogy, see Aldbury and Oldroyd (1977).
26. Compare these lines with Hake's 'Thou settest th'unlearned in the learned Seat /.... Thou makest the fool the wiseman to disgrace' (1604, 52).
27. On anti-mining rhetoric in the Renaissance, see Merchant (1980, 29–41) and Jowett (2004b).
28. See Derrida's glosses on the 'monetary spectre' (1993, 42), and Smith (2017, 101–16).
29. On the play's sense of wealth as a rhetorical performance and of gold as a 'bad poet', see Kolb (2018, 411).
30. Since this chapter was written, a similar reading of *Timon* as anticipating the Capitalocene has been advanced by Gillen (2018).
31. A conversation with Drew Daniel helped me to formulate this idea. For a contrasting view of the susceptibility of the book to organic decay and of Renaissance notions of bibliographic survival, see Calhoun (2020).

Chapter 3

1. It may seem unlikely that a tavern-keeper such as Wilkins would possess the requisite Latin to translate *Justine*. But much of the text is pilfered from Arthur Golding's translation and Wilkins's evident interest in the Mediterranean makes him a strong candidate for the G. W. credited on the title-page.
2. In a 2018 governmental report, Michael Gove (whose family once ran a fish-processing factory) declares that Brexit will 'promote a more competitive, profitable and sustainable fishing industry across the whole of the UK' (6). However, some fear the order of Gove's adjectives betrays the fishing lobby's real priorities, and the report's proposed shift from the benchmark of 'relative stability' to 'Maximum Sustainable

Yield' or 'Total Allowable Catch' (7) hardly sounds like enlightened ecological policy. Some commentators (Phillipson and Symes 2018) have warned that uncoordinated, nation-first policies toward management of our collective oceanic resources could further jeopardize the Atlantic's already depleted fishing stocks.

3. The dwindling of freshwater fish stocks contributed to a 'marine-fishing revolution' during the Medieval Warm Period, as Roberts demonstrates in his history of overfishing (2007, 20).
4. Plutarch reports that Pericles invested heavily in the navy so that Athens kept 'all the coastes of the sea under their obedience' (1579, 180) and triumphed in a contest with the Samians 'for the seignory by sea' (182).
5. For more on Dee's naval policies, see Baldwin (2006).
6. Considering that four of the six Greek names in the play not found in Gower come from Plutarch's Life of Pericles, it is evident that the playwrights wished to evoke the legacy of the Athenian leader, and the numerous scenes on sea-coasts and shipboard would stir up memories of his naval conquests. Early in the play Pericles orders his courtiers to 'o'erlook / What shipping and what lading's in our haven' (1.2.48), arranging an inspection of the nation's fleet like those endorsed by Dee, and Marina later recounts how he 'gall[ed] his kingly hands with haling ropes' (4.1.53) during the storm.
7. 'Afterward, you may passe on to the 37 page: and there in the 15th lyne from the end of that page you may begynne againe to reade, thus, *And surely yf there be any Brytish or English Pericles now living*, And so you may hold on till you have attenifely red over the 38 page, wholy' (95ᵛ italics added). The British Library holds three manuscript witnesses of this text (Harley MS 249 ff. 95–105; Royal MS 7 C.xvi ff. 158–66; c.21 e.12). For more on the *Thalattokratia Brettaniki*, see Sherman (1995, 192–200).
8. Grotius insists princes can only impose levies or rents for fishing rights on their own subjects, but 'the right of fishing everywhere ought to be free to foreigners' (2004, 32).
9. These estimates can be found in Winwood (1725, 3.49).
10. Although Welwood's magnum opus appeared in print five years after *Pericles*, he had apparently been working on the text for a considerable amount of time before it went to print, and both it and his *The Sea-Law of Scotland* look to the ancient Mediterranean and the 'remains of the Rhodian lawe (1590, A4ʳ) for juridical precedents for Scottish maritime policy.
11. For more on river angling in early modern England, see Wright (2018).
12. On the possible locations of Pentapolis in the Mediterranean, see Gossett (2004, 129).
13. Daniel's phrase alludes to a famous line from Virgil's *Aeneid*: 'And these will be your arts [to impose the ways of peace]' (6.852).
14. Munday praises the fishermen, whose 'labour doth returne rich golden gain' (1616, C2ᵛ), but the fishmongers' pageant apparently featured actual fish instead of the ersatz golden ones in Daniel's masque.
15. According to Pliny, fishers harvested murex in early spring before it lays its eggs. While this supposedly improved the quality of the dye it could have not improved the long-term stability of the sea-snail population.
16. See *PPMF* 359. Although the name Purpoole derives from the old manor of Portpool, which became the site of Gray's Inn, the early modern spelling and pronunciation

unmistakably evokes the regal shade of purple. Anna of Denmark's wardrobe inventory includes a 'purple satin gown stripped with orrenge colour green and white silck' and a 'nighte gown' decorated with 'Flowers of white wachett carnation and purple silk' (Field 2017, 8–9).

17. 'Whelks or murex shells' appear in Jonson's 1605 *Masque of Blackness* (*CWBJ* 2:514.43), also written for Queen Anna.
18. The Scottish poet Drummond describes purple as the dark lustre of 'Tyrian fish' (1616, 11), 'Tyrian grain' (24), and the 'purple faire of Tyre' (G2^v).
19. Confusingly, the shellfish Pliny calls *purpura* or *taeniense* is now classified as *murex* whereas Pliny's *bucinum* or *murex* is now categorized as *thais*, a genus name that closely resembles Shakespeare's Thaisa but appears to originate with Peter Röding in 1798 (Marzano 2013, 143). Due to the Mediterranean's temperature rise, the red-mouthed rocksnail (*thais haemastoma*) has now vanished from the waters near Tyre; global warming may prove more fatal than millennia of intensive snail-harvesting (Rilov 2016).
20. If this sounds far-fetched, recall that a character named Periwinkle had recently appeared (alongside Shrimp) in *The Family of Love*, acted by the Children of the King's Revels *c*.1607 and printed in 1608 (E3^v). Pericles also imagines retreating into a shell when he when he says 'in our orbs we'll live so round and safe' (1.2.120).
21. Archaeological evidence confirms playgoers at the Globe consumed large quantities of periwinkles, and the name of this sea-snail would have resounded from oyster-wives in and around Shakespeare's playhouse (Korda 2011, 144–73). Bede lists dye from crushed whelks and winkles among England's valuable natural resources. This marine mollusc is found all around the British coast, but large-scale attempts to extract dye from them seem to have occurred mainly in the Irish counties of Galway, Mayo, Sligo, and Donegal, and the island of Inishkea, where archaeologists have found evidence of a 'purple dye factory' from the Anglo-Saxon era (Biggam 2006, 33). The process was rediscovered by William Cole in his *Purpura Anglicana* (1686).
22. These lines glisten differently in the quarto: 'Silke Twine, with the rubied Cherrie, / That pupels [pun on purples?] lackes she none' (1609, H2^r). The Levant Company imported raw silks and large quantities of indigo, which could be combined with madder or kermes to make purple dye. By the 1630s the company was exporting over 20,000 pieces of cloth per year 'mostly purple or crimson in colour' (Wood 1964, 43) to Constantinople, Smyrna, and Aleppo. Klein (2016, 151) sniffs in Cerimon's spices an allusion to the Levantine spice trade.
23. Thaisa's resurrection by Cerimon, whose name connotes ceremony and who appears in 'rich tire' (3.2.22) in Ephesus, a place associated with Popish ritual during the Reformation, may have an added significance given that some Puritans opposed the liturgical use of purple during Lent.
24. Archaeological excavations of fishbones in London indicate that this shift was already underway by the late thirteenth century (see Barret and Orton 2016). Test (2008) sniffs out references to the cod industry in Shakespeare's *The Tempest*.
25. Carleton made this quip after watching Jonson's *Masque of Blackness* (Herford and Simpson 1925–52, 10:448).
26. Bacon cites the famous opening of Lucretius's *De rerum natura* in *The Advancement of Learning* (1605, 44). Blumenberg's (1997) masterful account of the shipwreck metaphor

has propelled Mentz's (2015) sparkling work on the topic, while Maisano (2014, 181) examines Miranda's Lucretian allusion to support his reading of *The Tempest* as a scientific romance. For an elegant analysis of the Renaissance playhouse as a ship and the ethics of spectating shipwreck in *Pericles*, see Degenhardt (2020).

27. In February 1287, a storm of such hurricane-like force slammed England's southeastern coast that Winchelsea was deluged and had to be relocated three miles inland. Memories of this event were still vivid in the Elizabethan era, as a map made in the 1590s shows the location of the old town, and proposes cutting a channel to protect the new harbour, which was already silting up.
28. The 1609 Act (c. 20) was preceded by similar legislation from 1553 (c. 11) to check the 'outrageous course and rage of the sea' in Glamorganshire and 1585 (c. 24) to repair 'sea-works on the sea-coasts in the county of Norfolk'.
29. For more on the history of early modern floods, see Morgan (2015), who observes that the Commission of Sewers convened an unprecedented twenty-four times in 1607 (more than double the number of the next highest year) to discuss flood control measures.
30. In an interesting crux, Shakespeare seems to have confused Thetis, the sea-nymph and mother of Achilles, with Tethys, the mother of the oceans, the eponymous heroine of Daniel's masque.
31. The fisherman's jest about a landwhale that 'swallowed the whole parish, church, steeple, bells' (2.1.34) satirizes lawyers or enclosing landlords, but adds to the play's iterative imagery of ocean devouring earth.
32. Marina is again likened to food in Bolt's blazon of her in the market, at which 'a Spaniard's mouth watered' (4.2.92), and the procurer's comparison of her to a 'joint' from which he hopes to 'cut a morsel' (4.2.122–3).
33. *Pericles*'s debt to *Rudens* was recognized over two centuries ago by Thomas Holt White (Sherbo 1992, 97), the brother of Gilbert White, author of the first work of English nature writing, but it remains an underappreciated inter-text for the play.
34. For more on the trope of the devouring ocean, see Brayton: 'if the ocean is hungry, it is so because we see in it a mirror of our hungry selves' (2012, 162).

Chapter 4

1. Notable studies include Jones (1961); Yates (1978, 41–61); Marcus (1988, 106–59); McEachern (1996, 189–95); Boling (2000); and Mottram (2013). For more on the Welsh elements in Shakespeare, see Maley and Schwyzer (2010).
2. Following Edward I's overthrow of Llywelyn ap Gruffydd (aka Llywelyn the Last), the heir to the English throne became the nominal ruler of Wales.
3. The earliest usage recorded by the *OED* is Thomas Nashe's reference to a 'dim far off launce-skip' (1599, 4). Dekker, who may have heard the Dutch term *lantskop* from his connections among London's Dutch community, provides another early citation in 1606. Drayton uses it once in the 1612 *Poly-Olbion*, and thrice in the 1622 continuation. One of Drayton's disciples, William Browne, penned an early comparison of a vista to a landscape in *Britannia's Pastorals* (1613, 42). See Fitter (1995); Morse (2008); and Trevisan (2013).

236   ENDNOTES

4. There are in fact two different versions of this painting, one at the Metropolitan Museum in New York and the other in the Royal Collection Trust (Fig. 5.1). In the second, the rocky outcrop in the left middle-ground is considerably higher.
5. See Strong (1986, 184–219); National Portrait Gallery (2012); and MacLeod (2012, 119).
6. As the mountain bedwarfs the castle in the foreground, the composition of Savery's painting reveals that nature constructs fortifications on a scale human engineering cannot match. Henry may have known of Savery's work since the official Keeper of his collection was Abraham van der Doort, who had previously worked for Emperor Rudolf II (Strong 1986, 186).
7. For more on the song, see Hammond (2010, 328–35) and Taylor (2012, 28–9, 47–8).
8. Johnson's song may have prompted lines in *Cardenio* similar to these in *Double Falsehood*:

> How much more grateful are these craggy mountains
> And these wild trees than things of nobler natures;
> For these receive my plaints and mourn again
> In many echoes to me.
>
> (4.2.38–41)

9. On the authorship of *Double Falsehood*, see Hammond (2010) and Taylor (2012).
10. Although Drayton's *The Famous Wars of Henry I and the Prince of Wales*, co-written with Henry Chettle and Thomas Dekker in 1598 (*HD* 88), is lost, it is tempting to speculate that the text could have included similar hymns to the Welsh mountains. Some theatre historians have lumped this play with another work mentioned by Henslowe, 'The Welshman's Price', sometimes retitled as 'The Welshman's Prize' (*LPD*). The connection is even more appealing given that the original title may very well have been 'The Welshman Price', the common Anglicization of the Welsh surname of Henry I's opponent, Gruffydd ap Rhys (Price).
11. For other examples of the alpine pastoral set in Wales, see William Shenstone's 'Taking a View of the Country, He is Led to Meditate on the Character of the Ancient Britons' (1746); Thomas Gray's 'The Bard' (1757); and Percy Shelley's 'On Leaving London for Wales' (1812).
12. My reading chimes with Morse's observation that Shakespeare's 'prospects tell us about characters' ethos in ways that might entail an ecological responsibility, or at least ethical respect' (2008, 69).
13. Innogen uses the same word in a derogatory sense when she suspects savage 'mountaineers' (4.2.369) of murdering her husband.
14. On geo-humoralism in the play, see Floyd-Wilson (2003, 161–81) and Iyengar (2014).
15. On *Cymbeline* and Prince Henry, see Cull (2014) and Wayne (2017, 33–42).
16. 'Orders established to be observed by all gentlemen and officers of the Prince's household'. MS 17, f. 218; transcribed in Birch (1760, 427–43). In contrast to the gruelling schooling in Latin and Greek James had received under George Buchanan, Henry only applied himself to books two hours a day, well below the norm for Renaissance princes, so as to devote more time to outdoor pursuits. See Pollnitz (2015, 346).
17. Cleland's treatise was republished in 1611 with the title *The Scottish Academy* in recognition of the efforts of the Scotsmen Adam Newton (Henry's Latin preceptor) and

Sir David Murray (Henry's Groom of the Stool) rather than its geographic location (chiefly at Nonsuch and Oatlands), but both the 1607 and 1611 texts repeatedly refer to this educational programme as 'British' at a time when British often signified Wales. On the title-page of his 1611 tragedy *Sophonisba*, Murray identified himself as a 'Scoto-Britaine'.

18. Together with his cousin, confusingly also named Thomas Chaloner, a botanist and chemist, he founded the English chemical industry after discovering alum deposits on the family's Yorkshire estate (allegedly inferring the presence of minerals by the surface vegetation), thus breaking the alum monopoly of the Papacy.
19. According to Henry Peacham, Chaloner had been 'kept to view, unseen this many year' (35) while supervising the Prince's education, which fits with Belarius's exile.
20. See Yates's (1978, 59) argument that the sense of rejuvenation in Shakespeare's late romances derives from the hopes invested in Prince Henry and Princess Elizabeth.
21. In 1571 the Queen granted Robert Dudley, Baron Denbigh, the rights 'to pasture on the mountain land' in Wales while 'reserving timber, woods, and mines' (NLW Deeds 1889) for the Crown. English investors also began to lease Welsh uplands or buy them outright: in 1595, Leonard Baker of Bedfordshire and Thomas Andrew of London purchased a ten-acre parcel 'of the waste called Moel Develog extending in breadth from the top of the mountain of Devclog to the brook of Belog' (Arthur Ivory Price 1595 March 20); in 1607 Edmund Sawyer of London acquired a 'lease of waste lands on the mountain in the comote of Isallett' (Coed Coch and Trovarth Estate Records, 248).
22. Sphagnum moss is crucial to the ecology of Welsh peatlands and the key biological ingredient in the preservation of bog bodies.
23. Gerald of Wales records a popular legend crediting the appearance of a large eagle on a certain rock in the Snowdonia mountains as an omen of impending war (2.9). 'The Prophecies of Merlin Silvester' with which Shakespeare seems to have been acquainted was alternatively entitled 'The Prophecy of the Eagle', and at least five Welsh versions of it survive, including one in *The Red Book of Hergest*, which belonged to Henry Sidney during his tenure as President of the Council of the Marches. The eagle prophecy (and Mount Paladour) is also referenced in Holinshed. See Flood (2018). Holinshed assumes 'Aquila' was the name of a Roman poet rather than an actual eagle (1587, 12).
24. On eagle place names in Britain, see Yaldon (2007, 472–3).
25. In 1879, a squabble erupted in the pages of the prestigious journal *Nature* when J. J. Murphy faulted Shakespeare for calling the eagle's eye 'green' in *Romeo and Juliet*. This triggered a series of retorts in which one correspondent claimed that eagle eyes can indeed be green, a second remarked that green means hazel or yellowish green, while a third insisted that green must be a compositor's error for 'keen'. In *The Ornithology of Shakespeare,* James Edmund Harting questions whether Shakespeare could distinguish between the golden and white-tailed species, while Geikie remarks that 'his allusions hardly suggest any personal familiarity' with the eagle, although the meticulous description of a starved eagle in *Venus and Adonis* forces him to revise this statement and propose Shakespeare had seen either a stuffed or captive specimen (1916, 44, 52). Maurice Pope sides with the sceptics: 'there is nothing in Shakespeare

about eagles to make us suppose that he need have actually seen one any more than he need have seen a lion or wolf' (1992, 137–8). Of course, Shakespeare may have seen all three in the royal menagerie.
26. Sullivan (1998, 146). Also see Marcus (1988, 118–24) and Hopkins (2010).
27. 'Species loneliness' appears to have been coined by Robert Pogue Harrison in 1996 and popularized by McGinnis (1999, 206).

Chapter 5

1. For a run-down of the staging of the bear scene, see Dunbar (2010, 49–50, 78, 98, 122, 165, 231).
2. For responses to Coghill, see Biggins (1962, 3–13) and Orgel (1996, 155–6n).
3. Taken from the wild and their mother before they were weaned, the cubs would have been accustomed to humans and could have been trained to obey basic commands; the Clown in *The Winter's Tale* alludes to such practices when he compares authority to 'a stubborn bear...oft led by the nose with gold' (4.4.807).
4. See Kotilaine (2005, 98–9). Fur imports to England declined after 1581, possibly due to overhunting, but seem to have climbed in the early seventeenth century as Russia wrested much of Western Siberia from the Tatar khanate. See Fisher (1943, 200–1) and Richards (2003, 517–25). While fur imports fell off again in 1609–10 due to the Polish-Muscovite war, they rose swiftly over the next decade (Dunning 1989, 213).
5. On *The Winter's Tale*'s interest in Russian politics, see Palmer (1995). Hermione's Russianness may have been signalled on stage by her wearing of furs, and her desirability as a match for Leontes would, from the court's point of view, stem in part from her family's ability to secure favourable trading terms for Russian furs. If a polar bear cub or white-fur-clad human did trundle across the stage at the Globe or Whitehall, Jacobean audiences might confound the play's notorious sea-coast in landlocked Bohemia with a port on the White Sea.
6. Notable studies of the interplay between Renaissance drama and the bear-pit include Dickey (1991); Fudge (2000); Scott-Warren (2003); Höfele—who calls the bear 'a figure of uncertainty' (2011, 32); and de Somogyi (2018).
7. As Shannon (2017) observes, whether performances featured bears trained to walk upright or human actors in fur crawling on all fours, both scenarios would undercut human bipedalism and the privileges it allegedly confers. On 'indistinction', see Bartolini (2011, 104) and Feerick and Nardizzi (2012). For a critique of some problematic aspects of Agamben's terminology, see Wolfe (2012).
8. Also see Mennell (2017).
9. The best-known screed against sheep-farming and its negative impact on bio-diversity is George Monbiot's *Feral* (2013). On the global fur trade, see Richards (2003, 463–546).
10. Early dates for the beaver's extirpation have been proposed by Raye (2014). Its disappearance from England helped propel the North American fur trade. In 1637, Thomas Morton reports that a Captain Kirk sent 25,000 beaver pelts from Canada back to England (97).
11. See Aubrey's *Natural History of Wiltshire* (Bodleian Aubrey MS 1 f. 131).

12. Sadly, Britain was not the only country to experience a stark decline in fur-bearers. In the early seventeenth century, the brown bear was already an endangered species in Bohemia, the site of the notorious bear encounter in *The Winter's Tale*, and the nation's last surviving bear was shot in 1856 (Servheen 1999, 96).
13. Giles Fletcher reports that the best 'white & dun [fox]' were exported from Pechora (in the present-day Komi Republic), 'whence also come the white wolfe, and white Beare skin' (1591, 7ᵛ).
14. This information on royal wardrobe purchases is derived from Veale (1966, 133–55). On 'the almost inexhaustible medieval demand for furs' and the extermination of English wildlife, see Lovegrove (2007, 24).
15. On *The Winter's Tale*'s deployment of ethnic stereotypes about Russians and Sicilians, see Desai (1996). Wickman (2008) explores the implications of casting a white Hermione and a black Leontes.
16. In Renaissance Italy, artists used the ermine as a symbol of fidelity and pregnancy—it has been suggested the one in Leonardo Da Vinci's *Lady with an Ermine* not only puns on the sitter's surname but hints that she is expecting (Musacchio 2001, 172–87)—which further explains the ermine's ghostly presence in Shakespeare's portrait of Hermione. On Anna's wardrobe, see Field (2017, 7).
17. On Elizabethan nostalgia at the Stuart court, see Perry (1997, 153–87) and Tsukada (2019).
18. On whiteness as a signifier of Russia in Webster's drama, see Connolly and Hopkins (2015).
19. Boleyn defied the verdict by wearing ermine to her execution (Ives 1986, 410). On the parallels between her trial and Hermione's, see Kaplan and Eggert (1994).
20. Since skinning is easier when the animal's body is still warm, some early modern skinners may have flayed animals while still alive in the belief it improved the quality of the pelts. See Fairnell (2008, 56). On the continuing illegal practice of flaying animals alive in the Chinese fur trade, see Cao (2015).
21. The forthcoming Box Office Bears project (https://boxofficebears.com) promises to unearth further archival evidence of ursine performance in early modern London.
22. See *HD* (128) and the entry for 'Arcadian Virgin' in the *LPD*.
23. Arcadia was christened after Callisto's son, Arcas, whose name derives from the Greek for bear, and thus shares an etymological root with Arctic, named for the northern constellation of the Great Bear, into which Callisto was stellified after her death.
24. While *Mucedorus* has long been derided as lowbrow fare, Kirwan (2013) observes that the 1610 text shows signs of being adapted for court performance, and derived prestige from its dedication to King James.
25. Citations from *Mucedorus* are taken from Bate and Rasmussen (2013).
26. Ravelhofer (2002) concedes that not all performances would have featured actual bears, a point seconded by Rooney (2007).
27. On Leontes as the bear, see Bristol (1991).
28. For the play's recurrent puns on 'bear', see Hunt (2004).
29. The recognition scene in *Valentine and Orson* was almost certainly part of the lost play, as the brothers' kinship is revealed by an oracular brazen head, a property the Admiral's Men already owned.
30. Aristotle describes children as governed by pleasure rather than reason in his *Nicomachean Ethics* 3.1119b.

31. Orgel claims Frederick's candidacy could not have been known before 1613 since the Spanish ambassador was ignorant of it then (1996, 16n). But since the point of the Palatine match was to secure a Protestant alliance the Spanish ambassador is precisely the person the English court would wish to keep in the dark. Alternatively, it is conceivable *The Winter's Tale* could have been revised in early 1613 in the wake of Prince Henry's death and the run-up to Princess Elizabeth's marriage, as Bergeron (1985) has proposed.

32. While the revision hypothesis is tempting, Pitcher (2010, 92) questions it, and one cannot discount the possibility that Shakespeare chose to adapt *Pandosto* in the first place in order to support the marriage negotiations, which were mooted as early as 1607, heated up when rival candidates to the Palatine match emerged in 1610, and were cinched the following spring (Akkerman 2011, 1:9; Anderson 2021), which overlaps with *The Winter's Tale* provenance of late 1610–11.

33. In 1595 James appointed John Erskine, Earl of Mar, to raise Prince Henry at Stirling Castle, which greatly angered Anna. His role in separating mother and child invites comparison with Antigonus. Clearly, the plot of *Pandosto* would have resonated with the Stuart court. The possibility that Frances Erskine's account contains reliable information on Elizabeth's upbringing is also boosted by the fact that Thomas Erskine was James's Captain of the Guard, Gentlemen of the Bedchamber, Groom of the Stool, and his 'most trusted friend' since childhood (Thurley 2021, 109–10). Elizabeth's most recent biographer concludes 'Erskine's account should not be completely discounted' (Akkerman 2021, 40).

34. Even if the *Memoirs* are contaminated by memories of *The Winter's Tale* or Garrick's adaptation *Florizel and Perdita*, it nonetheless illustrates how Shakespeare's romance could provide a forum for exalting the child's rapport with nature.

35. In reality, aristocratic women often did hunt in Stuart England. Queen Anna, for instance, frequently hunted at her country estate at Oatlands (Thurley 2021, 67–70), and Princess Elizabeth was also a keen hunter by the age of 14 (Akkerman 2021, 30, 75–6).

36. Traherne (2014, 6:23). On Traherne's sophisticated idealization of childhood innocence, see Watson (2006, 305–6).

37. Perdita exemplifies how Renaissance culture associated women with non-human nature 'in ways that were simultaneously marginalizing and empowering' (Laroche and Munroe 2017, 9). On Shakespeare's sense of an affinity between young girls and animals, see Higginbotham (2013, 104–43).

38. While girls were not permitted to perform on the Jacobean stage, Princess Elizabeth was something of an exception: she participated in court masques and in 1611 became the patron of a new acting company whose apprentices supplied the King's Men with fresh recruits (Syme 2019, 251) who may have played female roles.

39. Deane is listed as a creditor of the company in a petition dated 23 May 1626 (HL/PO/JO/10/1/32).

40. For more on the Roman triumph in Renaissance literature, see Miller (2001).

41. James received two live sables from Tsar Mikhail Fyodorovich in 1617 (Grigson 2016, 20), and it is possible his menagerie could have included ermine as well.

ENDNOTES   241

42. Langley (2013); Vanita (2000); and Tigner (2006).
43. Poliquin (2012) offers an incisive meditation on taxidermy and outlines its development in the Renaissance (26–7).
44. On Rudolf's Wunderkammer, see Friehs (2010). London's skinners may have displayed crude taxidermic specimens at Bartholomew Fair, where the Skinners' company formerly staged plays in honour of their patron saint (who had been flayed alive) as noted by Chapman (2004).
45. This song is cited in Cushing (1977, 150). For more research on Khanty bear ritual done in consultation with Indigenous expertise, see 'Waking the Bear' (2021).

Chapter 6

1. For some landmark works on *The Tempest* and colonialism, see Lamming (1960); Mannoni (1964); Marx (1964); Fielder (1973, 230–40); Barker and Hulme (1985); Brown (1985); Greenblatt (1990, 16–39); and Gillies (1994). Some complex perspectives are provided in the collection edited by Hulme and Sherman (2000)—particularly the essays by Vaughan, Gillies, and Seed. On the appropriation of *The Tempest* by authors from the Caribbean, South America, and Africa, see Nixon (1987); Vaughan and Vaughan (1991, 144–71); Zabus (2002); and Goldberg (2004).
2. Brotton (1998) seizes on the allusions to *The Aeneid* to recover *The Tempest*'s literal Mediterranean context, an approach shared by Hess (2000) and Wilson-Okamura (2003). Kastan also views the post-colonial interpretation as overblown and highlights the 'European courtly context' (1999, 183–97).
3. My approach is informed by Helgerson (1992) and his work on Drayton's *Poly-Olbion*, and Marcus's advocacy of 'local reading' (1988, 36–8).
4. When King James visited Stamford, Lincolnshire, in 1603, he was greeted by a party of fenmen on stilts that to one observer 'seemed like the Patagones' (Aitken 1822, 1:103–4).
5. See, for instance, Allewaert's reading of Ariel as personifying the tropical plantation (2013, 1). It should be noted that Bermuda, too, boasts its share of wetlands. Rather than deny the relevance of William Strachey's letter, I would encourage more ecocritical scrutiny of it as an uneasy reflection on anthropocratic imperialism. The narrative arc of 'The Wreck and Redemption of Sir Thomas Gates' traces the ordained triumph of both English and human ingenuity over a foreign and hostile ecology—a conflict all the more legible in the absence of native human inhabitants. Yet Strachey also speaks anxiously of the colonists who had the 'hot bloods and tall stomachs to *murder* thousands' (Purchas 1625, 1739, italics added) of the island's palm trees, and documents their reckless overhunting of indigenous species like the Bermuda petrel. Strachey reports witnessing the colonists slaughter 'three hundred in an hour' and 'twenty dozen' in two hours (1625, 1741), which explains why the Bermuda petrel was thought to be extinct for three centuries.
6. On the 'infracontexts' and sources of *The Tempest*, see Mowatt (2000) and Gurr (2014).
7. Doubts about Balfour's fieldwork have been voiced by Philips (1992, 156), but James (2013) mounts a stalwart defence of the authenticity of the legends on linguistic and

historical grounds, even consulting parish records to identify a likely candidate for the Tiddy Mun storyteller in one Mary Whelpton (168).
8. The word 'Tiddy' is a dialect word that means 'tiny'. This fits with the elderly woman later describing the bogey as the size of a 3-year-old. While the shape-shifting Ariel can squeeze inside a cowslip's bell, there is no corresponding evidence to indicate that Caliban is likewise diminutive. The text never suggests that Caliban has long white hair or an unkempt beard. Nor does grandfatherly seem a fit adjective for Shakespeare's cantankerous servant monster. Nevertheless, due to the ambiguous or conflicting nature of the descriptions we receive about Caliban, the objections listed above are far from definitive. It is possible to imagine Caliban as small in stature, as Brinsley Nicholson did over a century ago. Malone reported the stage tradition that Caliban 'is usually represented with long shaggy hair' (1821, 15:13), a tradition that survived into the twentieth century: see, for instance, the portraits of Sir Herbert Beerbohm Tree as a Neanderthal-like Caliban in his celebrated 1904 production. Tiddy Mun reportedly wears a grey gown, while Shakespeare dresses Caliban in a 'gaberdine' (2.2.38), a kind of loose overcoat. Tiddy Mun walks slowly, as does the otiose Caliban whom the impatient Prospero calls a 'tortoise' (1.2.318). Prior to learning English, Caliban seems to 'gabble' like a beast; Tiddy Mun is nameless and his voice is conflated with the inhuman soundscape of the swamp. In *Waterland*, Graham Swift describes a stagnant pool in the fens as exuding 'a smell which is half man and half fish' (4), and a life-long inhabitant of the region as stinking of 'fish slime, mud and peat smoke' (11). A similar ichthyoid odour clings to Caliban (2.1.25).
9. For Caliban as Native American or African, see n. 1. On Caliban as exotic fauna or a marine creature, see Warner (2000) and Test (2008). Studies of Caliban as a caricature of the wild Irish can be found in Fuchs (1997); Baker (1997); and Callaghan (2000, 97–138).
10. Briggs (1967, 54–5) reprints and modernizes an excerpt from Balfour's Tiddy Mun story in a chapter entitled 'Forgotten Gods and Nature Spirits'.
11. On the etymology and literary origins of Sycorax, see Orgel (1987, 19–20) and Warner (2000, 100–5).
12. In one of the few scholarly studies on the legend, Horn (1987) interprets Tiddy Mun's curse as an etiological fable about the actual environmental damage inflicted by the draining.
13. Residents of the fens carried on a lucrative trade exporting sedge, willow, and osiers to market towns throughout the East Midlands just as Caliban fetches in logs for Prospero. In 1618 efforts to drain the fens would be opposed by the Vice Chancellor of Cambridge, who feared that siphoning off the water would render the Cam and other shipping routes unnavigable during the summer and cut off the university's fuel supply (Ravensdale 1974, 54–7). The majestic cathedrals at Ely and Peterborough stand as towering monuments to the economic prosperity of the medieval fenlands—a prosperity that occurred 'not in spite of the survival of a vast undrained marshland but *because* of it' (Boyce 2020).
14. The use of scamel as a regional name for the godwit is first recorded in the *OED* in 1870 but is undoubtedly much older.
15. On this textual crux, see Kermode (1954, 97n).

16. Bevington reads the wedding masque-within-the-play as evidence of Shakespeare's wish to appeal to the court while also asserting his 'artistic independence' (1998, 237) from it.
17. Expanding on Egan, Nardizzi brilliantly implicates *The Tempest* in England's extraction of timber from its colonies, unmasking Prospero as a 'magical lumberjack' (2013, 112–35, 122).
18. The notable exception to this neglect of the fens is Hiltner (2011, 133–55). His account, however, focuses on the late seventeenth century and does not touch on Shakespeare. I briefly consider Caliban as a dispossessed fen-dweller (Borlik 2011, 4). Eklund (2017) has edited a pioneering collection on brown eco-studies, and is currently at work on a study of representations of the wetlands in early modern transatlantic literature.
19. The information in this paragraph is indebted to the following sources: Darby (1940); Lindley (1982); Richards (2003, 214–21); Hiltner (2011, 133–55); and Ash (2017, 139–247).
20. In 1561 Pope Pius IV commissioned the algebraist and hydraulic engineer Rafael Bombelli to drain these coastal swamps. After some initial success, the project failed (Jaywardene 1965).
21. The Italian fascists eventually drained the Pontine Marshes in 1934, though a small section was preserved and renamed Parco Nazionale del Circeo, after the sorceress Circe.
22. For more on *The Devil Is an Ass* as a satire on fen-draining, see Marcus (1988, 99–102); Evans (1994, 74–7); Sanders (1998, 107–22); and Borlik (2021).
23. Dee's manuscript on fen-draining is at the Bodleian Library, Oxford, Ashmolean MS 242/45. Dee also investigated 'The True Cause, and account (not vulgar) of Floods and Ebbs'. See French (1972, 32–3, 214).
24. Thorndike (1923–58) conducted the first serious investigation into the continuity between magic and science, an idea developed by Yates (1964) and Rossi (1978) and qualified by Copenhaver (1992) and Clucas (2003). The most through study of the subject in relation to *The Tempest* is by Sokol (2003), who compares Prospero to Thomas Harriot and Cornelius Drebbel. See also Sisson (1958); Orgel (1987, 20–3); Albanese (1996, 59–91); and Bate, who proposes *The Tempest* 'may be read as an allegorical anticipation of the project of mastery which came to be called Baconian method' (2000, 78–9).
25. Details can be found on *The Great Fen Project* website.
26. See the 'Royal letter to the Commissioners to assist the undertakers', 25 July 1620. CUA, CUR. 3.3/64. For more on the prehistory of eminent domain, see Reynolds (2010).
27. Despite the knighthood, Vermuyden's hydro-engineering was in fact far from perfect; he succeeded in draining Hatfield Level only by diverting water onto other lands that had not previously been inundated (Ash 2017, 156–8).
28. Latham (1992) is an exception.
29. Saenger (1995), however, presents a strong case that Caliban's costume was recycled from a royal pageant on the Thames devised by Anthony Munday to celebrate Prince Henry's investiture.

30. 'Monster', the word most often hurled at Caliban, is unhelpfully generic, and probably indicates some kind of physical deformity; the list of dramatis personae from the 1623 Folio tells us as much: 'Caliban, a salvage and deformed slave'. But apart from the 'long nails' (2.2.165) Caliban himself mentions, the text remains ambiguous as to the abnormality that demarcates him as a sub-human 'mooncalf' (2.2.105) and 'abominable' (2.2.156).

31. William Strachey's attempt to correct the popular misconception that the tropical islands of the New World 'can be no habitation for men, but are given over to devils and wicked spirits' (Purchas 1625, 1737-8) may have reminded Shakespeare of similar legends about Crowland. The story of Guthlac's enslaving demons, possibly based on 'local tradition' (Colgrave 1956, 22), is found in Ranulf Higden's *Polychronicon*. The text was Englished by John of Trevisa in the late fourteenth century and printed in 1482 by William Caxton, before being retold by Camden in his 1586 *Britannia*.

32. This addition to the story—found in a thirteenth-century manuscript at the University Library, Cambridge—perhaps originates from the psalter displayed as one of Guthlac's relics at Crowland Abbey. On accretions to the Guthlac legend, see Black (2007).

33. For a good overview of the furore enkindled by White's essay, see Atfield (2009). For a positive assessment of Guthlac as a St Francis-like figure, see Brooks (2019).

34. Colgrave is sceptical that a Celtic population still inhabited the fens in the eighth century, but cites a number of scholars who do subscribe to this theory (1956, 1-2, 185-6).

35. See Haigh (1993) and Duffy (2005, 155-205).

36. Cotton appears to have bound Felix's *Vita Guthlaci* in a copy of Higden's *Polychronicon*, a work of interest to Protestant antiquarians. Camden also consulted Henry of Avranches's life of Guthlac in Cotton's manuscript Vitellius D.xiv (Summit 2008, 172-83).

37. The most thorough monograph on the subject is by Allen (1990), who looks primarily at *Pericles*, *Measure for Measure*, and *As You Like It*. Felperin (1967) reads *Pericles* as an homage to the genre while Wilcox (2007) does the same for *All's Well That Ends Well*. For studies on Catholicism in *The Tempest*, see Beauregard (1997) and Wilson (2004, 206-29).

38. The day after All Saints was All Souls Day, a holiday not only for remembering the dead but also—as Shakespeare dramatizes in *Richard III*—for clemency and forgiveness. These virtues are of course crucial to the resolution of *The Tempest*, which further suggests that Shakespeare wrote the play with the holiday performance in mind.

39. Kermode mentions the 'fabulous holy voyages of the Golden Legend' (1954, xxxiv) as a possible analogue for the play, but efforts to pursue this line of inquiry to date have been few and, to be blunt, fanciful. Still (1921) considers *The Tempest* alongside medieval miracle plays, but his eccentric book mainly offers an allegorical reading of it as an initiation rite into ancient Eleusinian mysteries. Hall (1999) has uncovered some broad parallels with mystery plays at Coventry and York. Neither study mentions Guthlac or considers the saint play in depth.

40. On the Cutlack/Guthlac connection, see Bardsley (1877, 455-6) and McDougall (2002). There is even a character from the fens named 'Cutlack' in Swift's *Waterland* (1983, 84).

41. The *Lost Plays Database* conjectures that Cutlack might allude to the mythical Guichtlacus, the king of the Danes, mentioned by Geoffrey of Monmouth, a view strongly seconded by Matthew Steggle (2015, 61–76), who has now edited the *LPD* entry. The suggestion is plausible and worth considering. Guichtlacus does have a dramatic cameo in the *Historia Regum Britanniae*, although his story is subsidiary to that of two warring brothers Belinus and Brennius. Moreover, the Cutlake and Guthlack spelling of the saint's name are particularly common prior to the twentieth century, whereas the name of the Danish king is, as the *LPD* notes, 'subject to a bewildering variety of spellings' (including Ginchtalacus and Guilthdacus as well as Cutlake) but all derived from Geoffrey of Monmouth's Guichtlacus, the first syllable of which differs notably from Cutlack. While Steggle reasonably assumes that Guilpin's reference to 'Cutlacks gait' (63) must connote the martial stride of a warrior rather than a hermit, it should be noted that Guthlac (whose name means 'spoils of war'), besides repeatedly engaging in fisticuffs with demons, had been a battle-hardened warrior in his youth. Drayton reports that Guthlac 'liv'd a Souldier long' (1622, 2:94), while the *Vita Guthlaci* describes him as a Tamburlaine-like figure: he 'devastated the towns and residences of his foes' assembling a marauding army that pillaged 'villages and fortresses, with fire and sword' (81). Guthlac could well have had a swaggering gait.
42. Malone records a stage-tradition that Caliban's costume consisted of 'a large bearskin, or the skin of some other animal' (15:13). Where Malone gathered this bit of theatre-lore is unknown. The closure of the theatres during the Civil War makes the survival of original staging practices from Shakespeare's time unlikely. But Felix's statement that Guthlac 'passed all the days of his solitary life clad in the garment of animal skins' (185) suggests there might be some truth to Malone's claim. If true, it would provide another visual cue linking Caliban to the saintly fen-dweller.
43. See Anonymous (1586). Due to the drainage of the fens, the ruff virtually vanished from Britain in the late nineteenth century, and the population is now under 1,000 (Robinson 2005).
44. Qtd in Borlik (2019, 455); Borlik and Egan (2018) offer an overview of the ballad.
45. For an ecocritical reading of Césaire, see Bate (2000, 79–80).

Chapter 7

1. Burckhardt's oversight was corrected by French urban historian Henri Pirenne. For perceptive studies on how London's population boom galvanized English Renaissance literature, see Manley (1995) and Howard (2007).
2. In a study of Shakespeare's crowds, Egan acknowledges that they can 'behave badly' (2015, 130) but celebrates the collective knowledge of the hive mind over the individual.
3. 'Yet did their multitudes so oppress the country, and make provision so deare, that he was faine to publish an inhibition against the inordinate and dayly access of people's coming' (*PPMF* 76).
4. In 2019 the entire population of all Scotland (5.4 million) could fit comfortably within the London metropolitan area (which houses 8.6 million), and a similar imbalance existed in Shakespeare's day. In 1600, Edinburgh's inhabitants numbered roughly

25,000 (Whyte 2010), whereas historical demographers estimate London's population at this time in the vicinity of 200,000—and that figure would have swollen considerably in early 1603 from all the people who flocked there to attend the coronation festivities. Moreover, Scottish crowds maintained a respectful stillness and silence as the monarch passed, in contrast to the frenzied hullabaloo of the English.

5. Two centuries ago, Edmond Malone glossed the Duke's reluctance to 'stage' (1.1.68) himself before the multitude and his love of the 'life removed' (1.3.8) as a 'courtly apology for the stately and ungracious demeanour of King James' (1821, 2:383–7); scholars have since linked it to James's begrudging recognition in *Basilikon Doron* that kings stand 'upon a public stage' (*KJSW* 202). See Stevenson (1959), Lever (1965, xxxiii–v); Bennett (1966); and Goldberg (1983, 230–9).

6. Although Vincentio may not be a perfect likeness of England's new monarch, as Kevin Quarmby (2012, 112-19) cautions, the parallels would be striking enough for a Jacobean audience to draw comparisons. The editors of the Arden 3 edition grant that *Measure for Measure* should not be misconstrued as Stuart propaganda, but insist that this in no way nullifies the abundant evidence that when Shakespeare penned a play likely destined to be presented at court before his new patron he did 'what anybody in his position would have been strongly tempted to do: consider the monarch' (Braunmuller and Watson 2020, 115). The Norton editor concedes the play is 'far more than a staged version of *Basilikon Doron*' but emphasizes Shakespeare's 'direct flattery' of James (Iopollo 2010, x–xiii). The Bedford editors likewise maintain 'we should not discount the possibility of meaningful links between the king and the play' (Kamps and Raber 2004, 126). Also see Lawrence (2019).

7. See sources listed in n. 3. Mardock offers a valuable corrective to the '*Measure for Measure* version of King James' (2010, 114).

8. As Kamps and Raber note, 'while there was no clear understanding in the period of the vectors that spread the disease (primarily the black rat, *Rattus rattus*, and its fleas, a fact only discovered in the 1890s), there was a profound understanding of its demographics' (2004, 265).

9. See Bertram (2013, 480, 488).

10. Also see Heise (2001).

11. The case that the Folio text presents Thomas Middleton's modest revision of the play in 1621 was defended at length by Taylor and Jowett (1993), and subsequently developed for the *TMCW*, which presents versions of *Measure for Measure* before and after Middleton's tinkering. The Arden 3 editors deem it 'an intriguing hypothesis'—plausible but not proven (Braunmuller and Watson 2020, 117–23, 372).

12. Scholars attribute most of the poem, including these lines, to Dekker (*TMCW*, 129), but Middleton's involvement means he must have been familiar with the idea of plague as a population check. For a reappraisal of this plague pamphlet as 'environmental literature', see Whitney (2010).

13. See Cox (2008) and Mardock (2010).

14. In Plutarch, however, the first riot at which Menenius delivers his parable of the belly speech only targets usurers. Shakespeare shifts this oration to a second protest against exorbitant food prices due to grain-hoarding. For more on *Coriolanus* and the Midlands Rising, see George (2000); Hindle (2008, 41–51); Holland (2013, 56–68); and Boehrer (2013, 80–91).

15. On early modern demography, see Stangeland (1904); Bonar (1931); Hutchinson (1967); Slack (2011); and McCormick (2016).
16. Bodin was not a proto-Malthusian in that he believed that the most populous states were the most powerful, but he did tout the benefits of the census as a political tool (1606, 640).
17. Holland glosses the line in both senses, noting 'the concept of war as an efficient means of controlling population was as much an Elizabethan [sic] commonplace as a modern one' (2013, 169n).
18. Interestingly, Plutarch offers the counterargument that Roman wars brought about famine by converting too many ploughshares to swords:

   > Bicause the most parte of the errable lande within the territorie of ROME, was become heathie and barren for lacke of plowing, for that they had no time nor meane to cause corne, to be brought them out of other countries to sowe, by reason of their warres which made the extreme dearth. (1579, 243)

19. See Muir (1959).
20. On naming in *Coriolanus*, see Gordon (1964).
21. On animals in *Coriolanus*, see Elden (2018, 207–11).
22. For more on blood-letting in Shakespeare's England, see Decamp (2018).
23. On the play's appeal to Henry and Stuart hawks, see Wells (2000, 149–54).
24. Although Botero does not mention Coriolanus by name, he was likely thinking of this event when he praised the Romans for finding an outlet for population pressure through empire:

   > for the which inconvenience, the Romanes willing to provide a remedy; they made choyse of a number of poore Citizens, and sent them into *Colonies;* where, like trees transplanted, they might have more roome to better themselves both in condition and commoditie, and by that meanes encrease and multiply the faster. (1606, 94)

25. James's belief in the ancient legend that the Irish king Fergus founded the Scottish monarchy steeled his conviction in his claim to rule Ireland.
26. I have unearthed only a single passing reference to *Coriolanus* as appealing to 'colony hunters' in Ireland: Kiernan (1996, 185).
27. On Ralegh and Essex, see Holland (2013, 98–101).
28. 'It is no wisedome yet, to set up Colonies far off, in places too remote from your state and government... it being no easie thing for you to succor them' (Botero 1606, 100).
29. See Bacon (1641, 9–10).
30. See Bacon (1625, 182).
31. Given the intense focus on Ulster in Jacobean politics and the fact that early modern texts, including the Folio *Coriolanus*, follow Latin spelling conventions in using capital V in lieu of U, Shakespeare's early readers may have spied an orthographic resemblance between the Volsces and the Irish rebels of Vlster, also written Vlcister and Vlcester.
32. The details are set forth in the anonymous *Orders and Conditions to be observed by the Undertakers* (1609).
33. City authorities agreed to build 200 houses at Derry and another 100 at Coleraine, with plans to erect 500 more (Orr 2019, 90).
34. 'Phillips emerged as a character in keeping with William Shakespeare's Caius Martius....He was not a man given to the "gentle words" or "fair speech" necessary for

successfully negotiating the diverse array of local regimes through which the English actually governed themselves' (Orr 2019, 97).
35. The conqueror of Ulster, Henry Dowcra, confessed in his memoirs that without O'Doherty's assistance it would have been 'utterlie impossible that wee could have made that sure and steady progress in the Warress [against the Irish] that afterwards we did' (2003, 54).
36. Around this time O'Doherty applied to join the retinue of Prince Henry Frederick, apparently in a bid to bolster his influence at the Stuart court.
37. On Bartlett, see Klein (2001, 125–8), who notes the conflicting tendencies of English cartographers to depict Ireland either as a place of savagery or 'the colonial fantasy of a spatial tabula rasa' (186). Barrett (2018), meanwhile, argues that Spenser registers a 'cartographic anxiety' that maps delude viewers into imagining colonization as easier on paper than it proves in reality.
38. This translation comes from Gillies (1969). Samuel Ferguson's looser rendition underscores the environmental havoc of the occupation: the English have 'disfigured' the landscape and expelled the wildlife—'no more shall repair / Where the hill foxes tarry / Nor forth to the air / Fling the hawk at her quarry'—so that 'in the uprooted wildwood' the Irish no longer recognize their homeland. See CELT: Corpus of Electronic Texts, http://www.ucc.ie/celt.
39. *Coriolanus* does not represent environmental degradation so directly. But recognizing it as an Irish tragedy adds a layer to its wolf imagery, since wolves still prowled Irish woodlands, and the Roman populace's animosity towards the aristocratic warrior foretokens the tragic fate of apex predators as an influx of British settlers colonized the wild. For a poem linking the English conquest to the absence of snakes in Ireland, see John Derricke's *Image of Ireland* (1581), reprinted in Borlik (2019, 136–7).
40. See n. 14. Hindle argues that Martius's rhetoric 'echoes the punitive policies advocated by the Crown and administered by the Lords Lieutenant of Leicestershire and Northamptonshire in the immediate aftermath of the Midland Rising' (2008, 46). In contrast, Marcus suggests that the play champions the City's liberties, so that 'local law and privilege win out against the more global and arbitrary claims of absolutism' (1988, 202). Sadly, the same cannot be said for Ulster.
41. The revolt had been a painful reminder of 'how precarious their hold on the province had actually been' (Harris 1980, 305).
42. Everett (2015, 98–108) and D'Arcy (2021) document the environmental havoc wrought by the Ulster Plantation. The Crown licensed the felling 100,000 ash, 50,000 oaks, and 10,000 elms in Killetra woods but soon became alarmed at the scale of deforestation.
43. The phrase is recorded in Tacitus, *Agricola* 30.
44. On Petty and Ireland, see Fox (2009) and McCormick (2016, 33–6). For more on Petty and Swift, see Briggs (2005).

Chapter 8

1. This statistic comes from Bogard (2013, 7, 25).
2. Ecologists have identified light pollution as a prime culprit behind the precipitous decline of the world's insect population (Owens et al. 2019; Stewart 2021). On Bakhtin's chronotope, see Müller (2010).

3. For an application of Morton's theories to dark weather in *Macbeth* and *Lear*, see Whiteley (2020).
4. On Heming, see Ekirch (2005) and Koslofsky (2011).
5. Bronfen identifies the proto-Gothic elements in *Romeo and Juliet* and *A Midsummer Night's Dream* (2008, 21–41); Estok theorizes sleep as a state of animal-human hybridity (2011, 111–15); Shannon holds a candle to the nocturnal landscapes of *A Midsummer Night's Dream* and *King Lear* (2013, 174–217) as dramatizing the boundaries of human empire.
6. The 1599 Act is described in de Beer (1941, 314).
7. Of course, night-walking was a problem prior to 1599. The feline narrator of William Baldwin's *Beware the Cat* (c.1553) observes human night-walkers conducting illicit affairs and (punning on cat and Catholic) illegal midnight masses, while Nashe laments the sins afoot in London at night in *Christ's Tears over Jerusalem* (1593, 160–1).
8. On *Truth's Supplication to Candlelight*, which presumably satirized the wickedness of the city at night, see Steggle (2015, 91–3).
9. Stewart (2003, 24, 36, 124–5, 132). For more on James's insomnia, see Parris (2012).
10. 'I do walk / Methinks like Guido Faux, with my dark Lanthorne / Stealing to set the town afire' (Fletcher 1640, D4^v).
11. One might add John Dowland's 'Welcome Black Night' (composed shortly before his appointment as James's court lutenist in 1612) to Fitter's list of literary nocturnes.
12. Subsequent research would complicate Orgel's initial view of a monolithic state by revealing the Stuart masque's negotiations between competing power bases within the distinct courts of the king, queen, and prince, which had their own divergent views on religion, foreign policy, and gender politics: see Bevington and Holbrook (1998); Butler (1998).
13. See Hall (1995, 128–41); Andrea (1999); Vaughan (2005, 65–9); Iyengar (2005, 80–6); McDermott (2007).
14. The masque's title is somewhat misleading in that it features a diverse array of colours and depicts a remarkably prismatic Africa. The masque envisions the 'appropriation of African fertility and wealth' (Hall 1995, 137) through Britain's maritime empire and would have encouraged James to support the founding of the Guinea Company, which sought to import dyes from African sandalwood as well as exotic luxury goods such as gold, pearl, coral, murex, ivory, etc. that were all the more desirable for the way they glimmered under torchlight. Research emerging from the Sam Wanamaker Playhouse is revealing how performers would have exploited candlelight to shimmer off their colourful costumes (Dustagheer 2014), jewellery, and cosmetics (Karim-Cooper 2014), the last of which would include the body paint applied to mimic darker skin.
15. The popularity of using Africans or actors in blackface as torchbearers (as illustrated in the famous 1596 portrait of Sir Henry Unton) suggests a fetishizing of black skin aglisten. Yet Campion's anti-masque is also an egregious example of a tendency in Jacobean drama to represent the nocturnal environment 'as an object analogous to the vilified black Other' (Estok 2011, 118).
16. The eagle-owl is mentioned in a description of the royal menagerie reprinted in Strong (1986, 212). See the engraving of the owl in Conrad Gesner's *Icones animalium quadrupedum* (1560), reproduced in Swenson (2020). On Renaissance iconography featuring bats, see Riccucci and Rydell (2017).
17. Middleton's attack on coal is elucidated by Boehrer (2013, 33–5).
18. On tallow, see Graves (1999, 15) and Shannon (2011). On whale oil, see Fouquet and Pearson (2006, 154–5).

19. On owls in Renaissance culture, see Hirsch (2010) and Swenson (2020).
20. Ekirch's seminal research on segmented sleep patterns in early modernity (2005, 300–23) indicates many people were awake in the pre-electrified night. Drayton and Milton speak for a demographic that wanted the night to remain a private time for devotion or intimacy and resisted the growing colonization of night as public space in the seventeenth century.
21. Ekirch observes that early moderns regarded 'wasting candlelight [as] synonymous with extravagance' (2005, 109).
22. Flouting the custom of nocturnal sleep was by no means a brand-new phenomenon in the seventeenth century, as the classical setting reveals, nor is it unprecedented in Shakespeare: the debauched knight and diurnal sleeper Falstaff famously boasts of having heard the 'chimes at midnight' in *2 Henry IV*. Nonetheless, nocturnalization appears to have elicited greater concern in James's reign as can be inferred from the facts that Falstaff is an outcast from the court whose nocturnal habits betray his marginality whereas Antony and Cleopatra's night-time revels normalize this behaviour at court, obliging high society to follow suit.
23. Since the Solomon and Sheba story could serve as a warning against 'erotic entanglements with foreign women' (Hall 1995, 108), it is awkward that James and Anna had been compared to them in an entertainment performed at Holyroodhouse in 1590 to celebrate her coronation (Stevenson 1997, 117–20). Also see Loomba (2002, 112–34).
24. On Caesar's plan for cost-cutting royal expenses, see Cramsie (2002, 80–2).
25. Antipathy towards corvids was also heightened by the belief that they, along with night mists, were carriers of plague. In *Jew of Malta*, the night-walking Barabas compares himself to a raven 'that in the shadow of the silent night, / Doth shake contagion from her sable wings' (2.1.3–4).
26. The legislation obliged every English village of more than ten households to employ nets to 'kill and utterly destroy all manner of Choughes, Crowes, and Rookes', including 'all the yong brede'. A traditional English folk saying advises farmers to plant 'Four seeds in a hole / One for the rook, one for the crow, / One to rot and one to grow' (Lovegrove 2007, 154), but an agrarian society prone to harvest failures could not always be so generous.
27. Shakespeare again badmouths corvids when Ross comments how ambition 'will raven up / Thine own life's means' (2.4.28–9), conflating the bird with the verb ravin.
28. For a piercing discussion of startle in this play in comparison to its use in Kurosawa's *Throne of Blood*, see Tribble (2005).
29. Robert Baird captures startle's complexity when he asserts that it is 'at once genetically hard-wired, socially constructed, and personally expressed' (2000, 20–1).
30. Not long before *Macbeth* was performed the London council had passed a regulation imposing a three-shilling fine on anyone who emitted a 'sudden outcry in the still of the night' (Ekirch 2005, 62–3).
31. Lindsey Row-Heyveld has shown that the play dramatizes an 'embodied knowledge of disability', one that challenges narrow constructions of it through the multiplicity of its representations: the Fool's neurodivergence, Edgar's feigned madness, Lear's dementia, and Gloucester's blindness (2019, 173–8). On a less optimistic note, Robert

Pierce contends that 'much of the power of Shakespeare's most overwhelming tragedy is intimately bound up in outmoded assumptions about blindness' (2012, 163) as a living death. While *Lear* invokes the ableist metaphor 'knowing is seeing' (Vidali 2010), the tragedy also debunks this pat formula in Gloucester's declarations, 'I stumbled when I saw' and 'our mere defects prove our commodities' (4.1.21–3).

32. On the storm, see Mentz (2011a); Jones (2015, 59–78); Hamilton (2017;) and Chiari (2019, 150–75). Registering the play's fascination with the dark, Chiari observes that 'a new aesthetic of darkness influenced by northern mannerism probably encouraged Shakespeare' to develop 'the black pastoral of *King Lear*' (2019, 150).
33. Tom's strange outburst, 'Purr, the cat is grey' (3.6.45), likely alludes to the folk saying 'all cats are grey in the dark' (a proverb first recorded in 1546), and so serves as another reminder of the nocturnal setting and of the fallibility of the human eye at night.
34. Kent presumably excludes humans from the category of 'things that love night' (3.2.42), and this recognition that other species are far better equipped for noctivagation contributes to Shannon's insightful reading of the tragedy as an exposé of humanity's extraordinary maladaptedness, or 'negative exceptionalism' (2013). However, 'such nights as these' disorient and 'gallow' (an odd verb implying menace with death) even those creatures endowed with night vision, so that the play here imagines disability as a universal condition that extends across the species line.
35. 'Darkling' appears in Shakespeare on two other occasions. In *A Midsummer Night's Dream*, a frightened Helena whimpers, 'O wilt thou darkling leave me?' (2.2.92), implying that Lysander carried away their only light source, and Cleopatra compares Antony's death to a universal eclipse: 'darkling stand[s] the varying shore of the world' (4.15.10). It is suggestive that the word's disappearance from English usage in the early twentieth century coincides with the advent of electric light.
36. Other thinkers have already hit upon the phrase cosmic sublime (Lu 2018).
37. Peter Usher's intriguing theories on Shakespeare's crypto-Copernicanism are summarized in Falk (2014, 170–217). On revisions to *Hamlet* for court, see Dutton (2016).

Conclusion

1. On corruption at the Stuart court, see Peck (1993). James's culpability for the Civil War remains contested by historians but the revisionist exoneration of James has cooled since the millennium as more moderate voices grant he bears some responsibility: e.g. Stewart (2003, 348); Croft (2003, 186–7); Houlbrooke (2006); Matusiak (2015).
2. The myths that Brute founded Britain and the Irish king Fergus Scotland bolstered James's belief in imperial kingship (Cramsie 2006, 43).
3. Modern readers might assume 'worm' means earthworm, the mole's favourite food, but the context (the tyrant's power to silence opposition) indicates that it more likely refers to the mole, in accordance with the broader early modern usage of worm to designate any creeping animal.
4. Patriarchal culture's reluctance to confer full humanity on early modern women could allow them to act as privileged mediators or interlocutors between culture and nature

advocating for hybridity, as explored by Bowerbank (2004); Munroe and Laroche (2011, 1–9); and Nesler (2015). On the risks of presuming to speak for nature, see Munroe (2015).

5. Bacon decodes the Orpheus myth in his 1609 *De Sapientia Veterum*. For more on Orphic poetry and science, see Mann (2021). On the Orphic in Verlaine and Rilke, see Louth (2015).
6. The phrase 'deconsecration of sovereignty' is borrowed from Moretti (1983). On Shakespeare and Lucretius, see Shoaf (2014); Pollock (2017); and Chiari (2019).
7. Morton, in contrast, defends it as 'the first truly anti-anthropocentric concept' (2014, 262). In considering alternative labels such as Capitalocene and Plantationocene, *Shakespeare Beyond the Green World* heeds Mentz's call to 'break' or 'pluralize' (2019) the Anthropocene, allowing multiple conceptions of it to circulate and perform different cultural work.
8. For ecocritical suspicion of tragedy, see Meeker (1972) and Estok (2011).
9. On the ecological stakes of genre in Shakespeare, see Mentz (2011a).

References

Adams, Carol J. 1990. *The Sexual Politics of Meat*. London: Continuum.
Adorno, Theodore. 1978. *Minima Moralia*, trans. E. F. N. Jephcott. London: Verso.
Adrian, John. 2011. *Local Negotiations of English Nationhood 1570–1680*. Basingstoke: Palgrave Macmillan.
Agamben, Giorgio. 1993. *Infancy and History: The Destruction of Experience*, trans. Liz Horton. London: Verso.
Agamben, Giorgio. 2004. *The Open: Man and Animal*, trans. Kevin Attell. Stanford: Stanford University Press.
Agamben, Giorgio. 2005. *State of Exception*, trans. Kevin Attell. Chicago: University of Chicago Press.
Aitken, Lucy, ed. 1822. *Memoirs of the Court of King James I*. London.
Akrigg, G. P. V. 1984. *The Letters of King James VI and I*. Berkeley: University of California Press.
Alaimo, Stacy. 2016. *Exposed: Environmental Politics and Pleasures in Posthuman Times*. Minneapolis: University of Minnesota Press.
Albanese, Denise. 1996. *New Science, New World*. Durham: Duke University Press.
Albertson, Clinton, ed. 1967. *Anglo-Saxon Saints and Heroes*. New York: Fordham University Press.
Aldbury, W. R. and D. R. Oldroyd. 1977. 'From Renaissance Mineral Studies to Historical Geology in Light of Michel Foucault's *Order of Things*'. *British Journal for the History of Science* 10(3): 187–215.
Allen, Gary. 1990. *Shakespeare and the Saint's Life Tradition*. Pullman, WA: Washington State University Press.
Allewaert, Monique. 2013. *Ariel's Ecology: Plantations, Personhood, and Colonialism in the American Tropics*. Minneapolis: University of Minnesota Press.
Alsop, J. D. 1980. 'William Welwood, Anne of Denmark, and the Sovereignty of the Sea'. *Scottish Historical Review* 59(2): 171–4.
Akkerman, Nadine. 2011. *The Correspondence of Elizabeth Stuart, Queen of Bohemia*. 2 vols. Oxford: Oxford University Press.
Akkerman, Nadine. 2021. *Elizabeth Stuart, Queen of Hearts*. Oxford: Oxford University Press.
Anderson, Christy. 2000. 'Wild Waters: Hydraulics and the Forces of Nature'. In *The Tempest and Its Travels*, ed. Peter Hulme and William H. Sherman, 41–8. Philadelphia: University of Pennsylvania Press.
Anderson, Roberta. 2021. 'A Bridegroom for Elizabeth: Diplomatic Negotiations for the Marriage of Princess Elizabeth 1610–13'. *Gender and Diplomacy*, ed. Roberta Anderson et al., 115–48. Vienna: Holitzer.
Andrea, Bernadette. 1999. 'Black Skin, the Queen's Masques: Africanist Ambivalence and Feminine Author(ity) in the *Masques of Blackness* and *Beauty*'. *ELR* 29(2): 246–81.
Anonymous. 1586. *A most wonderful and true report… of diverse unknown fowles… latelie taken at Crowley*. London.
Anonymous. 1605. *The Bloudy Booke*. London.

Anonymous. 1606. *The most cruell and bloody murther committed by an Inkeepers wife, called Annis Dell*. London.
Anonymous. 1607. *True Report of Certain Wonderful Overflowings of Waters*. London.
Anonymous. 1608. *Newes from Ireland...Concerning the late treacherous action and rebellion of Sir Carey Adoughterie*. London.
Anonymous. 1608. *Overthrow of an Irish Rebell*. Dublin.
Anonymous. 1609. *A Collection of Such Orders and Conditions to be observed by the Vndertakers upon the distribution and Plantation of the Escheated Lands in Vlster*. Edinburgh.
Anonymous. 1626. *A Discription of Scotland*.
Anonymous. 1652. *A Cat May Look upon a King*. London.
Anonymous. 1657. *Nature's Cabinet Unlocked*. London.
Anonymous. 1688. *Gesta Grayorum*. London.
Archer, Elizabeth Jayne et al. 2012. 'The Autumn King: Remembering the Land in *King Lear*'. *Shakespeare Quarterly* 63(4): 518–43.
Archibald, Elizabeth. 1991. *Apollonius of Tyre: Medieval and Renaissance Themes and Variations*. Woodbridge, Suffolk: Boydell and Brewer.
Aristotle. 1964. *Politics and Poetics*, trans. Benjamin Jowett. New York: Heritage.
Armin, Robert. 1605. *Foole upon Foole*. London.
Armitage, David. 2000. *The Ideological Origins of the British Empire*. Cambridge: Cambridge University Press.
Arnold, Oliver. 2008. *The Third Citizen: Shakespeare's Theatre and the Early Modern House of Commons*. Baltimore: Johns Hopkins University Press.
Ash, Eric H. 2017. *The Draining of the Fens: Projectors, Popular Politics, and State Building in Early Modern England*. Baltimore: Johns Hopkins University Press.
Atfield, Robin. 2009. 'Social History, Religion, and Technology: An Inter-disciplinary Investigation into Lynn White Jr.'s "Roots"'. *Environmental Ethics* 31(1): 31–50.
Atkins, William. 2014. *The Moor: Lives, Landscape, Literature*. London: Faber and Faber.
Aubrey, John. *Natural History of Wiltshire*. Aubrey MS 1.
Aubrey, John. 1687–9. *Three Prose Works*, ed. John Buchanan Brown. Carbondale, IL: Southern Illinois University Press, 1972.
Aytoun, Robert. 1844. *The Poems of Sir Robert Aytoun*. Ed. Charles Roger. Edinburgh: A & C Black.
Bach, Rebecca Ann. 2018. *Birds and Other Creatures in Renaissance Literature: Shakespeare, Descartes, and Animal Studies*. New York: Routledge.
Bacon, Francis. 1605. *The Advancement of Learning*. London.
Bacon, Francis. 1625. *The Essayes*. London.
Bacon, Francis. 1641. *A Speech Used by Sir Francis Bacon...Concerning the Article of Naturalization*. London.
Badcoe, Tamsin. 2017. 'Richard Carew and the Matters of the Littoral'. In *Ground-work*, ed. Hillary Eklund, 41–58. Pittsburgh: Duquesne University Press.
Baggs, A. P. and A. R. J. Jurica. 1996. 'Forest of Dean: Forest Administration'. In *A History of the County of Gloucester*. Vol. 5: *Bledisloe Hundred, St. Briavels Hundred, the Forest of Dean*, ed. C. R. J. Currie and N. M. Herbert, 354–77. London.
Bagnall, Roger et al., ed. 2012. *The Encyclopaedia of Ancient History*. Oxford: Wiley-Blackwell.
Bailey, Amanda. 2011. '*Timon of Athens*, Forms of Payback, and the Genre of Debt'. *English Literary Renaissance* 41(2): 375–400.
Baird, Robert. 2000. 'The Startle Effect: Implications for Spectator Cognition and Media Theory'. *Film Quarterly* 53(3): 12–24.

Baldwin, Robert. 2006. 'John Dee's Interest in the Application of Nautical Science, Mathematics, and Law in English Naval Affairs'. In *John Dee: Interdisciplinary Studies in English Renaissance Thought*, ed. Stephen Clucas, 97–130. Berlin: Springer.
Bale, John. 1538. *The Dramatic Writings of John Bale*, ed. John S. Farmer. London: Early English Drama Society, 1907.
Balfour, M. C. 1891. 'Legends of the Lincolnshire Cars, Part I'. *Folklore* 2(2): 145–70.
Balfour, M. C. 1891. 'Legends of the Lincolnshire Cars, Part II'. *Folklore* 2(3): 257–83.
Baker, David. 1997. 'Where Is Ireland in *The Tempest*?' In *Shakespeare and Ireland: History, Politics, Culture*, ed. Mark Thornton Burnett and Ramona Wray, 68–88. New York: Palgrave Macmillan.
Baker, Tawrin et al., eds. 2015. *Early Modern Color Worlds*. Leiden: Brill.
Bardsley, C. W. 1877. 'Cutlack'. *Notes & Queries* 8: 455–6.
Barker, Francis and Peter Hulme. 1985. '"Nymphs and Reapers Heavily Vanish": The Discursive Con-texts of *The Tempest*'. In *Alternative Shakespeares*, ed. John Drakakis, 191–205. London: Routledge.
Barrata, Lucca. 2013. 'Lancashire: A Land of Witches in Shakespeare's Time'. *Journal of Early Modern Studies* 2: 185–208.
Barret, James H. and David C. Orton, eds. 2016. *Cod and Herring: The Archaeology and History of Medieval Sea Fishing*. Oxford: Oxbow.
Barrett, Chris. 2018. *Early Modern English Literature and the Poetics of Cartographic Anxiety*. Oxford: Oxford University Press.
Barroll, Leeds. 1991. *Politics, Plague, and Shakespeare's Theatre: The Stuart Years*. Ithaca: Cornell University Press.
Barroll, Leeds. 2001a. *Anna of Denmark, Queen of England: A Cultural Biography*. Philadelphia: University of Pennsylvania Press.
Barroll, Leeds. 2001b. 'Assessing Cultural Influence: James I as Patron of the Arts'. *Shakespeare Studies* 29: 132–62.
Barry, John. 2019. 'Green Republicanism and a "Just Transition" from the Tyranny of Economic Growth'. *Critical Review of International Social and Political Philosophy* 24(5): 725–42.
Bartolini, Paolo. 2011. 'Indistinction'. In *The Agamben Dictionary*, ed. Alex Murray et al., 102–4. Edinburgh: Edinburgh University Press.
Barton, Anne. 2017. *The Shakespearean Forest*. Cambridge: Cambridge University Press.
Bate, Jonathan. 2000. *The Song of the Earth*. London: Picador.
Bate, Jonathan. 2009. *Soul of the Age: A Biography of the Mind of William Shakespeare*. New York: Random House.
Bate, Jonathan and Eric Rasmussen, eds. 2013. *William Shakespeare and Others: Collaborative Plays*. London: Palgrave Macmillan.
Bates, Catherine. 2013. *Masculinity and the Hunt: Wyatt to Spenser*. Oxford: Oxford University Press.
Beaumont, Matthew. 2016. *Nightwalking: A Nocturnal History of London*. London: Verso.
Beauregard, David. 1997. 'New Light on Shakespeare's Catholicism: Prospero's Epilogue'. *Renascence* 49: 159–74.
Beer, E. S. de. 1941. 'The Early History of London Street Lighting'. *History* 25(100): 311–24.
Behringer, Wolfgang. 1999. 'Climatic Change and Witch-Hunting: The Impact of the Little Ice Age on Mentalities'. *Climate Change* 43(1): 335–51.
Bellany, Alastair and Andrew McRae, eds. 2005. *Early Stuart Libels: An Edition of Poetry from Manuscript Sources*. Early Modern Literary Studies Text Series. Web. http://www.earlystuartlibels.net/htdocs/index.html
Belsey, Catherine. 2007. *Why Shakespeare?* New York: Palgrave Macmillan.

Bender, John. 1980. 'The Day of *The Tempest*'. *English Literary History* 47(2): 235–58.
Bennett, Jane. 2010. *Vibrant Matter*. Durham: Duke University Press.
Bennett, Josephine. 1966. *Measure for Measure as Royal Entertainment*. Ithaca: Cornell University Press.
Bentham, J. 1763. *The Statutes at Large*. London.
Berger, Harry. 1990. *Second World and Green World: Studies in Renaissance Fiction-Making*. Berkeley: University of California Press.
Bergeron, David. 1985. *Shakespeare's Romances and the Royal Family*. Lawrence: University of Kansas Press.
Bergeron, David. 2019. 'Pericles: A Performance, a Letter (1619)'. In *Performances at Court in the Age of Shakespeare*, ed. Sophie Chiari and John Mucciolo, 107–19. Cambridge: Cambridge University Press.
Berry, Edward. 2001. *Shakespeare and the Hunt: A Cultural and Social Study*. Cambridge: Cambridge University Press.
Bertram, Benjamin. 2013. '*Measure for Measure* and the Discourse of Husbandry'. *Modern Philology* 110(4): 459–88.
Bertram, Benjamin. 2018. *Bestial Oblivion: War, Humanism, and Ecology in Early Modern England*. New York: Routledge.
Bevington, David, ed. 1975. *Medieval Drama*. Boston: Houghton Mifflin.
Bevington, David and Peter Holbrook, eds. 1998. *The Politics of the Stuart Court Masque*. Cambridge: Cambridge University Press.
Bevington, David. 1998. '*The Tempest* and the Jacobean Court Masque'. In *The Politics of the Stuart Court Masque*, ed. David Bevington and Peter Holbrook, 218–43. Cambridge: Cambridge University Press.
Bevington, David and David L. Smith. 1999. 'James I and Timon of Athens'. *Comparative Drama* 33(1): 56–87.
Bicks, Caroline. 2021. *Cognition and Girlhood in Shakespeare's World*. Cambridge: Cambridge University Press.
Biggam, Carol P. 2006. 'Knowledge of Whelk Dyes and Pigments in Anglo-Saxon England'. *Anglo-Saxon England* 35: 23–55.
Biggins, Dennis. 1962. '"Exit Pursued by a Bear": A Problem in *The Winter's Tale*'. *Shakespeare Quarterly* 13(1): 3–13.
Billington, Michael. 2012. '*Timon of Athens*—Review'. *The Guardian*, 18 July 2012. Web. https://www.theguardian.com/stage/2012/jul/18/timon-of-athens-review-olivier
Birch, Thomas. 1760. *The Life of Henry, Prince of Wales*. London.
Black, John. 2007. 'Tradition and Transformation in the Cult of St Guthlac in Early Medieval England'. *The Heroic Age* 10.
Blumenberg, Hans. 1997. *Shipwreck with Spectator*, trans. Steven Rendall. Cambridge, MA: MIT Press.
Boehrer, Bruce. 2013. *Environmental Degradation in Jacobean Drama*. Cambridge: Cambridge University Press.
Bogard, Paul. 2013. *The End of Night: Searching for Natural Darkness in an Age of Artificial Light*. New York: Little, Brown, and Co.
Boling, Ronald J. 2000. 'Anglo-Welsh Relations in *Cymbeline*'. *Shakespeare Quarterly* 51(1): 33–66.
Bonar, James. 1931. *Theories of Population from Raleigh to Arthur Young*. London: George Allen & Unwin.
Bonneuil, Christophe and Jean-Baptiste Fressoz. 2016. *The Shock of the Anthropocene*. London: Verso.

Borlik, Todd Andrew. 2011. *Ecocriticism and Early Modern English Literature: Green Pastures*. New York: Routledge.
Borlik, Todd Andrew. 2015. 'Teaching Timon of Walden'. In *Ecological Approaches to Early Modern English Texts: A Field Guide to Reading and Teaching*, ed. Jennifer Munroe et al., 169–80. Farnham: Ashgate.
Borlik, Todd Andrew, ed. 2019. *Literature and Nature in the English Renaissance: An Ecocritical Anthology*. Cambridge: Cambridge University Press.
Borlik, Todd Andrew and Clare Egan. 2018. 'Angling for the "Powte": A Jacobean Environmental Protest Poem'. *ELR* 48(2): 256–85.
Borlik, Todd Andrew. 2021. 'Magic as Technological Dominion: John Dee's Hydragogy and the Draining of the Fens in Ben Jonson's *The Devil Is an Ass*'. *Neophilogus* 105: 589–608.
Botello-Ordinas, Eva. 2010. 'Debating Empires, Inventing Empires: British Territorial Claims against the Spaniards in America'. *Journal for Early Modern Cultural Studies* 10(1): 142–68.
Botero, Giovanni. 1606. *A Treatise concerning the causes of the magnificence and greatness of cities*, trans. Robert Peterson. London.
Bowerbank, Sylvia. 2004. *Speaking for Nature: Women and Ecologies of Early Modern England*. Baltimore: Johns Hopkins University Press.
Bowsher, Julian and Pat Miller. 2009. *The Rose and the Globe—Playhouses of Shakespeare's Bankside, Southwark: Excavations 1988-90*. London: Museum of London Archaeology.
Bowyer, Robert. 1930. *The Parliamentary Diary of Robert Bowyer 1606-07*, ed. David Harris Wilson. New York: Octagon.
Boyce, James. 2020. *Imperial Mud: The Fight for the Fens*. London: Icon.
Brandt, Stefan. 2019. 'The Wild Ones: Ecomasculinities in the American Literary Imagination'. In *Ecomasculinities*, ed. Rubén Cenamor and Stefan Brandt, 1–28. London: Rowman and Littlefield.
Braunmuller, A. R. and Robert Watson, eds. 2020. *Measure for Measure*. London: Bloomsbury.
Brayton, Dan. 2011. 'Shakespeare and the Global Ocean'. In *Ecocritical Shakespeares*, ed. Lynne Bruckner and Dan Brayton, 173–92. Aldershot: Ashgate.
Brayton, Dan. 2012. *Shakespeare's Ocean: An Ecocritical Exploration*. Charlottesville: University of Virginia Press.
Briggs, K. M. 1959. *The Anatomy of Puck*. London: Routledge.
Briggs, K. M. 1967. *The Faeries in Tradition and Literature*. London: Routledge.
Briggs, Peter M. 2005. 'John Graunt, Sir William Petty, and Swift's Modest Proposal'. *Eighteenth-Century Life* 29(2): 3–24.
Bristol, Michael. 1991. 'In Search of the Bear'. *Shakespeare Quarterly* 42(2): 145–67.
Bryant, Levi. 2013. 'Black'. In *Prismatic Ecology*, ed. Jeffery Cohen, 290–310. Minneapolis: University of Minnesota Press.
Bronfen, Elizabeth. 2008. 'Shakespeare's Nocturnal World'. In *Gothic Shakespeares*, ed. John Drakakis and Dale Townshend, 21–41. New York: Routledge.
Brooke, Nicholas, ed. 1990. *Macbeth*. Oxford: Oxford University Press.
Brooks, Britton Elliot. 2019. *Restoring Creation: The Natural World in the Anglo-Saxon Saints' Lives of Cuthbert and Guthlac*. Martlesham: Boydell and Brewer.
Brotton, Jerry. 1998. '"This Tunis, sir, was Carthage": Contesting Colonialism in *The Tempest*'. In *Post-Colonial Shakespeares*, ed. Ania Loomba and Martin Orkin, 23–42. London: Routledge.
Brown, Paul. 1985. '"This Thing of Darkness I Acknowledge Mine": *The Tempest* and the Discourse of Colonialism'. In *Political Shakespeare: New Essays in Cultural Materialism*, ed. Jonathan Dollimore and Alan Sinfield, 48–71. Manchester: Manchester University Press.

Buell, Lawrence. 2005. *The Future of Environmental Criticism*. Oxford: Wiley.
Buell, Lawrence. 2013. 'Foreword'. In *Prismatic Ecology*, ed. Jeffrey Cohen, ix–xii. Minneapolis: University of Minnesota Press.
Buell, Lawrence. 2016. 'Anthropocene Panic: Contemporary Ecocriticism and the Issue of Human Numbers'. *Frame* 29(2): 1–15.
Burgess, Glenn et al. 2006. *The Accession of James I: Historical and Cultural Consequences*. Basingstoke: Palgrave Macmillan.
Burnet, Thomas. 1684. *Sacred Theory of the Earth*. London.
Butler, Martin. 1998. 'Courtly Negotiations'. In *The Politics of the Stuart Court Masque*, ed. David Bevington and Peter Holbrook, 20–40. Cambridge: Cambridge University Press.
Calderwood, David. 1842–9. *History of the Kirk of Scotland*, ed. T. Thomson and D. Laing. 8 vols. Edinburgh.
Calhoun, Joshua. 2020. *The Nature of the Page: Poetry, Papermaking, and the Ecology of Texts in Renaissance England*. Philadelphia: University of Pennsylvania Press.
Callaghan, Dympna. 2000. *Shakespeare without Women: Representing Gender and Race on the Renaissance Stage*. London: Routledge.
Camden, William. 1610. *Britannia*, trans. Philemon Holland. London.
Cao, Deborah. 2015. *Animals in China: Law and Society*. New York: Springer.
Cardano, Geronimo. 1550. *De subtiltate*. Paris.
Cawdry, Robert. 1600. *A Treasury or Storehouse of Similes*. London.
Cella, Matthew. 2013. 'The Ecosomatic Paradigm in Literature: Merging Disability Studies and Ecocriticism'. *ISLE* 20(3): 574–96.
Cèsaire, Aimè. 1969. *A Tempest*, trans. Richard Miller. Paris: Editions du Seuil.
Chakrabarty, Dipesh. 2009. 'The Climate of History: Four Theses'. *Critical Inquiry* 35: 197–222.
Chambers, E. K. 1903. *The Medieval Stage*. Oxford: Oxford University Press.
Chambers, E. K. 1923. *The Elizabethan Stage*. 4 vols. Oxford: Oxford University Press.
Chapman, Alison. 2004. 'Flaying Bartholomew: Jonson's Hagiographic Parody'. *Modern Philology* 101(4): 511–41.
Charnes, Linda. 2000. 'The Hamlet Formerly Known as Prince'. In *Shakespeare and Modernity*, ed. Hugh Grady, 189–210. New York: Routledge.
Charney, Maurice. 1961. *Shakespeare's Roman Plays: The Function of Imagery in the Drama*. Cambridge, MA: Harvard University Press.
Chiari, Sophie. 2015. '"The Dyer's Hand": Colours in Early Modern England—General Introduction, 'Chamelion like' England'. *Revue Électronique D'Études Sur Le Monde Anglophone* 12(2). Web. https://journals.openedition.org/erea/4331
Chiari, Sophie. 2019. *Shakespeare's Representation of Weather, Climate, and Environment: The Early Modern 'Fated Sky'*. Edinburgh: Edinburgh University Press.
Chiari, Sophie and John Mucciolo, eds. 2019. *Performances at Court in the Age of Shakespeare*. Cambridge: Cambridge University Press.
Chorost, Michael. 1991. 'Biological Finance in *Timon of Athens*'. *English Literary Renaissance* 21(2): 349–70.
Clover, Charles, 2004. *The End of the Line: How Overfishing Is Changing the World and What We Eat*. London: Ebury Press.
Clucas, Stephen. 2003. '"Wondrous Force and Operation": Magic, Science, and Religion in the Renaissance'. In *Textures of Renaissance Knowledge*, ed. Philippa Berry and Margaret Tudeau-Clayton, 35–57. Manchester: Manchester University Press.
Coghill, Nevill. 1958. 'Six Points of Stage-Craft in *The Winter's Tale*'. *Shakespeare Survey* 11: 31–41.
Cohen, Jeffery J., ed. 1996. *Monster Theory: Reading Culture*. Minneapolis: University of Minnesota Press.

Cohen, Jeffrey J., ed. 2013. *Prismatic Ecology: Ecotheory beyond Green*. Minneapolis: University of Minnesota Press.
Cohen, Jeffrey J. 2015. *Stone: An Ecology of the Inhuman*. Minneapolis: University of Minnesota Press.
Coldewey, John C. 1994. 'The Non-Cycle Plays and the East Anglian Tradition'. *The Cambridge Companion to Medieval English Theatre*, ed. Richard Beadle, 189–210. Cambridge: Cambridge University Press.
Colgrave, Bertram, ed. 1956. *Felix's Life of Saint Guthlac*. Cambridge: Cambridge University Press.
Connolly, Annaliese and Lisa Hopkins. 2015. 'A Darker Shade of Pale: Webster's Winter Whiteness'. *Revue Électronique D'Études Sur Le Monde Anglophone* 12(2). Web. https://journals.openedition.org/erea/4331
Conrad, Joseph. 1899. *Heart of Darkness and Other Tales*. Oxford: Oxford University Press, 2002.
Constantini-Cornède, Anne-Marie. 2015. 'Green Worlds: Shakespeare's Plays and Early Modern Imagery'. *Revue Électronique D'Études Sur Le Monde Anglophone* 12(2). Web. https://journals.openedition.org/erea/4331
Cooper, Helen. 2005. 'Pursued by Bearists'. *London Review of Books* (6 January 2005). https://www.lrb.co.uk/the-paper/v27/n01/letters.
Copenhaver, Brian. 1992. 'Did Science Have a Renaissance?' *Isis* 83(3): 387–407.
Cormack, Bradin. 2007. *A Power to Do Justice: Jurisdiction, English Literature and the Rise of Common Law*. Chicago: University of Chicago Press.
Cormack, Bradin et al. 2013. *Shakespeare and the Law*, Chicago: University of Chicago Press.
Corrigan, Bruce Jay. 2004. *Playhouse Law in Shakespeare's World*. Madison, NJ. Farleigh Dickinson.
Cottingham, John. 1990. 'Descartes on Colour'. *Proceedings of the Aristotelian Society* 90: 231–46.
Cox, Catherine. 2008. '"Lord Have Mercy Upon Us": The King, the Pestilence, and Shakespeare's *Measure for Measure*'. *Exemplaria* 20(4): 430–57.
Cramsie, John. 2002. *Kingship and Crown Finance under James VI and I*. Woodbridge: Boydell and Brewer.
Cramsie, John. 2006. 'The Philosophy of Imperial Kingship and the Interpretation of James VI and I'. In *James VI and I: Ideas, Authority, and Government*, ed. Ralph Houlbrooke, 43–60. Aldershot: Ashgate.
Crane, Mary Thomas. 2014. *Losing Touch with Nature: Literature and the New Science in Sixteenth-Century England*. Baltimore: Johns Hopkins University Press.
Creighton, Charles. 1965. *A History of Epidemics in Britain*. 2 vols. Cambridge: Cambridge University Press.
Cressy, David. 2011. 'Saltpetre, State Security, and Vexation'. *Past & Present* 212: 73–111.
Cressy, David. 2016. 'Trouble with Gypsies in Early Modern England'. *Historical Journal* 59(1): 45–70.
Croft, Pauline. 2003. *King James*. New York: Palgrave Macmillan.
Crosse, Henry. 1603. *Vertues Commonwealth*. London.
Cull, Marisa. 2014. *Shakespeare's Prince of Wales: English Identity and the Welsh Connection*. Oxford: Oxford University Press.
Curran, Kevin. 2009. *Marriage, Performance, and Politics at the Jacobean Court*. Aldershot: Ashgate.
Curry, W. C. 1959. *Shakespeare's Philosophical Patterns*. Albany: State University of New York Press.

Cushing, G. F. 1977. 'The Bear in Ob-Ugrian Folklore'. *Folklore* 88(2): 146–59.
Dahl, Marcus, Marina Tarlinskaya, and Brian Vickers. 2010. 'An Enquiry into Middleton's Supposed "Adaptation" of *Macbeth*'. Web. https://thomasmiddleton.org/wp-content/uploads/2014/04/enquiry.pdf.
Daly, Peter M. 1978. 'Of Macbeth, Martlets, and Other Fowles of Heaven'. *Mosaic* 12(1): 23–46.
Darby, H. C. 1940. *The Draining of the Fens*. Cambridge: Cambridge University Press.
D'Arcy, Gordon. 2021. 'Glenconkeyne: How Ireland's Largest Native Woodland Became the Timber Yard of the Plantation of Ulster'. *New Hibernia Review* 25(2): 89–107.
Davenant, William. 1674. *Macbeth*. London.
Davidoff, J., I. R. L. Davies, and D. Roberson. 1999. 'Colour Categories in a Stone-Age Tribe'. *Nature* 398: 203–4.
Davison, Francis, ed. 1602. A *Poetical Rhapsody*. London.
Dawson, Anthony and Gretchen Minton, eds. 2008. *Timon of Athens*. London: Cengage.
Decamp, Eleanor. 2018. 'In Such Abundance…That It Fills a Bason: Early Modern Bleeding Bowls'. In *Blood Matters*, ed. Bonnie Lander Johnson and Eleanor Decamp, 167–80. Philadelphia: University of Pennsylvania Press.
Dee, John. 1577. *The Perfecte Art of Navigation*. London.
Degenhardt, Jane Hwang. 2020. 'Performing the Sea: Fortune, Risk, and Audience Engagement in *Pericles*'. *Renaissance Drama* 48(1): 103–29.
Dekker, Thomas. 1608. *Lanthorne and Candlelight*. London.
Dekker, Thomas. 1628. *Britannia's Honor*. London.
De Quincey, Thomas. 1949. *Selected Writings*, ed. Philip Van Doren Stern, 1090–5. New York: Random House.
Derrida, Jacques. 1993. *Spectres of Marx*, trans. Peggy Kamuf. London: Routledge.
Derrida, Jacques. 2011. *The Beast and the Sovereign*, trans. Geoffrey Bennington. 2 vols. Chicago: University of Chicago Press.
Desai, R. W. 1996. '"What Means Sicilia? He Something Seems Unsettled": Sicily, Russia, and Bohemia in *The Winter's Tale*'. *Comparative Drama* 30(3): 311–24.
De Somogyi, Nick. 2018. 'Shakespeare and the Naming of Bears'. *New Theatre Quarterly* 34(3): 216–34.
Dickey, Stephen. 1991. 'Shakespeare's Mastiff Comedy'. *Shakespeare Quarterly* 42(3): 255–75.
Dillon, Janette. 2010. *The Language of Space in Court Performance 1400–1625*. Cambridge: Cambridge University Press.
Doelman, James. 2000. *King James I and the Religious Culture of England*. Woodbridge: D. S. Brewer.
Dowcra, Henry. 2003. *Dowcra's Derry: A Narration of Events in Northwest Ulster 1600–04*, ed. William Kelly. Belfast: Ulster Historical Foundation.
Dowden, Edward. 1876. *Poems*. London: Henry King.
Dowden, Edward. 1878. *Shakespeare*. New York: D. Appleton.
Dowden, Edward, ed. 1903. *Cymbeline*. London: Methuen.
Drayton, Michael. 1612, 1622. *Poly-Olbion*, ed. J. Willam Hebel. Oxford: Shakespeare Head Press, 1933.
Duckert, Lowell. 2013. '"Exit Pursued by a Bear": More to Follow'. *Upstart: A Journal of English Renaissance Studies*. Web. https://upstart.sites.clemson.edu/Essays/exit-pursued-by-a-polar-bear/exit-pursued-by-a-polar-bear.xhtml.
Duckert, Lowell. 2017. *For All Waters: Finding Ourselves in Early Modern Wetscapes*. Minneapolis: University of Minnesota Press.
Duckert, Lowell. 2019. '*Pericles*'s Deep Ecology'. *Studies in English Literature* 59(2): 367–81.

Duffy, Eamon. 2005. *The Stripping of the Altars: Traditional Religion in England 1400–1580*. New Haven: Yale University Press.
Dugdale, Gilbert. 1604. *The Time Triumphant*. London.
Dugdale, William. 1662. *History of Imbanking and Drayning of Divers Fenns and Marshes*. London.
Dulac, Anne-Valérie. 2020. 'The Impact of Climate on Early Modern Watercolours'. *The Representation of Natural Disasters in Early Modern Literature Conference*. 1–3 October 2020. Université Clermont Auvergne. https://weather.hypotheses.org/2981.
Dunbar, Judith, ed. 2010. *The Winter's Tale: Shakespeare in Performance*. Manchester: Manchester University Press.
Duncan-Jones, Katherine. 2001. *Ungentle Shakespeare: Scenes from His Life*. London: Thomson.
Dugan, Holly. 2013. '"To Bark with Judgment": Playing Baboon in Early Modern London'. *Shakespeare Studies* 41: 77–93.
Dunning, Chester. 1989. 'James I, the Muscovy Company, and the Plan to Establish a Protectorate over North Russia'. *Albion* 21(2): 206–26.
Dunning Chester. 2007. '"A Singular Affection for Russia": Why King James Offered to Intervene in the Times of Troubles'. *Russian History* 34: 277–302.
Dustagheer, Sarah. 2014. 'Acoustic and Visual Practices Indoors'. In *Moving Shakespeare Indoors*, ed. Andrew Gurr and Farah Karim-Cooper, 137–51. Cambridge: Cambridge University Press.
Dutton, Richard, ed. 1995. *Jacobean Civic Pageants*. Bodmin: Keele University Press.
Dutton, Richard. 2016. *Shakespeare, Court Dramatist*. Oxford: Oxford University Press.
Edelman, Lee. 2004. *No Future: Queer Theory and the Death Drive*. Durham: Duke University Press.
Egan, Gabriel. 2006. *Green Shakespeare: From Ecopolitics to Ecocriticism*. New York: Routledge.
Egan, Gabriel. 2015. *Shakespeare and Ecocritical Theory*. London: Bloomsbury.
Ekirch, E. Roger. 2005. *At Day's Close: Night in Times Past*. New York: Norton.
Eklund, Hilary, ed. 2017. *Ground-Work: English Renaissance Literature and Soil Science*. Pittsburgh: Duquesne University Press.
Elden, Stuart. 2018. *Shakespearean Territories*. Chicago: University of Chicago Press.
Emery, Frank. 1967. 'The Farming Regions of Wales'. In *Agrarian History of England and Wales*, ed. Joan Thirsk, 113–60. 4 vols. Cambridge: Cambridge University Press.
Ensor, Sarah. 2012. 'Spinster Ecology: Rachel Carson, Sarah Orne Jewett and Nonreproductive Futurity'. *American Literature* 84(2): 409–35.
Erskine, Frances. N.d. *Memoirs relating to the Queen of Bohemia*. Privately Printed.
Es, Bart van. 2014. 'Reviving the Legacy of Indoor Performance'. In *Moving Shakespeare Indoors: Performance and Repertoire in the Jacobean Playhouse*, ed. Andrew Gurr and Farah Karim-Cooper, 237–51. Cambridge.
Estok, Simon. 2011. *Ecocriticism and Shakespeare: Reading Ecophobia*. New York: Palgrave Macmillan.
Estok, Simon. 2015. 'Queerly Green: From Meaty to Meatless Days and Nights in *Timon of Athens*'. In *Ecological Approaches to Early Modern English Texts: A Field Guide to Reading and Teaching*, ed. Jennifer Munroe et al., 91–8. Farnham: Ashgate.
Evans, Robert C. 1994. *Jonson in the Context of His Time*. Lewisburg, PA: Bucknell University Press.
Evans, William David, ed. 1836. *A Collection of Statutes*. 10 vols. London.
Everett, Nigel. 2015. *The Woods of Ireland: A History, 700–1800*. Dublin: Four Courts.
Falk, Dan. 2014. *The Science of Shakespeare*. New York: St Martin's.

Fanon, Frantz. 1967. *Black Skin, White Masks*, trans. C. L. Markmann. New York: Grove.
Fairnell, E. H. 2008. '101 Ways to Skin a Fur-Bearing Animal'. In *Experiencing Archaeology by Experiment*, ed. P. Cunningham et al., 47–60. Oxford: Oxbow.
Feerick, Jean and Vin Nardizzi, eds. 2012. *The Indistinct Human in Renaissance Literature*. New York: Palgrave Macmillan.
Felperin, Howard. 1967. 'Shakespeare's Miracle Play'. *Shakespeare Quarterly* 18(4): 363–74.
Ferguson, Arthur B. 1969. 'John Twyne: A Tudor Humanist and the Problem of Legend'. *Journal of British Studies* 9(1): 24–44.
Field, Jemma. 2017. 'The Wardrobe Goods of Anna of Denmark, Queen Consort of Scotland and England'. *Costume* 51(1): 3–27.
Fielder, Leslie. 1973. *The Stranger in Shakespeare*. New York: Stein and Day.
Finlay, Roger and Beatrice Shearer. 1986. 'Population Growth and Suburban Expansion'. In *London 1500–1700: The Making of the Metropolis*, ed. A. L. Beier and Roger Finlay, 37–59. London: Longman.
Fischlin, Daniel and Mark Fortier, eds. 2002. *Royal Subjects: Essays on the Writings of King James VI and I*. Detroit: Wayne State University Press.
Fisher, R. H. 1943. *The Russian Fur Trade 1550–1700*. Berkeley: University of California Press.
Fitter, Chris. 1995. *Poetry, Space, Landscape: Towards a New Theory*. Cambridge: Cambridge University Press.
Flahiff, Frederick T. 1986. 'Lear's Map'. *Cahiers Elisabethains* 30: 17–33.
Fletcher, Giles. 1591. *Of the Russian Commonwealth*. London.
Fletcher, John. 1640. *The Night-walker*. London.
Flood, Victoria. 2018. 'Prophecy as History: A New Study of the Prophecies of Merlin Silvester'. *Neophilogus* 102(4): 543–59.
Floyd-Wilson, Mary. 2003. *English Ethnicity and Race in Early Modern Drama*. Cambridge: Cambridge University Press.
Floyd-Wilson, Mary. 2006. 'English Epicures and Scottish Witches'. *Shakespeare Quarterly* 57(2): 131–61.
Forker, Charles. 1985. 'The Green Underworld of Early Shakespearean Tragedy'. *Shakespeare Studies* 17: 25–47.
Forman, Valerie. 2013. *Tragicomic Redemptions: Global Economics and the Early Modern English Stage*. Philadelphia. University of Pennsylvania Press.
Foucault, Michel. 1979. *Discipline and Punish: The Birth of the Prison*, trans. Alan Sheridan. New York: Pantheon.
Fouquet, Roger and Peter Pearson. 2006. 'Seven Centuries of Energy Services: The Price and Use of Light in the United Kingdom (1300–2000)'. *Energy Journal* 27(1): 139–77.
Fox, Adam. 2009. 'Sir William Petty, Ireland, and the Making of a Political Economist, 1653–1687'. *Economic History Review* 62: 388–404.
Fremaux, Anne. 2019. *After the Anthropocene: Green Republicanism in a Post-Capitalist World*. New York: Springer.
French, Peter. 1972. *John Dee: The World of an Elizabethan Magus*. London: Routledge.
Freud, Sigmund. 1930. *Civilization and Its Discontents*. New York: Norton, 2010.
Friehs, Julia T. 2010. 'The Kunst-und Wunderkammer of Emperor Rudolf II'. *The World of the Habsburgs*. Web. https://www.habsburger.net/en/chapter/kunst-und-wunderkammer-emperor-rudolf-ii.
Frye, Northrop. 1957. *Anatomy of Criticism*. Princeton: Princeton University Press.
Fuchs, Barbara. 1997. 'Conquering Islands, Contextualizing *The Tempest*'. *Shakespeare Quarterly* 48(1): 45–62.
Fudge, Erica. 2000. 'Screaming Monkeys: The Creatures in the Bear Garden'. In *Perceiving Animals*, ed. Erica Fudge, 11–33. Basingstoke: Palgrave Macmillan.

Fudge, Erica. 2004. *Animal*. London: Reaktion.
Fudge, Erica. 2012. 'Renaissance Animal Things'. *New Formations* 76: 86–100.
Fuller, Thomas. 1840. *History of the University of Cambridge*. London.
Galeano, Eduardo. 2009. *Mirrors: Stories of Almost Everyone*, trans. Mark Fried. New York: Nation Books.
Garganigo, Alex. 2002. '*Coriolanus*, the Union Controversy, and Access to the Royal Person'. *Studies in English Literature* 42(2): 335–59.
Geikie, Archibald. 1916. *Birds of Shakespeare*. Glasgow: James Maclehose.
Geisweidt, Edward. 2015. 'The Bastard Bomb: Illegitimacy and Population in Thomas Middleton's *Chaste Maid in Cheapside*'. In *Ecologcal Approaches to Early Modern English Texts*, ed. Jennifer Munroe et al. Farnham: Ashgate.
George, David. 2000. 'Plutarch, Insurrection, and Dearth in *Coriolanus*'. *Shakespeare Survey* 53: 63–72.
Gerald of Wales. 1978. *The Journey through Wales and the Description of Wales*, ed. Lewis Thorpe. London: Penguin.
Gesner, Conrad. 1937. *On the Admiration of Mountains*, trans. H. D. B. Soulè. San Francisco: Grabhorn Press.
Giblett, Rod. 2016. *Cities and Wetlands: The Return of the Repressed in Nature and Culture*. London: Bloomsbury.
Giesekes, Edward. 2007. ' "From Wronger and Wronged Have I Fee": Thomas Middleton and Early Modern Legal Culture'. In *Thomas Middleton and Early Modern Textual Culture*, ed. Gary Taylor and John Lavagnino, 110–18. Oxford: Clarendon.
Gillen, Katherine. 2018. 'Shakespeare in the Capitalocene: *Titus Andronicus, Timon of Athens*, and Early Modern Eco-Theater'. *Exemplaria* 30(4): 275–92.
Gillies, John. 1994. *Shakespeare and the Geography of Difference*. Cambridge: Cambridge University Press.
Gillies, John. 2003. 'Place and Space in Three Late Plays'. In *A Companion to Shakespeare's Works: Vol. IV, The Poems, Problem Comedies, Late Plays*, ed. Richard Dutton and Jean Howard, 175–93. Oxford: Blackwell.
Gillies, W., ed. 1969. 'A Poem on the Downfall of the Gaoidhil'. *Éigse* 13: 203–10.
Goldberg, Jonathan. 1983. *James I and the Politics of Literature*. Baltimore: Johns Hopkins University Press.
Goldberg, Jonathan. 2004. *Tempest in the Caribbean*. Minneapolis: University of Minnesota Press.
Goodare, Julian. 1999. 'Thomas Foulis and the Scottish Fiscal Crisis of the 1590s'. In *Crises, Revolutions and Self-Sustained Growth: Essays on Fiscal History, 1130–1830*, ed. W. M. Ormrod et al., 170–97. Stamford: Paul Watkins.
Goodare, Julian. 2004. 'Thomas Foulis'. *ODNB*. Web.
Gordon, D. J. 1964. 'Name and Fame: Shakespeare's *Coriolanus*'. In *Papers Mainly Shakespearian*, ed. G. I. Duthie, 40–57. London: Oliver and Boyd.
Gossett, Suzanne, ed. 2004. *Pericles*. London: Bloomsbury.
Grady, Hugh. 1993. 'Containment, Subversion, and Postmodernism'. *Textual Practice* 7: 31–49.
Grady, Hugh. 2009. *Shakespeare and Impure Aesthetics*. Cambridge: Cambridge University Press.
Grant, Teresa. 2001. 'White Bears in *Mucedorus, The Winter's Tale*, and *Oberon*'. *Notes and Queries* 246: 311–13.
Grantley, Darryll. 'Saints' Plays'. 1994. *The Cambridge Companion to Medieval English Theatre*, ed. Richard Beadle, 265–89. Cambridge: Cambridge University Press.
Graves, Robert B. 1999. *Lighting the Shakespearean Stage 1567–1642*. Carbondale, IL: Southern Illinois University Press.

The Great Fen Project. 2010. Web. www.greatfen.org.uk.
Greenblatt, Stephen. 1990. *Learning to Curse: Essays in Early Modern Culture.* New York: Routledge.
Greenfield, Amy Butler. 2007. *A Perfect Red: Empire, Espionage, and the Quest for the Color of Desire.* New York: Harper Collins.
Griffin, Emma. 2007. *Blood Sport: Hunting in Britain since 1066.* New Haven: Yale University Press.
Griffiths, Paul. 1998. 'Meanings of Nightwalking in Early Modern England'. *The Seventeenth Century* 13(2): 212–38.
Griffiths, Paul. 2008 *Lost Londons: Change, Crime, and Control in the Capital City, 1550–1660.* Cambridge: Cambridge University Press.
Grigson, Caroline. 2016. *Menagerie: The History of Exotic Animals in England, 1100–1837.* Oxford: Oxford University Press.
Griswold, Jeffrey. 2019. 'Macbeth's Thick Night and the Political Ecology of a Dark Scotland'. *Critical Survey* 31(3): 31–43.
Grossman, Joanna. 2014. 'Timon of Ashes'. *Journal of Ecocriticism* 6(2). Web. https://ojs.unbc.ca/index.php/joe/article/view/569
Grotius, Hugo. 1609. *Mare Liberum,* trans. Richard Hakluyt. Indianapolis: Liberty Fund, 2004.
Guerzoni, Guido Antonio. 2012 'The Use and Abuse of Beeswax in the Early Modern Age'. In *Waxing Eloquent: Italian Portraits in Wax,* ed. A. Daninos, 43–59. Milan: Officina Libraria.
Guilpin, Edward. *Skialethia.* London, 1598.
Gurr, Andrew. 1983. 'The Bear, the Statue, and Hysteria in *The Winter's Tale*'. *Shakespeare Quarterly* 34(4): 420–5.
Gurr, Andrew. 1987. 'Intertextuality at Windsor'. *Shakespeare Quarterly* 38(2): 189–200.
Gurr, Andrew. 1996a. *Play-Going in Shakespeare's London.* Cambridge: Cambridge University Press.
Gurr, Andrew. 1996b. *The Shakespearian Playing Companies.* Oxford: Clarendon.
Gurr, Andrew. 2004. 'Bears and Players: Philip Henslowe's Double Acts'. *Shakespeare Bulletin* 22(4): 31–41.
Gurr, Andrew. 2009a. *The Shakespearean Stage 1574–1642.* Cambridge: Cambridge University Press.
Gurr, Andrew. 2009b. *Shakespeare's Opposites: The Admiral's Company 1594–1625.* Cambridge: Cambridge University Press.
Gurr, Andrew. 2014. 'Sources and Creativity in *The Tempest*'. In *The Tempest: A Critical Reader,* ed. Alden and Virginia Vaughan, 93–114. London: Bloomsbury.
H. C. 1629. *A Discourse Concerning the Drayning of the Fennes.* London.
Hadfield, Andrew. 2003. 'Timon of Athens and Jacobean Politics'. *Shakespeare Survey* 56: 215–26.
Hadfield, Andrew. 2005. *Shakespeare and Republicanism.* Cambridge: Cambridge University Press.
Haigh, Christopher. *English Reformations: Religion, Politics, and Society under the Tudors.* New York: Oxford University Press, 1993.
Hall, Grace R. W. 1999. *The Tempest as Mystery Play: Uncovering the Religious Sources of Shakespeare's Most Spiritual Work.* Jefferson, NC: McFarland & Co.
Hall, Joseph. 1630. *Occasional Meditations.* London.
Hall, Kim. 1995. *Things of Darkness: Economies of Race and Gender in Early Modern England.* Ithaca: Cornell University Press.

Hamilton, Jennifer Mae. 2017. *This Contentious Storm: An Ecocritical and Performance History of* King Lear. London: Bloomsbury.
Hammond, Brean, ed. 2010. *Double Falsehood*. London: Methuen.
Hammond, Paul. 1986. 'The Argument of *Measure for Measure*'. *ELR* 16(3): 496–516.
Haraway, Donna. 2007. *When Species Meet*. Minneapolis: University of Minnesota Press.
Haraway, Donna. 2016. *Staying with the Trouble: Making Kin in the Cthulucene*. Durham: Duke University Press.
Harbage, Alfred, Samuel Schoenbaum, and Sylvia Wagonheim, eds. 1989. *Annals of English Drama*. London: Routledge.
Harington, John. 1804. *Nugae Antiquae*, ed. Henry Harrington. 2 vols. London.
Harkness, Deborah. 2007. *The Jewel House: Elizabethan London and the Scientific Revolution*. New Haven: Yale University Press.
Harris, F. W. 1980. 'The Rebellion of Sir Cahir O'Doherty and Its Legal Aftermath'. *Irish Jurist* 15(2): 298–325.
Harris, Jonathan Gil. 2009. *Untimely Matter in the Time of Shakespeare*. Philadelphia: University of Pennsylvania Press.
Harrison, Robert Pogue. 1992. *Forests: Shadows of Civilization*. Chicago: University of Chicago Press.
Harrison, William. 1577. *The Description of England*, ed. Georges Edelen. Washington, DC: Folger, 1994.
Harsnett, Samuel. 1599. *A Discovery of the Fraudulent Practices of John Darrell*. London.
Hart, Vaughan. 1994. *Art and Magic in the Court of the Stuarts*. London: Routledge.
Harting, James Edmund. 1871. *The Ornithology of Shakespeare*. London: John Van Voorst.
Hartlib, Samuel. 1655. *His Legacy of Husbandry*. London.
Harvey, John. 1588. *A Discoursive Problem Concerning Prophecies*. London.
Hawkins, Shearman. 1967. 'The Two Worlds of Shakespearean Comedy'. *Shakespeare Studies* 3: 62–80.
Hazlitt, William. 1838. *Characters of Shakespeare's Plays*. London: Templeman.
Hazlitt, William. 1882. *Second Series of Bibliographic Collections and Notes on English Literature*. London.
Heidegger, Martin. 1993. *Basic Writings*, ed. David Krell. San Francisco: HarperSanFrancisco.
Heise, Ursula. 2001. 'The Virtual Crowds: Overpopulation, Space and Speciesism'. *ISLE: Interdisciplinary Studies in Literature and the Environment* 8(1): 1–29
Heise, Ursula. 2008. *Sense of Place, Sense of Planet: The Environmental Imagination of the Global*. Oxford: Oxford University Press.
Helgerson, Richard. 1992. *Forms of Nationhood: The Elizabethan Writing of England*. Chicago: University of Chicago Press.
Hengerer, Mark and Nadir Weber, eds. 2020. *Animals and Courts: Europe c. 1200–1800*. Berlin: De Gruyter.
Herford, C. H. and Percy and Evelyn Simpson, eds. 1925–52. *Ben Jonson*. 11 vols. Oxford: Clarendon.
Heresbach, Conrad. 1577. *Four Books of Husbandry*. London.
Hess, Andrew C. 2000. 'The Mediterranean and Shakespeare's Geopolitical Imagination'. In *The Tempest and Its Travels*, ed. Peter Hulme and William H. Sherman, 121–30. Philadelphia: University of Pennsylvania Press.
Higginbotham, Jennifer. 2013. *The Girlhood of Shakespeare's Sisters*. Edinburgh: Edinburgh University Press.

Hill, Christopher. 1972. *The World Turned Upside Down*. London: Penguin.
Hiltner, Ken. 2011. *What Else Is Pastoral?* Ithaca: Cornell University Press.
Hinchman, Lewis and Sandra Hinchman. 2001. 'Should Environmentalists Reject the Enlightenment?' *Review of Politics* 63(4): 663–92.
Hindle, Steve. 2008. 'Imagining Insurrection in Seventeenth-Century England: Representations of the Midlands Rising of 1607'. *History Workshop Journal* 66: 21–61.
Hirsch, Brett. 2010. 'From Jew to Puritan: The Emblematic Owl in Early English Culture'. In *'This Earthly Stage': World and Stage in Late Medieval and Early Modern England*, ed. Brett Hirsch and C. Wortham, 131–71. Turnhout: Brepols.
Höfele, Andreas. 2011. *Stage, Stake, and Scaffold: Humans and Animals in Shakespeare's Theatre*. Oxford: Oxford University Press.
Holinshed, Raphael. 1587. *Chronicles of England, Scotland, and Ireland*. London: Folio. 2012.
Holland, Peter. 2005. 'Coasting in the Mediterranean: The Journeyings of *Pericles*'. In *Charting Shakespearean Waters: Text and Theatre*, ed. Sos Haugaard, 11–30. Copenhagen: Museum Tusculanum.
Holland Peter, ed. 2013. *Coriolanus*. London: Bloomsbury.
Honigmann, E. A. J. 1985. *Shakespeare: The 'Lost Years'*. Manchester: Manchester University Press.
Hopkins, Lisa. 2004. 'Cleopatra and the Myth of Scota'. In *Antony and Cleopatra: New Critical Essays*, ed. Sara Munston Deats, 231–42. London: Routledge.
Hopkins, Lisa. 2005. *Shakespeare on the Edge: Border-Crossings in the Tragedies and the Henriad*. London: Routledge.
Hopkins, Lisa. 2010. '*Cymbeline*, the *translatio imperii*, and the Matter of Britain'. In *Shakespeare and Wales*, ed. Willy Maley and Philip Schwyzer, 143–56. London: Routledge.
Hopkins, Lisa. 2011. *Drama and the Succession to the Crown 1561–1633*. Farnham: Ashgate.
Horn, Darwin. 1987. 'Tiddy Mun's Curse: The Ecological Consequences of Land Reclamation'. *Folklore* 98(1): 11–15.
Houlbrooke, Ralph. 2006. 'James' Reputation: 1625–2005'. In *James VI and I: Ideas, Authority, and Government*, ed. R. Houlbrooke, 163–90. Farnham: Ashgate.
Howard, Deborah. 1992. 'Elsheimer's Flight into Egypt and the Night Sky in the Renaissance'. *Zeitschrift für Kunstgeschichte* 55(2): 212.
Howard, Jean. 2007. *Theater of a City: The Places of London Comedy*. Philadelphia: University of Pennsylvania Press.
Howell, James. 1907. *Epistolae Hoeliane*. Boston: Houghton Mifflin.
Hull, Robin. 2007. *Scottish Mammals*. Edinburgh: Birlinn.
Hulme, Peter and William H. Sherman, eds. 2000. *The Tempest and Its Travels*. Philadelphia: University of Pennsylvania Press.
Hunt, Maurice. 2004. 'Bearing Hence: Shakespeare's *The Winter's Tale*'. *Studies in English Literature* 44(2): 333–46.
Hutchinson, E. P. 1967. *The Population Debate: The Development of Conflicting Theories Up to 1900*. New York: Houghton Mifflin.
Hutson, Lorna. ed. 2017. *The Oxford Handbook of English Law and Literature*. Oxford: Oxford University Press.
Ingamells, John. 2008. *Dulwich Picture Gallery Collections*. London: Unicorn.
Iopollo, Grace, ed. 2010. *Measure for Measure*. New York: Norton.
Ives, E. W. 1986. *Anne Boleyn*. Oxford: Blackwell.
Iyengar, Sujata. 2005. *Shades of Difference: Mythologies of Skin Color in Early Modern England*. Philadelphia: University of Pennsylvania Press.

Iyengar, Sujata. 2014. 'Shakespeare's Embodied Ontology of Gender, Air, Health'. In *Disability, Health, and Happiness in the Shakespearean Body*, ed. Sujata Iyengar. New York: Routledge.
James I. 1965. *The Political Works of James I*, ed. Charles Howard McIlwain. New York: Russell & Russell.
James I. 1994. *Political Writings*, ed. Johann Sommerville. Cambridge: Cambridge University Press.
James, Maureen. 2013. Investigating *The Legends of the Carrs*: A Study of the Tales as Printed in *Folklore* in 1891'. PhD Thesis, University of Glamorgan.
James, Richard. 1636. *Iter Lancastrense*, ed. Thomas Courser. Chetham Society. 1845.
Jayne, Sears and Francis R. Johnson, eds. 1956. *The Lumley Library: The Catalogue of 1609*. London: British Museum.
Jaywardene, S. A. 1965. 'Rafael Bombelli, Engineer-Architect: Some Unpublished Documents of the Apostolic Camera'. *Isis* 56(3): 298–306.
Jones, Anne Rosalind and Peter Stallybrass. 2000. *Renaissance Clothing and the Materials of Memory*. Cambridge: Cambridge University Press.
Jones, Emrys. 1961. 'Stuart Cymbeline'. *Essays in Criticism* 11: 84–99.
Jones. Gwilym. 2013. 'The Problem of the Heath'. *Globe Education*. Web
Jones, Gwilym. 2015. *Shakespeare's Storms*. Manchester: Manchester University Press.
Jones, Gwilym. 2017. 'Environmental Renaissance Studies'. *Literature Compass* 14(10): e12407.
Jordan, Constance. 1997. *Shakespeare's Monarchies: Ruler and Subject in the Romances*. Ithaca: Cornell University Press.
Jordan, Constance and Karen Cunningham, eds. 2006. *The Law in Shakespeare*. Palgrave Macmillan.
Jowett, John, ed. 2004a. *Timon of Athens*. Oxford.
Jowett, John. 2004b. 'Timon and Mining'. *Seideri* 14: 77–92.
Kahn, Coppelia. 1987, '"Magic of Bounty": *Timon of Athens*, Jacobean Patronage, and Maternal Power'. *Shakespeare Quarterly* 38(1): 34–57.
Kamps, Ivo and Karen Raber, eds. 2004. *Measure for Measure*. Boston: Bedford/St Martins.
Kaplan, M. Lindsay and Katherine Eggert. 1994. '"Good Queen, My Lord, Good Queen": Sexual Slander and the Trials of Female Authority in *The Winter's Tale*'. *Renaissance Drama* 25: 89–118.
Karim-Cooper, Farah. 2014. '"To Glisten in a Playhouse": Cosmetic Beauty Indoors'. In *Moving Shakespeare Indoors*, ed. Andrew Gurr and Farah Karim-Cooper, 184–200. Cambridge, Cambridge University Press.
Kastan, David Scott. 1999. *Shakespeare after Theory*. New York: Routledge.
Katritzky, M. A. 2014. '"A Plague o' These Pickle Herring": From London Drinkers to European Stage Clowns'. In *Renaissance Shakespeare/Shakespeare Renaissances: Proceedings of the Ninth World Shakespeare Congress*, 159–68. University of Delaware Press.
Kermode, Frank, ed. 1954. *The Tempest*. London: Methuen.
Kernan, Alvin. 1995. *Shakespeare, the King's Playwright: Theater in the Stuart Court, 1603–1613*. New Haven: Yale University Press.
Kerridge, Richard. 2011. 'An Ecocritic's *Macbeth*'. In *Ecocritical Shakespeare*, ed. Lynne Bruckner and Dan Brayton, 193–210. Farnham: Ashgate.
Kerrigan, John. 2008. *Archipelagic English*. Oxford: Oxford University Press.
Kiernan, Victor. 1996. *Eight Tragedies of Shakespeare: A Marxist Study*. London: Verso.
Kippis, Andrew. 1784. *Biographia Britannica*. 3 vols. London.
Kirwan, Peter. 2013. '*Mucedorus*'. In *The Elizabethan Top Ten*, ed. Andy Kesson and Emma Smith, 223–34. Farnham: Ashgate.

Klein, Bernhard. 2001. *Maps and the Writing of Space in Early Modern England and Ireland*. Basingstoke: Palgrave Macmillan.
Klein, Bernhard. 2016. 'The Sea in *Pericles*'. In *Shakespeare and Space. Theatrical Explorations of the Spatial Paradigm*, ed. Ina Habermann and Michelle Witen, 121–40. Basingstoke: Palgrave Macmillan.
Knapp, Margaret and Michal Kobialka. 1984. 'Shakespeare and the Prince of Purpoole: The 1594 Production of *The Comedy of Errors* at Gray's Inn Hall'. *Theatre History Studies* 4: 70–81.
Knight, G. Wilson. 1947. *The Crown of Life: Essays in the Interpretation of Shakespeare's Final Plays*. Oxford: Oxford University Press.
Knight, Leah. 2014. *Reading Green in Early Modern England*. Farnham: Ashgate.
Koelb, Janice Hewlett. 2009. '"This Most Beautiful and Adorn'd World": Nicholson's *Mountain Gloom and Mountain Glory* Reconsidered'. *ISLE* 16(3): 443–68.
Kolb, Laura. 2018. 'Debt's Poetry in *Timon of Athens*'. *Studies in English Literature* 58(2): 399–419.
Korda, Natasha. 2011. *Labors Lost: Women's Work and the Early Modern English Stage*. Philadelphia: University of Pennsylvania Press.
Koslofsky, Craig. 2011. *Evening's Empire: A History of the Night in Early Modern Europe*. Cambridge: Cambridge University Press.
Kotilaine, J. T. 2005. *Russia's Foreign Trade and Economic Expansion in the Seventeenth Century*. Leiden: Brill.
Kurland, Stuart. 1992. '"A Beggar's Book Outworths a Noble's Blood": Politics of Faction in *Henry VIII*'. *Comparative Drama* 26(3): 237–52.
Kurland, Stuart. 2013. 'Shakespeare and James I: Personal Rule and Public Responsibility'. In *Late Shakespeare, 1608-13*, ed. Chrystine Brouillet et al., 209–24. Cambridge: Cambridge University Press.
Kuzner, James. 2007. 'Unbuilding the City: *Coriolanus* and the Birth of Republican Rome'. *Shakespeare Quarterly* 58(2): 174–99.
Laing, Malcolm. 1800–4. *The History of Scotland*. 4 vols. London.
Lamming, George. 1960. *The Pleasures of Exile*. Ann Arbor: University of Michigan Press, 1992.
Langland, William. 1377. *Piers Plowman*, ed. A. V. C. Schmidt. London: Dent, 1978.
Langley, Eric. 2013. 'Postured like a Whore? Misreading Hermione's Statue'. *Renaissance Studies* 27(3): 318–40.
Laroche, Rebecca and Jennifer Munroe. 2017. *Shakespeare and Ecofeminist Theory*. London: Bloomsbury.
Latham, Jaqueline E. M. 1992. '*The Tempest* and King James' *Daemonologie*'. In *Caliban*, ed. Harold Bloom, 151–8. New York: Chelsea House.
Latour, Bruno. 2004. *Politics of Nature*, trans. Catherine Porter. Cambridge, MA: Harvard University Press.
Lawrence, Jason. 2019. 'Jacobean Royal Premeries? *Othello* and *Measure for Measure* at Whitehall in 1604'. *Performances at Court in the Age of Shakespeare*, ed. Sophie Chiari and John Mucciolo, 92–106. Cambridge: Cambridge University Press.
LePerle, Carol Mejia. 2017. '"An Unlawful Race": Shakespeare's Cleopatra and the Crimes of Early Modern Gypsies'. *Shakespeare* 13(3): 226–38
Lever, J. W., ed. 1965. *Measure for Measure*. London: Methuen.
Levin, Richard. 1978. 'The King James Version of *Measure for Measure*'. *Clio* 7: 129–63.
Lewalski, Barbara. 1993. *Writing Women in Jacobean England*. Cambridge, MA: Harvard University Press.

Lewis, Simon L. and Mark A. Maslin. 2018. *The Human Planet: How We Created the Anthropocene*. London: Pelican.
Lindley, Keith. 1982. *Fenland Riots and the English Revolution*. London: Heinemann.
Lloyd, Humphrey. 1584. *The historie of Cambria, now called Wales*. London.
Lomax, Marion. 1987. *Stage Images and Traditions: Shakespeare to Ford*. Cambridge: Cambridge University Press.
Loomba, Ania. 2002. *Shakespeare, Race, and Colonialism*. Oxford: Oxford University Press.
Louth, Charlie. 2015. 'Rilke's Sonette An Orpheus, The Tombeau, Dance, and the Adonic'. *Modern Language Review* 110(3): 724–38.
Love, Heather. 2011. 'Milk'. In *Shakesqueer: A Queer Companion to the Complete Works of Shakespeare*, ed. Madhavi Menon, 201–8. Durham: Duke University Press.
Lovegrove, Roger. 2007. *Silent Fields: The Long Decline of a Nation's Wildlife*. Oxford: Oxford University Press.
Loveridge, Andrew et al. 2006. 'Does Sport Hunting Benefit Conservation?' In *Key Topics in Conservation Biology*, ed. David W. MacDonald and Katherine J. Willis, 224–40. Oxford. Wiley-Blackwell.
Lu, Mingjun. 2018. 'The Cosmic Sublime in the Aesthetics of Longinus and Zhuangzi' *Neohelicon* 45: 689–709.
Macfarlane, Robert. 2004. *Mountains of the Mind: A History of a Fascination*. London: Granta.
MacFaul, Tom. 2015. *Shakespeare and the Natural World*. Cambridge: Cambridge University Press.
MacGregor, Arthur. 2000. 'The Household Out of Doors: The Stuart Court and the Animal Kingdom'. In *The Stuart Courts*, ed. Eveline Cruickshanks, 86–117. Stroud: History Press.
MacLeod, Catherine. 2012. *The Lost Prince: The Life and Death of Henry Stuart*. London: National Portrait Gallery.
MacRitchie, David. 1894. *Scottish Gypsies under the Stewarts*. Edinburgh.
Magnus, Olaus. 1555, 1658. *A Compendious History of the Goths, Swedes, Vandals, and Other Northern Nations*. London.
Maguin, Jean-Marie. 1995. 'Rise and Fall of the King of Darkness'. In *French Essays on Shakespeare and His Contemporaries: 'What Would France with Us?'*, ed. Jean-Marie Maguin and Michele Willems, 247–70. Newark: University of Delaware Press.
Maguire, Laurie. 2009. *Shakespeare's Names*. Oxford: Oxford University Press.
Maisano, Scott. 2014. 'Shakespeare's Revolution: *The Tempest* as Scientific Romance'. In The Tempest: *A Critical Reader*, ed. Alden and Virginia Vaughan, 165–94. London: Bloomsbury.
Malay, Jessica L. 2010. *Prophecy and Sibylline Imagery in the Renaissance*. London: Routledge.
Maley, Willy and Andrew Murphy, eds. 2004. *Shakespeare and Scotland*. Manchester: Manchester University Press.
Maley, Willy. 2007. '"A Thing Most Brutish": Depicting Shakespeare's Multi-Nation State'. *Shakespeare* 3(1): 79–101.
Maley, Willy and Philip Schwyzer, eds. 2010. *Shakespeare and Wales: From the Marches to the Assembly*. London: Routledge.
Malone, Edmond. 1808. *An Account of the incidents from which the title and part of the story of Shakespeare's* Tempest *were derived*. C & R. Baldwin: London.
Malone, Edmond et al., eds. 1821. *The Plays and Poems of William Shakespeare*. 21 vols. London: F. C. and J. Rivington, et al.
Mancall, Peter. 2007. *Hakulyt's Promise: An Elizabethan's Obsession for an English America*. New Haven: Yale University Press.

Manley, Lawrence, 1995. *Literature and Culture in Early Modern London*. Cambridge: Cambridge University Press.
Mann, Jenny C. 2021. *The Trials of Orpheus: Poetry, Science, and the Early Modern Sublime*. Princeton: Princeton University Press.
Manning, Roger. 1988. *Village Revolts: Social Protest and Popular Disturbances in England, 1509–1640*. Oxford: Clarendon.
Mannoni, Octave. 1964. *Prospero and Caliban: The Psychology of Colonization*, trans. Pamela Powesland. New York: Praeger.
Marcus, Leah. 1988. *Puzzling Shakespeare: Local Shakespeare and its Discontents*. Berkeley: University of California Press.
Mardock, James. 2010. '"Thinking to Pass Unknown": *Measure for Measure*, the Plague, and the Accession of James I'. In *Representing the Plague in Early Modern England*, ed. Rebecca Totaro and Ernest Gilman, 113–29. New York: Routledge.
Marion, Jean-Luc. 2002. *Being Given: Towards a Phenomenology of Givenness*, trans. Jeffrey Kosky, Stanford: Stanford University Press.
Marland, Pippa. 2013. 'Ecocriticism'. *Literature Compass* 10(11): 846–68.
Markham, Gervase. 1613. *The English Husbandman*. London.
Markham, Gervase. 1620. *Markham's Farewell to Husbandry, or the Enriching of All Sorts of Barren and Sterill Grounds in our Kingdome*. London.
Markham, Gervase. 1621. *Hunger's Prevention: or, The Whole Arte of Fowling*. London.
Martin, Randall. 2015. *Shakespeare and Ecology*. Oxford: Oxford University Press.
Martin, Randall. 2020. 'Ecocritical Studies'. In *Arden Research Handbook of Contemporary Shakespeare Criticism*, ed. Evelyn Gajowski, 189–204. London: Bloomsbury.
Marx, Karl. 1844. *Economic and Philosophic Manuscripts of 1844*. Moscow: Progress. 1974.
Marx, Karl. 1867. *Capital: A Student Edition*. London: Lawrence and Wishart, 1992.
Marx, Leo. 1964. *The Machine in the Garden: Technology and the Pastoral Ideal in America*. Oxford: Oxford University Press.
Marzano, Annalisa. 2013. *Harvesting the Sea: The Exploitation of Marine Resources in the Roman Mediterranean*. Oxford: Oxford University Press.
Matusiak, John. 2015. *James I: Scotland's King of England*. Stroud: History Press.
Maynard, John? 1646. *The Anti-Projector*. London.
Mbembe, Achille. 2003. 'Necropolitics'. *Public Culture* 15(1): 11–40.
McClure, Norman, ed. 1939. *The Letters of John Chamberlain*. 2 vols. Philadelphia: American Philosophical Society.
McCormick, Ted. 2016. 'Who Were the Pre-Malthusians?' In *New Perspectives on Malthus*, ed. Robert J. Mayhew, 25–51. Cambridge: Cambridge University Press.
McDermott, Kristen, ed. 2007. *Masques of Difference: Four Court Masques by Ben Jonson*. Manchester: Manchester University Press.
McDougall, Elizabeth. 2002. *Cambridgeshire Family History Society Magazine* 13(8). Web. https://www.cfhs.org.uk/index.cfm.
McEachern, Claire. 1996. *The Poetics of English Nationhood 1590–1612*. Cambridge: Cambridge University Press.
McGinnis, Michael Vincent. 1999. *Bioregionalism*. New York: Routledge.
McIlwain, Charles Howard, ed. 1965. *The Political Works of James I*. New York: Russell & Russell.
McManus, Clare. 2002. *Women on the Renaissance Stage: Anna of Denmark and Female Masquing in the Stuart Court 1590–1619*. Manchester: Manchester University Press.
McPhee, Shamus. 2017. *Gypsy Traveller History in Scotland*. https://www.iriss.org.uk/sites/default/files/2017-06/gt-timeline-A4-web.pdf.

McRae, Andrew. 2009. *Literature and Domestic Travel*. Cambridge: Cambridge University Press.
Meeker, Joseph. 1972. *The Comedy of Survival: Studies in Literary Ecology*. New York: Scribner.
Mennell, Nicole. 2017. 'Zibellini as Animal- Made Objects'. *Society for Renaissance Studies*. Web. https://www.rensoc.org.uk/2128-2.
Mentz, Steve. 2008. '"Shipwreck and Ecology": Toward a Structural Theory of Shakespearean Romance'. *Shakespearean International Yearbook* 8: 165–82.
Mentz, Steve. 2009a. 'Towards a Blue Cultural Studies: The Sea, Maritime Culture, and Early Modern English Literature'. *Literature Compass* 6(5): 997–1013.
Mentz, Steve. 2009b. *At the Bottom of Shakespeare's Ocean*. London: Continuum.
Mentz, Steve. 2010. 'Strange Weather in *King Lear*'. *Shakespeare* 6(2): 139–52.
Mentz, Steve. 2011a. 'Tongues in the Storm: Shakespeare, Ecological Crisis, and the Resources of Genre'. In *Ecocritical Shakespeare*, ed. Lynne Bruckner and Dan Brayton, 155–72. Farnham: Ashgate.
Mentz, Steve. 2011b. 'Shakespeare's Beach House, or the Green and Blue in Macbeth'. *Shakespeare Studies* 39: 84–93.
Mentz, Steve. 2015. *Shipwreck Modernity*. Minneapolis: University of Minnesota Press.
Mentz, Steve. 2018. 'Green Comedy: Shakespeare and Ecology'. In *The Oxford Handbook of Shakespearean Comedy*, ed. Heather Hirschfield, 250–62. Oxford: Oxford University Press.
Mentz, Steve. 2019. *Break up the Anthropocene*. Minneapolis: University of Minnesota Press.
Merchant, Carolyn. 1980. *The Death of Nature: Women, Ecology, and the Scientific Revolution*. San Francisco: HarperCollins.
Merkley, Wyatt. 2018. '"The Multiplying Villainies of Nature": Northrop Frye's Green World and the Red World of the Shakespearean Tragedy'. Western University. Web. https://ir.lib.uwo.ca/undergradawards_2018/13/.
Miglietti, Sara and John Morgan, eds. 2017. *Governing the Environment in the Early Modern World*. New York: Routledge.
Mikalachki, Jodi. 1995. 'The Masculine Romance of Roman Britain: *Cymbeline* and Early Modern English Nationalism'. *Shakespeare Quarterly* 46(3): 301–22.
Mikhaila, Ninya and Jane Malcolm-Davies. 2006. *The Tudor Tailor: Reconstructing Sixteenth-Century Dress*. London: Batsford.
Miller, Anthony. 2001. *Roman Triumphs and Early Modern English Culture*. Basingstoke: Palgrave Macmillan.
Miller, Gemma. 2017. '"He Has No Children": Changing Representations of the Child in Stage and Film Productions of *Macbeth* from Polanski to Kurzel'. *Shakespeare* 13(1): 52–66.
Miller, George. 1833. *Later Struggles in the Journey of Life*. Edinburgh.
Milton, John. 1957. *Complete Poems and Major Prose*, ed. Merritt Y. Hughes. New York: Odyssey.
Mitchell, David and Sharon Snyder. 2013. 'Narrative Prosthesis'. In *The Disability Studies Reader*, 4th edn, ed. Lennard Davis, 222–35. New York: Routledge.
Mitchell, William and Kevin Colls. 2016. 'What Was Life Like in Shakespeare's New Place?' In *Finding Shakespeare's New Place: An Archaeological Biography*, ed. Paul Edmonson et al., 166–9. Manchester: Manchester University Press.
Monbiot, George. 2013a. *Feral: Searching for Enchantment on the Frontiers of Rewilding*. London: Penguin.
Monbiot, George. 2013b. 'The Naturalists Who Are Terrified of Nature'. Web. https://www.monbiot.com/2013/07/16/the-naturalists-who-are-terrified-of-nature.
Montaigne, Michel de. 1603. *Essayes*, trans. John Florio. London.

Moore, J. W. 2017. 'The Capitalocene, Part I: On the Nature and Origins of Our Ecological Crisis'. *Journal of Peasant Studies* 44(3): 594–630.
Moretti, Franco. 1983. 'The Great Eclipse: Tragic Form as Deconsecration of Sovereignty'. *Signs Taken for Wonders*, 42–82. London: Verso.
Morgan, John 2015. 'Understanding Flooding in Early Modern England'. *Journal of Historical Geography* 50: 37–50.
Morse, Ruth. 2008. '"A dim farr of launce-skippe": The Ethics of Shakespeare's Landscapes'. In *Shakespeare's World/World Shakespeares*, ed. Richard Fotheringham et al., 58–72. Cranbury, NJ: Associated University Press.
Morton, Thomas. 1637. *New English Canaan*. Amsterdam.
Morton, Timothy. 2012. *The Ecological Thought*. Cambridge, MA: Harvard University Press.
Morton, Timothy. 2014. 'How I Learned to Stop Worrying and Love the Term Anthropocene'. *Cambridge Journal of Postcolonial Literary Inquiry* 1(2): 257–64.
Morton, Timothy. 2016. *Dark Ecology: For a Logic of Future Coexistence*. New York: Columbia University Press.
Mottram, Stewart. 2013. 'Warriors and Ruins: *Cymbeline*, Heroism, and the Union of the Crowns'. In *Celtic Shakespeare*, ed. Willy Maley and Rory Loughnane, 169–83. Farnham: Ashgate.
Mowatt, Barbara. 2000. '"Knowing I Loved My Books": Reading *The Tempest* Intertextually'. In *The Tempest and Its Travels*, ed. Peter Hulme and William Sherman, 27–36. Philadelphia: University of Pennsylvania Press.
Muir, Kenneth. 1959. 'The Background of Coriolanus'. *Shakespeare Quarterly* 10(2): 137–45.
Mullaney, Steven. 1988. *The Place of the Stage: License, Play, and Power*. Chicago: University of Chicago Press.
Müller, Timo. 2010. 'Notes Toward an Ecological Conception of Bakhtin's "Chronotope"'. *Ecozon* 1(1): 98–102.
Munro, Lucy. 2005. *Children of the Queen's Revels: A Jacobean Theatre Repertory*. Cambridge: Cambridge University Press.
Munro, Lucy. 2020. *Shakespeare in the Theatre: The King's Men*. London: Bloomsbury.
Munroe, Jennifer. 2011. 'It's All about the Gillyvors: Engendering Art and Nature in *The Winter's Tale*'. In *Ecocritical Shakespeare*, ed. Lynne Bruckner and Dan Brayton, 139–54. Farnham: Ashgate.
Munroe, Jennifer and Rebecca Laroche, eds. 2011. *Ecofeminist Approaches to Early Modernity*. New York: Palgrave Macmillan.
Munroe, Jennifer. 2015. 'Is It Really Ecocritical If It Isn't Feminist?': The Dangers of "Speaking For" in Ecological Studies and Shakespeare's *Titus Andronicus*'. In *Ecological Approaches to Early Modern English Texts*, ed. Jennifer Munroe et al., 37–50. Farnham: Ashgate.
Murdoch, Steve. 2010. *The Terror of the Seas? Scottish Maritime Warfare 1513–1713*. Leiden: Brill.
Murray, Catriona. 2020. 'The Queen's Two Bodies: Monumental Sculpture at the Funeral of Anna of Denmark, 1619'. *The Sculpture Journal* 29(1): 27–43.
Musacchio, Jacqueline. 2001. 'Weasels and Pregnancy in Renaissance Italy'. *Renaissance Studies* 15(2): 172-87.
Nardizzi, Vin. 2013. *Wooden Os: Shakespeare's Theatres and England's Trees*. Toronto: University of Toronto Press.
Nashe, Thomas. 1594. *Terrors of the Night*. London.
Nashe, Thomas. 1599. *Lenten Stuff*. London.

National Portrait Gallery. 2012. 'Princely Collecting'. *The Lost Prince: The Life & Death of Henry Stuart*. Web. https://www.npg.org.uk/whatson/the-lost-prince-the-life-and-death-of-henry-stuart/exhibition/princely-collecting.

Natural England. 2002. 'Lowland Heathland: A Cultural and Endangered Landscape'. *Natural England*. Web. http://publications.naturalengland.org.uk/publication/81012.

Nesler, Miranda G. 2015. 'Hybrids: Animal Law and the Actaeon Myth in *Titus Andronicus*'. *The Shakespearean International Yearbook* 15: 65–80.

Netzloff, Mark. 2001. 'Counterfeit Egyptians and Imagined Borders: Jonson's *The Gypsies Metamorphosed*'. *ELH* 68(4): 763–93.

Newman, Cathy. 2017. "What Will Become of Scotland's Moors?" *National Geographic*. May 2017. Web. https://www.nationalgeographic.com/magazine/article/scotland-moors-highlands-conservation-land-management.

Nicholl, Charles. 2007. *The Lodger Shakespeare: His Life on Silver Street*. New York: Viking.

Nichols, John. 1828. *The Progresses, Processions, and Magnificent Festivities of King James the First*. London.

Nicholson, Brinsley. 1868. 'Shakespeare Illustrated by Massinger'. *Notes and Queries* 1: 289–91.

Nicholson, Marjorie Hope. 1997. *Mountain Gloom, Mountain Glory: The Development of the Aesthetics of the Infinite*. Seattle: University of Washington Press.

Nixon, Rob. 1987. 'Caribbean and African Appropriations of *The Tempest*'. *Critical Inquiry* 13: 557–78.

Nixon, Rob. 2011. *Slow Violence and the Environmentalism of the Poor*. Cambridge, MA: Harvard University Press.

Norden, John. 1607. *Surveyor's Dialogue*. London.

Norman, A. V. B. and Ian Eaves. 2016. *Arms and Armour in the Collection of Her Majesty the Queen*. London: Royal Collections Trust.

North Wales Live. 2004. 'Can the Eagle Come Home?' *North Wales Daily Post*. 21 June 2004. Web. https://www.dailypost.co.uk/news/north-wales-news/can-the-eagle-come-home-2928381.

Nosworthy, J. M. 1965. *Shakespeare's Occasional Plays: Their Origin and Transmission*. London: Edward Arnold.

Notestein, Wallace. 1971. *The House of Commons 1604–1610*. New Haven: Yale University Press.

Novitsky, Grigory. 1715. *A Short Description of the Ostyak People*, ed. L. N. Maikov. St Petersburg, 1884.

Oakley-Brown, Liz. 2016. 'Writing on the Borderlines: Anglo-Welsh Relations in Thomas Churchyard's *The Worthiness of Wales*'. In *Writing Wales*, ed. Stewart Mottram, 39–58. London: Routledge.

O'Dair, Sharon. 2007. 'The Life of Timon of Athens'. In *Thomas Middleton: The Collected Works*, ed. Gary Taylor and John Lavagnino, 467–70. Oxford: Clarendon.

O'Dair, Sharon. 2011. 'Is It Shakespearean Ecocriticism if It Isn't Presentist?'. In *Ecocritical Shakespeare*, ed. Lynne Bruckner and Dan Brayton, 71–85. Farnham: Ashgate.

O'Farrell, Brian. 2011. *Shakespeare's Patron: William Herbert, Third Earl of Pembroke*. London: Continuum.

Ogden, James. 1997. 'Lear's Blasted Heath'. In *Lear from Study to Stage: Essays in Criticism*, ed. James Ogden and Arthur Scouton, 135–45. Madison, NJ: Farleigh Dickinson University Press.

Oki-Siekierczak, Ayami. 2015. '"How Green!": The Meanings of Green in Early Modern England and *The Tempest*'. *Revue Électronique D'Études Sur Le Monde Anglophone* 12(2). https://journals.openedition.org/erea/4331.

O'Malley, Evelyn. 2021. *Weathering Shakespeare: Audiences and Open-Air Performance*. London: Bloomsbury.

Orgel, Stephen and Roy Strong. 1973. *Inigo Jones: Theatre of the Stuart Court*. Berkeley: University of California Press.
Orgel, Stephen. 1975. *The Illusion of Power: Political Theater in the English Renaissance*. Berkeley: University of California Press.
Orgel, Stephen, ed. 1987. *The Tempest*. Oxford: Oxford University Press.
Orgel, Stephen, ed. 1996. *The Winter's Tale*. Oxford: Oxford University Press.
Orgel, Stephen. 1999. '*Macbeth* and the Antic Round'. *Shakespeare Survey* 52: 143–53.
Orr, D. Alan. 2019. 'Protestant Military Humanism in Early Stuart Ireland'. *The Historical Journal* 62(1): 77–99.
Owen, George. 1603/1994. *The Description of Pembrokeshire*. Llandysul: Gomer P.
Owens, Avalon et al. 2019. 'Light Pollution Is a Driver of Insect Declines'. *Social Science Research Network*. Web. https://ssrn.com/abstract=3378835.
Pafford, J. H. P., ed. 1963. *The Winter's Tale*. London: Arden.
Palmer, Daryl. 1995. 'Jacobean Muscovites: Winter, Tyranny, and Knowledge in *The Winter's Tale*'. *Shakespeare Quarterly* 46(3): 323–39.
Palsgrave, John. 1530. *L'esclaircissement de la langue francoys*.
Parker, Geoffrey. 2013. *Global Crisis: War, Climate Change, and Catastrophe in the Seventeenth Century*. New Haven: Yale University Press.
Parris, Benjamin. 2012. '"The Body Is with the King, but the King Is Not with Body": Sovereign Sleep in *Hamlet* and *Macbeth*'. *Shakespeare Studies* 40: 101–42.
Pastoureau, Michel. 2014. *Green: The History of a Color*. Princeton: Princeton University Press.
Paul, H. N. 1950. *The Royal Play of Macbeth*. New York: MacMillan.
Peacham, Henry. 1612. *Gentlemen's Exercise*. London.
Peacock, John. 2005. *The Stage Designs of Inigo Jones*. Cambridge: Cambridge University Press.
Peck, Linda L. 1993. *Court Patronage and Corruption in Early Stuart England*. New York: Routledge.
Pericles: Maritime Cultural Heritage. 2018. Web. https://www.pericles-heritage.eu/.
Perry, Curtis. 1997. *The Making of Jacobean Culture*. Cambridge: Cambridge University Press.
Petty, William. 1691. *The Political Anatomy of Ireland*. London.
Petty, William, ed. 1807. *Bibliotheca manuscripta Lansdowniana*, 2 vols. London.
Pfeifer, Theresa H. 2009. 'Deconstructing Cartesian Dualisms of Western Racial Systems: A Study in the Colors Black and White'. *Journal of Black Studies* 29(4): 528–47.
Philips, Neil. 1992. *The Penguin Book of English Folktales*. London: Penguin.
Phillipson, Jeremy and David Symes, 2018. 'A Sea of Troubles: Brexit and the Fisheries Question'. *Marine Policy* 90: 168–73.
Pierce, Robert B. 2012. '"I Stumbled When I Saw": Interpreting Gloucester's Blindness in *King Lear*'. *Philosophy and Literature* 36(1): 153–65.
Pitcher, John, ed. 2010. *The Winter's Tale*. London: Arden.
Plautus. 1995. *The Comedies*. 4 vols, trans. David R. Slavitt and Palmer Bovie. Baltimore: Johns Hopkins University Press.
Plutarch. 1579. *The Lives of the Noble Grecians and Romans*, 2 vols, trans. Thomas North. New York: Heritage Press, 1941.
Poliquin, Rachel. 2012. *The Breathless Zoo: Taxidermy and the Cultures of Longing*. State College: Pennsylvania State University Press.
Pollnitz, Aysha. 2015. *Princely Education in Early Modern Britain*. Cambridge: Cambridge University Press.
Pollock, Jonathan. 2017. 'Of Mites and Motes: Shakespeare's Reading of Epicurean Science'. In *Spectacular Science, Technology, and Superstition in the Age of Shakespeare*, ed. Sophie Chiari and Mickaël Popelard, 119–32. Edinburgh: Edinburgh University Press.

Pope, Maurice. 1992. 'Shakespeare's Falconry'. *Shakespeare Survey* 44: 131–44.
Potts, Thomas. 1613. *The Wonderful Discovery of Witches*, ed. Robert Poole. Lancaster: Palatine, 2011.
Prior, Roger. 1972. 'The Life of George Wilkins'. *Shakespeare Studies* 25: 137–52.
Pryme, Abraham de la. 1870. *The Diary of Abraham de la Pryme, the Yorkshire Antiquary*. Durham: Andrews & Co.
Prynne, William. 1641. *Mount Orgueil*. London.
Purchas, Samuel. 1625. *Purchas His Pilgrims*.
Purkiss, Diane. 2000. *At the Bottom of the Garden: A Dark History of Faeries, Hobgoblins, and Other Troublesome Things*. New York: New York University Press.
Quarmby, Kevin. 2012. *The Disguised Ruler in Shakespeare and His Contemporaries*. Farnham: Ashgate.
Quiller-Couch, Arthur, ed. 1931. *The Winter's Tale*. Cambridge: Cambridge University Press.
Quilligan, Maureen. 2016. '"Exit Pursued by a Bear": Staging Animal Bodies in *The Winter's Tale*'. In *The Oxford Handbook of Shakespeare and Embodiment: Gender, Sexuality, and Race*, ed. Valerie Traub, 506–22. Oxford: Oxford University Press.
Raber, Karen. 2018. *Shakespeare and Posthumanist Theory*. London: Bloomsbury.
Rackham, Oliver. 1986. *The History of the Countryside: The Classic History of Britain's Landscape, Flora, and Fauna*. London: Dent.
Ralegh, Walter. 1650. *Discourse of the Original and Fundamental Cause of... War*. London.
Ravelhofer, Barbara. 2002. '"Beasts of Recreacion": Henslowe's White Bears'. *English Literary Renaissance* 32: 287–323.
Ravelhofer, Barbara. 2006. *The Early Stuart Masque: Dance Costume, Music*. Oxford: Oxford University Press.
Ravensdale, J. R. 1974. *Liable to Floods: Village Landscape on the Edge of the Fens AD 1450–1850*. Cambridge: Cambridge University Press.
Raye, Lee. 2014. 'The Early Extinction Date of the Beaver (Castor fiber) in Britain'. *Historical Biology* 27: 1029–41.
Rees, Ioan Bowen, ed. 1992. *The Mountains of Wales*. Cardiff: University of Wales Press.
Remien, Peter. 2019. *The Concept of Nature in Early Modern English Literature*. Cambridge: Cambridge University Press.
Reynolds, Susan. 2010. *Before Eminent Domain: Towards a History of Expropriation of Land for the Common Good*. Chapel Hill: University of North Carolina Press.
Riccucci, Marco and Jens Rydell. 2017. 'Bats in the Florentine Renaissance: From Darkness to Enlightenment'. *Lynx* 48: 165–82.
Richards, John F. 2003. *Unending Frontier: An Environmental History of the Early Modern World*. Berkeley: University of California Press.
Rickard, Jane. 2007. *Authorship and Authority: The Writing of King James VI and I*. Manchester: Manchester University Press.
Rickard, Jane. 2015. *Writing the Monarch in Jacobean England: Jonson, Donne, Shakespeare, and the Works of King James*. Cambridge: Cambridge University Press.
Riding, Laura and Robert Graves. 1927. 'William Shakespeare and ee cummings'. In *A Survey of Modernist Poetry*. London: Heinemann. 59-82.
Ridley, Thomas. 1607. *A View of the Civil and Ecclesiastical Law*.
Rilov, Gil. 2016. 'Multi-species Collapses at the Warm Edge of a Warming Sea'. *Scientific Reports* 6.
Risdon, Tristram. 1633. *Chorographical Description or Survey of the County of Devon*. London: 1811.
Roberts, Callum. 2007. *The Unnatural History of the Sea*. Washington, DC: Island Press.

Roberts, Peter S. 2006. 'The Business of Playing and the Patronage of Players at the Jacobean Courts'. In *James VI and I: Ideas, Authority, and Government*, ed. Ralph Houlbrooke, 81–106. Aldershot: Ashgate.

Robinson, R. A. 2005. 'Ruff'. *BirdFacts: Profiles of Birds Occurring in Britain & Ireland*. BTO, Thetford. http://www.bto.org/birdfacts.

Robson, Lynn. 2010. '"We'll Build Sonnets in Pretty Rooms": Early Modern Literary Studies, the Spatial Turn, and Ecocriticism'. *Literature Compass* 7/12: 1062–76.

Rooney, Tom. 2007. 'Who "Plaid" the Bear in *Mucedorus*?' *Notes and Queries* 54(3): 259–62.

Rossi, Paolo. 1978. *Francis Bacon: From Magic to Science*. Chicago: University of Chicago Press.

Row-Heyveld, Lindsey. 2019. 'Known and Feeling Sorrows: Disabled Knowledge and *King Lear*'. *Early Theatre* 22(2): 169–95.

Saenger, Michael. 1995. 'The Costumes of Caliban and Ariel Qua Sea Nymph'. *Notes and Queries* 240: 334–6.

Sanders, Julie. 1998. *Ben Jonson's Theatrical Republics*. London: MacMillan.

Sanders, Julie. 2001. 'Ecocritical Readings and the Seventeenth-Century Woodland: Milton's *Comus* and the Forest of Dean'. *English* 50: 1–18.

Sanders, Julie. 2011. *The Cultural Geography of Early Modern Drama, 1620–50*. Cambridge: Cambridge University Press.

Santer, Eric L. 2016. *The Weight of All Flesh: On the Subject-Matter of Political Economy*. Oxford: Oxford University Press.

Schanzer, Ernest, ed. 1966. *The Winter's Tale*. Hammondsworth: Penguin.

Schoenbaum, Samuel. 1981. *Shakespeare: Records and Images*. Oxford: Oxford University Press.

Schoenbaum, Samuel. 1991. *Shakespeare's Lives*. 2nd edn. Oxford: Clarendon.

Schwyzer, Philip. 2004. *Literature, Nationalism, and Memory in Early Modern England and Wales*. Cambridge: Cambridge University Press.

Scot, Reginald. 1584. *Discoverie of Witchcraft*. New York: Dover, 1972.

Scott, Alison. 2006. *Selfish Gifts: The Politics of Exchange and English Courtly Literature*. Madison, NJ: Farleigh Dickinson.

Scott, Charlotte. 2014. *Shakespeare's Nature: From Cultivation to Culture*. Oxford: Oxford University Press.

Scott, Walter, ed. 1811. *The Secret History of the Court of James the First*. Edinburgh: J. Ballantyne.

Scott-Warren, Jason. 2003. 'When Theatres Were Bear-Gardens, or What's at Stake in the Comedy of Humours'. *Shakespeare Quarterly* 54(1): 63–82.

Scottish Environmental Protection Agency. 2011. 'Review of metal concentrations data held for Glengonnar Water and Wanlock Water, South Scotland'. Web. http://www.sepa.org.uk/media/163236/metals_glengonnar__wanlock_waters_review.pdf.

Servheen, Christopher. 1999. *Bears: Status Survey and Conservation Action Plan*. Cambridge: IUCN.

Seymour, Nicole. 2013. 'Down with People: Queer Tendencies and Troubling Racial Politics in Antinatalist Discourse'. In *International Perspectives in Feminist Ecocriticism*, ed. Greta Gaard, Simon Estok, and Serpil Opperman, 203–20. New York: Routledge.

Sgroi, R. C. L. 2003. 'Piscatorial Politics Revisited: The Language of Economic Debate and the Evolution of Fishing Policy in Elizabethan England'. *Albion* 35(1): 1–24.

Shannon, Laurie. 2011. 'Greasy Citizens. And Tallow-Catches'. *PMLA* 126(2): 311–13.

Shannon, Laurie. 2013. *The Accommodated Animal: Cosmopolity in Shakespearean Locales*. Chicago: University of Chicago Press.

Shannon, Laurie. 2017. 'Shakespeare's Comedy of Upright Status: Standing Bears and Fallen Humans'. *Shakespeare Survey* 70: 213–18.
Shapiro, James. 2016. *1606: The Year of Lear*. London: Faber and Faber.
Sharpe, Robert B. 1935. *The Real War of the Theatres: Shakespeare's Fellows in Rivalry with the Admiral's Men 1594–1603*. Boston: D. C. Heath.
Sharpe, Will. 2013. 'Authorship and Attribution'. In *Collaborative Plays*, ed. Jonathan Bate and Eric Rasmussen, 641–745. London: Palgrave Macmillan.
Sherbo, Arthur. 1992. *Shakespeare's Midwives: Some Neglected Shakespeareans*. Newark, DE: University of Delaware Press.
Shell, Alison. 2001. 'Autodidacticism in English Jesuit Drama: The Writings and Career of Joseph Simons'. *Medieval and Renaissance Drama in England* 13: 34–56.
Shell, Marc. 2014. *Islandology: Geography, Rhetoric, Politics*. Stanford University Press.
Sherman, William H. 1995. *John Dee: The Politics of Reading and Writing in the English Renaissance*. Amherst: University of Massachusetts Press.
Shoaf, Richard A. 2014. *Lucretius and Shakespeare on the Nature of Things*. Newcastle: Cambridge Scholars.
Siewers, Alfred. 2006. 'Landscapes of Conversion: Guthlac's Mound and Grendel's Mere as Expressions of Anglo-Saxon Nation Building'. In *The Postmodern Beowulf: A Critical Casebook*, ed. Eileen Joy and Mary K. Ramsey, 199–257. Morgantown: University of West Virginia Press.
Siewers, Alfred. 2013. 'The Green Otherworlds of Early Medieval Literature'. In *The Cambridge Companion to Literature and the Environment*, ed. Louise Westling, 31–44. Cambridge: Cambridge University Press.
Sisson, C. J. 1958. 'The Magic of Prospero'. *Shakespeare Survey* 11: 70–7.
Skeel, Caroline. 1926. 'The Cattle Trade between Wales and England from the Fifteenth to the Nineteenth Centuries'. *Transactions of the Royal Historical Society* 9: 135–58.
Skura, Meredith. 1989. 'Discourse and the Individual: The Case of Colonialism in *The Tempest*'. *Shakespeare Quarterly* 40(1): 42–69.
Slack, Paul. 2011. *Plenty of People: Perceptions of Population in Early Modern England*. Reading: University of Reading Press.
Slovic, Scott. 2016. 'The Fourth Wave of Ecocriticism: Materiality, Sustainability, Applicability'. 1–6. Web. http://sunrise-n.com/transatlantic_ecology/wp-content/uploads/2016/09/SlovicThe-Fourth-Wave-of-Ecocriticism.doc.pdf.
Smith, Bruce. 2009. *The Key of Green: Passion and Perception in Renaissance Culture*. Chicago: University of Chicago Press.
Smith, Christian A. 2017. '"Verdammt metal": Marx's use of Shakespeare in His Critique of Exchange Value'. *Critique* 45(1–2): 101–16.
Smith, Emma. 2013. *Macbeth: Language and Writing*. London: A & C Black.
Smith, Emma. 2020. 'What Shakespeare Teaches Us about Living with Pandemics'. *New York Times*. 28 March 2020. Web. https://www.nytimes.com/2020/03/28/opinion/coronavirus-shakespeare.html.
Smuts, R. Malcolm. 1996. 'Art and the Material Culture of Majesty in Early Stuart England'. *The Stuart Court and Europe: Essays in Politics and Political Culture*, ed. R. Malcolm Smuts, 86–112. Cambridge: Cambridge University Press, 1996.
Snyder, Susan. 1966. 'Marlowe's *Doctor Faustus* as an Inverted Saint's Life'. *Studies in Philology* 63: 514–23.
Sokol, B. J. 2003. *A Brave New World of Knowledge: Shakespeare's* The Tempest *and Early Modern Epistemology*. Cranbury, NJ: Associated University Press.

Solomon, Julie R. 1999. *Objectivity in the Making: Francis Bacon and the Politics of Inquiry.* Baltimore: Johns Hopkins University Press.
Somos, Mark. 2012. 'Selden's *Mare Clausum*: The Secularisation of International Law and the Rise of Soft Imperialism'. *Journal of the History of International Law* 14: 287–330.
Speed, John. 1612. *The Theatre of the Empire of Great Britaine.* London.
Spenser, Edmund 1949. *Prose Works,* ed. Rudolf Gottfried. Baltimore: Johns Hopkins University Press.
Spurgeon, Caroline. 1961. *Shakespeare's Imagery and What It Tells Us.* Cambridge: Cambridge University Press.
Standish, Arthur. *Commons Complaint.* 1611.
Stannard, David. n.d. 'The Timing of the Destruction of Eccles Juxta Mare'. Academia.edu. https://www.academia.edu/26800157/The_Timing_of_the_Destruction_of_Eccles_juxta_Mare_Norfolk.
Steevens, George, ed. 1803. *Dramatic Writings of William Shakespeare.* 21 vols. London: John Bell.
Steggle, Matthew. 2015. *Digital Humanities and the Lost Drama of Early Modern England.* Farnham: Ashgate.
Stephen, Leslie. 1909. *The Playground of Europe.* New York: Putnam.
Stevenson, David L. 1959. 'The Role of James I in *Measure for Measure*'. *ELH* 26(2): 188–208.
Stevenson, David. 1997. *Scotland's Last Royal Wedding: The Marriage of James VI and Anne of Denmark.* Edinburgh: John Donald.
Stewart, Alan. 2003. *The Cradle King: A Life of James VI & I.* London: Chatto & Windus.
Stewart, Alan J. A. 2021. 'Impacts of artificial lighting at night on insect conservation'. *Insect Conservation and Diversity* 14(2): 163–66.
Still, Colin. 1921. *Shakespeare's Mystery Play: A Study of* The Tempest. London: Cecil Palmer.
Stokes, James, ed. 2009. *Records of Early English Drama: Lincolnshire.* Toronto: University of Toronto Press.
Stradling, John. 1607. *Epigrammatum,* trans. Dana Sutton. Philological Museum. Web. https://philological.cal.bham.ac.uk/.
Stangeland, Charles Emil. 1904. *Pre-Malthusian Doctrines of Population: A Study in the History of Economic Theory.* New York: Columbia University Press.
Strain, Virginia. 2015. 'Shakespeare's Living Law: Theatrical, Lyrical, and Legal Practice'. *Literature Compass* 12(6): 249–61.
Strong, Roy. 1975. *Nicholas Hilliard.* London: Michael Joseph.
Strong, Roy. 1986. *Henry Prince of Wales and England's Lost Renaissance.* London: Thames and Hudson.
Sullivan, Garrett. 1998. *The Drama of Landscape: Land, Property, and Social Relations on the Early Modern Stage.* Stanford University Press.
Sullivan, Garrett. 2005. 'Sleep, Epic, and Romance in *Antony and Cleopatra*'. In Antony and Cleopatra: *New Critical Essays,* ed. Sarah Munson Deats, 259–73. New York: Routledge.
Summit, Jennifer. 2008. *Memory's Library: Medieval Books in Early Modern England.* Chicago: University of Chicago Press.
Sweeney, Anne R. 2011. *Snow in Arcadia: Redrawing the English Lyric Landscape, 1586–95.* Manchester: Manchester University Press.
Swenson, Haylie. 2020. 'Owls in the Early Modern Imagination: Ominous Omens and Pitiable Sages'. *Folger Shakespeare Library.*
Swift, Graham. 1983. *Waterland.* New York: Vintage.

Syme, Holger Schott. 2019. 'The Jacobean King's Men: A Reconsideration'. *The Review of English Studies* 70: 231–51.
Tacitus. 2009. *Agricola*, trans. A. R. Birley. Oxford: Oxford University Press.
Taylor, Gary and John Jowett. 1993. *Shakespeare Reshaped, 1606–1623*. Oxford: Clarendon Press.
Taylor, Gary and John Lavagnino. 2007. *Thomas Middleton and Early Modern Textual Culture: A Companion to the Collected Works*. Oxford: Clarendon.
Taylor, Gary. 2012. 'The History of the History of Cardenio'. *The Quest for* Cardenio, ed. David Carnegie and Gary Taylor, 11–78. Oxford: Oxford University Press.
Taylor, Gary. 2014. '*Macbeth* and Middleton'. In *Macbeth*, ed. Robert S. Miola, 296–305. New York: Norton, 2007.
Teramura, Misha. 2015. 'Silver Mine'. *Lost Plays Database*. Web. https://lostplays.folger.edu/Silver_Mine.
Test, Edward M. 2008. '*The Tempest* and the Newfoundland Cod Fishery'. In *Global Traffic: Discourses and Practices of Trade in English Literature and Culture from 1550 to 1700*, ed. Barbara Sebek and Stephen Deng, 201–20. London: Palgrave Macmillan.
Theis, Jeffrey. 2009. *Writing the Forest in Early Modern England: A Sylvan Pastoral*. Pittsburgh: Duquesne University Press.
Thirsk, Joan. 1997. *Alternative Agriculture: A History*. Oxford: Oxford University Press.
Thomas, Keith. 1971. *Religion and the Decline of Magic*. New York: Oxford University Press.
Thomas, Keith. 1983. *Man and the Natural World 1500–1800*. London: Penguin.
Thorndike, Lynn. 1923–58. *A History of Magic and Experimental Science*. 8 vols. New York: Columbia University Press.
Thurley, Simon. 2021. *Palaces of Revolution: Life, Death, & Art at the Stuart Court*. London: William Collins.
Tigner, Amy. 2006. '*The Winter's Tale*: Gardens and the Marvels of Transformation'. *English Literary Renaissance* 36(1): 114–34.
Traherne, Thomas. 2014. *The Works of Thomas Traherne*, ed. Jan Ross. 6 vols. Woodbridge: Boydell & Brewer.
Tsing, Anna Lowenhaupt. 2015. *The Mushroom at the End of the World: On the Possibility of Life in Capitalist Ruins*. Princeton: Princeton University Press.
Tsukada, Yuichi. 2019. *Shakespeare and the Politics of Nostalgia*. London: Bloomsbury.
Trevisan, Sara. 2013. 'The Impact of the Netherlandish Landscape Tradition on Poetry and Painting in Early Modern England'. *Renaissance Quarterly* 66(3): 866–903.
Tribble, Evelyn. 2005. ' "When Every Noise Appalls Me": Sound and Fear in *Macbeth* and Akira Kurosawa's *Throne of Blood*'. *Shakespeare* 1(1–2): 75–90.
Tricomi, Albert. 2001. 'Joan de la Pucelle and the Inverted Saints Play in *1 Henry VI*'. *Renaissance and Reformation* 25(2): 5–31.
Turner Henry. 1997. '*King Lear* Without: The Heath'. *Renaissance Drama* 28: 161–83.
Turner, Henry. 2006. *The English Renaissance Stage: Geometry, Poetics, and the Practical Spatial Arts 1580–1630*. Oxford: Oxford University Press.
Twyne, Lawrence, trans. 1607. *The Patterne of Painefull Adventures*. London.
Tyson, Leslie Owen. 1996. 'Sir Bevis Bulmer: An Elizabethan Adventurer'. *British Mining* 57. Sheffield: Northern Mines Research Society.
Tyson, Leslie Owen. 2004. 'Sir Bevis Bulmer, Courtier and Mining Projector'. *ODNB*. Web.
Ulrich, Roger S. 1986. 'Human Responses to Vegetation and Landscapes'. *Landscape and Urban Planning* 13: 29–44.
Vanita, Ruta. 2000. 'Mariological Memory in *The Winter's Tale* and *Henry VIII*'. *Studies in English Literature* 40(2): 331–7.

Vaughan, Adam. 2009. 'Polar Bears Sail down Thames'. *Guardian. Environmental Blog*. 26 January 2009. Web. https://www.theguardian.com/environment/blog/2009/jan/26/conservation-poles?CMP=gu_com.

Vaughan, Alden and Virginia Vaughan. 1991. *Shakespeare's Caliban: A Cultural History*. Cambridge: Cambridge University Press.

Vaughan, Virginia Mason. 2005. *Performing Blackness on English Stages 1500–1800*. Cambridge.

Veale, Elspeth. 1966. *The English Fur Trade in the Later Middle Ages*. Oxford: Oxford University Press.

Vermuyden, Cornelius. 1642. *A discourse touching the drayning of the great fennes*. London.

Vickers, Brian. 2010. 'Disintegrated: Did Middleton Adapt *Macbeth*?' *Times Literary Supplement* 28 May 2010.

Vidali, Amy. 2010. 'Seeing What We Know: Disability and Theories of Metaphor'. *Literary and Cultural Disability Studies* 4(1): 33–54.

Waage, Frederick. 2005. 'Shakespeare Unearth'd'. *ISLE: Interdisciplinary Studies in Literature and the Environment* 12(2): 139–64.

Wade, Nicholas. 2003. 'Why Humans and Their Fur Parted Ways'. *New York Times*. 19 August 2003. Web. https://www.nytimes.com/2003/08/19/science/why-humans-and-their-fur-parted-ways.html.

'Waking the Bear: Understanding Circumpolar Bear Ceremonialism'. 2021. ELOKA: Exchange for Local Observation and Knowledge of the Arctic. University of Colorado. Web. https://eloka-arctic.org/bears/introduction.

Walsham, Alexandra. 2011. *The Reformation of the Landscape: Religion, Identity, and Memory in Early Modern Britain and Ireland*. Oxford: Oxford University Press.

Warde, Paul. 2018. *The Invention of Sustainability: Nature and Destiny c. 1500–1870*. Cambridge: Cambridge University Press.

Warner, Marina. 2000. ' "The Foul Witch" and "Her Freckled Whelp": Circean Mutations in the New World'. In *The Tempest and Its Travels*, ed. Peter Hulme and William Sherman, 97–113. Philadelphia: University of Pennsylvania Press.

Warren, Christopher. 2015. *Literature and the Law of Nations 1580–1680*. Oxford: Oxford University Press.

Warren, Roger, ed. 2008. *Cymbeline*. Oxford: Oxford University Press.

Wasson, John. 1986. 'The Secular Saint Plays of the Elizabethan Era'. In *The Saint Play in Medieval Europe*, ed. Clifford Davidson, 241–60. Kalamazoo: Medieval Institute.

Watson, Robert. 1984. *Shakespeare and the Hazards of Ambition*. Cambridge, MA: Harvard University Press.

Watson, Robert. 2006. *Back to Nature: The Green and the Real in the Late Renaissance*. Philadelphia: University of Pennsylvania Press.

Watson, Robert. 2015. 'Tell Inconvenient Truths but Tell Them Slant'. In *Ecological Approaches to Early Modern English Texts*, ed. Jennifer Munroe et al., 17–28. Farnham: Ashgate.

Wayne, Valerie, ed. 2017. *Cymbeline*. London: Bloomsbury.

Weber, Alan, ed. 2003. *Because It's There: A Celebration of Mountaineering from 200 B. C. to Today*. Lanham, MD: Taylor Trade.

Weis, René. 2015. 'His granddaughter, Lady Elizabeth Barnard'. In *The Shakespeare Circle: An Alternative Biography*, ed. Paul Edmondson and Stanley Wells, 122–34. Cambridge: Cambridge University Press.

Wells, Robin H. 2000. *Shakespeare on Masculinity*. Cambridge: Cambridge University Press.

Welwood, William. 1590. *The Sea-Law of Scotland*. Edinburgh.

Welwood, William. 1613. *An Abridgement of All Sea Laws*. London.

Welwood, William. 1615. *De domino maris*. London.
West, Russel. 2002. *Spatial Representations on the Jacobean Stage: From Shakespeare to Webster*. New York: Palgrave Macmillan.
Westby-Gibson, John. 2004. 'Chaloner, Sir Thomas, the Younger (1563/4–1615), Chemist and Courtier'. *ODNB*. Web.
White, Lynn. 1967. 'The Historic Roots of Our Ecologic Crisis'. *Science* 155.3767: 1203–7.
White, Martin. 2014. '"When Torchlight Made an Artificial Noon": Light and Darkness in the Indoor Jacobean Theatre'. In *Moving Shakespeare Indoors*, ed. Andrew Gurr and Farah Karim-Cooper, 115–36. Cambridge, Cambridge University Press.
Whiteley, Giles. 2020. 'Shakespeare's Dark Ecologies: Rethinking the Environment in *Macbeth* and *King Lear*'. In *Shakespeare's Things*, ed. Brett Gamboa and Lawrence Switzky, 134–49. New York: Routledge.
Whitney, Charles. 2010. 'Dekker and Middleton's Plague Pamphlets as Environmental Literature'. In *Representing the Plague in Early Modern England*, ed. Rebecca Totaro and Ernest Gilman, 201–18. New York: Routledge.
Whyte, I. D. 2010. 'Urbanization in Early Modern Scotland: A Preliminary Analysis'. *Scottish Economic and Social History* 9(1): 21–37.
Wickham, Glynne. 1972. 'The Staging of Saints Plays in England'. In *The Medieval Drama*, ed. Sandro Sticca, 99–120. Binghamton: SUNY Press.
Wickman, Tom. 2008. '"Make your garden rich in gillyvors, / And do not call them bastards": Perdita and the Possibilities for Redemptive Interracialism'. *Borrowers and Lenders* 4 (1). https://ojs01.galib.uga.edu/borrowers/article/view/2304/2281.
Wilcox, Helen. 2007. 'Shakespeare's Miracle Play? Religion in *All's Well, That Ends Well*'. In *All's Well That Ends Well: New Critical Essays*, ed. Gary Waller, 140–54. New York: Routledge.
Wilkins, George. 1606. *The Historie of Justine*. London.
Williams, Gwyn, trans. 1974. *Welsh Poems: Sixth Century to 1600*. Berkeley: University of California Press.
Williams, Raymond. 1983. *Keywords*. New York: Oxford University Press.
Wilson, Richard. 2004. *Secret Shakespeare: Studies in Theatre, Religion, and Resistance*. Manchester: Manchester University Press.
Wilson-Okamura, David Scott. 2003. 'Virgilian Models of Colonization in Shakespeare's *Tempest*'. *ELH* 70: 709–37.
Winwood, R. 1725. *Memorials of Affairs of State in the Reigns of Q. Elizabeth and K. James I*. 3 vols.
Wolfe, Cary. 2012. *Before the Law: Humans and Other Animals in a Biopolitical Frame*. Chicago: University of Chicago Press.
Wood, Alfred. 1964. *A History of the Levant Company*. London: Frank & Cass.
Wood, Gillen D'Arcy. 2008. 'Introduction: Eco-Historicism'. Journal for Early Modern Cultural Studies 8(2): 1–7.
Wortham, Christopher. 1996. 'Shakespeare, James I, and the Matter of Britain'. *English* 145(182): 97–122.
Wright, Myra. 2018. *The Poetics of Angling in Early Modern England*. London: Routledge.
Yachnin, Paul. 2001. 'The Populuxe Theatre'. In *The Culture of Play-going in Shakespeare's England: A Collaborative Debate*. Cambridge: Cambridge University Press.
Yaldon, Derek. 2007. 'The Older History of the White-Tailed Eagle in Britain'. *British Birds* 100: 471–80.
Yates, Frances. 1964. *Giordano Bruno and the Hermetic Tradition*. Chicago: University of Chicago Press.
Yates, Frances. 1978. *Majesty and Magic in Shakespeare's Last Plays*. Boulder: Shambhala.

Yates, Frances. 1979. *The Occult Philosophy in the Elizabethan Age*. London: Routledge.
Yates, Julian. 2013. 'Orange'. In *Prismatic Ecology: Ecotheory beyond Green*, ed. Jeffrey Cohen, 83–105. Minneapolis: University of Minnesota Press.
Yuran, Noam. 2014. *What Money Wants: An Economy of Desire*. Palo Alto: Stanford University Press.
Yusoff, Kathryn. 2019. *A Billion Black Anthropocenes or None*. Minneapolis: University of Minnesota Press.
Zabus, Chantal. 2002. *Tempests after Shakespeare*. New York: Palgrave Macmillan.

Index

For the benefit of digital users, indexed terms that span two pages (e.g., 52–53) may, on occasion, appear on only one of those pages.

Adam 20, 219–20
Adams, Carol J. 83–4
Adders 163, 199–200
Adrian, John 7
Aethelbald, King of Mercia 156–7
Africa 197–9, 241n.1, 249n.14
Agamben, Giorgio 115–16, 126–8, 130–3, 135–7, 183, 238n.7
Agricola, Georgius 232n.24
Alaimo, Stacy 3, 84–5
Allewaert, Monique 241n.5
Alleyn, Edward 112–13, 115–16, 123–4, 162–3, 222, 226nn.12–13
Alum 102–3, 237n.18
Akkerman, Nadine 240nn.32,33
Anderson, Christy 148
Anderson, Roberta 240n.32
Andrea, Bernadette 249n.13
Animal-baiting 14, 112–13, 116, 123–4, 135
Anna of Denmark, Queen of Scotland, England, and Ireland 7–10, 67–8, 73–7, 79, 85–6, 102, 121–3, 134–5, 197–8, 200–1, 204–6, 215, 228n.23, 233n.16, 234n.17, 239n.16, 240nn.33,35, 250n.23
Anthropocene 1, 14–15, 20, 45, 61–2, 79, 113, 134, 136–7, 151–2, 192–4, 215–17, 219–20, 222–4, 252n.7
Anthropomorphism 84–5, 94–5
Anti-natalism 44–5
Arctic 3–4, 6–7, 11, 22, 112–15, 125, 134
Aubrey, John 116–17
Apes 61–2, 163, 221–2
Aristophanes 47
Aristotle 59–60, 127–8, 182, 221–2
Armin, Robert 35
Ash, Eric 152, 243n.27
Astrology 215–16
Astronomy 2–3, 215
Atkinson, Stephen 49–53, 55, 232n.22
Aytoun, Robert 55–6

Bach, Rebecca Ann 38–9, 119–20
Bacon, Francis 14–15, 78–9, 156–7, 177–9, 185–6, 219–20, 222–3
Badcoe, Tamsin 231n.7
Badgers 106–7, 116–17
Baker, David 242n.9
Baker, Tawrin 226n.11, 227n.14
Baldwin, Robert 233n.5

Baldwin, William 249n.7
Balfour, M. C. 142–4
Barad, Karen 3
Barentsz, William 113–14
Barker, Francis 241n.1
Barrett, Chris 248n.37
Barroll, Leeds 7–8, 227nn.17,20, 229n.1
Bartlett, Richard 187–8
Barton, Anne 225nn.5,7
Bate, Jonathan 8, 107–8, 243n.24, 245n.45
Bates, Catherine 228n.28
Bates, Katherine Lee 89–90
Bats 199–200, 249n.16
Bears 14, 22, 112–17, 123–7, 130–1, 134–6
Beaumont, Matthew 208–9
Beauregard, David 244n.37
Beavers 110, 116–17, 238n.10
Bees 200, 221–2
Beetles 110, 154, 208–9
Belsey, Catherine 164–5
Bender, John 161–2
Bennett, Jane 3, 231n.2
Berger, Harry 225n.2
Bergeron, David 227n.17, 240n.31
Berry, Edward 228n.28
Bertram, Benjamin 2–3, 173–4
Bevington, David 46–7, 243n.16, 249n.12
Bicks, Caroline 131–2
Biopolitics 168
Bitterns 142
Blackface 197–9, 205–6, 249n.15
Blackfriars 9–10, 23, 27–8, 54–6, 194–5, 202–3, 210–11, 214
Boar 12, 163, 223–4
Bodin, Jean 178–9, 247n.16
Boehrer, Bruce 2–3, 6–7, 177–8, 218, 249n.17
Bohemia 114–16, 127–8, 130–2, 217–18, 238n.5, 239n.12
Boleyn, Anne 123, 239n.19
Botany 4–5, 107–8, 131–2, 237n.18
Botero, Giovanni 178–80, 247nn.24,28
Bowsher, Julian 85
Bradbrook, M. C. 55
Braumuller, A. R. 173–4, 246nn.6,11
Brayton, Dan 2–3, 63, 83–4, 148, 235n.34
Briggs, K. M. 153–4
Bronfen, Elizabeth 194–5, 249n.5
Brotton, Jerry 138, 241n.2
Browne, Sir Thomas 59–60, 84–5

284   INDEX

Browne, William 235n.3
Bruno, Giordano 214–15
Bryant, Levi 193–4
Buchanan, George 12–14, 236n.16
Buell, Lawrence 1–4, 174
Bulmer, Sir Bevis 21, 47–57
Burckhardt, Jacob 167–8
Burnet, Thomas 88
Butchers 43–4, 181
Butler, Martin 228n.23, 249n.12

Caesar, Sir Julius 206–7
Caius, John 110
Calgacus 189–90
Callaghan, Dympna 242n.9
Camden, William 79–80, 95–6, 108–10, 146, 148–50, 154–7, 160–1, 241n.6, 244n.31
Campion, Thomas 66–8, 199
Capitalization 21, 57–60, 62, 209–10, 212, 232n.23
Capitalocene 46, 62, 232n.30
Cardano, Girolamo (Geronimo) 59–60
Carew, Richard 20–1, 229n.3
Carleton, Dudley 51, 78, 234n.25
Caron, Noel 91
Carr, Robert 1st Earl of Somerset 152, 228n.30
Carroll, Lewis 131–2
Cats 123–4, 199–200, 208, 217–18, 249n.7, 251n.33
Cattle 35, 105, 144, 175
Caus, Saloman de 91
Cavendish, Margaret 218
Cecil, Robert, 1st Earl of Salisbury 18, 51, 54, 231n.10
Cecil, William, 1st Baron Burghley 18
Cella, Matthew 211–12
Césaire, Aimé 165–6, 245n.45
Cervantes, Miguel de 92–4
Chaloner, Sir Thomas 102–4, 237nn.18–19
Chamberlain, John 230n.24
Chapman, Alison 241n.44
Chapman, George 54, 197
Charcoal 150–1
Charles I, King of England 95–6, 102–3, 107, 127–8, 152–3
Charnes, Linda 220–1
Chester, Robert 101
Chiari, Sophie 2–3, 7–8, 227nn.14,17, 251n.32, 252n.6
Chorography 6–7, 17–18, 20–1, 29, 95–6, 154, 252n.9
Chorost, Michael 46–7
Churchyard, Thomas 88–90, 96–8, 101–2, 104–5
Christian IV, King of Denmark 67–8, 73–4, 205–6
Christianity 61, 72, 121–3, 156–7, 205–6, 219–20
Cleland, John 102–3
Clidro, Robin 106
Climate 10–14, 27, 30, 79–80, 117–18, 148, 166, 185, 195–6, 212, 215–18
Clucas, Stephen 243n.24
Coal 9–10, 17–18, 50–4, 56–7, 88, 105–7, 146, 200, 222–3, 249n.17

Cockayn, Sir William 132–3
Cod 72, 77, 85, 234n.24
Cohen, Jeffrey J. 1–2, 97, 142
Coke, Edward 42–3
Coleridge, Samuel Taylor 127
Colonialism 4–7, 19–20, 131–2, 138–40, 157, 165–6, 184–7, 219
Commission of Sewers 148–52, 235n.29
Connolly, Annaliese 239n.18
Conrad, Joseph 139
Coombe Abbey 128–9, 131–2, 134
Cooper, James Fenimore 107
Copenhaver, Brian 243n.24
Cormack, Bradin 65–6, 228n.26
Cotton, Robert 156–7, 160–1, 244n.36
Cowley, Abraham 218
Cox, Catherine 246n.13
Cramsie, John 206–7, 227n.19, 250n.24, 251n.2
Crane, Mary Thomas 2–3, 215
Cressy, David 230nn.16,31
Crimson (Kermes) 177, 182, 226n.13, 234n.22
Croft, Pauline 18, 251n.1
Crowland 146, 150–1, 153–60, 164, 244n.31
Crows 35–6, 39, 98, 208, 250n.26
Cull, Marisa 103–4
Curran, Kevin 199
Curry, W. C. 153–4

Daniel, Samuel 73–4, 77, 81, 85, 233nn.13,14, 235n.30
Darkness 23, 37–8, 45, 154, 193–216
Dartmoor 25–6, 32–5, 37, 229n.3
Da Vinci, Leonardo 121–3, 239n.16
Davison, Francis 67
Deane, Richard 133, 240n.39
Decamp, Eleanor 247n.22
Dee, John 65–8, 73, 95, 151, 233n.6, 243n.23
Deer 12–14, 35, 91–2, 102–4, 106–7, 188–9, 221–4
Deforestation 7, 17–18, 27, 37–8, 105–7, 171, 189–90, 248n.42
Degenhardt, Jane 234n.26
Dekker, Thomas 56, 235n.3, 236n.10
  Britannia's Honor 115–16, 133–4
  Lanthorne and Candlelight 31–2, 195, 202
  The Magnificent Entertainment 5–6
  News from Gravesend 176–7, 246n.12
Demographics 167–70, 172–3, 175–86, 189–92
Denmark 67–8, 79–80, 195–8, 215
Dennys, John 68
De Quincey, Thomas 211
Derrida, Jacques 14, 232n.28
Desai, R. W. 239n.15
Descartes, Rene 4–5, 205–6, 226n.11
De Somogyi, Nick 238n.6
Devereux, Robert 2nd Earl of Essex 185–7, 247n.27
Digges, Dudley 180
Digges, Thomas 214–15
Dillon, Janette 225n.9
Dogs 84–5, 110, 174, 181, 221–2
Dollimore, Jonathan 173–4

INDEX 285

Donne, John 74–5, 87–8, 110–11, 197
Dotterels 150–1
Doves 20–1, 40–3, 221–2
Dovecotes 38–45, 230n.30
Dover 87–8, 98, 213
Dowden, Edward 87–8, 98, 161–2
Drayton, Michael 17–18, 20–1, 35, 79–80, 88–90, 94–6, 110–11, 146, 148–50, 158–61, 201–2, 205, 235n.3, 245n.41, 250n.20
Du Bartas, Guillaume de Salluste 19–20, 219–20
Duckert, Lowell 2–3, 63, 115
Dudley, Robert, Earl of Leicester 237n.21
Duffy, Eamon 199–200, 244n.35
Dugdale, Gilbert 170–1
Dugdale, William 156–7
Dustagheer, Sarah 249n.14
Dutton, Richard 7–8, 73, 203, 227n.20, 229n.1, 251n.37
Dyes 4–5, 21, 63–4, 74–7, 165, 226nn.11,13, 233n.15, 234n.21, 249n.14
Dyer, Edward 66
Dyer, Richard 121–3

Eagles 12, 42–3, 62, 101, 107–11, 136, 181, 221–4, 237nn.23–25
Ecofeminism 3, 121–3, 129–30
Eco-historicism 1, 10–11, 24, 46, 63, 79, 86–8, 139–40, 165, 224
Eco-materialism 4–5, 11–12, 20–1, 57, 62, 76–7, 105, 118–19, 200, 219–20
Edelman, Lee 44–5, 181, 231n.34
Edward I, King of England 85–6, 108–9, 116–17, 195, 235n.2
Eels 140–1, 186, 223–4
Egan, Gabriel 24, 146–8, 186, 225n.7, 245n.2
Egerton, Sir Thomas 178–9
Ekirch, E. Roger 193–4, 249n.4, 250nn.20,21
Eklund, Hilary 2–3, 243n.18
Elden, Stuart 225n.9, 247n.21
Elsheimer, Adam 197
Elizabeth, Princess, Queen of Bohemia 9–10, 75–6, 114–16, 127–32, 134, 161–2, 203, 217–18, 224, 237n.20, 240nn.31–35,38
Elizabeth I, Queen of England and Ireland 8, 49–50, 67–8, 118, 121–3, 131–2, 171, 195–6, 199, 201, 203, 227n.17
Enclosure 7, 26–7, 35–6, 105, 107, 142, 145, 167–8, 177–8, 189–90, 218, 222–3, 225n.9
Ermine (Stoat) 114–23, 126–7, 130–1, 133–7
Erskine, Frances 128–32, 240n.34
Erskine, John, Earl of Mar 240n.33
Estok, Simon 2–3, 46–7, 148, 194–5, 249nn.5,15, 252n.8
Evelyn, John 218

Fanon, Frantz 205–6
Fawkes, Guy 196
Fens 4–5, 11, 15, 20, 22, 30, 109–10, 140–57, 160–1, 163–5, 167–8, 221–3, 229n.4
Fielder, Leslie 241n.1

Field, Jemma 233n.16, 239n.16
Fishing 43–4, 63–74, 77, 82–6, 148–50, 186, 232n.2, 233nn.3,8,14, 234n.24
Fitz, Sir John 32–4
Fletcher, Giles 239n.13
Fletcher, John 94, 196, 249n.10
Fletcher, Phineas 70
Floods 21, 63–4, 79–82, 144–5, 148–51, 165, 224, 235n.29
  Noah's flood 89
Flowers 5–6, 129–30, 146–7, 200, 210–11
  Cowslips 107–8
  Daffodils 129–30
  Harebells 107–8
  Violets 4–5, 76–7, 99
Floyd-Wilson, Mary 207–8
Forests 1–2, 16, 30, 37–8, 217, 225n.5
  Arden 1, 98
  Dean 105–7, 228n.37
Forman, Simon 30, 42–3, 125–6, 230n.15
Forman, Valerie 86
Foulis, Thomas 46–7, 52–6
Foxes 27, 116–17, 133, 239n.13, 248n.38
Fremaux, Anne 219–20
Freud, Sigmund 224
Frogs 164–5, 199–200
Frye, Northrop 1–2, 225n.2
Fudge, Erica 116, 124, 238n.6
Fuller, Nicholas 183–4
Fur 4–5, 22, 110, 112–24, 132–7, 189–90, 219, 238nn.4,7–12, 239nn.13,14,20

Galeano, Eduardo 139
Garganigo, Alex 183–4
Garrard, Greg 192
Geisweidt, Edward 172–3
Georgic 12–14, 21, 24–5, 34, 104–7
Gerald of Wales 96–7, 110, 237n.23
Gesner, Conrad 84, 134–5, 232n.24, 249n.16
Giblett, Rod 139
Gillen, Katherine 232n.30
Gillies, John 78, 241n.1
Giovane, Palma 91
Godwits 146, 242n.14
Gold 4–6, 18, 21, 23, 46–52, 55–62, 74–7, 105, 150–1, 222, 249n.14
Goldberg, Jonathan 19, 227n.17, 241n.1, 246n.5
Golding, Arthur 144–5, 232n.1
Goltzius, Hendrik 90–2
Goodare, Julian 53–4
Gossett, Suzanne 71, 233n.12
Grady, Hugh 225n.2
Grant, Teresa 112–13, 126
Green 1–7, 12, 18, 26–7, 37–8, 91, 99, 101–2, 107, 165, 187–8, 219–20, 225nn.2–4,7, 226n.11, 237n.25
Greene, Robert 114–15, 162–3
Grotius, Hugo 64–5, 67–8, 233n.8
Gurr, Andrew 126–7, 162, 210, 227n.20, 228n.31, 241n.6
Guthlac 139, 155–66, 244–5nn.32,33,36,39–42

Hadfield, Andrew 46–7, 221–2
Hake, Edward 58–9
Hall, Joseph 90–1
Hall, Kim 197–8, 204, 249nn.13,14, 250n.23
Hamilton, Jennifer Mae 251n.32
Hamilton, Sir Thomas 52–3, 231n.11
Hands, Terry 112
Haraway, Donna 63–4, 84–5, 127, 224
Hares 12–14, 116–17, 181
Harington, Sir John 196–7, 205–7
Harington, John 1st Baron of Exton 128–9, 240n.34
Harkness, Deborah 228n.33
Harriot, Thomas 243n.24
Harris, Jonathan Gil 27–8
Harrison, Robert Pogue 24, 231n.33, 238n.27
Harrison, William 29–30, 71, 146
Hartlib, Samuel 230n.29
Hay, James 1st Earl of Carlisle 55–6, 199
Hazlitt, William 27–8, 230n.21
Heaths 11, 20–1, 24–39, 44–5, 96, 156–7, 193–4, 200, 229nn.3–10,12
Heidegger, Martin 7, 61–2, 133
Heise, Ursula 225n.8, 246n.10
Helgerson, Richard 7, 17–18, 225n.9, 241n.3
Henry Frederick, Prince of Wales 9–10, 17–18, 72–9, 88–92, 95–6, 102–4, 107, 127–8, 160–1, 183, 189–90, 196–7, 224, 236nn.6,15–16, 237n.20, 240n.33, 247n.23, 248n.36
Henry I, King of England 236nn.9,10
Henry II, King of England 96
Henry III, King of England 112–13, 148
Henry IV, King of England 118
Henry V, King of England 101–2, 118
Henry VI, King of England 118
Henry VIII, King of England 35, 110, 118, 158, 196–7
Henslowe, Philip 112–13, 115–16, 123–5, 162, 226n.12, 232n.21, 236n.10
Herbert, William 3rd Earl of Pembroke 106–7, 158
Herrick, Robert 197
Herring 63, 67–72, 77, 85–6
Higginbotham, Jennifer 240n.37
Hilliard, Nicholas 122, 232n.22
Hindle, Steve 228n.35, 246n.14, 248n.40
Hiltner, Ken 2–3, 243nn.18,19
Hirsch, Brett 249n.19
Höfele, Andreas 123, 228n.31, 238n.6
Hole, William 148–50
Holinshed, Raphael 29–30, 33–4, 40–1, 178, 237n.23
Holland (Lincolnshire) 148–50, 217–18
Holland, Peter 63, 246n.14, 247nn.17,27
Holland, Philemon 154
Hopkins, Lisa 32, 108–9, 230nn.18,19, 238n.26, 239n.18
Horses 9–10, 16, 61, 93, 110, 163, 221–2
Howard, Jean 167–8, 245n.1
Howard, Charles, 1st Earl of Nottingham 67, 72–3
Hulme, Peter 148, 241n.1

Hunt, Maurice 239n.28
Hunting 12–14, 16, 20–1, 24–5, 35–41, 44–5, 91–2, 100, 102–3, 110, 116–19, 121, 123–4, 129, 131–2, 136, 161, 171, 188–90, 203, 228n.28, 230n.27, 238n.4, 240n.35, 241n.5
Husbandry 12–14, 16, 34, 129, 173–4, 228n.29

Iopollo, Grace 246n.6
Iovino, Serenella 3
Ireland 5–7, 11–12, 19–20, 22, 55, 66, 139, 143, 165, 183–92, 222–3, 234n.21, 242n.9, 247nn.25,26,32–34, 248nn.41–42,44
Iyengar, Sujata 236n.14, 249n.13

James I of England/VI of Scotland, King
    Absolutism 9–12, 14–15, 18–20, 73–4, 152–3, 177, 219–23
    Alleged Agoraphobia 171
    Author 18–20, 77, 89–90, 102, 182–4, 196–7, 219–20
    Conservationist 7, 11–12, 17–18, 35–8, 40, 44, 64–5, 110, 228n.28, 230n.27
    Coronation 5–6, 118–19, 169–71
    Culpability for Civil War 217–18, 251n.1
    Debts 18, 46–7, 53–6, 206–7
    Dedicatee 14–15, 17–18, 58, 68, 239n.24
    Deified 9, 73–4, 199, 208–9, 217, 219, 222–3
    Diplomacy 85–6, 114–15
    Family 85–6, 102, 128–9, 196, 240n.33
    Favourites 12–14, 52, 54–6, 152, 195–6, 199, 217–18, 226n.13, 228n.30
    Hunter 12–14, 35–6, 40, 118, 228n.28, 230n.24
    Insomnia 249n.9
    Investor 50–1, 54–5, 139–40, 152, 228n.39
    Journey to Denmark 79, 215
    Knighthoods 32–3, 47–8, 50–1, 231n.8
    Late Hours 195–6, 203, 205–6
    Menagerie 14, 110, 112–13, 228n.32, 241n.41
    Pacificism 40–1, 72–3, 168–9, 183
    Petitions 15–17
    Proclamations 11–12, 35–8, 40, 42–3, 64–5, 67–8, 71–2, 171–2, 177–8, 183, 186
    Scotophobia 196
    Solomon 14–15, 19, 205–6, 250n.23
    Theatre Patron 6–7, 9, 24, 32, 54, 70, 126, 135, 147–8, 168, 196–7, 212, 246n.6
    Union 3–4, 6–7, 64–5, 67–8, 88, 183–4, 186
Jamestown 73, 139, 185, 219
Johnson, Robert 92–3
Johnson, Samuel 11
Johnson, Thomas 107–8
Jones, Gwilym 2–3, 28–9, 78–9, 213–14
Jones, Inigo 91–4, 197–8, 251n.32
Jonson, Ben
    The Alchemist 47–8, 56
    Bartholomew Fair 225n.1
    The Devil is an Ass 150–2, 228n.34, 243n.22
    For the Honour of Wales 95–6

INDEX

The Gypsies Metamorphosed 31–2
The Lady of the Lake (*The Speeches at Prince Henry's Barriers*) 161
Masque of Blackness 197–8, 205–6, 234nn.17,25
Masque of Queens 199–200, 208–9
Oberon 89–96, 112–13, 134
Pleasure Reconciled to Virtue 94–5
The Staple of News 47
Volpone 47–8, 55, 58
Jowett, John 46–7, 55, 57, 232n.27, 246n.11

Kahn, Coppélia 46–7
Karim-Cooper, Farah 249n.14
Kastan, David Scott 241n.2
Kermode, Frank 242n.15, 244n.39
Kernan, Alvin 7–9, 203–4, 227nn.17,20
Kerrigan, John 97, 226n.10
Keysar, Robert 56
Khanty 10–11, 135–6, 241n.45
Kirwan, Peter 239n.24
Klein, Bernhard 63, 234n.22, 248n.37
Knight, G. Wilson 219–21
Knight, Leah 225n.7
Knights, L. C. 172–3
Koelb, Janice Hewlett 89
Korda, Natasha 234n.21
Koslofsky, Craig 193–4, 197, 201–2, 249n.4
Kurland, Stuart 7–8, 227n.17, 231n.9
Kuzner, James 183

Lancashire 25–6, 31
Lapwings 143–4
Laroche, Rebecca 3, 24, 240n.37, 251n.4
Latour, Bruno 3, 218
Lawrence, Jason 227n.20, 246n.6
Lead mining 18, 48, 50, 53–4, 105–6
Leland, John 108–9
Lent 16, 43–4, 71–2, 84–5, 234n.23
Leopold, Aldo 12, 100
Levant Company 6–7, 219–20, 234n.22
Lewalski, Baraba 128–9
Lincolnshire 3–4, 22, 139–46, 148–51, 153–8, 162, 164–5, 241n.4
Lion 14, 22, 116, 123–4, 126–7, 130–1, 134–5, 155–6, 237n.25
Little Ice Age 2–3, 30, 79–80, 165, 167–8, 217, 222–3, 229n.13
London 2–3, 5–6, 15, 31, 35–6, 48, 54–6, 64–5, 67–8, 71, 85, 105, 112–13, 132–4, 167–80, 183–7, 189–97, 200–2, 207–8, 218, 222–3, 236n.11, 245nn.1,4, 249n.7
Lost Plays
The Arcadian Virgin 125
Cox of Collumpton 125
Cutlack 162–3, 244n.40, 245n.41
The Famous Wars of Henry I and the Prince of Wales 236n.10
Nebuchadnezzar 222
The Scottish Mine 54, 231nn.16,17
Truth's Supplication to Candlelight 195
The Welshman's Prize (The Welshman Price?) 236n.10
Lovegrove, Roger 109–10, 230n.26, 239n.14
Lucretius 78–9, 222–3, 234n.26, 252n.6
Lumley, John 1st Baron of Lumley 160–1

Macfarlane, Robert 87–8
MacFaul, Tom 20, 222
Machiavelli, Niccolo 178–80
Magic 143–5, 148, 151–2, 154–6, 164, 168, 199, 243n.24
Magnus, Olaus 123–4
Maguin, Jean-Marie 207
Maguire, Laurie 228n.27
Maisano, Scott 234n.26
Malay, Jessica 230n.20
Maley, Willy 95, 229n.2, 235n.1
Malone, Edmond 123–4, 138, 242n.8, 245n.42, 246n.5
Malthus, Thomas 22–3, 176–80, 192, 247n.16
Manley, Lawrence 245n.1
Manwood, John 37–8
Marcus, Leah 235n.1, 238n.26, 243n.22, 248n.40
Marion, Jean-Luc 61–2
Markham, Gervase 12–14, 34, 37–41
Marlowe, Christopher
  Doctor Faustus 162–3, 222
  Tamburlaine 133–4
Martens 116–18, 136, 189–90, 223–4
Martin, Randall 2–3, 24, 100, 177–8, 230n.31
Martin, Sir Richard 48
Marx, Karl 46, 57, 61–2, 231n.2
Marx, Leo 138
Massinger, Philip 161–2
Mbembe, Achille 38–9
McCarthy, Cormac 211–12
McCormick, Ted 247n.15, 248n.44
McEachern, Claire 235n.1
McManus, Clare 228n.23
McRae, Andrew 225n.9, 231n.8
Menagerie 14, 110, 112–13, 115–16, 128–9, 131–2, 228n.32, 239n.30, 241n.41
Mennell, Nicole 238n.8
Mentz, Steve 2–3, 24, 63, 86, 148, 225n.2, 251n.32, 252n.9
Merchant, Carolyn 232n.27
Meyrick, John 113–15
Middleton, Thomas
  A Chaste Maid in Cheapside 56, 105
  Macbeth 208–9
  Measure for Measure 176–7, 246n.11
  The Meeting of Gallants at an Ordinary 182
  More Dissemblers Beside Women 31–2
  News from Gravesend 176–7, 246n.12
  Timon of Athens 21, 46–52, 54–7, 204
  The Triumphs of Love and Antiquity 132–4
  The Triumphs of Truth 200, 249n.17
  The Witch 31–2
  The World Tossed at Tennis 226n.13

INDEX

Midlands Rising 177–8, 189–90, 246n.14, 248n.35
Miglietti, Sara 228n.38
Mikalachki, Jodi 102
Milton, John 205, 250n.20
  Masque Presented at Ludlow Castle (Comus) 106–7, 201–2
  Paradise Lost 201–2
Mining 18, 21, 35, 46–57, 61–2, 102–3, 231n.7, 232nn.22,27
Moles 221–2, 251n.3
Momper, Joos de 91, 94–5
Monopolies 7, 42–3, 201
Montaigne, Michel de 9
Moore, J. W. 46, 62
Moors 11–14, 24–9, 31–3, 35–7, 49–51, 57, 96, 105, 217–18, 222–3, 229nn.2,4,5
More, Sir Thomas 87–8, 116–17, 177–9, 185–6
Moretti, Franco 252n.6
Morgan, John 228n.38, 235n.29
Morton, Timothy 2–3, 24–5, 44–5, 193–4, 224, 249n.3, 252n.7
Moss 25–6, 107–8, 237n.22
Mostyn, Roger 105–6
Mottram, Stewart 235n.1
Mountains 11–12, 20–3, 87–111, 133, 185, 221–2, 236nn.6,8,10–11,13, 237nn.21,23
Mountjoy, Marie 75–6
Mucedorus 112–13, 123–4, 126
Munday, Anthony 74–5, 233n.14, 243n.29
Munro, Lucy 7–8, 231n.17
Munroe, Jennifer 3, 24, 129–30, 228n.29, 240n.37, 251n.4
Murray, Sir David 236n.17
Muscovy Company 11, 113–17, 133–6, 219–20
Myddleton, Hugh 105–6

Nardizzi, Vin 225n.7, 243n.17
Nashe, Thomas 69–71, 204, 207, 211–12, 235n.3, 249n.7
New Market 35–6
Newton, Adam 236n.17
Newton, Isaac 4–5
Nicholl, Charles 56, 75–6
Nicholson, Marjorie Hope 87–9, 104
Night
  Night blindness 212
  Nightscape 195, 198–200, 212
  Night scenes 194–5, 207, 210
  Night walking 195–7, 201–2, 208, 213–14
  Night watch 194–7
  Nyctophobia 23, 194–5, 207
Nixon, Rob 30, 225n.8, 241n.1
Nonsuch 102–3, 236n.17
Norden, John 34
Norris, John 197

Oatlands 236n.17, 240n.35
O'Dair, Sharon 46, 231n.1
Ó Dálaigh, Lochlann Óg 187–9
Ó Dochartaigh, Cathaoir (Sir Cahir O'Doherty) 186–7, 189–91, 248nn.35,36

Ó Gnímh, Fearflatha 187–9
O'Malley, Evelyn 227n.21
Opperman, Serpil 3
Orbis Spike 217–18
Orgel, Stephen 197–8, 229n.1, 238n.2, 240n.31, 242n.11, 243n.24, 249n.12
Osborne, Francis 12
Osborne, John 186–7
Ovid 9, 46–7, 61–2, 68, 97, 125, 144–5, 222
Owen, George 20–1, 95, 107
Owls 40–1, 106–8, 199–201, 204, 208–9, 211, 249n.16

Parker, Geoffrey 217–18
Parliament 9–14, 16–18, 35–7, 40–1, 43–4, 53–5, 79–80, 118, 148, 152, 182–5, 217, 219, 226n.13, 228n.24
Pastoral 2–3, 21–2, 87–8, 97–100, 103–5, 107–8, 110–11, 115–17, 128–9, 131–2, 136, 236n.11
Pastoureau, Michel 225nn.4,5
Paulet, Sir George 186–7
Peacham, Henry 35, 120–3, 225n.5, 239n.19
Peacock, John 91–2
Peake, Robert 91–2, 103–4
Periwinkles 76, 84–5, 234nn.20,21
Perry, Curtis 7–8, 227n.17, 239n.17
Pett, Phineas 72–3
Petty, Sir William 168, 190–2, 248n.44
Philip IV, King of Spain 222
Phillips, Sir Thomas 186, 248n.34
Plague 22–3, 167–77, 179–80, 183–5, 190–2, 222–3, 246nn.8,12, 250n.25
Plantationocene 166
Plat, Hugh 17–18, 228n.33
Plato 205–6
  Neo-platonic 151–2, 215
Plautus 84, 235n.33
Pliny 46–7, 59–61, 74–6, 84–5, 232n.24, 233n.15, 234n.19
Plutarch 65, 177–80, 184–7, 204–6, 233nn.4,6, 246n.14, 247n.18
Poole, Jonas 112–15, 126
Popham, Sir John 15–16, 228n.34
Porcellis, Jan 72–3, 78–9
Post-colonialism 138–40, 165–6
Post-humanism 46
'The Powte's Complaint' 10–11, 164–5
Privy Council 7–8, 14, 19–20, 32, 54, 114–15, 148, 152, 167–8, 178–9, 183, 189–90, 226n.13
Protest 17, 35, 148–50, 164–5, 177–8, 184–5, 218, 227n.21, 230n.23, 246n.14
Pryme, Abraham de la 142–3
Prynne, William 78
Purple 21, 63–4, 74–7, 84–5, 177, 233n.16, 234nn.18,21–23

Quarmby, Kevin 246n.6
Quilligan, Maureen 130–1

Rabbits 116–17, 133
Raber, Karen 175, 223–4, 246nn.6,8

INDEX

Rats 176, 179–81, 185–6, 246n.8
Ravelhofer, Barbara 112–13, 126, 134, 239n.26
Ravens 39, 163, 211–12, 250nn.25,27
Ralegh, Sir Walter 178–9, 185–7, 247n.27
Ramelius, Henry 67–8
Ray, John 109–10
Reformation 158–62, 175–6, 234n.23
Remien, Peter 228n.36
Rewilding 9, 12, 27, 57–8, 111, 123–4, 202, 209–10, 214
Rich, Barnaby 181, 189–90
Rickard, Jane 19, 227n.17
Ridgeway, Sir Thomas 189–90
Rilke, Rainer Maria 133, 222–3
Risdon, Tristram 35
Romani 31–2, 197–8, 229n.2, 230nn.16,19
Rooks 38–9, 208, 211, 250n.26
Rousseau, Jean-Jacques 87–8, 128–9
Rowley, Samuel 196–7
Rowley, William 226n.13
Royal Shakespeare Company 9, 112
Royal Society 14–15, 190–2, 219–20, 228n.33
Royston 15, 35–8, 230nn.24,25
Rubens, Peter Paul 9, 232n.22
Rudolf II, Holy Roman Emperor/King of Bohemia 91, 134–5, 236n.6, 241n.44
Ruff 164
Russell, Francis 4th Earl of Bedford 152–3
Russell, Thomas 180
Russia 3–4, 11–12, 113–15, 120–3, 133–5, 219, 238n.4, 239n.18

Sables 4–5, 118–19, 133–4, 241n.41
Sam Wanamaker Playhouse 210, 214
Sanders, Julie 106–7, 225n.9, 243n.22
Sandys, Edward 228n.39
Savage, Thomas 56
Savery, Roelandt 91, 93, 236n.6
Schwyzer, Philip 95, 235n.1
Scotland 3–7, 12–14, 19–20, 24–8, 32, 34, 37–8, 45–54, 67–8, 109–11, 116–17, 121–3, 169–70, 183–4, 186, 189–90, 195–9, 207–9, 219, 222–3, 229n.2, 231n.7, 232n.22, 233n.10, 236n.17, 245n.4, 247n.25
Scott, Charlotte 25–6, 228n.29
Selden, John 65
Shakespeare, William
  All's Well that Ends Well 215
  Antony and Cleopatra 23, 31–2, 69, 194–5, 204–7, 213–14, 250n.22, 251n.35
  As You Like It 1–3, 130–1, 221–2, 244n.37
  Cardenio (Double Falsehood) 92–4, 236n.8
  A Comedy of Errors 66, 84, 225n.2
  Coriolanus 22–3, 42–3, 146–7, 167–9, 177–92, 246n.14, 247nn.20–21,23,26,31, 248n.39
  Cymbeline 3, 6–7, 9–10, 19, 21, 87–92, 96–111, 127–9, 131–2, 200, 222, 236n.15
  Hamlet 8–9, 25–6, 118–19, 174–6, 195–6, 202, 215, 219, 224, 251n.37
  2 Henry IV 250n.22
  Henry V 96, 118, 172–3, 185
  Julius Caesar 183–4, 195, 215
  King John 123–4
  King Lear 9–10, 18–20, 23, 28–9, 33–4, 44, 46, 92–3, 116–17, 147–8, 194–5, 207–9, 212–15, 220–2, 249nn.3,5, 250n.31, 251nn.32–34
  Love's Labour's Lost 211, 225n.2
  Macbeth 19–21, 23–45, 86, 108, 172–3, 182, 194–5, 206–14, 221–2, 229nn.1,8–9,15, 230nn.19,31, 249n.3, 250nn.27,30
  Measure for Measure 22–3, 70, 161–2, 167–77, 196–7, 244n.37, 246nn.5–7,11,13
  Merchant of Venice 215
  Merry Wives of Windsor 96
  A Midsummer Night's Dream 1–2, 212, 249n.5, 251n.35
  Much Ado About Nothing 192
  Othello 31–2, 121–3, 130–1, 206–7
  Pericles 9–10, 19–21, 40, 63–6, 68–86, 161–2, 172–3, 221–2, 233nn.4,6, 234nn.20,26, 235nn.31–33, 244n.37
  'The Phoenix and Turtle' 42–3, 101
  Richard III 244n.38
  Romeo and Juliet 134–5, 192, 237n.25, 249n.5
  Sir Thomas More 71, 87–8
  The Sonnets 106–7, 192
  The Taming of the Shrew 31, 76–7
  The Tempest 5–6, 8, 19, 22, 77–9, 138–40, 142–58, 161–6, 203, 217–18, 222, 225n.4, 227n.16, 234nn.24,26, 241nn.1,2,5,6, 242nn.8–9,11,15, 243nn.16–18,24, 244nn.37,39, 245n.42
  Timon of Athens 9–10, 18–19, 21, 23, 46–62, 86, 179–80, 203–5, 222, 231nn.13,18, 232nn.21,29,30
  Titus Andronicus 133–4, 225n.2
  Twelfth Night 4–5, 84, 226n.13
  The Winter's Tale 9–10, 22, 42–3, 82, 112–17, 119–23, 126–32, 134–7, 162, 203, 238nn.3,5, 239nn.12,15, 240nn.31–32
Shannon, Laurie 116–17, 194–5, 238n.7, 249nn.5,18, 251n.34
Shapiro, James 205–6, 227n.17, 228n.24
Sharpe, Robert Boies 162
Sheep 1–2, 35, 80, 105, 116–17, 119–20, 130–1, 177–8, 221–2
Shelley, Percy Bysshe 87–8, 236n.11
Sherman, William H. 148, 233n.7, 241n.1
Sidney, Sir Philip 20, 65–6, 120, 224, 225n.1
Siewers, Alfred 156–7, 225n.2
Skura, Meredith 138
Smith, Bruce 225n.7
Smith, Emma 169, 209
Snails
  Murex 4–5, 74–7, 233n.15, 234nn.17–19
  Periwinkles 76, 84–5, 234nn.20,21
Solomon, Julie 14–15
Speed, John 20–1, 35, 95–6
Spenser, Edmund 46–7, 61, 74–5, 79–80, 87–8, 131–2, 187–8, 195–6, 248n.37
Squirrels 14, 106, 116–20, 133, 189–90
Standish, Arthur 17–18, 230n.30

Starch 4–5, 16–18, 226n.13
Steggle, Matthew 245n.41, 249n.8
Stirling Castle 32, 102, 196, 240n.33
Stoat (*see* Ermine)
Stradling, John 80–1
Stratford-upon-Avon 4–5, 31, 39, 42–3, 72, 107–8, 158, 167–8, 170, 227n.21
Strong, Roy 72–3, 161, 197, 232n.22, 236nn.5,6, 249n.16
Stuart, Henry, Lord Darnley 34, 196
Sullivan, Garrett 7, 98, 100, 206–7, 225n.9, 238n.26
Summit, Jennifer 156–7, 160–1, 244n.36
Swifts 40–1
Swift, Graham 141–2, 242n.8, 244n.40
Swift, Jonathan 190–2, 248n.44

Taylor, Gary 236nn.7,9, 246n.11
Teramura, Misha 231n.15, 231n.17
Theobald, Lewis 92–4
Theobalds 228n.32, 230n.27
Therfield 35–6
Thetford 35–6, 230n.25
Tigner, Amy 241n.42
Toads 199–200
Traherne, Thomas 130, 240n.36
Trees 9–10, 17–18, 27, 29–30, 34, 37–8, 44, 62, 103–7, 128–9, 226n.13, 228n.37, 236n.8, 247n.24
  Ashes 248n.42
  Elms 248n.42
  Hazel 146
  Logwood 4–5, 226n.13
  Oaks 156–7, 189–90, 224, 248n.42
  Palms 241n.5
  Pines 99
Tsing, Anna 224
Turner, Henry 28–9, 168–9, 225n.9

Ulster 3–4, 22–3, 168–9, 184–92, 248nn.35,39–40,42

Vaughan, Henry 108–9, 197
Vaughan, Virginia 138, 241n.1, 249n.13
Veer, Gerrit de 113–14
Vergil, Polydore 101
Vermin 38–9, 41–3, 45, 109–10, 208
Vermuyden, Cornelius 152–3, 243n.27

Virgil 73–4, 233n.13, 241n.2
Virginia 6–7, 11–12, 138–9, 219–20
Vos, Maerten de 158–60

Wales 3–4, 6–7, 19–21, 25–6, 50, 66, 85–6, 88–92, 94–111, 219, 235nn.1,2, 236nn.11,17, 237nn.21,23
Warren, Roger 103–4
Warwickshire 6–7, 31, 39, 115–16, 128–9, 177–8, 192, 218
Watson, Robert 2–3, 24, 130–1, 173–4, 218, 225n.7, 231n.33, 240n.36, 246nn.6,11
Webster, John 197, 200–1, 205, 239n.18
Welwood, William 68, 70–1, 73–4, 86, 233n.10
Whetstone, George 172
White, Lynn 156–7, 244n.33
White, Martin 210
White, Thomas Holt 235n.33
Whitehall 1, 8–10, 14, 22, 194–7, 203, 205–7, 209–10, 212–14, 238n.5
Whiteley, Giles 249n.3
Whitney, Charles 246n.12
Wilkins, George 21, 63–6, 71, 76–9, 83–4, 232n.1
Williams, Raymond 19–20
Willoughby, Frances 109–10
Wilson, Arthur 200–1
Winter 22, 27, 42–3, 72, 79–80, 100, 107–8, 119–23, 134, 136, 140–1, 150, 156, 195, 199–200, 203, 207–8, 226n.12
Winter, Edward 105–6
Witchcraft 24–5, 30–2, 37, 40–1, 44, 151, 156, 199–201, 207–8, 215, 229n.13
Woad 4–5, 16, 165, 226nn.11,13
Wolfe, Cary 238n.7
Wolverines 123–4
Wolves 12–14, 22, 110–11, 116–17, 127, 133, 163, 181, 199–200, 202, 208–9, 221–2, 237n.25, 239n.13, 248n.39
Wynn, John 105–6

Yachnin, Paul 77
Yates, Frances 151, 235n.1, 237n.20, 243n.24
Yates, Julian 4–5, 123
Yusoff, Kathryn 223

Zabus, Chantal 241n.1